José Martí, Cuban Patriot

RICHARD BUTLER GRAY

José Martí, Cuban Patriot

University of Florida Press
Gainesville-1962

To My Mother

A University of Florida Press Book

Foreword

*T*HE STUDENT OF HISTORY frequently speculates on
contemporary and future affairs in the light of past events, even
though he realizes that few persons ever learn anything from history.
Today, undoubtedly, Cubans of all ranks, who recognize and worship Martí as a great national hero and "apostle," are asking themselves, "What would Martí do if he were alive now?" In the light of his
vast affection for Cuba and its people, would Martí today advocate
logically and philosophically what should be done by the Cubans, by
the United States, and by Latin America? Faced with the myriad
problems of the present, would he propose remedies, advocate
methods, suggest actions, counsel care, caution against mistakes? Or
would he quietly prepare a plan of action, carefully thought out, to
be boldly executed by unilateral action or by multilateral cooperation in order to solve the "Cuban Problem" faced by the island's
people, by the United States, by the Latin American countries, and
by the communist bloc? In other words, would Martí the man as he
was, or would Martí the image as he is thought to be, be able to
achieve the results for which patriotic Cubans now so devoutly wish?

Martí's short life and untimely death did not prevent him from
expressing himself on an astonishing variety of topics or from examining in a penetrating and often critical fashion the perplexing facets
of life and thought with which the Cubans and the other Spanish
Americans in general were concerned. His mind ranged over the
whole universe and his opinions embraced all provinces of knowledge. After his death the "Cult of Martí" arose, and an ever increasing number of followers literally sought out his every word
until his collected writings number seventy-four volumes in Spanish.

At the risk of encroaching on Professor Gray's presentation and of repeating some of his observations and conclusions, I should like to reiterate an expression of personal opinion presented at the Congreso de Escritores Martianos, on the occasion of the Centenario de Martí in Havana, Cuba, in February, 1953, in a joint paper by my wife and myself. We wrote at that time:

Martí, possibly more than any other leading character in the drama of American hemisphere history, was all things to all men. Like Sarmiento, he was an inveterate reader as a child; and as a young scholar in his shabby clothes, he resembled a youthful Lincoln. Throughout his short lifetime he displayed the intelligent curiosity of a Benjamin Franklin, while his wide interests in learning in general reminds one of Brazil's Dom Pedro II. As he intensely observed the men and movements around him and recorded his innermost thoughts in diaries, he might be likened to a combination of a Samuel Pepys and a John Quincy Adams. He was able to formulate his philosophical principles as would a modern Plato, and he expressed them with the oratorical skill of a Demosthenes and the silver tongue of a William Jennings Bryan. As a writer of poetic elegy he surpassed Thomas Gray, and in his wide literary interests he resembled the great Andrés Bello. He wrote with the "dramatic realism" of a Victor Hugo, for whom, indeed, he had great admiration, and he had "the sharp and skeptical humor" of a Heinrich Heine. His ability to express himself in words rivaled that of a Daniel Webster. Martí had the patriotic fervor of a Patrick Henry, the ardent democratic ideals of a Thomas Jefferson, the ability to state his principles in essays and pamphlets like a Tom Paine. Like Voltaire, Martí was the leader of a new cult. He was an idealist reformer akin to Father Hidalgo of Mexico. In his interests in the underdog he rivaled the author of *Los de Abajo*, Mariano Azuelo. Like Beníto Juáres, he was a social reformer of the highest type. He had the restless zeal of a Bernardo O'Higgins, the intelligent political vision and leadership of a Simón Bolívar, and the organizing ability of a San Martín and a Napoleon Bonaparte. He was a schemer for revolution after the pattern of Francisco Miranda and he had the dogged determination in both defeat and victory of a George Washington. In exile he had the fortitude of an Eloy Alfaro. His interests in individuals led him, as it did Horace Mann, to work to improve the mind of the common people. He was a crusading journalist of the stamp of Bartolomé Mitre. As the apostle of Cuban independence he was suspicious of the United States, where he spent a third of his life, but knowing this country so well he had an appreciation for the Pan American ideals of a Henry Clay and a James G. Blaine.

These words, published in Spanish, have today perhaps a greater significance than a decade ago. Professor Gray has extended and reinforced their meaning with his own interesting study in hero worship and hero criticism. A careful reading of his volume will confirm the fact of the universality of Martí's ideas and ideology and will reward the reader with an understanding of the influence of one of the great minds of this hemisphere.

A. CURTIS WILGUS, *Director*
School of Inter-American Studies
University of Florida

October 10, 1962

Acknowledgments

I AM MAINLY INDEBTED in this study to two persons:
Dr. William S. Stokes, Professor of Political Science at Claremont
Men's College, and Dr. Gonzalo de Quesada y Miranda, Director of
the Martí Seminar at the University of Havana. During the twenty
months that I spent in Cuba, Professor Quesada gave me many hours
of his time and the hospitality of his home, as he furnished me with
valuable information from his extensive knowledge of the life of
Martí, original documents, and rich interpretations of the Cuban
scene. It is difficult to imagine how the work would have progressed
without their advice. I am also deeply obligated to Dr. Charles H.
Backstrom, of the University of Minnesota, for his numerous helpful
suggestions in emending the manuscript, and to Dr. Eduardo Neale-
Silva, of the University of Wisconsin, for his assistance.

Many persons in Cuba aided in this investigation of Martí. I am
particularly grateful to Ernesto Mercado of the Fragua Martiana for
his help in making books and other materials available. The staff of
the National Library of Cuba must be credited with many hours of
work on my behalf.

I am very grateful to the Cuban Ministry of Education, which,
in cooperation with the United States State Department, made my
stay in Cuba from 1955 to 1957 possible through an award under the
Buenos Aires Convention for the promotion of inter-American scholarship and understanding. For his aid and consideration in this program my appreciation also goes to Mr. Francis J. Donahue, who was
Cultural Affairs Officer of the American Embassy. My sincere gratitude, in addition, must be extended to the Cuban people in general,

who frequently demonstrated their interest in the study and willingness to help. Many more persons could be named, but unfortunately for lack of space must remain anonymous.

I also wish to thank the University of Wisconsin for the award of a Kemper Knapp Fellowship, which made my investigations in Cuba much easier.

The judgments that appear in this work, as well as the translations, all made by the author, may seem controversial to some persons. Naturally I accept full responsibility for all conclusions and language interpretations made in the book.

R. B. G.

The Florida State University
Tallahassee
July, 1962

Contents

Introduction

To Cubans the National Hero of the freedom movement that led to the Spanish-American War is José Martí, a figure who is relatively unknown in the United States. Although Martí died three years before the War took place, his compatriots have given him the major share of the credit in the organization and the arming of the Revolution. In fact, he may be considered by some to be the most important person in the history of Cuba, at least to judge by the extent of the homage paid to him. As the National Hero he has burst the bonds of mortality to achieve an afterlife in the thought, expressions, and public manifestations of a great number of Cubans.

Yet to North Americans the Cuban struggle for freedom in 1898 is usually characterized by three incidents: the sinking of the "Maine," the message to García, and the charge of Theodore Roosevelt up San Juan Hill in Santiago province. This is incomprehensible to Cubans who are proud of their long history of resistance to Spanish colonial domination. Correctly enough they refer to the conflict as the "Hispanic-Cuban-American War."

The complaint is often made by North Americans that they will never understand Cubans, and many Cubans respond with a similar statement about their northern neighbors, sometimes adding humorously that Yankees are completely mad. José Martí, during the fifteen years that he was a journalist in the United States (1880-95), often wrote about the lack of understanding between North Americans and Latin Americans. The articles that he sent to newspapers in many Central and South American countries about life in the United States, partly in an attempt to alleviate these differences, have frequently been compared in their insights to the interpretations made by Baron Alexis de Tocqueville for France and Lord James Bryce for England. Thus in consideration of the bonds that tied Martí to the United States through his career as a journalist, and the bonds that tie him strongly to the Cuban people, he becomes an ideal figure for study in an attempt to promote better understanding between Cubans and North Americans.

In order to analyze the role of Martí in Cuba it has been necessary, however, to comment upon some features of national politics that many North Americans will find unintelligible and perhaps unpleasant compared to their concepts of democracy. No attempt will be made to justify the political extremes that are sometimes resorted to in Cuba by asserting that an understanding of a neighbor's peculiarities will necessarily add to good feeling. What is important to keep in mind is that any criticism made by an outsider has probably been made much oftener and more acidly by Cubans themselves. For them Martí has become a standard by which to evaluate the conduct of those in public office. The critics do not hesitate to cite him, nor do those in government positions. It is important to know how the persons who represent political attitudes in Cuba have used the life and ideas of Martí as symbols to promote public and private interests.

In essence, research in this work on Martí is an examination of charismatic leadership. The first part will be devoted to a brief biography of Martí and a systematic exposition of his social, political, and economic ideas. An evaluation of the ideas of Martí is important because the statement has been made that he was the Word of the Revolution, and that it was as a philosopher and not as a soldier that he made his greatest contribution. The growth of Martí as a National Hero is closely linked with the interpretation and exposition of his ideas by the persons who have declared themselves to be his followers, or "Martianos." No attempt will be made to present an exhaustive treatment of Martí's philosophizings, but what is offered here may serve as a basis of departure for other students.

The second part of the book will be devoted to three chapters that will trace the development of Martí as the National Hero. One chapter will consist of statements by his contemporaries, an examination of the great volume of literature that has been produced on him, and his representation in busts, monuments, and coins. Another chapter will be devoted to the promotion of Martí as a patriotic symbol by special societies, and fraternal and religious organizations. Some characteristics of the Martí apotheosis, such as those expressed in language and literature, acts with special religious symbolism, representations on film, and the exaltation of Martí as not only the ideal Cuban but also as a universal type will be noted. This part will end with a discussion of the reaction of the Roman Catholic Church to the designation of Martí as the "Apostle."

No attempt will be made to analyze the phenomenon of charisma as applied to Martí in the way that a trained sociologist could do. This is beyond the scope of the study. The author has merely selected those aspects of the homage paid to Martí that have seemed in one way or another to have contributed to his exaltation as a "saint." A case study of charismatic leadership might well be a useful future addition to political science.

The third part of the book will consist of a chapter on the prevalence of Martí as a symbol in politics, particularly in the use of his ideas to win popular support and justification for political action. Political practices and party platforms will furnish a basis of departure for comments on the extent to which Martí's ideas have actually been carried out. The eighth chapter in this part will be devoted to a study of the viewpoints of leaders of various groups about the influence of Martí on selected public institutions, such as labor, education, and the press, ending with a record of conversations with various Cubans about their views on Martí. Another chapter will examine some of the ways in which Fidel Castro has found Martí useful. The final chapter of the book will attempt to draw some conclusions as to whether the evidence in the foregoing chapters shows that Cuba has achieved the republic Martí dreamed about, or whether Martí is only cited by many who never put his thoughts into action, as is the frequent charge.

The method used in this study has consisted of a careful examination of the writings of Martí in the original Spanish in the seventy-four volumes of his collected works, with concentration on his letters to prominent Cubans in the independence movement, his articles on politics in the United States, Latin America, and Europe, his poetry, and his notes. In addition, biographies and studies by authorities on Martí, historians, and other writers inside and outside of Cuba have been read in detail. Conversations with leaders in social and political organizations have been held. In an authoritarian society these are the opinions that are especially significant. Political speeches and political events have contributed an important source of information on the presence or absence of Martí as a vital guide to the conduct of Cuban government and society.

Further limitations on the scope of the study should be recorded. In the first place, no attempt has been made to present material relating to Martí's influence in current Cuban life as a scientific investigation along the lines of professional public opinion testing with its highly developed formulae for selecting samples and its elaborate development of schedules and interviewing techniques. Resources available precluded such efforts. A study of this nature should certainly be undertaken in the interests of progress in the field of political behavior in Latin America. It is hoped that some of the conclusions might serve as hypotheses for such an effort.

In the second place, every attempt has been made to avoid generalizations about the "Cuban people," who, after all, in many respects are many peoples, consisting as they do of Spanish and African cultures, and to a lesser degree, Chinese and Indian. It seems especially difficult to determine the answer to the question, "What is the attitude of Juan Criollo (the Cuban John Doe) toward Martí?" when the extreme individualism of the Latin American must be taken into account.

Furthermore, no assertion of cause and effect has been intentionally made. It would be difficult to prove, for instance, that the people in Cuba who hold certain beliefs do so because Martí gave them expression. Short of such an unwarranted conclusion, however, it should be worth while to establish some parallels. One generalization that the author feels competent to make about the Cuban people is that they have more than the usual share of charm, hospitality, and friendliness, which makes them one with their National Hero. The author hopes that his liking for the Cubans and for Martí will never be in doubt.

Since the author's major investigations were concluded, Fidel

Castro has come to power in Cuba. Ideally this book should include an investigation of the many ways in which Martí has been exploited by the new regime in power from January 1, 1959, to the present. Unfortunately relations between the United States and Cuba have deteriorated to the extent that serious scholarship there for this period on this subject must be postponed. Some material, however, is available to indicate the currency of Martí in Cuban politics.

*Trenches of ideas are worth more
than trenches of stone.*—José Martí

Chapter 1

*J*osé Martí was born January 28, 1853, in Havana, Cuba, the son of Mariano Martí y Navarro, a first sergeant in the Spanish Royal Artillery, and of Leonor Pérez y Cabrera. His father was a native of Valencia, Spain, and his mother came from Santa Cruz de Tenerife, in the Canary Islands. According to Spanish custom, Martí was given his father's name for his first surname, and that of his mother for his second surname. When he was baptized as a Roman Catholic on February 12, 1853, in the church of Santo Angel Custodio de la Habana, his full name became José Julián Martí y Pérez. Martí was born a citizen of Spain. Although from an early age he was to fight for liberation of Cuba from Spain, he never renounced his citizenship nor was he denied it by the Spanish government. An affidavit on "clearness of blood," requested at the time of Martí's entry into high school in Havana in 1866, showed that respected individuals who knew Martí's parents testified to the legitimacy of Martí's birth and to the lack of any colored blood on the part of either parent.[1]*

There were seven other children in Sergeant Martí's family, all girls, two of whom died in early childhood. When Martí was about four and a half years old, his father resigned as a local guard and uprooted his family to take them to Spain so that he could recover his health. They remained two years in Spain and then returned to Havana, where Mariano Martí secured employment as a guard.[2] There were complaints about his conduct, however, and he was released from duty in 1860.[3] The reason given was that Martí, in his capacity as a

*Notes section begins on page 263.

1

district watchman, had refused to take testimony from a dying man in a poisoning case in his district. In addition, he was cited in the letter concerning the disciplinary action taken as being a person of "little aptitude, scarce capacity, and lack of manners for the necessary fulfillment of his position." Two years later Mariano Martí appeared as a minor city official in Hanábana, Cuba. His numerous applications in 1866 and 1867 for a position as a policeman in Havana finally resulted in favorable action being taken in 1868 by the central prefecture of police for Cuba.[4]

One student of Martí as a child has advanced the interesting, if tenuous, theory that Martí's family group was a reproduction in miniature of Cuba confronting the Spanish regime. He writes: "At home Martí was exposed to a kind of Mother-Father relationship resembling the conflict he saw in his adult years between Cuba and the Spanish government." To this scholar Martí's mother represented Cuba in her understanding, admiration of her son's efforts, and capacity for sacrifice. On the other hand, in Martí's father he saw an upright conservatism, honest, and loyal in rejecting Cuban independence. Although the author admits that he is forcing the parallel, he compares Martí's sisters, in their indecisiveness, to Cuban public opinion of the time, unwilling to choose between revolutionary and conservative ideas.[5] There is very little evidence given, however, to bear out this novel simile, particularly in developing the role of Martí's mother as a revolutionary Mother Cuba. Furthermore, while Martí's father was apparently a stern disciplinarian, there is no indication that Leonor Pérez was constantly battling for independence. On the contrary, she seems to have been a loyal wife.

One of Martí's lifelong friends, Fermín Valdés Domínguez, wrote of Martí's parents that they "were honest, although possessing little intelligence or education."[6]

Early Education and Initiation into Politics

By the time José Martí was ready to enter high school in 1866 he had become acquainted with Rafael María de Mendive, a poet, teacher, and enthusiast for Cuban independence. Since Martí's parents, according to Valdés Domínguez, were satisfied to see him become a clerk without a future, Martí found in Mendive the under-standing and intellectual inspiration which were lacking at home.[7] Mendive intervened with Martí's father and urged him to allow José to continue his education in high school at a time when Mariano Martí was eager to have his son find a job to help out with the family's finances. Mendive, in offering to pay for Martí's education through high school, overcame the father's reluctance. He was also instrumental in arranging for Martí's being accepted for an entrance examination. On September 27, 1866, at the age of thirteen, Martí was admitted to the Institute of Secondary Education in Havana.[8]

From 1867 to 1868 he attended St. Paul's School, a branch of the Institute that was under the direction of Mendive. In all his courses he received the highest grades possible.[9] Martí and Valdés Domínguez became the devoted pupils of Mendive, who by thought, word, and deed inspired his young students to amateur literary efforts of a patriotic nature—patriotic, that is, in favor of Cuban inde-pendence from Spain. Early in 1869, January 19, to be exact, Martí and Valdés collaborated in printing a pamphlet, *El Diablo Cojuelo* (*The Limping Devil*). This was a brief collection of anecdotes, jokes, and puns intended to point up, in a humorous way, the lifting of the ban on the press. A decree by the Spanish Captain General, Domingo Dulce y Garay, had established freedom of the press on January 9, 1869. Gonzalo de Castañón, the Spanish editor of *La Voz de Cuba* (*The Voice of Cuba*), is being addressed:

"Mr. Castañón?"
"Yes?"
"There is a Miss Cuba here looking for you. She has come to reclaim her voice, which, as she says, you have taken without her permission."
"Oh, close the door, close the door, my friend! Tell her that I have moved, that I have gone to hell."

The editorial comment of Martí and Valdés is, "We do not know at this time whether Miss Cuba entered or did not enter in time. We'll let you know about this happy event."[10]

Four days later, January 23, Martí, this time on his own, set up a small newspaper. Called *Patria Libre* (*Our Free Country*), it lasted for one issue. *Patria Libre* contained Martí's first drama, *Abdala*. In it

"Nubia" is oppressed Cuba, and "Abdala" is probably a self-portrait of young Martí. Exclaims Abdala:

Finally my forehead will be fringed with glory. I will be the one to free my anguished country, and the one who will drag the oppressor from the people it is beginning to destroy between its claws. And the vile tyrant which threatens Nubia will beg for life and forgiveness at my feet. And the cowardly persons who help it will moan terrified at our effort.[11]

Political Situation in Cuba—1860's

The political situation in Cuba at this time was particularly tense. By the late 1860's Cuba and Puerto Rico were Spain's only remaining colonies in the New World. The disintegration of the Spanish Empire during the eighteenth century and its cataclysmic loss in the first part of the nineteenth century were too great a shock for Spain's inept rulers to grasp any concrete lessons for improving conditions to retain two small island possessions. Nevertheless Cuba was possessed all the more jealously as a remnant of a once great empire in the face of small but determined efforts by Cubans wishing to retire Spain conclusively from the New World. From 1849 to 1851 Narciso López, a Cuban revolutionary, had made three unsuccessful attempts to overthrow the Spanish regime by invading Cuba from the United States.[12]

By far the most serious effort to dislodge the Spanish, however, came on October 10, 1868, with the "Proclamation of Yara" on the part of Carlos Manuel de Céspedes, in the name of the Cubans. This action started a rebellion that was to last in guerrilla warfare for the next ten years, and to become known in Cuban history as the "Ten Years' War."[13]

After hostilities had begun, the Spanish authorities found it necessary to take security measures. In the general collection of "security risks" Martí's teacher, Rafael María de Mendive, was unjustly accused of being involved in a political rally at a theater in Havana, imprisoned, and exiled to Spain in 1869.[14]

Arrest and Imprisonment of Martí

In 1869 Martí himself was destined for trouble with the colonial regime. On October 4 a group of Spanish soldiers was marching past the home of Fermín Valdés Domínguez in Havana. Valdés Domínguez and his friends, joking among themselves, caused the soldiers to take offense. Later that day some of the soldiers returned and searched the house. They found a letter written by Martí and Valdés accusing a former friend of having decamped to the Spanish cause. The two friends were arrested, along with two companions and the brother of Valdés, and detained under a charge of *infidencia* (treason). Several weeks later, October 21, Martí was officially registered in prison. It was not until March 4, 1870, that Martí was sentenced to six years in prison, and his friend Valdés was sentenced to six months.[15]

Martí was not quite seventeen years old when he received this harsh punishment. The disparity in sentences between the two arose from Martí's claiming entire authorship of the letter in question, and a general recognition on the part of the Spanish authorities that Martí was the greater firebrand.[16] On April 5, 1870, Martí was finally processed through the colonial courts and prison administration.[17] He was given his number, 113, and eventually assigned to work at hard labor in a stone quarry in Havana, "Las Canteras de San Lázaro." He was chained from waist to ankle, and suffered severe hardships which had a lasting effect on his spiritual and physical being.[18]

Fortunately Mariano Martí was a friend of the contractor of the stone quarry, José María Sardá, and was able to persuade him to have the Spanish release his son to Sardá's custody on his estate, "El Abra," on the Isle of Pines, off the southern coast of Cuba. Martí was transferred there on October 13, 1870, approximately one year after his arrest in Havana.[19] Martí was well treated at "El Abra."[20] On December 18 of the same year he was returned to Havana for deportation to Spain.[21] Soon thereafter, on January 15, 1871, he left Havana.[22]

When Martí reached Spain he was placed at complete liberty. The Spanish authorities were not to bother him again until his second arrest in 1879, after he had returned to Cuba at the end of the Ten Years' War. At this time a general amnesty was accorded to political prisoners and exiles.

Exile and Political Activities in Spain

Martí soon joined other Cubans in exile in Spain, and began writing letters to the newspapers on behalf of freedom for Cuba.[23] One of his major efforts was an impassioned plea to the Spanish people and authorities to recognize how the liberties of the Cubans were being repressed by the colonial governors. Martí, in an idealistic outburst in his *El presidio político en Cuba* (*The Political Garrison in Cuba*), wrote that all that was lacking was for the truth to be made known. He thought that the lamentable conditions of political prisoners would then be immediately remedied as a result of one great outburst of public indignation.[24] Martí's pamphlet was published. The young revolutionary had established himself as a political writer with a cause.

On May 31, 1871, Martí entered Central University in Madrid to take up a course in law. During September he interrupted his studies long enough to engage in a political polemic with the Madrid newspaper *La Prensa,* with Martí skirmishing from the columns of *El Jurado Federal.* The gist of the battle was criticism by *La Prensa* of the Cuban filibusterers, who were accused of disguising much more radical theories behind the mask of democracy. Martí, along with other Cubans in Madrid, denying the charge, continued the debate throughout the month.[25]

During 1872 Martí pursued his studies in law. Late in the year a political handbill was circulated in Madrid, signed by Martí, Fermín Valdés, who had joined him in exile, and another accomplice. This document, entitled *¡27 de noviembre!,* condemned the shooting by Spanish authorities of eight medical students in Havana on that date in 1871. It was printed in Spain on the first anniversary of the affair.[26]

At this time both Martí and Valdés were suffering from illness. According to Valdés, faculty members decided that their health would be improved by a change in scene. They decided to leave Madrid and enroll at the University of Zaragoza.[27] Consequently, on May 17, 1873, Martí petitioned the administrative authorities at the Central University in Madrid to have his credits transferred to the University of Zaragoza,[28] where he planned to continue in law. As insurrectionists they were well received by the Aragonese, who have often reacted unfavorably to centralizing tendencies from Madrid. While there Martí finished writing a play, *Adúltera (Adultress)*,[29] an amateurish allegory extolling the joys of suffering for others and the nobility of grief.

The first Spanish Republic was proclaimed on February 11, 1873. Martí took this opportunity to publish his pamphlet, *La República española ante la Revolución cubana (The Spanish Republic Confronts the Cuban Revolution)*. Martí pointed out that the logic of republicanism called for one republic to recognize another, that one republic could not keep another by further military repression, which would surely be necessary in the face of the determined efforts that the Cubans were making to secure their freedom. He argued that for humanitarian reasons Spain should give up its hold on Cuba, even maintaining that there was a lack of common identity between the two countries. Pointing out that all the rest of the Latin American colonies of Spain had gained their independence, he found that there was actually much sympathy in Spain for Cuban independence. He claimed that there was a will to independence on the part of those who participated in a war for freedom that could not be downed after it had broken out. He asserted that once the Spanish soldiers realized why they were fighting, they would give up. He warned that the expense involved would result in an economic fiasco for Spain. To clinch his argument he wrote that independence for Cuba would be the inevitable result of all of Spain's errors in colonization.[30]

Journalistic and Literary Activities in Mexico

On June 30, 1874, Martí received his degree in law from the University of Zaragoza, following it later in the same year with a degree in the liberal arts.[31] After completing his studies, Martí, in the company of his friend Valdés, left Spain for Paris, where they remained about one month. From there Martí sailed for Mexico to join his parents, who were then living in that country.

On February 8, 1875, when he arrived in Mexico, Martí was met by members of his family and given the news that his favorite sister, Ana, had died. On this note of grief Martí rejoined the family circle, after having been away for over five years.[32]

Several months later through a friend of the family, Manuel Mercado, a government official, Martí secured a post on the *Revista Universal,* a leading newspaper of the capital city. Mercado was to become one of Martí's most intimate friends. Martí wrote articles and poems for the newspaper under the pseudonym of "Orestes."[33] His major contribution to the *Revista Universal,* however, was in his "Boletines" ("Bulletins"), in which he described Mexico's part in the birth of a new America. He also published articles under his own name. On several occasions he tilted with editors of local newspapers favoring Spain.[34] During this period Martí's translation into Spanish of Victor Hugo's *Mes Fils* was published.[35]

In December, 1875, his play, *Amor con amor se paga (Love Is Repaid with Love),* received its *première* in Mexico City.[36] In the final speech of the last act Martí wrote of one of his favorite themes, the corroding effect that exile has on a person. He said: "The soul without luster is the one of which I write. When one lives without his country, the soul receives neither the light of the sun nor does it enjoy life."[37] It was during this stay in Mexico that Martí became interested in Carmen Zayas-Bazán, his future wife, the daughter of a wealthy Cuban exile.[38]

Teaching and Politics in Guatemala

In January, 1877, Martí decided to return to Havana under an assumed name; but, once there, he was restless and unhappy.[39] He remained in Cuba only a month, and then was on his way to Guatemala. He was fortified with letters of recommendation from the father of Valdés Domínguez to the president, Justo Rufino Barrios, and to other persons in that country.[40] One was a Cuban, José María Izaguirre, the principal of a high school in Guatemala City. By May, 1877, Martí was teaching modern languages and the history of philosophy in Izaguirre's school.[41]

Before securing his teaching position, Martí wrote to Mercado of his impressions of Guatemala, saying:

I have come full of love for this land and these peoples, and if I do not overflow with how much I love them, it is so that I may not be accused of being servile and full of flattery. These are my skies and my people.

If there are not many minds developed, I come to animate them, not to shame or wound them.[42]

By September 21, 1877, Martí was writing to Mercado of the goals that he had marked out for himself. He said:

The terrible, and fortunately unjust, fears of not reaching the well-being which I desire, the bitter memories of my home, the extraordinary activity of a spirit which sees a great deal imperfectly, and which, degrading the characters of other people, displeases and irritates mine; this bed of waves upon which luck . . . obliges me to cast my house—all of this keeps my spirit in serious and sickly preoccupation, which, being mine, all of my griefs increase and exalt. To give life to America, to make the old live, to pour forth my excess of love, to write about serious matters in Paris, to study great things with my intelligence without prejudice . . . to make a warm reception for my voluntary martyr's soul—these are the grave tasks which have come to my pen.[43]

One of Martí's friends in Guatemala was General Miguel García Granados, a former president of the country. Much has been written about Martí's relations with María, the daughter of the General.[44] She is considered to have been Martí's deepest love, but his engagement to Carmen Zayas-Bazán prevented their marriage. Furthermore Martí thought of María as a kind of ideal woman, whom he could worship but not marry.[45]

At the end of the year Martí left Guatemala to return to Mexico and marry Carmen Zayas-Bazán. The marriage took place on December 20.[46] While in Mexico Martí arranged to have his short book, *Guatemala*, published.[47]

Shortly after Martí's marriage to Carmen and their return to Guatemala, María Granados died, probably from tuberculosis.[48] Martí, in a more romantic vein, however, wrote a poem about her in which he said:

> *Like burning bronze*
> *Was her forehead*
> *At my farewell kiss; the forehead*
> *Which I have loved most of all*
> *In my life.*
>
> . . . .
>
> *They say she died of cold;*
> *I know she died of love.*[49]

Meanwhile Martí ran into difficulties with the government, which had deposed Izaguirre from his post as principal of the school. Martí supported Izaguirre by resigning from the school on April 6.[50] Shortly before renouncing his teaching post Martí wrote to Mercado of his plans to publish a monthly magazine in Guatemala, "in which I will have to disfigure myself a great deal to put myself on the common level. Where there are many heads outstanding, one head more does not attract any attention, but where there are few that are prominent, vast plains without mountains, one exceptional head is a crime. The conservatives nail me to the cross, and they are right. I must seem like a devil to them. . . . I do not find any liberals with intelligence or heart here. . . . It is a battle in which I, as a soldier of light, am conquered beforehand, but I struggle as discreetly as I can, that is what my magazine is for."[51] The project, however, was never realized.

Several weeks later he wrote to Mercado that it was impossible for him to find work in Guatemala because the government would hire only Guatemalans in teaching jobs; he bitterly complained that he was being treated as a stranger.[52] On July 6, 1878, Martí wrote to Mercado of his decision to leave Guatemala because he was disgusted with the spectacle of petty individuals making themselves lackeys of the government in order to gain favors. During his first stay in Guatemala he had felt well received, but when he returned he had discovered a new tyranny in the land. Soon the way in which he was teaching made him unpopular with the authorities. Consequently he had decided to return to Cuba, "in answer to the tears of Carmen and the perspicacity of her father." Logic told him to go anywhere but to Cuba because the end of the war there was impossible. He reasoned as follows:

Shall I tell you . . . that I carry my unhappy people in my head, and that it seems to me that their liberty will some day depend upon one breath of mine? . . . They think that I am returning to my country. . . . I no longer have a country—until I conquer it. . . . I am to suffer much, and I am leaving . . . this means that I understand my duty, and I fulfill it. . . . There is in me a double man—the prudent one who does what he should, and the rebel thinker who urges himself on. Satisfied with this victory that I have won over myself, I mourn it with inexpressible bitterness.[53]

Return to Cuba and Second Deportation

In mid-1878 Martí and his wife left for Havana, taking advantage of the general amnesty granted to political exiles after the signing of the Pact of Zanjón on February 10, 1878, ending the Ten Years' War.[54] After their arrival, Martí secured a job as a clerk for two lawyers, Nicolás Azcárate and Miguel F. Viondi.[55] Meanwhile he sought authorization to practice as a lawyer, but was unable to secure permission because of technical difficulties in the certification of his degree. This disappointment was mitigated on November 22, 1878, with Martí's joy at the birth of a son, José, in Havana.[56]

Such an event, however, was only a temporary distraction in Martí's pursuit of the liberation of Cuba. With the failure of one liberation movement, the Ten Years' War, as an immediate example, Martí decided that he would undertake two modes of action—verbal combat in literary tourneys with Hispanophiles and conspiracy. Late in 1878 Martí was elected secretary of the literature section of the Artistic and Literary Society of Guanabacoa, which afforded him a forum for debate. Meanwhile he daily met with Juan Gualberto Gómez, a fellow conspirator.[57]

During 1879 Martí continued his revolutionary activities, not, however, without regret at having returned to Cuba. In a letter to Manuel Mercado, January 17, 1879, he wrote:

The first weakness and serious error of my life—returning to Cuba. Today my poor Carmen, who wept so much to return, now regrets having wept so much. But here I am, with no joy in my heart, my pen and lips in irons, leading a life which every day is more difficult. I was not born to live in these lands. I need breathing space . . . Spanish life, after having lived American life! . . . Exile in one's country is a thousand times more bitter for those, like myself, who have found a home in exile. Here I do not speak, nor write, nor do I have the energy to think. . . .If Cuba were not so unfortunate, I would love Mexico more than Cuba.[58]

A group of conspirators met in Havana, March 18, 1879, to draw up a plan of action against the Spanish regime, and Martí was among them. The document that remains from that meeting is interesting in that, while protesting the loyalty of the island rebels to the Cuban group in exile in New York, it called for the establishment of a provisional center in Cuba to coordinate local activities. The plan is also of significance in showing the importance of the role of patriotic clubs in the revolutionary movement.[59]

Sometime during 1879 Martí jotted down in his notebook some thoughts about the type of revolution that was necessary to free Cuba. He wrote:

This is not a revolution of anger. It is a revolution of reflection. It is the only form, the only way that we can reach, as soon as our necessities require, the realization of our brilliant and vibrant destinies. For, in this matter of the future, severe meditations and cold judgment dispel the phantoms which either timid interest, or pretentious ignorance, or trembling fear provoke.

In his notes Martí scourged the political opportunists for raising false hopes for a quick and easy liberation. He reflected, "The cost of liberty is very high. It is necessary either to resign one's self to live without it, or to decide to buy it at its price."[60]

Martí boldly followed his own advice when, on April 26, 1879, he spoke out against the autonomists at a banquet in honor of a prominent journalist, Adolfo Márquez Sterling.[61] The following day he openly advocated Cuban independence in the presence of General Ramón Blanco, the Spanish governor.[62]

On September 17, 1879, Martí was detained for conspiracy, along with Juan Gualberto Gómez. Eight days later he was deported once again to Spain. He remained in Spain only until December.[63] Then he left for France, on his way to New York, where he arrived on January 3, 1880.[64] He was not to set foot in Cuba again until the year of his death, 1895.

Exile, Politics, and Literary Activities in New York

Martí immediately joined the Cubans in exile in New York. There he proceeded to undertake his prodigious journalistic efforts, which were to make him known throughout Latin America as an interpreter of the United States, particularly in Argentina, Uruguay, and Venezuela in South America; Mexico; and in Guatemala, Honduras, and Costa Rica in Central America.

One of Martí's first acts was to join the Cuban Revolutionary Committee of New York, which had been organized in October,

1878, under the leadership of General Calixto García, a veteran of the Ten Years' War. In a speech to this group in Steck Hall in New York City on January 24, 1880, Martí inspired his listeners with such admiration for his opposition to the autonomist group of Cubans that he was appointed interim head of the New York Committee in the absence of its president, José Francisco Lamadriz. Up to then Martí had been little known. It was at this point, according to one biographer, that Martí seriously began his labor to organize the war of liberation.[65]

In the summer of 1879 the Cuban Revolutionary Committee on behalf of the Cubans, whose interests had not been served by the Pact of Zanjón, had begun a new rebellion, known as "La Guerra Chiquita" ("The Little War").[66] One of Martí's first official acts as interim president of the Committee was to give his enthusiastic approval to the expedition of General Calixto García. In a circular of the Revolutionary Committee Martí established in an un-mistakable way his democratic and civilian point of view toward the revolution. He wrote:

The military leader has gone, not only to battle. He will not monopolize total power in his own hands, whatever may be the reasons his friends may give him for it. To prepare us for peace, in the midst of war, without weakening the war effort, that is what he has gone for.[67]

Lacking popular support, the Little War began to lose its verve a little over a year after it had begun. On October 13, 1880, some time before the failure of the insurrection, Martí wrote to Emilio Núñez, a leading general, asking him to lay down his arms rather than to continue in useless attempts to rout the Spaniards. He said that a handful of men, supported by the people could succeed, but that abandoned by the people, they would soon seem to become a group of bandits.[68]

One of Martí's first journalistic efforts in 1880 was his "Impressions of America" in a magazine called the *Hour*. In this year he also began contributing to the *Sun*, under the editorship of Charles A. Dana.[69]

Later in 1880 Martí was joined in New York by his wife and their son, but soon the parents were quarreling. Carmen Martí was completely unsympathetic to her husband's dedication to revolutionary activities, and, in fact, indicated that she was satisfied with Spain's government of the island. Martí suffered with the picture of his son growing up contrary to his fervent beliefs. In January, 1881, Carmen returned to Cuba with their son, unable to reach an understanding with her husband. Martí dedicated himself increasingly to his work and wrote, "Work, and the spiritual well-being that it produces, are the sweetest vengeance on those who make us suffer."[70]

A more sympathetic partner Martí found in Carmen Miyares de Mantilla, a Cuban woman who operated a boarding-house where Martí stayed from time to time while in New York. Her daughter, María, born November 20, 1880,[71] is considered to be Martí's child. María's son is César Romero, a film star.[72]

On his decision to continue active in politics regardless of its effect on his marriage, Martí jotted down some thoughts in his notebooks in 1881. He wrote:

There is no life more bitter, more treacherous, and scarce in results, than public life. For one who knows the dark workshops in which fame is customarily wrought out, and who knows that vicious ambition is stronger there than modest virtue . . . for one who knows that people, today still largely ignorant, if governed sometimes by reason, are ruled more by their passions, and that those who flatter them make the greatest headway, for those honest men who do not know how to sacrifice a conviction for the pleasure of seeming acceptable to the intolerant public, these certainly can not seem to be tempting motives. There is no grief like leaving one's hidden and peaceful refuge, but there is no evil like feeling capable of doing good, although it may be to one's own detriment, and then failing to do it.[73]

Early in 1881 Martí left for Venezuela, where he took up writing for *La Opinión Nacional,* a major newspaper in Caracas, the capital city. He also began a magazine of his own, *La Revista Venezolana,* an ephemeral publication which saw only two issues.[74] The final number contained his famous article on Cecilio Acosta, written on the death of this outstanding Venezuelan man of letters. Martí's praise of Acosta, who had been in poor political standing, irritated the dictator of Venezuela, President Guzmán Blanco, and Martí found it expedient to leave for New York on July 28, 1881.[75] He continued to write under a pseudonym for *La Opinión Nacional,* however, until the editors told him to avoid attacking the Pope, and to include more news and less literary style in his articles.[76]

Although he was busy with his reporting activities, Martí still had time to write poetry, and in 1882 he published his book of verse, *Ismaelillo* (*Little Ishmael*), dedicated to his son José. In 1891 he published his *Versos sencillos* (*Simple Verses*), of an autobiographical nature. Many of his poems, however, were written without being published during his lifetime, and afterwards appeared in a collection as *Versos libres* (*Free Verses*).[77]

In 1882 Martí became a regular correspondent for the famous newspaper of Bartolomé Mitre, *La Nación,* in Buenos Aires. For his literary efforts with *La Nación* Martí received high praise from the great Argentine writer, Domingo Faustino Sarmiento, who wrote that he was "Latin America's representative of the Spanish language."[78] Martí contributed less regularly to *La Pluma,* in Bogotá, Colombia; *El Partido Liberal,* in Mexico City; *La República,* of Tegucigalpa, Honduras; *La Opinión Pública,* in Montevideo, Uruguay; and others.[79]

To supplement his meager income as a newspaper correspondent Martí found it necessary to work at numerous occupations. From 1883 to 1886 he translated four books for D. Appleton and Company in New York.[80] Martí was very impatient with newspaper work and translation, and said that he did it only because it was a way of earning his living. He wrote:

The daily writer can not pretend to be sublime. . . . The sublime is the essence of life: the mountain ends in a peak; the sublime is like a mountain top. The daily writer is like one who, should he decide to walk on mountain peaks, falls into an abyss. He must stick to the pavements of the city, which are not of summits but of stones. . . . The daily writer can be sublime once in a while, but most of the time he must be content with being agreeable.[81]

In 1882 Martí wrote to General Máximo Gómez, a citizen of the Dominican Republic and one of the leaders of the Ten Years' War, introducing himself as a young but enthusiastic Cuban revolutionary who wanted to enlist the General's aid once again to prepare for the liberation of Cuba. He wrote:

As you know, General, moving a country, however small it may be, is the work of giants. And he who does not feel gigantic in love, or valor, or thought, or patience, should not undertake it.

No doubt recalling the failure of the Little War, Martí emphasized the need for moving slowly and waiting for carefully laid plans. He stressed the danger lying with those timid persons in Cuba who, while wishing freedom from Spain, preferred annexation to the United States. He ended on the note that the General probably would not know him because of Martí's dislike of publicity, but that a mutual friend, Flor Crombet, who was on his way to Honduras, would tell him who he was.[82]

In a letter to General Antonio Maceo, another outstanding hero of the Ten Years' War, also in Honduras, Martí wrote the same way, introducing himself and telling him of the renewal of the revolutionary movement. He asked Maceo's opinion about recommencing the war, stating that he could not conceive of any serious matter in regard to Cuba in which Maceo would not figure.[83]

In 1883 Martí became editor of a business magazine, *La América,* in New York, a post he held until 1884.[84] In December he was rejoined by his wife and son, after two years of separation.[85] If Carmen Martí had read the letter to Manuel Mercado which Martí had written earlier in the year she might have thought that the goals Martí was writing about could very well have been supplied by herself and their son by Martí's return to Cuba. Martí wrote:

My only happiness, and I have known it since childhood, is in that some few noble souls may know and love me, and in returning to Cuba this body which it gave to me. For that reason and the lack of its fulfillment I look upon myself with ill will and displeasure, as if I were a very great rogue.[86]

Martí was not referring to his family, however, and in 1884 his wife and son returned to Cuba. Martí was always bitter about his wife's lack of comprehension of his ambitions. One of his poems, "¡Dios las maldiga!" ("God Curse Them!"), was written in tune with his sentiments on just such an occasion. In the first stanza he cries out:

> *God curse them! There are mothers in the world*
> *Who take their children from their fathers,*
> *And prepare their white souls for evil,*

And pour hatred into their ears!
God curse them! Oh, Heaven, will there not be
A God more cruel who may curse them more?[87]

Carmen and her son returned for a brief stay in New York in 1891,[88] but for the major part of their almost eighteen years of marriage she and Martí were separated.

On May 22, 1884, Martí was named vice-consul for Uruguay in New York City. Martí, however, did not officially receive his *exaquatur* until January 23, 1891.[89]

On October 18, 1884, Martí met with General Gómez and General Antonio Maceo in New York for the first time to discuss plans for continuing the revolutionary movement in and out of Cuba. The meeting broke up in failure, however, because Martí was unwilling to continue as an associate unless some clear understanding could be reached beforehand that liberated Cuba would not have a military form of government. Two days later Martí wrote a letter to General Gómez explaining his position, affirming that it was his determination not to contribute one iota toward bringing a personal despotism to Cuba in the wake of military conquest. In his opinion a people was not founded in the way a military camp was run, and he was shocked and displeased when General Maceo gave him to understand that they were to consider the Cuban war as the "exclusive property" of General Gómez. For that reason Martí stated that he would have to withdraw from collaboration with the two military leaders because of the incompatibility of their positions.[90]

Meanwhile Martí continued his literary efforts. In 1885 he published a short novel, *Amistad funesta* (*Sad Friendship*), under the pseudonym of "Adelaida Ral."[91] The work is regarded as of very little merit as a novel. Martí wrote it in seven days. A Mexican authority on Martí as a writer claims,

The most that can be said of this book is that it is dull, diffuse, if not artificial and false. Not even in its biographical aspect do we believe that it can be granted as much value as has been attributed to it. Martí can not pour forth his soul with full force, his tenderness is directed to things which do not matter to him, and he does not see the moral, apostolic, patriotic, and effective application which he considered essential in every work. For that reason this novel did not interest him, nor is he in it, or if he is, it is less than in any other of his pages.[92]

This point of view is not held by other writers on Martí. Félix Lizaso writes that "there are innumerable confessions of his own sentiments in writing these pages."[93] Mauricio Magdaleno, a Mexican writer, maintains that in the novel there are many breaths of Martí's own life.[94] Jorge Mañach finds that "in *Amistad funesta* he left much of himself and of his own life."[95] In the opinion of Gonzalo de Quesada y Miranda,

It is not mere chance, but a phenomenon psychologically explicable, that in that novel he empties his own person with transparent clarity, as perhaps he would not have been able to realize in any other moment of his life, in the almost autobiographical Juan Jerez.[96]

Numerous passages in the novel support the majority point of view. Among them is one in which Martí seemed to be identifying himself with one of his characters when he wrote:

He traveled because he was full of eagles, which gnawed at his body, and wanted wide spaces, and were suffocating in the prison of the city. He traveled because he was married to a woman whom he thought he had loved, and whom he then found like an insensible cup, in which the harmonies of his soul found no echo, from which there came to him such great dejection that he had not even strength to move his hands upon the keyboard.[97]

The following year, 1886, Martí was suffering from a similar despair. In a letter to Mercado he wrote that the memory of his old father, the love of his friends, and the love of children were the only things that moved "his terrified soul," in addition to his affection for all that suffered, which was a "vice" in him. He wrote that everything tied him to New York, which he found to be a "cup of poison," and that he was grieving over the political situation in Cuba, so near and yet so far away. He could not think of returning to Cuba, however, because every political misdeed he would take as a personal affront. Sunk in a slough of despond, he wrote, "Miserable wretch that I am, I am not the master of my life, nor can I . . . fulfill private duties."[98]

On February 2, 1887, Martí's father died in Havana. Shortly before, Martí had written a eulogy as an expression of his reconciliation with his father. He wrote to Mercado that he was extremely sad because it had taken him so long to understand his father and venerate him.[99]

Family griefs, however, never kept Martí from his dedication to the Cuban revolution. In May, 1887, he wrote in an open letter to Ricardo Rodríguez Otero his belief that Cuba would never secure the reforms promised by Spain, and also that the Autonomist party would never achieve success. He saw that war was inevitable and he declared his inalterable opposition to annexation of the island by the United States.[100]

On October 10, 1887, Martí initiated his yearly speech to commemorate the Tenth of October, 1868, the date from which the Cuban independence movement is usually reckoned. According to one authority on Martí it is in these speeches better than in any other place that Martí reveals himself as a statesman, sociologist, and especially as a true leader of people, and as a person capable of evoking mass sentiment.[101] He regularly gave these discourses until 1894.

Worry over the political situation in Cuba, personal problems, and the daily struggle for existence would have left many lesser individuals without energy for further activity, but Martí found release from these burdens by translating for his own satisfaction. In 1887, on his private account, he translated and published Helen Hunt Jackson's *Ramona*.[102] His Spanish translation is considered superior to the original in literary style. Martí saw in the novel a unique and sympathetic treatment of a Latin American people, the Indians of Lower California. He wrote:

Our race, often disdained without reason, [is] treated with ingenuous affection, and recognized in all of its goodness by a famous writer among those who have most disdained us.[103]

In 1887 Martí added *El Economista Americano* to the list of periodicals to which he was contributing.[104] By this time Martí's attitude toward journalism had been modified to the extent that he wrote:

The newspaper [in the United States], among other things, . . . has the habit of often publishing articles of good sense, of moderation in form, and practical, and broad-minded in politics, which is different from the impassioned jargon in use . . . there [Mexico].

He felt that this reflected a politically superior attitude in the United States. In addition, the financial and prestige aspects pleased him.

More than twenty newspapers publish my letters, with compliments that please me very much. Although still poor, I am able to pay all my debts. At other times I have earned more, but with such martyrdom and on such a tight schedule that I almost did not have time to eat.[105]

Organizing for the Revolution

Late in 1887, to further the revolutionary movement, a Provisional Executive Commission was formed with Martí at its head. It had a decidedly civilian complexion, although General Máximo Gómez was invited to help in its work. In a letter to the General, December 16, 1887, signed by Martí and twenty-one other Cuban patriots, it was announced that the Commission had been formed. It stated that the time seemed appropriate to group their forces since the principle of the new revolution had caught on in Cuba and in the emigration centers in New York City, Philadelphia, and Florida. It was necessary to act while the enemies of the revolution were divided. Furthermore it maintained that the benevolent disposition of the General was essential to the efficacy of the work. While Martí thereupon showed himself willing to heal the breach made in 1884 between himself and General Gómez, the letter reaffirmed the necessity of having a civilian government once the revolution had achieved success.[106]

Three days earlier Martí had written to Mercado in Mexico:

My country is agitated, and very much disposed to suffer from the machinations of foreigners and from its own people. I am restless and I bleed, thinking about how I could cover it all and shelter it with my own body, which can not be, and I do not have a tranquil moment. . . . If mythology were true, and a man could convert himself into a tree or a flower, I would be a weeping willow.[107]

Once again, February 19, 1888, Martí wrote to Mercado of his state of depression, only this time over the sentiment on the part of the United States in proposing to buy Cuba from Spain. He maintained that if this should happen he would be on the verge of suicide.[108]

On March 21, 1889, Martí spent some of his journalistic fervor in answering an attack on Cuban honor in the *Evening Post* of Philadelphia. This newspaper, following the lead of the *Manufacturer* of the same city, had written that it was against the best interests of the United States to annex Cuba because the Cubans as a people would be an undesirable addition to the population of the United States. It was a slanderous attack on the character of the Cubans, and Martí struck back in a letter to the *Post* in his "Vindicación de Cuba" ("Vindication of Cuba").[109]

In this letter Martí wrote that there were some Cubans with respectable motives who desired annexation to the United States, but those who had fought in the Ten Years' War could never accept annexation because they saw that it was not necessary. Furthermore, he said that the admiration of the Cubans for the United States was very great, making its heroes their own. Although they desired the success of the United States as the greatest glory of humanity, he could not honestly believe that the excessive individualism of the North Americans, the worship of wealth, and the prolonged celebration of a terrible victory in the Civil War prepared the United States to be the "typical nation of liberty." He maintained that the Cubans were not that people of miserable vagabonds nor immoral pygmies that the *Manufacturer* was pleased to describe, nor were they useless verbalizers, incapable of action. He showed that the Cubans had fought valiantly against an empire of corruption, but in the process they had somehow managed to avoid contamination. He asserted that the political knowledge of the average Cuban could be compared not unfavorably with that of the average citizen of the United States. Furthermore, he wrote:

The absolute lack of religious intolerance, the love of man for property acquired with the work of his hands, and familiarity in practice and theory with the laws and procedures of liberty, will accustom the Cuban to rebuild his country on the ruins in which he will receive it from his oppressors.[110]

The ill-natured attack on Cuban honor by the *Post* caused Martí to write to Manuel Mercado of his plans to publish a newspaper in English in defense of the Latin American nations. He stated his purpose:

What I want is to demonstrate that we are good people, industrious and capable. For each offense, a reply, of the type which I can write, and more effective by its moderation. For each false assertion about our countries, an immediate correction. For each defect, apparently just, which is thrown in our faces, the historical explanation which will excuse it, and proof of the capacity to remedy it. One can not live without defenses. It would seem to me that I were being derelict in my duty if I should not realize this plan.[111]

Unfortunately the plan was never carried out, just as other projects of Martí for books and magazines were short-lived.

In July, 1889, Martí began publication of a monthly magazine for children, *La Edad de Oro* (*The Age of Gold*), in which he included poetry and stories of historical interest about Latin America. He wrote that his purpose in beginning the magazine was to fill Latin America with men of originality, brought up to be happy in the land in which they were living, and to live by conforming to it, without being separated from it, or living barrenly in it. He wrote, "We must bring up our children to be men of their time, and men of America. If I had not had my eyes on this high proposition, I would never have begun the enterprise."[112] The publication of the magazine, however, was suspended after the fourth number because of a "lack of atmosphere and income."[113]

Martí as a Diplomat in the United States

The last issue of *La Edad de Oro* appeared as the first Pan-American Congress—October 2, 1889, to April 19, 1890—was opening its meetings. Martí was very much interested in this conference. A young Cuban, Gonzalo de Quesada y Aróstegui, who had previously caught Martí's attention as an enthusiastic patriot for Cuban liberation, was the secretary to Argentina's delegate. Quesada soon became Martí's favorite disciple, and it was in his letters to Quesada during the conference that Martí expressed his most intimate feelings about North American politics. Quesada was Martí's source of information for what was happening during the conference.[114] In a letter of October 19, 1889, Martí wrote to Quesada of his fears that the conference would afford an opportunity for the United States to seek again the annexation of Cuba.[115]

On July 24, 1890, Martí was named consul for Argentina in

New York.[116] He also became Paraguay's representative in New York July 30.[117]

On December 23, 1890, Martí was named Uruguay's representative to the first American International Monetary Conference, which was to meet in Washington the following year.[118] The Conference was called to gain the support of the Latin American countries on the issue of bimetallism, and specifically on the circulation on equal terms of gold and silver on a world-wide basis. As a large silver-producing country the United States would have profited from such an international agreement. It sought the backing of the Latin American nations in its proposal, especially the aid of the silver-rich countries, Mexico and Peru. According to one authority on Martí, "A quick glance at the detailed Index of the *Minutes* reveals that he was the most active delegate of the Conference and the one who played the most decisive role.[119]

Martí's major contribution to the Conference as Uruguay's delegate was to read a speech at the March 30 session opposing United States Secretary of State James G. Blaine's proposal that the Latin American nations support the United States. In his speech on behalf of the committee of Latin American delegates Martí showed that since most of their countries lacked silver the committee could not see any advantage for Latin America in the plan. The main reason Martí gave for the committee's opposing its adoption, however, was that two recent conferences on the same issue had failed to produce any results, and conditions in the meantime had not changed to the extent that a new meeting was justified.[120]

The report was unanimously accepted, and Martí is given credit for having "thwarted the designs of the Department of State,"[121] although other factors may have contributed to the failure of the Conference.

Martí's prominent role in the activities of the Conference led the Spanish ambassador in Washington to complain on September 18, 1891, to his superiors in Madrid that it was an incongruous situation for a Cuban revolutionary to be holding the position of consul in New York for another country.[122] Repercussions of this reached Martí and he subsequently resigned from all three positions in October in order to devote more time to the revolutionary movement.[123]

Martí and the Cuban Revolutionary Party

On November 25, 1891, Martí was in Tampa, Florida, at the invitation of the Ignacio Agramonte Club, a Cuban patriotic group, to take part in a benefit for the organization. The following day he gave an important speech in the Cuban Lyceum, known as "Con todos y para el bien de todos" ("Everyone Together and for the Well-being of All"). In it Martí discussed the Cuba that should be the dream of every Cuban aspiring to its freedom. He wrote, "Cuba must be taken as an altar, to offer our lives on it; and not as a pedestal, to lift ourselves upon it." He envisioned a Cuba in which there would be justice for all, including the Negroes and even the Spaniards, many of whom he considered to be good Cubans.[124]

Martí was admitted to the Cuban Patriotic League of Tampa on November 27. On this occasion he gave his speech known as "Los pinos nuevos" ("The New Pines"), in commemoration of November 27, 1871, the date of the shooting of the eight medical students in Havana. In this speech he began with a eulogy of death, saying that others lamented necessary death, but that he believed in it as a "pillow, as the yeast, as the triumph of life." Then he asked:

Who, who was the first one in the procession of sacrifice, when the tambour of death rolled, and one could hear the wave of sobs, and the assassins lowered their heads, who was the first, with a smile of peace on his lips, and with firm step, and almost happy, and all of him tinged with light?

It was Martí. He wrote of himself, "The youth of sixteen years went ahead, smiling, tinged as if with light, looking back, to see if anyone should accuse him of cowardice." He then went on to a general praise of the heroism needed in the struggle ahead to save Cuba, and the need for sacrifice, ending on a note of optimism. Referring to a recent storm scene etched in his memory of a burst of light on a young pine tree, he exclaimed in a final note, "That is what we are: new pines!"[125]

The next day the leaders of the Cuban emigrants in Tampa approved the *Resoluciones* (*Resolutions*), a statement of the aims of the Cuban revolutionary movement. It is almost certain that they were written or at least outlined by Martí. Martí returned to New York, but was back in Florida by the end of December, in ill health but eager to meet with the insurrectionist clubs in Tampa and Key West. On January 5, 1892, the leaders of the patriotic clubs met in Key West with Martí and drew up the *Bases y estatutos secretos del Partido Revolucionario Cubano* (*Bases and Secret Statutes of the Cuban Revolutionary Party*). This document is the cornerstone of the Cuban revolutionary movement.[126] The following month Martí wrote to Mercado:

Now I will only tell you that I have been working, with my soul dragging along, on patriotic organization, from bed to rostrum, on evangelizing trips, suffering a long and serious illness, and polemicizing, and in daily struggle. . . . When I have no strength for myself, I have it for my country.[127]

On March 14, 1892, the first number of Martí's newspaper *Patria,* a weekly publication, appeared in New York City. Martí was its editor and publisher until his death.

The Cuban Revolutionary party was formally proclaimed on April 10, 1892, by all the Cuban and Puerto Rican groups in exile in the United States.[128] At the same time Martí was elected the delegate of the body. Thereupon he officially became the major leader of the Cuban revolutionary movement, since the position of "delegate" meant the presidency of the party. Benjamín J. Guerra was elected treasurer. Martí designated Gonzalo de Quesada y Aróstegui as secretary.[129]

In May Martí wrote from New York to the presidents of clubs in the advisory body of Key West, elaborating on the organization of the Cuban Revolutionary party. He said that one of the bases of good government was to allow as much internal independence to its subsidiary organizations as was possible, but that at the same time it was necessary for these groups not to contradict the major goals of the whole movement.[130]

Meanwhile Spanish agents were attempting to sow discord between the Cuban civilian and military revolutionaries. In an article in *Patria* June 4, 1892, Martí warned against this treachery, at the same time acclaiming the solidarity existing between these patriotic groups. In Cuba the political situation was becoming worse. On August 27, 1892, Martí wrote in *Patria*:

Havana is now not a good university nor is there any reason for perfect men to come from that theater of vice, where there is no justice without bribery, nor honor without its price, nor a breath of air without adulation, nor bread without a stain, and who would like it without stains, is left without bread.

In the same article, however, Martí saw hope for Cuba in its good citizens. He said, "Of these men a people is made, even though today they have one political motto and tomorrow another." He wrote that the sin was not in being mistaken about the route, and believing in a remedy which was not the right one, but in perpetuating the weak and indecisive character of the colony.[131]

Plans for the Invasion of Cuba

At the end of August, 1892, Martí left New York for Gonaives and Cap Haïtien, Haiti, and from there on horseback to Montecristi, in the Dominican Republic, for an interview and further reconciliation on September 11 with General Máximo Gómez, with whom Martí had broken eight years before.[132] They had corresponded but had not met since then. In a formal letter to Gómez, dated September 13, 1892, Martí, in the name of the Cuban Revolutionary party, asked the General to be the supreme chief of the military branch of the revolutionary movement. He wrote:

I invite you without fear of a negative answer to this new work, and today I have no more remuneration to offer you than the pleasure of sacrifice and the probable ingratitude of men.[133]

After this meeting General Gómez wrote in his diary that many prominent Cubans were fearful that he would refuse to help Martí in his effort to revive the revolution because of their past differences. He added, however, that this was out of the question because Martí came in the name of Cuba, and that there was no reason to doubt his political honesty.[134] The reunion was a success and Gómez agreed to head another military attempt of the Cubans to wrest independence from Spain. Martí returned to New York by way of the capital cities of Santo Domingo, Haiti, and Jamaica.[135]

After his arrival in New York Martí reported on October 23 to the assembled revolutionary clubs on his trip.[136] In December he was re-elected delegate of the Cuban Revolutionary party.[137]

During the first half of 1893 Martí was constantly on the road between Florida and New York, reporting to the New York clubs on the results of his propaganda efforts, and conferring with Tomás Estrada Palma, a distinguished Cuban exile and later first President of a liberated Cuba.[138]

One of Martí's major fears was that a premature uprising in Cuba by rebels would jeopardize the success of the general movement. In an article in *Patria* April 1, 1893, Martí wrote of the inalterable opposition of the Cuban Revolutionary party to a precipitant uprising of scattered revolutionary elements.[139] These fears were soon realized when a small group, led by the Sartorius brothers, rose up in arms in Oriente province April 27. The rebellion soon dissolved without a shot being fired.[140] A long manifesto of the party was issued and published in *Patria* on May 27. It roundly censured the isolated uprising as playing directly into the hands of the Spaniards. Another ill-starred revolt took place later in the year in Cienfuegos. Martí was disposed to aid this one as long as it seemed to have some chance for success, but it also failed.[141]

Meanwhile, on May 26, 1893, Martí left once again for Montecristi for a conference with Máximo Gómez. From there he went to Costa Rica, by way of Haiti, for a fence-mending conference with General Antonio Maceo, the Cuban mulatto leader with whom Martí had broken in 1884. Maceo was won over and agreed to support a new uprising.[142]

In September Martí was back in New York reporting to the advisory body of the party of his travels on behalf of the revolution.[143] During the fall and winter of 1893 the editions of *Patria* and Martí's letters show that he spent much of his time traveling between Florida and New York coordinating the revolutionary effort, collecting funds, and animating his countrymen.[144]

General Gómez arrived in New York April 8, 1894, to confer with Martí on future action for the liberation of Cuba. The plan, according to Gómez' *Diario de campaña* (*Field Diary*), was as follows: at the decisive moment a ship was to pick up Gómez, accompanied by at least two hundred Cubans and Dominicans, and take them to Cuba.

An expedition was to leave from Key West for Santa Clara, Cuba. Antonio Maceo and Flor Crombet were to leave with another group from Costa Rica for the eastern part of the island. Throughout Cuba cohorts were to be posted to rise up at the signal for the revolution to start.[145]

By the middle of July Martí was in New Orleans on his way to Mexico to obtain funds for the revolutionary treasure chest.[146] It is claimed that while in Mexico he also visited President Porfirio Díaz to enlist his support in the Cuban invasion.[147] There is no documentary evidence that this interview was ever held, but one Mexican writer insists that he has talked with persons who claim that the interview was held.[148]

Failure of the Fernandina Filibuster

By Christmas Day, 1894, Martí had completed all details for the expedition to Cuba. Three ships had been rented, provisioned with arms, and were waiting to set sail from Fernandina, Florida. One ship was to pick up General Antonio Maceo and General Flor Crombet in Costa Rica and take them and their volunteers to Cuba. Another was to carry Martí and his men to the Dominican Republic, then invade Cuba from the south, with Maceo's group invading from the north. The third ship was to go to Key West, pick up volunteers there, and take them to Santa Clara.[149]

Unfortunately for the conspirators, one of their trusted members, Colonel Fernando López de Queralta, revealed the plan, and the United States government closed in on them on January 12, 1895, and confiscated the ships and arms.[150] Martí was most distraught at this unexpected disaster, but his friends rallied to his support. In particular, the mother-in-law of his best friend, Gonzalo de Quesada y Aróstegui, offered to furnish bail for those arrested in connection with the debacle. Horatio S. Rubens, the young lawyer engaged as counsel for the revolutionists, was able to save part of the supplies of the expedition.[151] In some ways the confiscation was a blessing, because the publicity convinced the cigar makers of the Cuban emigrant colonies in Florida that Martí was in earnest and had invested their contributions in arms.[152] He became "positively an idol" to them.[153]

The Manifesto of Montecristi

Slowly Martí began to gather together the pieces and to make new plans for the invasion. On January 29, 1895, Martí signed an order for a general uprising in Cuba directing Juan Gualberto Gómez, representative of the Cuban Revolutionary party in Havana, to take charge of the arrangements in Cuba.[154]

Martí left New York on January 31 for Montecristi to meet with General Máximo Gómez to consolidate their plans to launch another invasion attempt.[155] They met on February 7 and spent the rest of the month awaiting news of an uprising in Cuba. On February 26 word came that the revolution had begun.[156]

Meanwhile in Costa Rica Antonio Maceo refused to undertake his part of the expedition unless $5,000 was forthcoming, rather than the $2,000 which was his share of the revolutionary funds. Flor Crombet was anxious to begin the operation, but Maceo had again lost faith in Martí. On February 26 the latter found it necessary to write him a sharp letter pulling him into line.[157] Maceo responded, but never forgave Martí.[158]

One month later Martí was still in Montecristi, where, on March 25, he and General Máximo Gómez signed *El Manifiesto de Montecristi*. Martí did the actual drafting of the document.[159] The *Manifiesto* was the message of the Revolutionary party to the Cuban people. In an exposition of the principles of the revolution it called for a just war, which could not be against the individual Spaniard, but against the colonial regime. It urged understanding and appreciation of the Negro, not fear, and foresaw a vigorous and healthful war to give Cuba a rebirth. It read:

The revolution will tomorrow fulfill the duty of explaining once more to the country and to all nations the local causes, on the basis of universal interest, with which the veterans of Yara and Guáimaro renew for the advancement and service of humanity a war worthy of the respect of its enemies and the help of its peoples, according to the rigid concept of the rights of man, and its abhorrence of sterile vengeance and useless devastation.[160]

At this time Martí wrote his "political will" in a letter to Federico Henríquez y Carvajal, a close friend and prominent public figure in

the Dominican Republic. This letter reflects Martí's preoccupation with the necessity of his taking part in the actual liberation of Cuba. He wrote:

I was dying of shame, apart from my conviction that my presence in Cuba is as useful there as elsewhere, as long as I believed that because of the great risk involved I could convince myself that it was my obligation to allow him [Máximo Gómez] to go alone, and that a people allows itself to be served, although with a certain disdain and indifference, by one who preached the necessity of dying and did not begin by risking his own life. Wherever my greater duty may be, within or without, there I will be. . . . I will lift up the world. But my only desire will be to stick there, to the last tree trunk, to the last fighter; to die silent. For me, the hour has arrived.[161]

On April 1, 1895, Martí wrote his "literary will," leaving all his papers and manuscripts to Gonzalo de Quesada y Aróstegui, with instructions for editing.[162]

The Invasion: from Playitas to Dos Ríos

The same day that Martí wrote his literary will he left Montecristi for Cuba, accompanied by Máximo Gómez and four companions, of which three were Cubans, and one a Dominican.[163] This number of volunteers was considerably less than the 200 men called for in General Gómez' original plan. Gómez was reluctant to have Martí in the expedition and urged him to return to New York to direct operations from there. Martí, however, was determined to be part of the expedition.[164] After numerous delays and false starts the ship on which they finally took passage hove in sight of the southern coast of Cuba on April 11, 1895, at Maisí Cape. The six members of the expedition rowed under the cover of darkness to the beach, Playitas, in a small boat. They made their way inland the following day, and two days later made contact with a representative of the guerrilla forces of Maceo.[165]

On April 15, 1895, Gómez, after a conference with his officers, called Martí to his side, and, to his great surprise conferred upon him the rank of major general. Martí wrote on the same day:

Up until today I have not felt that I was a man. I have lived ashamed

and have dragged the chain of my fatherland all of my life. The soul's divine light lightens my body. This rest and well-being explains the constancy and jubilation with which men offer themselves for sacrifice.[166]

The small party continued on its way—its destination to find Antonio Maceo. On April 20, according to Martí's diary, they learned that they were being followed by Spanish forces; the next day Flor Crombet was killed. They reached the vicinity of Guantánamo April 25, and the following day met José Maceo, the brother of Antonio. The latter had just sustained a skirmish with Spanish forces. The following day, while a camp was being established, Martí and Gómez issued an order that there would be no surrender of the insurrectionary forces without absolute recognition of the independence of Cuba. The same day in another communication they called for the naming of Cuban representatives to constitute an assembly of delegates to choose a government for the new Republic.[167]

The march was resumed on May 1. The next day Martí was interviewed by a war correspondent of the *New York Herald,* George E. Bryson. Martí and Gómez then wrote a long letter to the *Herald* with a statement of the aims of the Cuban revolutionary movement, in general following the *Manifiesto de Montecristi.* Bryson left for New York with the message.[168]

On May 5, 1895, Gómez and Martí finally met Antonio Maceo for a council of war. It was agreed that the military campaign would be carried on from the eastern to the western part of the island. The problem of a future government was discussed. Martí maintained his point of view that an assembly of delegates of the Cuban revolutionaries should be formed, while Maceo insisted that all matters of the country should be under the direction of a military junta. Maceo and Martí could not agree, and the former, recalcitrant, ended the meeting by refusing to let them review his troops. Gómez and Martí left, with Martí in low spirits.[169] The following day, however, Martí and Gómez again joined Maceo, and this time they were received by Maceo's troops.[170] The same day, after leaving Maceo's camp, Martí, Gómez, and their small party slowly traveled westward, establishing camp for a few days, and then moving on.[171]

On May 17, General Gómez received intelligence reports that a Spanish convoy was in the vicinity. He left with a small group of

soldiers to harass the Spaniards, leaving Martí in camp.[172] On May 18, the day before his death, Martí wrote a long, but uncompleted, letter to Manuel Mercado saying, "every day I am in danger of giving my life for my country and for my duty." He said that his sacrifice would consist in impeding by means of the independence of Cuba the extension of the United States through the Antilles. He wrote: "However much I have done up to today, and will do, is for that purpose." He also reaffirmed his strong desire that an assembly of delegates of the Cuban people be called after the war to establish a republican form of government in Cuba.[173]

The Death of Martí in Battle

Gómez returned May 19, having failed to make contact with the Spanish column. Their party was joined by reinforcements in time to meet the attack of Spanish forces which had meanwhile discovered the presence of Gómez' troops and were in pursuit of them. Gómez and his lieutenants grouped their forces and left to attack the Spaniards. Before departing the General ordered Martí not to leave the camp.[174] Gómez' troops, however, soon found themselves in difficulty. In the confusion Martí, astride a white horse, rode into the melee with only one aide. Martí was recognized by a Spanish soldier, who directed fire on him. Martí fell, mortally wounded, near Dos Ríos. His body was taken by the Spaniards for burial in Santiago de Cuba, May 27, 1895.[175]

Many versions of Martí's death have been given. A frequent one is that Martí by his brash action deliberately committed suicide. This argument is strongly rejected by one writer who has drawn up a convincing array of evidence, based on Martí's diary of the campaign for liberation and his last letters. He shows that Martí was looking forward to greater activity on behalf of a freed Cuba and therefore could not have taken flight in suicide.[176]

According to another biographer's firm belief, however,

the death of Martí was no "tragic mishap," but rather was a conscious sacrifice on his part, in accordance with his most intimate feeling and with the deep conviction that his fall, far from weakening the revolution, would give it the supreme and necessary example to triumph, not

momentarily in a military victory, but in its most important and transcendental psychic aspect, that of leaving his immortal imprint on the Cuban soul. . . . Any other ending to his life is inconceivable.[177]

The "nonsuicide" point of view, to be completely acceptable, must overlook Martí's frequent references to his preoccupation with his own death and martyrdom. The "conscious sacrifice" point of view must discount Martí's many remarks about his interest in participating in the future of the Republic of Cuba. The two theories can be reconciled, perhaps, by advancing the thesis that Martí himself held them balanced in his own mind, and that whatever might happen he foresaw himself as the winner. Death in battle would bring him martyrdom. A safe delivery would give him an honorable service record. He could hardly have been the loser in either circumstance.

Postscript to the Revolution

The revolution did not collapse with Martí's death. Gómez and Maceo continued to wage guerrilla warfare from the eastern to the western tip of the island. Maceo fought heroically until his death in action on December 7, 1896, in San Pedro, as he was about to attack Havana. Gómez and Calixto García carried on the struggle, preparing the ground for the final victory which came with the arrival of United States forces in 1898. The events of the Spanish-American War and the several interventions of the United States in Cuban affairs under the Platt Amendment to the Cuban Constitution (1903) will not be discussed in detail here.[178] During the period of United States intervention in Cuban politics, with the exception of the administration of the first President, Tomás Estrada Palma, Cuba suffered under a succession of corrupt administrations which finally culminated in the harsh dictatorship of General Gerardo Machado, a veteran of the War of Independence. President Machado fell from power August 12, 1933.[179] The Platt Amendment, which had kept Cuba subject to American intervention, was abrogated in a treaty between Cuba and the United States on May 29, 1934.[180]

* * * * *

The force of Martí's personality, his profuse writings, his brilliant

oratory, and his many sacrifices on behalf of the revolution contributed an inestimable amount to the freeing of Cuba from Spain. Others gave their share to the cause, but today, while some like Maceo and Gómez are honored, the total homage paid to Martí eclipses by far that paid to all the other heroes of Cuba combined. When the question is asked of the average Cuban who the outstanding patriots of Cuba are, the answer is invariably, "Martí and Maceo." Maceo is cited for his military exploits and Martí for his mental ability. Intellectuals often have heroes, as in the case of Ralph Waldo Emerson's admiration for great men, but they themselves seldom become heroes, unless they are associated with some patriotic cause. The most that generals and presidents usually accomplish in the field of scholarship is to write their memoirs. Martí, therefore, occupies a unique position in Cuban politics.

Before examining the evidence of the impact of Martí upon the Cuban people it is necessary to look into his ideas on philosophy, sociology, politics, and economics to determine the intellectual basis for his appeal to the Cubans. This involves studying in some detail the seventy-four volumes of Martí's collected works and seeing in what ways Cuban scholars have interpreted his writings.

Chapter 2

MORAL AND SOCIAL IDEAS

*T*HE IDEAS OF JOSÉ MARTÍ are disorganized and contradictory. The task of running down and bringing order to this mass of data is beyond the scope of this study.[1] At most, perhaps, one is limited to a judicious selection of Martian thoughts which can be considered most representative of Martí, with the uneasy reservation that in such an enormous and undigested amount of data better selections might have been chosen to point up similar conclusions, or worse still, to arrive at opposite ones. There is no denying that the prolixity of Martí's writings has resulted in his becoming "all things to all men." The most that one can do is to recognize that fact and then proceed to discover in what ideas Martí seems to have been most consistent. Clearly his ideas on every subject can not be considered. An attempt will be made in this chapter to touch upon the most important ones, and to emphasize those areas of his thought which may be shown later to have had a bearing on his impact upon the Cuban people. These ideas will in turn furnish points of departure for discussion in later chapters. An attempt will be made to follow Martí's ideal of methodology in this respect: "Isolated facts should not be cited—the easy way of a light and useless erudition—rather, facts in order, of a solid whole, knit together and certain."[2]

Martí wrote that one's best ideas did not issue from meditation, but from improvisation. He believed that ideas broke out in conversation in an unexpected and spontaneous fashion, even involuntarily. Some of these ideas he elaborated upon, arranged, contrived, and polished, but he admitted that these were poorer than the ideas that burst forth fully finished. He wrote, "Others go to bed with their mistresses; I with my ideas."[3]

35

Martí was aware that the importance and effectiveness of ideas are related to the manner in which they are received. He said:

Each thought has its mold; but, just as the lithographer's plate is worn when it is used to print numerous examples, and the figure printed loses line and ink, so does the thought which falls upon other thoughts in a used mold lose its force to influence and shine. And what began as the lion's roar ends up a little like a dog's bark.[4]

Because most of Martí's writings appear without sources given for the ideas contained therein, it is difficult to determine what thoughts occurred to him spontaneously. He took a rather cavalier attitude toward citing references when he jotted down in his notes in 1894:

You will pardon me for not citing books, not because I do not read them . . . but because the book which most interests me is the book of life, which is also the hardest to read, and the one which one is to consult most in all that which refers to politics.[5]

For the sake of convenience Martí's thought may be arranged in the general fields of moral philosophy, sociology, politics, and economics, although, to repeat, this is attributing an organization to it that does not exist. Perhaps a truer picture might be obtained if his ideas were merely strung along alphabetically, as they do appear in one anthology.[6]

Moral Philosophy

Martí was an inveterate moralizer about man, his mind, character, love, and friendship; the good life, and death. One of his major literary and philosophical projects, as revealed in a letter to his friend Miguel Viondi, was to write a three-volume work called *El concepto de la vida (The Concept of Life)*, although he admitted that he would never have time to do it. Volume I was to be on the universe up to the present, the world as it was and why it had come to be that way. Volume II was to be an expression in verse of the eternal human soul, from the Greeks up to the present. Volume III was to be a study of the essence and soul of history, with a prognostication of the future world and final destiny of man's spirit. In this work he hoped to distinguish the artificial life from the natural one. He wrote:

The world today is a vast dwelling place of people wearing masks. One comes to earth like so much wax and chance places us in preformed molds. Existing conventions deform our true existence, and our real life comes to be like a quiet current running beneath our apparent existence, at times not even felt by the one in whom it is doing its silent work.

One of his plans in this project was to write in an attempt to promote human liberty. Political liberty, he felt, would never be assured so long as spiritual liberty was not secure, and it was urgent to free men from tyranny and convention.[7]

Concept of Man

Martí's concept of man varied. In 1877 he wrote, "I believe above all . . . in the absolute good of man. I work to deserve it." Elsewhere, however, he was less optimistic: "Each man is a sleeping beast. It is necessary to place reins on the beast. And man is an admirable beast, he is able to govern himself." Also, "Men, seen from above, or seen from any point of view, make one feel sad." Martí wrote in a similar passage on Mark Twain, "He must have, and I believe that he does have, the incurable melancholy of all those who know men profoundly."[8]

Human virtues.—Martí was in favor of all the human virtues: truth, it is better "to keep silent than not to speak the truth"; honor, "Honor must always be a religion in our souls"; honesty, "Honest men are my circle, and the rest are knaves"; decorum, "Dignity is like a sponge, it is pressed, but it always retains its power of resilience"; virtue, "The heart becomes bitter when it does not recognize virtue in time"; fraternity, "Every man is to feel on his cheek the blow received on the cheek of any other man"; and compassion, "And if I kill a fly, in anguish I begin to argue with my conscience whether I had the right to kill it."[9]

Martí once summed up his ideal of the virtuous man in a creed that reads:

To live in these times and to be pure, to be eloquent, brave and beautiful, and not to have been bitten, tortured and crushed by passions, to reach the maturity of mind which is necessary, and to keep one's heart in healthful vigor; to triumph over hunger, over one's own vanity, and the hatred which discord engenders; and to triumph without hiding one's conscience nor trafficking at the expense of dignity; to brace, in short,

with the bitter sea, . . . and to drink foul air and water, and remain healthy—these are the great things in life.[10]

Other human qualities occupied his pen from time to time: piety, "Piety is the stamp of chosen souls"; charity, "It is a marvelous law of Nature that only the one who gives himself becomes whole, and does not begin to possess life until he empties his own, without objection and reflection, for the good of others." He commented at the same time, however, in a mordant passage, that whoever gave himself to men would be devoured by them.[11]

INTELLIGENCE: Martí believed that human intelligence was the only definitive power on earth. He affirmed, "Intelligence produces goodness, justice, and beauty, and like a wing, it raises the spirit; like a crown, it makes a monarch of the one who displays it."[12]

HAPPINESS: Martí was certain that the only way to be happy was to be good. He wrote, "Being good is pleasing, and makes one strong and happy." An important ingredient in doing good was in being generous. He said, "Happiness does exist on earth; and it is conquered with the prudent exercise of reason, knowledge of harmony in the universe, and the constant practice of generosity." Martí even found possibilities for the exercise of virtue in the absence of generosity and good, "Great crimes are useful because they demonstrate to what extent nobility may be necessary to pardon them."[13]

LOVE: To Martí only one key opened the door to happiness—love. He defined it as follows:

Love is two spirits knowing each other, caressing, blending, helping each other to arise from the earth in a single being. It is born with the pleasure of looking at each other, it is fed with the necessity of seeing each other, it is concluded with the impossibility of separation![14]

In 1881 he saw the world equally divided between love and hate. He wrote: "Life on earth is a hand-to-hand mortal combat, an eye for an eye, a tooth for a tooth, between the law of love and the law of hate." By 1893, however, he wrote, "The only truth in this life, and the only force, is love. In it lies salvation, and in it lies power. Patriotism is no more than love. Friendship is no more than love."[15]

FRIENDSHIP: One of the strong threads running through Martí's life was his deep capacity for friendship and his ability to express it in

deeds and in writing. His most famous poem, known as "La Rosa Blanca" ("The White Rose"), is concerned with the generous, or "turn the other cheek" attitude in friendship. It reads:

> I cultivate a white rose,
> In July as in January,
> For the sincere friend
> Who gives me his open hand.
>
> And for the cruel one who tears out
> The heart that gives me life,
> I cultivate neither thistle nor weed,
> I cultivate a white rose.[16]

In 1889 he wrote that five just men would have been enough to have saved Gomorrah; but that to be immortal being remembered by a sincere friend was sufficient. In 1894 he wrote, "Love has not, to my recollection, given me any supreme moment; friendship has." In the same year he said that a great proof of the excellence of the Greeks was the value that they gave to friendship.[17] He once summed up his feelings on the subject of friendship when he wrote in a friend's album, "If they ask me what word is most beautiful, I will say that it is 'country'; and if they ask me for another, almost as beautiful as 'country,' I will say 'friendship.' "[18]

To Mercado, one of his most intimate friends, he wrote:

You entered my soul in my hour of greatest grief, and you divined it without obliging me to the imprudence of showing it to you, and since that time you have a royal throne there.[19]

GRIEF: If there is any one characteristic that marks Martí's concept of life, it is that life is one great bowl of sorrow mitigated only by grief. In *Adúltera* he wrote, "If they should ask me what it is to live, I would say, 'Grief, grief is life.' " In fact, "Man needs to suffer. When he does not have real griefs he creates them. Griefs purify and prepare him." In his notes he jotted down, "Griefs, like benevolent angels, draw the curtains of my life"; and, "I am like those plains in Siberia which give abundant fruit in the midst of cold. From grief, flowers." In another notebook he wrote that for suffering, just like thinking, he needed to be alone. In a letter to Mercado he wrote in 1889, "Women are never more beautiful than when they suffer."[20] Elsewhere, "There

is only one pleasure—grief." In 1894 he wrote again in his notes, "I rejoice in sorrow. There is deep joy in sorrow—in our own sorrow."[21]

This predilection for the expression of suffering, which is so evident in Martí, has been traced by Medardo Vitier, a Cuban professor of philosophy, to the influence of Seneca's writings in Spanish letters in general and specifically in Martí.[22] In addition, Félix Lizaso has written, "Stoicism offered Martí the best resonance for his thought . . . especially in his reading of Seneca."[23] Although these references are probably well based, Martí was undoubtedly influenced just as much if not more in his writings by having all the characteristics of a "born sufferer." To hazard an irreverent statement, Martí could have taught Seneca a few points about the art of suffering.

Concept of Self

It is at this point, on a note of grief, so to speak, that one may explore the areas of Martí's more personal philosophy, his concept of himself. In a passage in 1881, showing signs of the influence of Walt Whitman, he wrote:

I was born of myself, and from my own eyes the world itself opened up. Now, when man is born, surrounding his cradle, with strong bonds to encircle him, are all the philosophies, the religions, the political systems. And they tie him up . . . and man is now, for all of his life on earth, a bridled horse, and I am a horse without a saddle. From no one do I receive a law nor do I intend to impose one on anybody. I save myself from men, and I save them from me. . . . But I suffer. One does not live except in the community.[24]

Martyrdom.—Henry David Thoreau, the American philosopher, whom Martí admired, once wrote that the mass of men lead lives of quiet desperation. While Martí was inclined to write, "Grief is life," it seems clear that he was thinking less about the lot of man in general than he was about himself. In fact, whether consciously or not, Martí sought martyrdom at a very early age, as is evidenced by his exaltation of the glories of sacrifice for one's country in *Abdala,* and his eagerness to take all the blame for the letter which resulted in his being sentenced to six years in prison. From that time until his death his writings are replete with references to his eventual martyrdom. For instance, in a passage from his notes he philosophized upon the re-

lationship of the body and the soul, concluding that what he called the "body" was a collection of ideas, prime among them being passion for duty and for a "voluntary martyrdom." When these duties were fulfilled the result would be a "soul that would rise to heaven."[25]

In 1878 Martí wrote to Mercado from Guatemala:

In Spain I was keeping myself for a martyrdom; in Mexico I was fulfilling it; here, since I am working for my happiness, I have no right to it.[26]

The very word "martyrdom" is a stock item in the language of Martí, as can be seen in another letter to Mercado in the same year, in which he wrote, "It is a terrible martyrdom this matter of seeing a great work necessary, to feel oneself with the force to carry it through, and not being allowed to do it."[27]

Martí elaborated his ideas of martyrdom to the point where he identified himself with the stigmata of Christ, saying, "I bear on my left side a rose of fire, which burns me, but I live and work with it, in the hopes that some heroic, or at least difficult, labor will redeem me." Once he wrote to Mercado that a letter he had just received from him had found him tormented and on "the cross in the hour of martyrdom for good Christians." This point was also developed in *Amistad funesta,* in which Martí described the hero of the novel, Juan Jerez (with whom Martí has been closely identified by many writers), as follows: "There was in his character a strange and violent necessity for martyrdom."[28]

Although it is probably true that the use of the word "martyrdom" in Spanish is often lightly invoked, along with many other expressions of a religious origin, there can be no doubt that Martí's attitude was of a much more serious nature. The average Latin American, for example, does not feel that "an apostleship is a daily and constant duty."[29]

Duty.—This concept of duty as an apostleship was another strong force in Martí's life. Félix Lizaso, whose major work on Martí is called *Martí, místico del deber (Martí, Mystic of Duty),* has written in another study, "It was his idea of duty, and not a romantic impulse, which gave him [Martí] his status of apostle."[30] This opinion was affirmed five years later by Jorge Mañach.[31] Andrés Iduarte finds that

Martí's formula in life is sacrifice and, "above all, duty."[32] While still in his twenties Martí wrote that he was not a hardhearted revolutionary merely dedicating his life to troublemaking. Nevertheless when it became necessary to engage in rebellion it did not matter to him if the fulfillment of his duty made him unpopular; he would do it. In 1881 he wrote, "I love my duty more than my son." His notes of the same year read in part:

From human institutions, which I find already formed and among which I live, I do not recognize, nor remember, nor require other duties than my own. I do not even consider that the duties of others toward myself exist.[33]

Martí's preoccupation with suffering—one of the main threads running through his life—often led him to give it an undue amount of attention in his writings. Occasionally, however, he would make an effort to sublimate personal feelings for the greater cause. Consider the following passage from his notes:

One should not lose time in suffering: one should use it in fulfilling our duty. Thus, I feel that I am dying, and I lift my head, I tremble from a horrible cold, and I continue forward—I will die a whole man.[34]

Although Martí's suffering seems to have left him without any sense of humor, some amusement can be gleaned from the following passage of his worry about age creeping up to hinder him in his work. He complained:

I have something important to tell you. . . . It is that I am becoming bald, and I am afraid of leaving this life without having had an opportunity to fulfill my duty. It is not reasonable that one who has strength to carry a hundred pounds on his back should be employed in drawing water from an empty well with a bucket without a bottom. That is what I have been thinking about in the midst of these trifling business tasks.[35]

For Martí the act of doing was the only effective way of censuring those who would not work. He also wrote:

The person who is contented with his own well-being, and does not care for the misery which is destroying the rest, is neither a man by rights, nor will he be able to prevent infamy and public misery from reaching himself.[36]

He once wrote that he served no other master except duty, and

that with this he would always be powerful enough. In 1895 he said, "Wherever may be my greatest duty, inside or out, there I will be."[37]

Towards the end of his life Martí wrote that the good individual feels an inexpressible bitterness about his deeds when he sees that men are dazzled by pomp, that the truth does not interest them, that strong virtue bothers and displeases them, that they follow the one who praises them for their vices, and abandon those who would do them the most good. He wrote:

All of that is true, but from these pains a good man grows, he gains greater strength while those most needful of him let him remain in solitude.

According to Martí, the lesson to be gained from this is that one must persevere in the service of mankind in spite of an aching heart.[38]

Death.—For a person who had set such a monumental task for himself in life, Martí was preoccupied to an unusual extent with death. He wrote frequently about it, saying that as night is the recompense for day, death is the recompense for life. In a passage which is representative of his attitude he exclaimed:

Death! Generous death! Death, my friend! Sublime bosom where all the sublime kingdoms are wrought; fear of the weak; pleasure of the brave; satisfaction of my desires; dark passage to the remaining episodes of existence; immense mother at whose feet we stretch out to gain new strength for the unknown way where heaven is wider, limitless horizons, where unworthy feet are dust, truth at last, wings; tempting mystery, . . . harbinger of liberty.[39]

At times, however, he resisted death and wrote, "Death is not true," or, "It is a crime not to oppose all possible obstacles to death." His notes in 1881 read:

Death is no rest. There is no rest until the entire job is completed, and the world purified, and the canvas in its frame. I do not want to rest; because there is pleasure in suffering well, and what is to be shall be. . . . I am afraid of dying before having suffered enough.[40]

Again in his notes, probably sometime during 1894, he wrote down the Spanish word *postrimerías* (theological term for the last stage of life), adding, "I like this word in an extraordinary way. I love it like a person: it has produced a friend for me."[41]

Martí frequently wrote poems on the subject of death. A well-known one, composed in 1894, reads:

> *I wish to leave the world*
> *By its natural door;*
> *In my tomb of green leaves*
> *They are to carry me to die.*
> *Do not put me in the dark*
> *To die like a traitor;*
> *I am good, and like a good being*
> *I will die with my face to the sun.*[42]

Thus it can be seen that Martí was mentally preparing himself for death and martyrdom, which finally caught up with him at Dos Ríos. The apotheosis of Martí and the cult to him which has developed will be discussed in a later chapter. It should be kept in mind that the conditioning process for this phenomenon was started in Martí's own writings. This opinion, however, is not shared by Andrés Iduarte, who writes, "He is mistaken—some have already made the mistake—who believes that Martí was a seeker after glory. He did not want power while alive nor glory after death."[43] The evidence does not seem to support this point of view.

Philosophy of Religion

In addition to Martí's conviction of his approaching martyrdom, his philosophy of religion was a curious compound of oriental mysticism, pantheism, and anti-Roman Catholicism. While it may be difficult to determine with certainty just what Martí's religion was, it does appear that he was basically not irreligious. In fact, one Cuban writer, Raquel Catalá, claims that Martí was "supremely religious."[44] Whether or not this statement is quite accurate, it seems clear that when Martí was writing about the great human virtues of love, honoring father and mother, charity, truth, honor, generosity, and piety, he was doing so with a religious base. He said:

Morality is the basis of a good religion. Religion is the form of natural belief in God and the natural tendency to investigate Him and reverence Him. Being religious is deeply engrained in human beings.

Another of his definitions of religion reads:

There is in man a vague and intimate knowledge, constant and imposing, of a Great Creative Being. This knowledge is religious sentiment, and its form, expression, the manner with which each group of men conceive this God and worship Him, is what is called religion.[45]

Martí believed that God existed in the idea of good, which watched over the birth of every being and left in the soul that was incarnate "a pure tear."[46]

Transmigration of souls.—Miguel Jorrín, among other Cuban writers, has pointed out that Martí's religious philosophy was very much influenced throughout his life by the "ideas of India."[47] An example of Martí's inclination toward a philosophy of transmigration of souls is his poem "Yugo y Estrella" ("Yoke and Star"). Martí wrote in part:

> *When I was born, without sun, my mother said:*
> *Flower of my breast, generous Homagno,*
> *Substance and reflex of Creation and me,*
> *Fish which becomes bird, horse, then man,*
> *Look at these two insignias of life*
> *Which I give you: look and choose.*[48]

This sentiment also appeared in *El presidio político en Cuba.* One part reads:

And when I suffer, and the pleasure of mitigating the suffering of others does not lessen my own, it seems to me that in previous worlds I must have committed a grave misdeed which, in my unknown wanderings through space, it has become my lot to atone for here.[49]

Félix Lizaso does not believe, however, that Hindu philosophy had a direct influence on Martí. He feels that Indian thought came to Martí through the writings of Ralph Waldo Emerson, and that at all events it was "not a guide-rule but only a resonance" in his thought.[50]

Perhaps Martí's greater preoccupation was in his certainty of another existence after death. He wrote, "Idealism is not a vague desire for death, but the conviction of an afterlife, which one is to merit with the calm practice of virtue in this life." He believed that human life would be a barbarous and repugnant invention if it were

limited to existence on earth. He wrote, "It is a lie that memory ends with death, because that would be such a profound grief that it would be inconceivable in one's life."[51]

Martí found evidence all around him of a future life: the miracle of the brain, and even electricity, which announced "the permanent beatific light" which the spirit would enjoy in better worlds. He saw in the imperfection of the human tongue to express precisely the judgments, affections, and designs of man a perfect and absolute proof of the necessity of a future existence. He found that suffering was an augury of things to come; and he saw postlife in the magic words of music.[52]

God and Nature.—Many references to a philosophy of pantheism exist in Martí's writings, which, it is alleged, show the influence of a German philosopher of the early nineteenth century, Karl Christian Krause. Krause was popular in Spain during the second half of the nineteenth century, and Martí came into contact with his philosophy while a student there.[53] For Krause, God, or Conscience, was not a personality but an essence containing the Universe within itself. He called his philosophy panentheism, a variation of pantheism, asserting that God contained the Universe without being exhausted in it.[54]

A Cuban writer, José A. Béguez César, although admitting that Martí was familiar with the doctrine of Krause, insists that that does not by any means indicate his adherence to it, nor even his sympathy for it. In fact, he comes to the conclusion that, in view of Martí's "frank and simple confession that his spiritualism was learned in the materialist books of Luis Buchner, it is sufficient proof to deny that he was a follower of Krause inasmuch as the two doctrines are irreconcilable in form and base." This writer believes that Martí's manner of work is identical to that of the German philosopher Leibnitz.[55]

Whether Martí was a follower of Leibnitz or Krause is not a matter for extended consideration here. The fact remains that Martí's religious philosophy was often Nature-oriented. Félix Lizaso finds that "Nature is his great center of spiritual resonance, only that which conforms to the natural life can satisfy him."[56] Martí's concept of Nature is to be seen in the following excerpt from his notes:

Apply without fear to each act of life the general laws of Nature: in

medicine, in the development of peoples, in the creation of character, in the medicine of the soul. The laws of a locomotive are the same as those of the human body. The laws of the tides are those of one's thoughts. And the laws that govern the existence of a people are the same as those which rule the life of a flower.

Martí then asked where this admired wisdom of field and sea came from. The answer he gave was that it was an instinctive wisdom that at times impelled people, and at times detained them.[57]

The foregoing quotation from Martí's notes can be traced to the influence of Ralph Waldo Emerson. At the death of Emerson, Martí with consummate skill and appreciation wrote an obituary that undoubtedly stands as one of the most sensitive evaluations of this American philosopher and poet in any language. In the essay Martí's discussion of Emerson's philosophy of transcendentalism is taken by many writers to represent Martí's own beliefs.[58] Martí wrote that a moral character existed in all the elements of Nature that quickened the character of man. He commented:

Nature inspires, cures, consoles, fortifies, and prepares man for virtue. And man does not find himself complete, nor is revealed to himself, nor sees the invisible, except in his intimate relation with Nature.[59]

Miguel Jorrín, although accepting Martí's admiration for Emerson, believes that Martí already had his own philosophy formed before coming into contact with the New England Sage. Also, Jorrín writes, "I do not find in him that identification of man with Nature... since he always places man above Nature."[60] The passage quoted from Martí's essay on Emerson, however, would seem to indicate the contrary. In it Nature is certainly the performer, and man the object, with a seemingly close identification between the two.

At any rate, Martí unquestionably and deeply admired Emerson. On one occasion he asked, "Why can not the whole world be like Emerson, who wrote in one place, 'The world is mind precipitated'?"[61]

Félix Lizaso is of the opinion, "If Martí had written in English, and had not been Hispanic-American, it is possible that the North would consider him as the last of the transcendentalists."[62]

The Roman Catholic Church.—In his letters, newspaper articles,

and novel, Martí evidenced a hostility to the Roman Catholic Church that is unmistakable. He was convinced that no people could be happy without the separation of Church and State.[63] He was opposed to priests entering homes with the "unquestionable and infallible" teachings of Christ to use influence in political matters. He thought that it was a perversion of religion and would even result in the corruption of souls.[64]

There are instances in Martí's reporting on European affairs that show anti-Roman Catholic sentiment in his discussion of the Church in Italy and in Spain. As an example in Spain, he wrote that he had seen the members of a Roman Catholic youth organization in Madrid remain seated when the orator mentioned God or Jesus Christ, but stand up when the Pope was mentioned.[65]

Other examples of Martí's anti-Roman Catholic feeling may be cited. One is a short tract, "Hombre del campo" ("The Countryman"), which is an attack against an organized church, presumably the Roman Catholic. Martí addressed himself to the average farmer, advising him to stop going to the priest and to cease paying for services, such as baptism, which he could perform just as well for himself. Martí cautioned, "The first duty of a man is to think for himself. For that reason I do not want you to respect the priest, because he will not let you think."[66]

Elsewhere Martí continued his attack, writing that Christianity had died under Roman Catholicism, and that in order to love Christ it was necessary to wrench Him from the heavy hands of the priests.[67] He once referred to them as the merchants of divinity.[68]

The *cause célèbre*, however, in Martí's writings on the Roman Catholic Church as an institution in society is found in his "North American Scenes" for 1887, where he defended a priest by the name of Father Edward McGlynn. The clergyman had been suspended by Rome for having publicly defended Henry George, the famous but controversial author of *Progress and Poverty*. Martí wrote:

The parish priest, it is true, owes obedience to his Archbishop in ecclesiastical matters; but in political opinions, in matters of simple economy and social reform, in affairs that do not pertain to the Church, why is the priest to owe absolute obedience to his Archbishop?[69]

Martí wrote in detail of the meetings of Father McGlynn's parish-

ioners with Henry George to support the erring priest, and on the position of the Roman Catholic Church in the United States, without seeming to realize the anomalous position in which his approval of a priest in politics placed him.[70] The controversy lasted into the summer of 1887 and furnished Martí with good copy.[71]

Agnosticism.—Tolerance, however, was sometimes stressed in Martí's attitude toward all organized religion in society. He once wrote, "Everybody has the right to his own conscience. Tyrant is the Catholic who imposes himself on a Hindu, and the Methodist who sneers at a Catholic."[72] Martí even pushed his tolerance to the point of cheering on the atheism of Robert G. Ingersoll in New York in September, 1883, along with favorable comments on a meeting of freethinkers.[73]

At times Martí himself found it difficult to reach God, saying, "One would believe that the Creator of man is a vain creature—he places so many obstacles in the way of those who try to approach him." Also, he saw that men invented deities in their own likenesses, and that each people imagined a different heaven, with divinities who lived and thought the same as the people who created them. He wrote:

The sky was always a copy of mankind, and populated with serene images, joyful or vengeful, according to whether the nations creating them lived in peace . . . or in slavery and torment: every jolt in the history of a people altered its Olympus.

In his notes he once projected writing a "good and transcendental" work on Christian mythology.[74]

Opinion on the bases of Martí's religion varies widely. To Raquel Catalá "the spiritualism of Martí is perfectly thought out."[75] To Emilio Roig de Leuchsenring he is "heterodoxical, a freethinker, laic, antitheocratic, and anticlerical."[76] Miguel Jorrín, to repeat, does not find Martí's "identification of man with Nature," while to Félix Lizaso "Nature is his great center of spiritual resonance." Where does the answer lie? Probably somewhere in between these extremes.

Social Philosophy

Martí projected his moral philosophy into the major portion of

his writings on social institutions and relationships. His interest was not particularly as a social scientist, but as a writer in aphoristic style about the home, husband and wife relationships, divorce, adultery, parental obligations to children, education, and race relationships.

Marriage and the Family

On marriage he declaimed, "The only pillow on which one may rest from the pain and ugliness which one sees is in the home, where modesty has placed its crown of honor and where abnegation and sincerity are smiled upon." He recognized the importance of pleasant home surroundings when he wrote that every clean and ventilated house was a school. Elsewhere, however, he wrote that school and home were the two formidable jails of man, and that it was necessary, while leaving the roof on to shelter their occupants, to open the doors to let fresh air come in.[77]

In spite of a generally favorable attitude toward the institution of marriage, Martí often commented on the lack of understanding between husbands and wives, writing, "If there were a lens which would permit women to see just how thoughts pass through men's brains, and what is in their hearts, they would love them much less." In a tone distinguished by a certain air of self-righteousness, Martí asked:

What is the knowing husband to do except to look away with horrified and grief-stricken eyes from that one who does not understand his language, nor care about his anxieties, nor can reward his noble qualities, nor sense his griefs, nor reach with her eyes where he is looking?[78]

He wrote that in one day a man could stop loving the woman whom he worshipped when a definite and unexpected act revealed to him that in her soul there did not exist that sweetness and superiority with which his fancy had first invested it. In the early 1880's, when he was still deeply upset over his incompatibility with his wife, he wrote, "The question in life is reduced to a simple statement—either to seek victims or be one."[79] There was no question in Martí's mind that he was being victimized.

Nothing was lower in his estimation than a woman who did not measure up to expectations. He wrote, "A woman without tenderness is a glass of flesh full of poison." Martí was fond of this rather gruesome simile. He sighed:

Ah, in those markets where generous youths, searching for bluebirds of happiness, are accustomed to link their lives to pretty glasses of flesh, in the first flush of life, the astute fox, the venomous snake, the cold and impassive cat, reveal themselves.[80]

Martí was not ill-equipped to paint an unattractive picture of womankind when he was in the mood.

And then again, at times, Martí's lyricism about women knew no bounds, as when he compared a good woman to a perpetual rainbow, and asserted that the only sound force in life was the love of a woman.[81]

Martí's unfortunate relationship with his wife did not blind him, however, to seeing a more productive role for women in society. He wrote that by lifting up the mind of woman with solid studies she would live on a par with man as a companion and not as a plaything. He thought that education would make women more pure. He asserted that it was not true, as teachers and observers said, that it was a proven fact that the feminine mind was weak in understanding matters of art, law, and science. In a passage with purple overtones he wrote:

Oh, the day in which women will not be frivolous! How happy that will be for mankind! How, instead of a mere plate of fragrant meat, they will become a spiritual urn, to which men will always have their anxious lips pressed.[82]

Martí was interested in the subject of adultery. As has already been seen, he wrote a play on this theme when he was only twenty-one years old. In one of the passages a character is made to exclaim, "A woman stained by desire is flesh, she is dust, she is mud, she is vile!" And, "Stupid frivolities cheer on the woman who deceives her husband." Elsewhere in the play, in lines full of smugness, Martí wrote, "When man falls, being strong, he redeems himself. When woman falls, being weak, the fall insults her and cheapens her."[83]

In a more objective vein he wrote later that it was necessary to study the source of the ulcer of adultery. He found that society did not look upon it as a moral crime, but rather a right considered as an absolute necessity in women, and a required social "baptism" in men. He wrote that exchanging wives was becoming as frequent as lending

books, and that even among persons with superior minds confusion on this point had reached a frightening stage. He rejected the offer of the Roman Catholic Church of religion as a remedy on the grounds that in the periods of greatest strength of the Church adultery was widely practiced. Martí's explanation was that ideals were lacking, as well as knowledge of one's self, that belief in a future existence was needed, as well as spiritual development.[84]

Martí's concept of parenthood was as follows, "As necessary to people as the one who pushes is the one who restrains, and as necessary to the child is the father of the house, always active, in contrast to the mother, always timid." He thought that parents should be the friends and not the implacable censors of their children. As for one's mother, "Whether she is near or far away, she is the sustaining force in our lives. . . . The earth, when she dies, opens beneath our feet."[85]

Martí spoke kindly of old people. He wrote, "Old people are like an ornament, and the best fountain of force in life. What an example, a serene old man! . . . How good it is to have reached that age smiling."[86]

Martí loved children and was very much interested in them, as his magazine *La Edad de Oro* and his poems to his son, José, in *Ismaelillo*, indicate. On one occasion Martí wrote:

For our children, who make us ambitious and delirious, and make our hearts giddy as if with wine, and give us the strength of the conquistadores, for them, oh, for them the whole world seems little enough.[87]

Martí once wrote that when he wrapped up in newspaper the little straw hat and shoes that his son had used, he looked to see whether the paper contained stories of man's ignoble passions, or whether it defended instances of justice. Then he would enclose his son's possessions only in the latter. He explained: "I believe in these contacts."[88]

EDUCATION

A profession that Martí esteemed very highly was that of the educator, and as frequently as he is called "Apostle," is he also called "Maestro," a term difficult to translate into English. He stated his ideal of education as follows:

To educate is to deposit in each man all the human work which has preceded him: it is to make each man the abstract of the living world up until the day of his death: it is to put him at the level of his time, so that he may float upon it . . . that is preparing man for life.[89]

Martí believed that one of the best ways to accomplish this was to substitute scientific study for scholasticism, so prevalent in Latin American schools. He wrote that a radical revolution in education was necessary if the Latin Americans did not want to see themselves "forever atrophied and deformed like the monster of Horace, with a huge head and heart, but dragging weak feet, and with arms of skin and bones." He proposed that physics be taught instead of theology, that mechanics should replace rhetoric, and instead of the precepts of logic he would offer the practical arts. Courses of public teaching were to be prepared and classified in such a way that from the primary to the final grades they would develop so that man would be allowed to make a practical application of his knowledge to Nature. Once left on his own the youth would be able to apply his learning to a known world instead of being loaded down with "useless Greek and Latin letters." This seems a strange request for an avowed humanist. It is interesting to note that Martí used an example from the classics to emphasize his point. He said:

Education is to go where life goes. . . . Education must give the means of resolving the problems that life presents. The great human problems are: self-preservation and the attainment of the means of making life pleasing and peaceful.[90]

Martí's opposition to scholasticism was also apparent in his hostility toward religious instruction in the schools. He wrote:

No one has the right to teach either the Catholic or anti-Catholic religion in schools; honor should be the greatest virtue in religion, and as long as the schools promote it they will be religious enough.[91]

Martí felt that another grave error was being committed in education in Latin America. Among populations that lived almost completely on agricultural products, men were being educated exclusively for urban life rather than for living in the country. The result was that with the overpopulated cities existing only at the expense of the country and trafficking in its products, the current system of education

was creating a great army of unemployed. He advised, "Sow chemistry and agriculture and you will reap grandeur and riches."[92]

Martí was particularly interested in teaching the student appreciation of Nature, and wrote that behind every school there should be an area where each student could plant a tree. He said, "We need elementary education to be purely scientific: instead of the history of Joshua, let them teach the formation of the land." Martí placed his greatest emphasis on education in agriculture. He wrote:

Teaching in agriculture is the most urgent of all, but not in technical schools, rather in experimental stations, where the parts of the plow will not be described except where the student may see it in operation; and where the composition of the fields will not be explained in formulas on the blackboard, but rather in the layers of the earth itself.

As an immediate solution for the lack of education in the country, Martí urged the establishment of traveling teachers.[93]

Martí's emphasis upon scientific education in conformity with the principles of Nature raises the question of the influence on him of Auguste Comte's philosophy of Positivism, which was very much in vogue at this time in Latin America. This system of philosophy rejected everything but natural phenomena and experience as its base. According to Miguel Jorrín, "Martí found Positivism useful as a science, but not as a philosophy."[94] Raquel Catalá, by pointing to a criticism by Martí of Positivism, asserts that he rejected this philosophy.[95] In addition Medardo Vitier writes that Martí never fell into the excesses of Positivism.[96] Jorge Mañach, however, is of the opinion that, although Martí's philosophy took its impetus from romanticism, "Positivism was its main channel."[97] Mañach's position is probably too strong here, although Martí's thoughts on education seem to be very much influenced by Positivism.

An additional tenet in Martí's philosophy of education was his irrevocable opposition to the practice of sending children away from the country for their education, particularly to the United States. He wrote:

The education of a son of these lesser countries amongst a people of opposite character and superior riches could bring the student to a fatal position in his native country, which is to make use of his education, or worse still . . . to the disdain of his countrymen.

Martí believed that a conflict would take place in their young minds at learning to speak another language, which they could never master. Being exposed to another civilization they would be left confused and inadequate to cope with life in Latin America. At the same time they would be unable to adapt themselves to the hurly-burly of life in the United States.[98]

Martí's zeal to introduce the practical arts into Latin American schools in the face of an overwhelming reliance upon scholasticism is understandable. What is not understandable, however, was his failure to appreciate the values to be gained from the study of classical and modern languages, and the broadening effects of exposure to another civilization.

Race

The Negro.—Martí frequently wrote on ethnological problems in the Americas. In Cuba he was concerned primarily with the Negro. Martí believed that the colored person had every right to be treated on his merits as a man, without any reference to his color.[99] He wrote that if the Negro were to be judged on any criterion, it would be to excuse him from the faults that the white race had prepared for him, and that it had invited him to commit because of its own unjust disdain. In Martí's analysis, "White persons scorn the Negroes because they see them as victims of the wrongs they themselves have perpetrated on them."[100]

Martí, in his eagerness to overcome differences between Negroes and white people, went so far as to insist that there was no such thing as race. Martí, himself, however, constantly used the term "race." In his article "Mi raza" ("My Race") in *Patria* in 1893 he wrote that to insist on racial divisions and differences merely made public progress difficult. He was unsympathetic to the Negroes adding to the problem by proclaiming their own racism, thereby neglecting to emphasize the spiritual unity of all races. This action justly provoked the white racist. He felt that the only fair racism was the right of the Negro to maintain and to prove that his color did not deprive him of any of the capacities and rights of the human species.[101]

Martí once expressed a feeling in notes on a projected book, *La raza negra* (*The Black Race*), that the Negroes in Cuba were not

ready to take a full part in the cultural life of the country because of their primitive background. He wrote that he had awakened one morning and had begun formulating some ideas he had received in a dream of the Negro as a social element and how he would be affected after the liberation of Cuba. He felt that there were elements in the race itself that could be employed to combat the savagery of their heritage.[102] Unfortunately the dream apparently ended right there, for Martí never specified what those elements might be. The foregoing notes by Martí have been cited by Fernando Ortiz, a leading sociologist of Cuba, as an indication of how "sociologically scientific his program was" for the role of the Negro in society.[103]

The Indian.—In addition to Martí's interest in the problem of the Negro in society, he was concerned with the lot of the Indian. He looked for his subject matter elsewhere than in Cuba, however, since the Indian population there disappeared under the pressures of the early conquistadores.

As a newspaper reporter in the United States Martí wrote articles on the treatment of the Indians in the West. He was especially critical of the Indian agents, whom he accused of neglect and robbery in dealing with their charges. On the favorable side, however, in his description of life on a Cherokee Indian reservation, he was very much impressed by the fact that 50 per cent of the public funds spent on them was devoted to education.[104] Although space does not permit further treatment here, the sympathetic penetration of Martí into the social and political problems of the United States in the 1880's and the skill with which he gave them literary form in Spanish can not be overemphasized.

As far as the Latin American Indians are concerned, they are mainly taken up in Martí's literary productions and in his reports from Mexico and Guatemala. It once occurred to Martí that an opportune book to write would be on the life and customs of the indigenous races of America. This work never materialized, but Martí's interest in the Indian appeared in his novel, *Amistad funesta*. In it he had the main character representing the Indians in a legal suit against a ranch owner who had been taking advantage of them.[105] Martí also wrote a play at the request of the Guatemalan government, in which he discussed the plight of the Indian. No copy of this

drama has ever been found, but Martí's notes indicate its contents.[106]

Martí translated Helen Hunt Jackson's novel *Ramona*, as has already been mentioned, because he found it to be a sympathetic treatment of the Indians of Lower California. Martí's concern over the Indian problem in the South American Andean countries and Central America caused him to state flatly:

Can it not be seen that the same blow that paralyzed the Indian paralyzed America? And until the Indian is made to walk forward, America will not progress?[107]

Martí's acumen here is evidenced by the fact that the Indian problem is still often largely ignored. For instance a Cuban student in a seminar on Latin American economic relations, upon hearing figures on the very grave status of health in Latin America, protested that these data "included Indians."[108]

In ethnological problems Martí recognized that social equality was not possible until cultural equality was achieved. On the question of race in general he wrote:

In this world there is only one inferior race, belonging to it are those who consult their own interest before all else, whether it be for their vanity, pride or material welfare. Likewise, there is only one superior race, that of the ones who consult before all else the interest of mankind.[109]

Martí's Status as a Philosopher

In discussing Martí's thought, Miguel Jorrín has advanced the opinion that Martí was not a philosopher in the sense of one who has organized a body of thought, but that he qualified for that appellation in that he was aware of problems that do not occur to ordinary persons.[110] Félix Lizaso wrote that Martí was not a philosopher, but that there was "undoubtedly philosopher's material in him."[111] Andrés Iduarte asserted that Martí was a philosopher in the sense that he was a lover of knowledge and a believer and propagandist of a moral decalogue.[112]

Humberto Piñera has also asked the question, "Was Martí really a philosopher? . . . The answer must be decidedly negative: Marti was not a philosopher." Piñera arrived at this conclusion by way of distinguishing between the philosopher, who attempts to create an

ideal state, and Martí, who sought to "idealize the real." In Piñera's opinion the philosopher must make no concession toward reality— an impossibility for Martí. He believes instead that Martí may be considered a "thinker." A "thinker," according to his definition, is one who seeks the "partial realization of what is real."[113]

An opposite point of view is expressed by José A. Béguez César, who writes, "José Martí was a philosopher and not a thinker, as has been said." Béguez believes that a "thinker" is one who rises above himself, whereas a "philosopher" is one who not only thinks but lives his philosophy. Béguez insists, "If Martí had been only a thinker, he would never have been able to unite all opinions for the liberation effort."[114]

The authorities on Martí seem to be divided between those who consider that he was a philosopher and those who do not.[115] As long as no single definition of "philosopher" is accepted, however, there is little value in carrying the debate beyond pointing out the disagreement. Be it as "thinker" or "philosopher" or inspired moralist the evidence is overwhelming that Martí produced a wide body of writings in matters of morals that have stimulated extensive comment. An attempt will be made later to assess the impact of this material upon the Cuban people.

Chapter 3

POLITICAL IDEAS

*A*LTHOUGH JOSÉ MARTÍ touched upon many philosophical and sociological topics in his writings, his major interest and dedication, when he was not brooding about his personal griefs and torturing his sensibilities to the breaking point, was in politics.

In about an hour and a half one can easily run through the two-volume index to Quesada y Miranda's *Obras completas de Martí,* and find references to many of the major political theorists of the Western world. By no stretch of charity, however, can Martí be considered to have thought out a consistent political theory. He had little time for closet philosophy in the matter of politics. He was, first and last, from his revolutionary tract *Patria libre* to the *Manifiesto de Montecristi,* an active revolutionist. Yet in the course of fulfilling this self-appointed mission in life he had occasion to include in his letters, newspaper articles, poetry, drama, and notes novel observations about political theory, public administration, comparative government, legislation, civil rights, law, economics, and through it all, a belief in a humanistic philosophy. Martí had an insatiable curiosity that led him to many insights into the practical workings of politics, which he seemed to prefer to the study of organized theory.

These references are to be found mainly in Martí's sixteen volumes on "North Americans and North American Scenes," his four volumes on "European Scenes," and in his three volumes of notes. Volumes I through IX of his collected works, which deal with Cuban politics and the Revolution, represent letters, documents, and newspaper articles largely from *Patria,* and contain many of Martí's ideas about politics, but they generally do not include abstract political philosophy.

59

Definition of Politics

How did Martí define politics? When writing on the political situation in France in 1881, he expressed himself in this manner:

Politics is the art of inventing a recourse to match every new contrary event, to convert reverses into fortune; to adapt oneself to the present moment, without having that adaptation result in sacrifice, or in a significant lessening of the idea which is being pursued; of relaxing to gain new energy; and, of falling upon the enemy before he may have his troops in order, and battle prepared.[1]

Elsewhere he wrote that politics was the art of bringing inhumanity to justice; of conciliating egotism with generosity; and of favoring and harmonizing interests for the general welfare, keeping virtue in mind.[2] In the same vein he wrote later, "Government is no more than the equilibrium of the natural elements of a country."[3] He further believed that politics was a resolution of equations, and that the solution would fail whenever the equation was badly put together.[4] In the study of politics Martí saw the necessity for the independence of political science as a discipline when he said, "Politics is not a borrowed science, but must be its own."[5]

One Cuban writer in defining politics referred to Martí as an "apostolic genius" in this field. He wrote:

Since every instruction for the good of man in relation to other men ends up at the art of leading one another toward a happy life together; and since that art is called politics, José Martí, builder of men, is nothing more than a politician—the greatest of politicians. To that, his sacred vocation—since it is a cult in Him [sic]—he consecrates all of his activity as in a perpetual mission—since it is liturgy in Him.[6]

Whether one is inclined to consider Martí an "apostolic genius," a "thinker," or a "politician," his aspirations and record as a revolutionist are well documented.

Martí's political goals in life, as frequently expressed in his writings, were to secure the complete liberation of Cuba and Puerto Rico from Spain, prevent their annexation by the United States, and establish democratic and free republics. His first goal was realized three years after his death. His second goal was not fully reached for Cuba

until the abrogation of the Platt Amendment in 1933. The third goal will be discussed in a later chapter.

Documents of the Cuban Revolution

Martí had occasion to express his ideas on the Cuban revolutionary movement in three important public papers. These were the *Resoluciones,* signed by the Cuban emigrants in Tampa, Florida, November 28, 1891;[7] the *Bases del Partido Revolucionario Cubano,* including the "Estatutos secretos," signed by the leaders of Cuban patriotic clubs in Key West, January 5, 1892; and the *Manifiesto de Montecristi,* written by José Martí, and signed by him as delegate (president) of the Cuban Revolutionary party, and General Máximo Gómez, military chief of the movement, at Montecristi, the Dominican Republic, March 25, 1895.

The *Resoluciones,* briefest of the three documents, contain a statement of purpose followed by four resolutions. The *Bases* contain nine articles, the first seven being of a general nature. Article 8 has five subpoints containing concrete proposals, and Article 9 asserts that the party was to be governed by the "Estatutos secretos," which followed. They are concerned with the internal organization of the party. The *Manifiesto* is a document written at full speed, which is apparent in its lack of organization, there being no numbered articles, in spite of the fact that it is the longest of the three papers. It has the greatest warmth and appeal, however, and is most obviously the work of Martí.

All three documents expressed the importance of unity in the struggle to free Cuba. The *Resoluciones* maintained that it was of urgent necessity to unite all "honest revolutionary elements." The *Bases* stated that all Cubans abroad were to be united, and the *Manifiesto* claimed that the unity of Cubans abroad and in Cuba had been achieved.[8]

The *Resoluciones* maintained that the war was not to be undertaken without accommodation to the realities, rights, and democratic spirit of the country, and in particular was to avoid inspiring fear among the Cubans that it was a war without a popular base. While not explicitly stating it, this implied the need for propaganda. The

same point was discussed in greater detail in the *Bases*, which asserted that the Cuban Revolutionary party was to avoid in its propaganda efforts offending the peoples with whom it was to deal. The *Bases* also clearly stated that it was one of the purposes of the party to "propagate in Cuba the knowledge of the spirit and the methods of the Revolution."[9]

More than from any other antecedent the *Manifiesto* was the result of this declaration, since the Montecristi document was written on the eve of the invasion of Cuba to prepare the Cubans for cooperation with the revolutionary movement. The *Manifiesto* as a propaganda document will be discussed in more detail as individual points are discussed.

The *Resoluciones* stated that the Revolution was not to overlook the "practical necessities derived from the constitution and history of the nation." The *Bases* echoed this purpose in the recommendation that the party should foment sincere relations between historical and political elements within and without the island in order to bring about the rapid triumph of the war and to assure the solid foundation of future institutions. This sentiment was repeated in the *Manifiesto* in the form that once the nation was free "it would be built up from its roots with viable forms."[10]

An important statement in the *Resoluciones* was that there was to be "no one class, present or future, which would be given a chance to dominate in the nation." This was repeated in the *Bases*, "The Cuban Revolutionary party does not have as its object to bring to Cuba a victorious group that would consider the island as its prize and dominion." The *Manifiesto* specified that the war was not to result in the "insane triumph of one party over another."[11]

One of the points most frequently mentioned in the *Manifiesto* was that the war to liberate Cuba was to be a just one. It stated, "It is only right that the party declare its faith that the Revolution is to find forms which may assure it . . . a cultured war."[12] Elsewhere in the same document Martí spoke of a "healthful and vigorous war." What makes a war "healthful" and "cultured"? Undoubtedly one of its characteristics, as stated in the *Resoluciones*, would be no "sterile vengeance" inflicted upon the Spaniards. This particular point was not raised in the *Bases*, but it was a prominent issue in the *Manifiesto*:

The war is not against the Spaniard, who, earning the security of his children and the esteem of the country, will be able to enjoy liberty with respect and even love.[13]

In a long paragraph Martí promised that the Spaniard was not to be mistreated, but, on the contrary, while "steel may answer steel, friendship responds to friendship." He continued:

. . . in the Antillean heart there is no hatred; and the Cuban salutes the Spaniard in death, whom forced military service tore from his home and land to come to kill in the hearts of men that liberty which he himself desires.[14]

On another occasion Martí elaborated on this point in *Patria*. He wrote:

The Republic, in Puerto Rico as in Cuba, should not be the unjust predomination of one class of citizens over the rest, but the open and sincere equilibrium of all the real forces of the country, and of the free thought and desire of all of the citizens.[15]

Martí declared that a people is made up of the rights and opinions of all its members, and not of the rights and opinions of a single class. Nor is it the "will of a single man, however pure it might be, nor the childish desire of realizing in a group of human beings the ingenuous ideal of a celestial spirit, the blind graduate of a tumbling university of the clouds."[16]

Martí spoke of the war to liberate Cuba in terms of a holy crusade, saying that to give one's life for one's country was the most beautiful and respectable form of human sacrifice. He wrote that war for the independence of a people was a sacred war and that the creation of a free people that was formed by it was a universal service.[17]

Although Martí glorified war as a means to an important end— the freedom of Cuba—he often expressed his opposition to military interference in politics. He wrote that the sword was to be taken from its scabbard only in defense of country, liberty, and honor. In an obituary on the death of General Philip H. Sheridan he wrote, "War does not make government impossible, but neither is it the proper school to learn the art of governing." At times Martí's pessimism about power politics extended beyond a fear of militarism, as when he wrote, "One does not know whose ambitions are more dangerous

for a country that is yet unborn—those of the militarist or of the civilians."[18]

The *Manifiesto* is unique among the revolutionary documents in that it alone mentioned the Negro. Martí scored the unjustified fears that had been expressed about the dangers of a race war being unleashed should the Revolution break out in full force. He wrote that the only ones who saw hatred in the Negro were the ones who hated the Negro, and with dread tried to subjugate the hands that could be lifted to expel "the corrupting occupant" from Cuban land.[19]

One of the major purposes of the *Manifiesto* as a propaganda piece was to animate the Cubans to accomplish a difficult task. This required boosting their morale with praise of their qualities. According to Martí the Cubans had not only the ability to carry out the war, but also had a bright future ahead of them. He wrote that the civilian attitude of their soldiers, the culture and kindness of their artisans, the modern and real employment of a vast amount of their intelligence and wealth, and the peculiar moderation of the laborer seasoned in exile and in war assured Cuba, without unjustified illusions, of a future free from the dislocations that often followed wars.[20]

The *Resoluciones* concluded with the proposal that the revolutionary organization should respect the constitutions of the local emigration centers in New York, Tampa, and Key West. This point was not repeated in the *Bases.* The "Estatutos secretos" did not provide a guide to any future constitution for the Republic. Emeterio S. Santovenia, a well-known Cuban historian, writes, "The *Bases* and 'Estatutos' of the Cuban Revolutionary party are conceived as a constitutional scheme."[21] Ramón Infiesta, however, maintains that it is difficult to discern in Martí a plan of constitutional organization for the future Republic.[22]

Since one of the characteristics of a republic is that it usually has a constitution, written or unwritten, it would seem that Martí missed a major point in not promising one in his appeal to the Cubans to support the Revolution. Instead the *Manifiesto* contained general references to the ability of the Cubans to govern themselves. An antecedent for this lay in the *Bases,* where the party promised not to continue the authoritarianism of the Spanish colony. The document read:

The Cuban Revolutionary party does not propose to perpetuate in the Cuban Republic, with new forms or with changes more apparent than real, the authoritarian spirit and bureaucratic composition of the colony, but to found in the free and cordial exercise of the legitimate capacities of man a new people and a true democracy capable of overcoming through hard work and the equilibrium of social forces the dangers of sudden liberty in a society composed for slavery.[23]

The *Manifiesto* briefly considered the avoidance of tyranny in the new Republic, but did not discuss the drawing up of a constitution.

The *Resoluciones* took into account the necessity of securing allies. This objective was repeated in the *Bases*. In the *Manifiesto* the statement was made that the war was to be "worthy of the respect of its enemies and the help of its allies."[24] This was a vague reference to the need for foreign aid, but there was nothing beyond this brief note.

The *Bases* promised that the economic disorder then existing in Cuba would be replaced by a system of public finance that would open up the country to the diverse activities of its inhabitants. This point was elaborated upon in the *Manifiesto,* where Martí declared that the errors of the other Latin American countries, such as concentration on only one industry, particularly on agriculture, were to be avoided in Cuba. The *Resoluciones* did not mention the need for economic revisions in Cuba.

The three documents discussed cover the period from November 28, 1891, to March 25, 1895. Each served a specific purpose: the *Resoluciones* to unite the Cuban groups in exile; the *Bases* to form the Cuban Revolutionary party to carry out the war of liberation; and the *Manifiesto* as a message to the Cuban people of the aims of the invasion and the projected war. Although serving distinct purposes, the three documents coincided on major political, sociological, and economic points.

The most optimistic of the three documents was the *Manifiesto,* in which Martí poured forth his faith in the character of the Cubans, their culture, and their devotion to the principles of democracy. If it is possible to summarize the content of the documents and arrive at a fair estimate of the future government envisioned by Martí for Cuba, it would be that he anticipated the complete withdrawal of Spain from Cuba, and that in its place would be left an exceptionally gifted

people, tolerant, cultured, intelligent, humane, and just, which, by its virtues would avoid the pitfalls suffered by other Latin American nations after they had gained their freedom from Spain. He expected that Cuba would be a republic dedicated to the principles of freedom, equality, and justice for all.

Martí and the Spanish Colony

Did Martí, however, have an intimate knowledge of the governmental system of the colony upon which to base concrete suggestions for bringing about an orderly transition from a colonial bureaucracy to a republic? It must be remembered that his only experience with the colonial government was at age sixteen, and was confined to the walls of a rock quarry. From that time until his death, twenty-four years later, he spent in two brief visits to Havana less than a year in Cuba. After his last trip in 1879 his information about Cuban politics reached him secondhand, from newspaper accounts, letters, and personal reports by emigrants from Cuba. The exiles were not, however, persons whose experience included extensive colonial administration, familiar as many of them may have been with the abuses and corruption of the regime. It was the habit of Spain to assign the major administrative positions to Spaniards, not to Cubans. Martí was never confronted with the problems of running a governmental organization. By profession he was a journalist. One searches in vain, therefore, to find any concrete proposals for the establishment of governmental institutions once the Spanish bureaucracy had been destroyed. Santovenia, however, is of the opinion that the *Bases* and "Estatutos secretos" were a point of departure for Martí's ordering of institutions capable of fundamentally changing Cuban society. The evidence to support this point of view is not conclusive.[25]

At times Martí had no thoughts about conserving any feature of the colony. He wrote in his notes, "My land must be *purified* like the Augean stables; it is necessary to let loose a river on it." In another passage, however, he said:

One's native land is something more than oppression, something more than pieces of land without liberty and without life, something more

than the right of possession by force. Country is a community of interests, unity of ends, a sweet and consoling mixture of loves and hopes.[26]

Thus Martí, apparently without realizing it, posed the dilemma of "letting loose a river" on Spanish institutions, at the same time building a new Cuba on a "community of interests," which in many instances reflected deep social and political patterns of Spanish origin. His frequent references to the importance of the past make it all the more difficult to understand his failure to grasp this problem. Instead he wrote grandly, "With their teachings, passions, and griefs, the spirits of past generations inhabit space, and from it impel its people and watch over it."[27]

Martí's Concept of the Future Republic of Cuba

What, then, were Martí's ideas for the new Republic of Cuba? In 1895 he wrote:

Each person is to undertake in the work of the world that which is most near at hand . . . because the influence of man is exercised best and most naturally in that which he knows, and from which there comes to him immediate pain or pleasure. That assignment of human labor, and nothing more, is the true and irrevocable concept of country. All of its parts must be satisfied to achieve a uniform whole. Country is humanity, that portion of humanity which we see most nearby.[28]

Perhaps Martí's writings on specific institutions for a future Cuba were vague, but his recurring philosophy was that whatever forms the government of the island should take they were to be completely indigenous to Cuba. In a frequently quoted passage from an article in *El Partido Liberal* in Mexico, January 30, 1891, Martí wrote that the young people of America were rolling up their shirt sleeves, plunging their hands into the bread dough of the nations and helping them to rise with the yeast of their perspiration. He wrote that they understood that too much was being imitated and that salvation lay in creating. "Banana wine," he said, "even if it turns out bitter, is still our wine." Forms of government of a country were to accommodate themselves to their natural elements. He added cryptically, "When a problem turns up in Cojímar [Cuba], do not look for the solution in Dantzig."[29] Elsewhere he said:

Either the Republic has as its base the whole character of each one of its sons, the habit of working with their hands and thinking for themselves, the integral employment and respect for one's self, as family honor, the integral employment of others, in short, the passion for the dignity of man, or the Republic is not worth a tear of our women nor a single drop of blood of our brave soldiers. We work for reality and not for dreams.[30]

Patriotism

At times Martí's passion for love of country reached unusual extremes. In 1886 he wrote:

This love of country is to be completely pure, without a mixture of personal interest, active, active to frenzy, to sacrifice, to the flag, but as a priest, without ever staining oneself with the spots of ambition.

He felt that patriotism was the most beautiful and vehement expression of man's love. In 1894 he asked:

Who would not give his life for the land in which he was born? Those who think that they would not give their lives, do so. But about such matters one must speak after one has been wounded on the battlefield. Being merely an onlooker is one thing, abusing it is another.[31]

Martí saw the Republic as being built from the ground up, with all of its citizens working to make a new Cuba, with opportunities for all, with everyone enjoying the fruits of self-respect, regard for others, and all imbued with a profound patriotism. A Cuban author, Raimundo Lazo, writes:

It can be said that for Martí politics in its entirety is patriotism in action. It is, therefore, an ethical projection of the individual into collective life, and for that reason, into his politics pass all the essential characteristics of his heroic morality.[32]

Martí's views on patriotism actually envisioned a subordination of the individual to the nation. He wrote that the first quality of patriotism was self-abnegation, the disappearance of personal passions or desires in deference to the realities of public needs. He wrote that to love one's country was to lay one's self before it at all hours. "A sincere patriot," he said, "must sacrifice everything to his country, even to the glory of falling, defending it before the enemy." He also wrote that the greatest worth in life was that of sacrificing one's own

impulses to the convenience of the rest. He once commented, "A single man is never worth more than a whole people." In 1893 he wrote, "We wipe out the Individual. We serve the Nation." Summing up, he said, "Obedience is government."[33]

Duties of the Citizen

Martí had much to say about the citizen and his duties. "Social discipline," he wrote, "dignifies the obedience of citizens, because it deprives public authority of all iniquitous force." Yet he also believed that the general felicity of a people rested in the individual independence of its inhabitants. "Whoever would wish a live nation," he asserted, "should help to establish the matters of his country in such a way that each man may work actively and enjoy personal independence."[34] The obligation of every individual was to bear his share of the burden of public service.

Martí recognized, however, that public service, while a noble duty, often meant deep personal sacrifices. He wrote, "The illustrious man suffers in political service more than the ignorant man in business relations." He found that it was only with agonizing and continuous servitude that one bought political prominence.[35]

On the other hand Martí was extremely critical of the self-seeking politician. He wrote that the greatest danger for a country was the voluntary abandonment on the part of the citizens of their natural gifts into the hands of the petty politicians, whom he considered repugnant criminals who made honest men in public affairs feel the same as devout persons would upon seeing a criminal at the altar.

Fat politicians, massive, smiling, glittering, like those who live in profitable ease, immensely resemble the high priests of long ago, only the politicians pray their Hours in the law of universal suffrage.[36]

He wrote that the beer hall and corner politician, the falsifiers of public opinion, and the vote merchants were the "pigs of political institutions." Martí contrasted the "pigs" with the "true man," who did not look on which side he would live best, but where duty lay. "If any citizen fails to fulfill his part of his duty," he wrote, "we must double ours so that part may not remain unfulfilled."[37]

As for the rights of the citizen, Martí had less to say on this subject, except to remark that rights are taken, not asked for; rooted out, not begged for. Although he considered that voting was a right of the citizen, he placed more emphasis upon it as a duty. Martí felt that the one who failed in his duty to vote ought to be punished with no less penalty than the one who abandoned his weapon in the face of the enemy. "Voting should be obligatory," he urged, "because nobody has the right to place his country in danger because of his indolence."[38]

Following Rousseau, Martí saw the incontestable "will of all" as an expression of the sovereignty of the people, which, when pacifically demonstrated, was the "yeast of republics." The natural expression of this was in voting, since "the Republic rises on the shoulders of universal suffrage, of the unanimous will of the people."[39]

Martí, however, was unable to see the connection between voting and arriving at an estimate of public opinion. He wrote:

Although it is said that government . . . is the manipulation of currents of opinion in a country to arrive at definite political solutions, the truth is that government is not that, but the direction of national forces in such a way that the individual may fulfill his ends in a dignified way and take advantage in the best way of all the elements of prosperity in a country.[40]

How Martí could think that national forces might be directed in a democracy without responding in part to public opinion, leaves a void in his understanding of public affairs.

One of the political curiosities in Latin America is the last minute abstention of opposition parties from the polls when their leaders feel that the party in power will not assure free elections. This is in the nature of a protest to call attention to their opinion that elections have been rigged. It is doubtful just what this abdication from responsibility accomplishes, unless, of course, it is to avoid physical violence. Although not specifically referring to this situation, Martí seems to have found a related malady, not only in Latin American politics, but in all constitutional forms of government when he wrote:

The most immediate relief to political evils is for educated persons, who today make a great show of staying away from the polls, to vote. If they disdain today the exercise of their right as proprietors, tomorrow, terrified, they will have to kneel before a tyrant to save themselves.[41]

Martí took a dim view of the lack of civic conscience of educated persons when their major interest in life was the pursuit of financial gain. He saw them as remembering their right to vote only when they saw their material interests in danger from the triumph of an unfriendly candidate.[42] For Martí the citizen could not avoid his duty whatever the excuse might be. He wrote:

When politics has as its object merely changing its form in a country, without changing the conditions of injustice in which the inhabitants suffer; when politics has as its object, under the name of liberty, of replacing those in power with even hungrier authorities, the duty of the honest man will never be to stand aside and permit unchained corruption.[43]

Should this happen, Martí felt that in nations composed of educated and uneducated elements, the illiterate would govern because of their habit of resolving difficulties by force whenever the educated did not learn the art of governing. Elsewhere, however, Martí pictured the "uncultured masses as lazy and timid in intelligence, although wanting to be well governed." In case the people were crossed, however, they would shake themselves free and take over the reins of government.[44]

Martí's opinions on law and justice at times reflected his admiration for the common man.[45] He wrote:

The natural man comes, indignant and strong, and overthrows the accumulated justice of books, because it is not administered in accordance with the evident needs of the country.[46]

At one time, however, Martí believed that only the general exercise of law freed people from the domination of the ambitious. He also wrote, "There is no worse country in which to resort to violence than that one where law is practiced."[47] Roberto Agramonte, a Cuban sociologist, finds, "Natural liberty is the metaphysical nucleus of Martí's conception of what was human. Natural law had no more exemplary representative or sponsor."[48]

Liberty and Tyranny

Martí wrote frequently of liberty, although in general and lyrical

terms. He believed that liberty was the right of every man to be honest and to think and speak without hypocrisy. He wrote, "Liberty and intelligence are man's natural atmosphere." In a passage on the blessings of liberty he soared:

Like bone to the human body, and the axle to a wheel, and the wing to a bird, and air to the wing, thus is liberty the essence of life. Whatever is done without it is imperfect.[49]

At one point Martí equated liberty of country with the "adjustment of interests of all of its citizens." He went so far as to define the Republic as no more than a burning and irrepressible desire in elevated souls to see man happy and free.[50] Martí did not believe, however, that liberty could be an isolated affair. He wrote:

Every man of justice and honor fights for liberty wherever he may see it offended, because that is to fight for his integrity as a man; and the one who sees liberty offended and does not fight for it, or helps those who offend it, is not a whole man.[51]

Martí did not take an unqualified view of liberty, however. He wrote, "If the liberty of tyranny is tremendous, the tyranny of liberty repels, makes one tremble, and horrifies."[52]

Martí wrote that one of the prerequisites of liberty was that every man should learn the use of firearms, not to turn them against brother peoples who were defenseless, but to discharge them against the forehead of the one who, in intending to make slaves of men, should dishonor the foreheads of all men. Martí recognized that where men had no sure and honest opportunity for earning their bread, "there is no hope that public liberties will be secure, because the necessity of earning a living will always make violations seem justified, and the lack of interests to defend will give rise to ambitious troublemakers."[53]

Martí saw education as indispensable to the enjoyment of liberty. He wrote, "To be cultured is the only way of being free. He also cautioned, "He who does not help to lift up the spirit of the enormous and ignorant masses, voluntarily renounces his liberty." He felt that nothing guaranteed the liberal sentiments of a government so much as the haste that it showed in spreading education.[54]

Considering the many references to be found in Martí's writings on the sacredness of patriotism to one's native country, and the obliga-

tion of obedience to authority, as contrasted to Martí's romantic concept of liberty, one is led to suspect that Martí's references to liberty were made as a propaganda device to whip up enthusiasm for overthrowing the Spanish oppressor. Once the Republic was established, however, Martí would seem to have advocated duty, obedience, and patriotism to replace liberty. In this respect Martí suffered from the faulty logic of all revolutionaries. Resistance is the supreme good until the "right" government is in power, then protest becomes treason before the "true wisdom" embodied by the rulers.

The Hero in History

Martí's admiration for great men also shows some inconformity with a fully developed philosophy of liberty. He often expressed his esteem for the outstanding military heroes of Latin America—Simón Bolívar, José de San Martín, and José Antonio Páez; for the great presidents of the United States and Mexico—George Washington, Abraham Lincoln, and Benito Juárez; outstanding humanitarians and individualists—Ralph Waldo Emerson, Walt Whitman, Peter Cooper, and Henry David Thoreau in the United States, Cecilio Acosta in Venezuela, and José de la Luz y Caballero, the Cuban educator. Martí read Carlyle and admired him because "Carlyle liked men of action, was not in conformity with his times, and loved humanity." Martí believed that respect for great persons helped one to be great.[55]

Martí even planned a dictionary of quotations from the works of great men. He also had in mind writing a book, *The Liberators of Humanity*, in which he intended to discuss the "heroes of thought" from Buddha to Comte, from Aristotle to Littre, of all those who had "labored for freedom" in philosophy.[56]

As an indication of his almost mystical identification with a great man, he wrote in his notes at the age of thirty:

I have knocked around in life and tried its tidbits, but the greatest pleasure, the only absolutely pure pleasure that I have enjoyed up until now, was that afternoon in which half-naked I saw from my room the prostrate city [New York], and thinking about Emerson I caught a glimpse of the future.[57]

Martí wrote that men capable of accomplishing universal tasks should not waste their time on trifling personal affairs. On the contrary, he wrote:

Great ideas and great actions are the natural family of a great man. They are great for their internal stature, which is the essential and real greatness, whether or not the occasion is found for them to become famous.[58]

Martí was critical of the people when they failed to pay proper homage to their heroes. He exclaimed:

What can people be doing who do not raise great temples to the redeemers of men, and who do not place their statues in niches; and make up a new book of saints, and meet on holidays to comment upon the virtues of their heroes? Are they clamoring for a church? . . . Well, here is the new church![59]

One of Martí's more curious ideas was that egotism was a characteristic of ancient times, and that humanitarianism was the keynote of his own age. This dubious premise is interesting because of the persons whom Martí considered to be qualified for the role of "humanitarians." He wrote:

I do not speak of the common people: these everywhere are packs of little beasts, the stomach of the Universe. I speak of superior spirits who exalt and represent these times.[60]

He was very impatient with "common spirits who pursued men of superior souls." He found that they never pardoned those whom they had seen themselves obliged to admire. He wrote, "At the foot of the most beautiful trees worms always make the deepest hollow." Martí found that the reason for this was that peoples tired of their pure men. Seeing them constantly held on high, they came to lose the respect that they first gave them. "Still," he wrote, "there is no deeper pleasure experienced by people than to feel that an extraordinary creature lives among them," adding, however, "Afterwards they bite, stone, disfigure, and abandon him."[61] Although these writings of Martí would seem to preclude on his part any deep appreciation of the masses of humanity, one authority finds that he was, "more than any other Hispanic-American writer of the nineteenth century, a populist and a democrat."[62]

Agramonte asserts that Martí's theory of society "rejects the idea

of the great man; he does not believe with Carlyle, who otherwise had a powerful influence on him, that history is nothing more than the biography of great men." Nevertheless Agramonte himself sees Martí as a superman in the mold established by Nietzsche. According to Agramonte's application of the Nietzschean idea, Martí's "supermanship" consisted precisely in being a great man without making a show of it. This, the Cuban sociologist believes, gives the key to Martí's whole life.[63]

Whether a superman can be a democrat is a moot point. It is possible but not likely. In view of Martí's writings on the subject of his martyrdom, his identification with Emerson, and his contempt toward "common spirits," it would seem that he was not exactly overwhelmed with a philosophy of democracy. The evidence seems to point in the direction of Martí's having had visions of the fame of greatness being accorded to himself at some future date.

Martí's admiration for great men, however, was not blind hero worship for mere military accomplishments, as is often found with the "man on horseback" in Latin America, but was directed toward their humanitarian philosophy and accomplishments.

Concept of Latin America

Martí's concept of a republic for Cuba was conceived in such general terms that it could be applied to any of the other Latin American nations. Although his ideas were strong for love of country, he did not profess a narrow nationalism.[64] In fact Martí wrote that patriotism was censurable when it was invoked to hinder friendship among all the men of good faith in the universe. Once he wrote:

Everything in "Nuestra America" is Cuban, and we fight for human liberty not only in Cuba, we fight to insure with our freedom the independence of all Hispanic America.[65]

Martí saw the Spanish heritage as a detriment not only to Cuba but also to the other Latin American republics. He once said, "What we have not done is what we have not had time to do because we have been so busy extracting from our blood the impurities that our parents willed us." He wrote that colonial institutions and attitudes still existed

in the Latin American republics, but that in spite of this the new nations were gradually becoming aware of the need to face the problems of a large and depressed Indian population, the concentration of persons and wealth in the large cities at the expense of the rest of the country, and the extensive importation of foreign culture.[66]

The following paragraph by Martí is a faithful, if florid, representation of his thinking on the "new" Latin America:

America, a giant savage . . . is tearing off its clothing, is disassociating itself from its inadaptable residue, is shaking off the moral oppression which different powers have left on it, is redeeming itself from its confusion and from the servility of imported doctrines, and is living its own life. Although hesitant then, it is firm now; always embattled, hindered, and envied, it travels toward itself. Original institutions are created, foreign ones are reformed and made to fit. Feeling is subordinated to thought, and counting its wounds, upon them it calculates its way of exercising liberty.[67]

This picture of Latin America as a noble savage, casting aside the old and awakening to a new life of its own, is largely a beatific vision. As such it did not represent the facts then, nor do the frequent and violent changes of government now indicate that "Nuestra America" has "redeemed itself from its confusion."

When writing somewhat more specifically about the "good governor" for America, Martí said that he should ignore how the French or Germans governed themselves, and concentrate on studying the native elements of his own country. Martí, however, once projected writing a book on comparative government to include Switzerland, the United States, France, and the republics of South America.[68] Using these native elements as guides, the administrator could direct his program toward maintaining the identity of the individual and exploiting the resources of the nation for the benefit of its citizens. Martí often recurred to this indigenous theme:

How are governors to come from universities if in America there is no university where the rudiments of the art of government, which is the analysis of the peculiar elements of the peoples of America, are taught?

On this subject it is interesting to observe that Martí in a letter to Mercado, March 30, 1878, wrote from Guatemala that he was going to be teaching the "science of legislation" in Izaguirre's school.[69]

Martí believed that the American nations, whose citizens up to then seemed more given to showing their bravery than to working the land's riches, would finally tire of wasting their forces in useless struggles. They would then turn their activity toward making agricultural and mercantile revolutions with "the same haste, generosity, and brilliance" with which they had been making political revolutions.[70]

In Martí's opinion the goal of the Americas in international relations was not "to raise one world against another, nor to hastily assemble diverse elements for an unjust and unnecessary conflict, but to treat peaceably and honorably with the peoples who in the dark hours sent us their soldiers, and in the upsetting epoch of reconstruction kept open their treasuries for us."[71] This passage refers particularly to the enlistment of Englishmen in the armies of liberation of the Latin American colonies in the 1820's and 1830's. The hostile attitude of the United States government toward the outfitting of Cuban expeditionary forces in the United States did not allow Martí to foresee active North American intervention as a likely possibility in the Cuban Revolution in 1895. Martí, however, in the excerpt quoted, is not expressing an anti-United States attitude.

The United States and Latin America

Martí saw two different peoples in the Western Hemisphere, very diverse in spirit because of origin, antecedents, and customs, and similar only in their fundamental human identity. He said that on one side was Latin America, with all of its peoples of one nature, and on the other was an America which was alien, but whose enmity it was "not feasible nor wise to foment." Martí thought, however, that with firm circumspection and wise independence it was not impossible to be friendly with the United States, although he also warned against "entangling alliances" and blind imitation of United States institutions. Martí made a few brief references to the Monroe Doctrine in his notes,[72] largely by way of definition, but there is no evidence that this important policy of gratuitous protection of Latin America by the United States was of much concern to him, at least by that title. In fact, one Cuban writer finds that Martí saw no inconvenience in close

relations between Cuba and the United States and in hoping for victory through its cooperation.[73]

Martí, nevertheless, often considered the United States as a danger to Latin America. He wrote, "The disdain of a formidable neighbor who does not really know us is the worst danger to our America."[74]

Economic Ideas

Martí's views on economics often revealed his fears of political domination of Latin America by the United States. He wrote that whoever spoke of economic union also meant political union. He saw that the nation that wanted economic independence would have to sell to more than one country, since where there was only one buyer the seller could not set the terms of the sale. He wrote that a people wanting to be free must be independent in its commercial relations.[75]

Martí was opposed to the economic policy of the United States whereby high tariffs discriminated against the entry of foreign products.[76] In this respect he was following the classic economic liberalism of Adam Smith and Baron Montesquieu.[77] Martí's fear of United States imperialism via its international monetary proposals has already been discussed. Martí's warnings against United States economic imperialism is considered by a Cuban economist as one of Martí's major economic preoccupations.[78]

Martí gave special importance to the intelligent exploitation of agricultural resources. He warned that a nation that trusted its subsistence to the cultivation of a single product would see itself in a serious crisis.[79] This meant, of course, in the case of Cuba, dependence upon the whims of the United States sugar market and tariff regulations.

Martí held that wealth was more rapidly produced in agriculture than in industry, and that it was more stable than mining. The nation that possessed thriving agriculture was assured "true well-being."[80]

Martí thought that the most direct way of resolving social problems was to study the forces of nature and to learn to manage them. Like Rousseau he believed that cultivation of the land was the only absolutely honest source of wealth. In a passage that would not have been well received had it been widely circulated while Martí was

soliciting funds for the revolutionary movement from the cigar makers in Florida, he exclaimed, "It is certainly not so pleasing to the eyes to see a man who rolls tobacco as the one who works the earth, or labors in a smithy." In addition, Martí would have required of every man, as a title to enjoy public rights, to plant a certain number of trees.[81]

Martí's recognition of the need for scientific agriculture has already been mentioned in the discussion of his views on education. The importance of this point may be seen in the assertion by a Cuban writer that Martí's social and economic philosophy may be summed up in two words: agriculture and education.[82]

The Worker in Society

Like Whitman, Martí glorified the manual laborer, writing, "I shake every calloused hand with pride." He believed that personal work was the root of self-respect and public liberty. "When the hands are busy," he counseled, "the mind is disturbed less." Work assumed almost a mystical aura to Martí. He exclaimed, "Here is a great priest, a live priest: the worker." In addition, he warned, "It is dangerous for a people to have the spectacle of and contact with a group of inactive men who do not create or inspire."[83]

Martí's writings on the role of the worker in society were based on situations in the United States rather than in Cuba and the rest of Latin America. It is largely in his articles on strikes in the United States that he demonstrated his opinions on this subject.

Labor troubles in Chicago in the 1880's had long been exploited by a group of anarchists led by August Spies, Albert R. Parson, Adolf Fischer, and George Engel. After the disastrous riot in Haymarket Square on May 4, 1886, Martí condemned the violent methods of the anarchist leaders, although he had previously shown himself to be sympathetic to workers in industrial disputes. Spies and his associates were later arrested for complicity in the plot to set off the bomb that resulted in the bloody massacre. At the end of a widely publicized trial seven of the leaders were sentenced to death. Although public opinion acclaimed the verdict, Martí wrote, "The stranger with the compassive soul, and the thinker who sees into causes was made sad and kept still."[84]

The following year Spies, Parson, Fischer, and Engel were hanged. By this time Martí was openly on the side of the victims, writing that their guilt had not been proven. He warned, "This Republic . . . has fallen into the injustice and violence of monarchies."[85]

One Cuban writer has established the Haymarket Massacre as the turning point in Martí's attitude toward socialism. His claim is that after this date no antisocialist writing appears in Martí.[86] Since socialism was not an issue in the trial, it is doubtful that this could have been responsible. At all events, it scarcely makes a socialist out of him. Like the good reporter that he was, Martí saw pathos in the trial and exploited it.

A good case can be established, nevertheless, for Martí as a firm believer in social justice. This is evident in his general philosophy and in particular in his essay on Peter Cooper. He deeply admired this prominent American philanthropist.[87] Ramón Infiesta asserts, nevertheless, that Martí's opinions on economic matters lack validity for any kind of socialist theory.[88]

Communism

Martí wrote sparingly on political systems based upon economic principles, his writings on these subjects comprising only a fraction of the entire body of his works. Iduarte finds that Martí wrote informatively rather than formulating an economic theory.[89] Raúl Maestri, a Cuban authority on economic matters, also writes, "Martí was certainly not an economist."[90]

When Martí wrote it was often under the inspiration of day-to-day events, as at the death of Karl Marx. His obituary on Marx was sympathetic. He wrote:

Karl Marx was not only a titanic mover of the anger of the European workers, but a profound seer in the reasons for human misery, and in the destinies of men. He was a man eaten with the desire to do good.

Martí showed how Marx had studied the ways to set the world upon new bases, but in his opinion Marx went too fast and in the dark.[91]

A commentary by Martí on the insecurity of the times making it difficult for poets to write lyrics or epics seems to have been in-

fluenced by a well-known passage from the Manifesto of the Communist party. Martí wrote:

A pale, immense man, with an austere face, sad eyes, and dry mouth, dressed in black, walks with grave steps, without rest or sleep, through all the land. And he is seated at all the firesides, and he has placed his trembling hand on everybody's head.[92]

Martí saw the world as being in violent transition from one social state to another, and in it peoples were disordered, ideas obscured, justice and vengeance mixed, and action and reaction increased in intensity. His solution for this situation was not, however, in any political system based upon economics. The world would not be reordered, he wrote, "until the sovereign power of reason, which dominates all else, bursts forth, like the dawn from night, sorts out the confused elements, dissipates the clouds of combat, and channels the original forces of the new state."[93] At times Martí found it difficult to bring his economic theory down to earth. The *tour de force* and *deus ex machina* were central in many of his outbursts of romantic thought.

Martínez Bello, a Cuban writer on Martí's ideas, insists, however, that Martí's romanticism disappeared from his thinking during the last eight years of his life.[94] Another authority, Portuondo, is certain that Martí's romanticism never abandoned him.[95] Félix Lizaso claims that Martí is "*por excelencia* the antiromantic."[96] To Jorge Mañach, Martí is the "practical romanticist."[97] Juan Marinello finds that Marti was a romantic.[98]

Other references by Cuban writers and selections from Martí's works might be cited at this point to develop the debate. To repeat the statement of purpose of this study made in the introduction, however, it is to assess the impact of the ideas and personality of José Martí upon the Cuban people. It does not include an attempt to present an exhaustive study, establishing, for example, when Martí ceased, if ever, being a romantic. The temptation to become involved in debates among authorities on Martí on the nuances and contradictions of his philosophical, sociological, political, and economic thinking must be avoided. It is important, however, to point out clearly the diversity of opinions existing to show how Martí has become "all things to all men."

What these chapters have attempted to do has been to present an objective montage of Martí's thought. For the purpose of this study the importance of what Martí has written lies not so much in what he said as in the way in which he has been interpreted, not only by intellectuals, but also by other segments of Cuban society. It was necessary to present Martí's ideas in some detail, however, to avoid total confusion on the subject of his philosophy. If the general impression gained from these pages is one of an avalanche of opinions by Martí on many subjects, unsystematized and often paradoxical, and of a Martí, humane, with an exquisite sense of justice, excruciatingly sensitive in his grief, thoroughly convinced of his patriotic destiny in life, and anticipating martyrdom in the service of his country, the purpose of these chapters has been achieved. What stands out in all of Martí's philosophy is a sustained humanism very well expressed in the following passage:

The reading of beautiful things, the knowledge of the harmonies of the universe, mental contact with great ideas and noble deeds, intimate contact with the best things which in every epoch have been adding to the human soul, quicken and extend intelligence ... produce pleasures much more profound and delicate than those of mere possession of fortune, sweeten and ennoble the life of those who do not possess it, and create the national soul for the union of all such men on high.[99]

Chapter 4

TRANSFIGURATION IN THE PLASTIC ARTS

*T*HE SHORT-LIVED and unequal struggle between Spain
on the one hand and Cuba and the United States on the other, the
freeing of Cuba, and the subsequent American occupation helped to
eclipse the exploits of José Martí from Cuban view. Most of the praise
lavished upon him soon after his death came from abroad, from
Cubans who had known him in the United States, and from Latin
American men of letters. It is often alleged that Martí was forgotten
in Cuba for many years after his death. To a certain extent this is true
until, roughly speaking, the abrogation of the Platt Amendment in
1934, when the right of the United States to interfere in Cuban affairs
ended. No attempt will be made to prove that there was any necessary
relationship between the Platt Amendment to the Cuban Constitution
and a lack of interest in Martí during this time, although it is logical
to assume that the reason for the new look at Martí after abrogation
was due to a heightened spirit of nationalism on the part of the
Cubans.

It is the purpose of this chapter to look into the biographical works
written in these years to estimate their share in building Martí as a
national hero, and to report any statements made to support or refute
the generally held thesis that Martí was largely ignored in Cuba
up to the early 1930's. This process will involve measuring the volume
of literary production from 1895 to 1955, including the collecting
and editing of Martí's own works, in and out of Cuba. In addition, the
record of Martí as he has appeared in statuary, on stamps, and on
coins will also be noted as an indication of progress toward his acceptance by the Cuban people as *the* National Hero.

Death and Transfiguration

José Martí was a consummate writer of obituaries. It is regrettable that he did not write the final draft of his own, or at least guide with an invisible hand the writing of a perfect eulogy. At any rate, with his death on May 19, 1895, his followers in Cuba, other Latin American countries, and the United States wrote in sorrow and in praise. A biographical sketch in the pro-Spanish newspaper *La Discusión* of Havana two days after his death paid grudging respect by referring to him as the "titular president of the Cuban Republic." It commented upon his exceptional record as a student and his excellence as a poet. The article ended with the comment that Martí's death had given the Revolution a rude shock since it could be said that Martí personified the separation of Cuba from Spain.[1]

Charles A. Dana, editor of the New York *Sun*, wrote that the news of the death of Martí had caused him great sorrow. He said:

We learn with poignant sorrow of the death in battle of José Martí, the well-known leader of the Cuban revolutionists. We knew him long and well and esteemed him profoundly. For a protracted period, beginning twenty-odd years ago, he was employed as a contributor to the *Sun*, writing on subjects and questions of the fine arts. In these things his learning was solid and extensive, and his ideas and conclusions were original and brilliant. He was a man of genius, of imagination, of hope, and of courage. . . . His heart was warm and affectionate, his opinions ardent and inspiring, and he died as such a man might wish to die, battling for liberty and democracy.[2]

Tomás Estrada Palma, the future President of Cuba, wrote:

If you ask where José Martí is, you will hear a chorus repeat: "In the hearts of every Cuban patriot." And thus it certainly is. . . . Humanity has lost an apostle; Cuba one of its most devoted and enthusiastic servants; I, I have lost a loyal friend *par excellence*. I could even say a loved son.[3]

The Dominican Federico Henríquez y Carvajal wrote that Martí was the Word of the Revolution, and "the Word was made man; and the man became a soldier; and the soldier, a hero; and the hero, an august martyr." He also wrote:

Ah! On the heights of Turquino [the highest mountain in Cuba] will be

raised the dawning figure of the greatest patriot, for such is José Martí, in the midst of the Pleiades of the heroes of the redeemed nation.[4]

In a speech at a memorial service for Martí in New York in 1895 Lincoln de Zayas spoke on the "Apotheosis of Martí." He said that in past centuries Martí would have been taken for a demigod, so marvelous were his gifts and extraordinary his achievements. He maintained that he said this in spite of the indifference of almost everybody toward Martí, with the exception of a few noble souls. He wrote of Martí:

His foresight was amazing, and while the rest of us wandered, erring and disheartened, surrounded by impenetrable darkness, he walked erect and enthusiastic, with his eyes fixed on the distant horizon, where there shone in his prophet's vision the bright reflection of his regenerated and free country.[5]

Homage from Mexico was paid by two great poets, Amado Nervo and Justo Sierra. Nervo wrote:

I knew him; I nourished my spirit with his radiant word; and, hearing the patriot speak, I believed in liberty. . . . He was not only the artist; not only the poet; he was something more; the hero. He was in love with liberty. His cause found a sympathetic response in Mexican hearts.[6]

Justo Sierra wrote his tribute in poetry:

> *The native soil will not hide forever*
> *Your sacred body from our view,*
> *Ah, in its absence may my fleeting lament*
> *Tell of the grief that saddens my heart.*
>
> *On the lyre of America we shall put*
> *Your body, thus shall we carry it*
> *On our own shoulders to History!*
> *In the peace of your funereal night,*
> *Perchance, like a lamp of glory,*
> *May your solitary star shine some day.*[7]

Another Mexican poet, Luis G. Urbina, writing twenty years later in homage to Martí, commented upon the circumstances in which he had first heard Sierra's poem:

One day in May, 1895, Justo Sierra, my father, my teacher, my guide . . . came to see me in my ministerial office. He sat down next to me; he

took from the pocket of his coat a small piece of paper, and resting his arms on the table, . . . read me a sonnet. He had just written it, his pulse trembling and a disturbed look in his eyes. . . . When he had finished reading it, we were silent and thoughtful. Justo Sierra remained bowed over, as if looking at the paper, but absorbed—who knows in what distant thoughts. . . . The verses still linger in my memory.[8]

Another Mexican writer, Alberto Leduc, wrote that if Cuba should some day be free, not only Martí's compatriots but all of the writers of Latin America and all of those who wished social betterment for the human race should make a pilgrimage to his tomb to pay their respects.[9]

Manuel de la Cruz, writing from New York in 1895, said:

When one feels the cold of his room, solitary and still, and one looks at his worktable, dusty and loaded with newspapers, pamphlets, and books, and then visualizes the smoking and bloody field in which he fell mortally wounded, the contrast between his life as an almost romantic apostle, a refined artist, and his end as a martyr, removes his legendary apotheosis to the realms of fantasy. And yet that legend, which surrounds his figure like a gold halo, is [becoming] a legend of the Americas.[10]

Gonzalo de Quesada y Aróstegui wrote that Martí's hand was the one which had guided the Cuban Revolution, and that he had foretold its direction and its triumph. Quesada said that Martí's originality consisted in his intuition in foretelling events with a mathematical exactitude. He extolled his former mentor:

His life is like the symbol of his country's history; in his diverse and versatile accomplishments, in the salient virtues of his character, he embodied those of his native land; even in his glorious death and his immortality we see the future of Cuba.[11]

Serafín Sánchez in a eulogy of Martí in 1896 spent much of his fervor in attacking the Cubans who, he maintained, had betrayed Martí through the insolence and cowardice of local leaders in accepting salaries from the Spanish colonial government. He spoke frankly:

It must be said—the immense majority of the Cubans who by their intelligence and social position could have effectively helped him turned their back on him, and most of the time fought him in his task of redemption.

He added that they charged Martí with being a "visionary and a

madman," but that he had felt compassionate towards them in his role of prophet and had dauntlessly continued his difficult work.[12]

Enrique José Varona, Cuban philosopher and successor to Martí as editor of *Patria*, wrote a year after Martí's death:

There is no life more worthy of admiration than that of the Cuban patriot José Martí. His intimate friends recognized this when they gave him the noble and affectionate title of maestro. We Cubans all recognize this when we venerate him with the worthy name of martyr. He was a maestro who taught doctrines of liberty, lessons of concord, and examples of moral dignity. And for his life of abnegation and for his heroic death he has deserved well in having his career synthesized in the glorious word . . . which immortalizes the Prometheuses chained to their racks, and the Christs nailed to their crosses, the word SACRIFICE.[13]

Máximo Gómez paused in his fight for the liberty of Cuba and wrote in 1896:

He died in a hard encounter [with the enemy] and at the first shots of the war as if with the awakening of this people to rise and stand erect and angry against tyranny, he might with his death give an example of resolution and bravery. Greater stature could not be expected of any man.[14]

Rubén Darío, the great Nicaraguan poet, wrote in 1897 in tribute to Martí:

I am not one . . . of those who believe in the existing riches of [Latin] America. . . . We are very poor. . . . So poor that our spirits, if nourishment did not come from abroad, would die from hunger. We should weep long for the one who has fallen. The one who died in Cuba was the best that we Latins have.

Darío went on to say that Martí was not only a man but rather a superman. He wrote that Martí lived in communion with God, having ascended to Him along the most certain of all ladders—the ladder of Grief.[15]

Rufino Blanco Fombona, the noted Venezuelan man of letters, wrote from Caracas four years after the death of Martí:

If men are measured by success, it is possible that there are greater ones than José Martí; but if sublimity of heart, and breadth of view, and a generous soul are worth something, José Martí is an illustrious memory. . . . Despair never took him captive because that Jesus, that preacher, had his ideal: the Republic; his apostleship: Liberty.[16]

Wenceslao Gálvez, a Cuban emigrant in Tampa, wrote in 1897:

Where is he? Everywhere. Is he God perhaps? Who knows? What is certain is that he is everywhere, in all homes, in the street, in the tribunal, in the clubs, in the newspapers; let us put it squarely, he is everywhere. . . . His picture is in every Cuban home, in all the stores; his name is read in flowers in the garden of fervent patriotism; women wear his miniature, like a jewel, at their necks; and the men wear his likeness in lapel buttons. . . . His shadow protects us; his presence extends everywhere, and there is no Cuban on all the surface of the Earth who does not feel at bedtime that he stands beside him; and it is because he is the Cuban soul, he is the soul of the nation.[17]

In addition to tributes that came from scattered admirers, praise for Martí regularly appeared in *Patria,* which continued to be published in New York until 1898. Another weekly newspaper dedicated to the principles of the Cuban Revolution existed in New York at this time. Its editor, Rafael Serra, chose for its title, *La Doctrina de Martí.* Containing news of the progress of the war in Cuba, items of interest about the revolutionary leaders, praise for Martí, and a column devoted to Martí reprints, it lasted until 1899.[18]

Thus Martí was memorialized by his followers after his death. In spite of all this praise from Cubans and foreigners, Emilio Roig de Leuchsenring wrote forty years later that in 1899 only sixteen representative Cubans understood and admired Martí. Roig de Leuchsenring arrived at this number by referring to a public opinion poll taken by the Havana newspaper *El Fígaro* in 1899 in which "the most outstanding political, revolutionary, and intellectual figures" of Cuba were asked whose statue should be placed in Central Park in Havana. José Martí received only sixteen votes out of 105 questionnaires returned. Among the high revolutionary officers, only Generals Emilio Núñez, Daniel Gispert, and Loynaz del Castillo responded for Martí. Counted in the sixteen favorable votes were those of Fermín Valdés Domínguez, who headed a committee to raise a monument in his memory, Juan Gualberto Gómez, and Miguel F. Viondi.[19]

Homages and Literary Interpretations of Martí, 1899-1933

Nevertheless Martí's name continued to appear in homages and

literary works. In 1899 Ana Maria Barnes came into print with her *Martí, A Story of the Cuban War*.[20] This book, however, has been something of an impostor. Erna Ferguson in her book in 1946 on Cuba reported that the first book on Martí was published in English in the United States in 1899.[21] Ana Maria Barnes' work is also listed in Peraza Sarausa's *Bibliografía martiana*.[22] As a matter of fact, Barnes' book on Martí had nothing to do with José Martí. It is a fictional account of a little Cuban boy by the name of Martí who was caught up in the Spanish-American War of 1898. What is interesting about the book, however, is that the name of Martí was of sufficient prominence to the author that she chose it for her main character and for the title.

Two years after the appearance of this book with the deceptive title, in Cuba another dubious work made its debut with the title *Martí, novela histórica por un patriota (Martí, a Historical Novel by a Patriot)*. Understandably anonymous, the author cavalierly wrote:

The inaccuracies of date should not be taken into account, since this is a historical novel, and liberties are permitted to the novelist which would be censurable in the historian.[23]

The plot of the novel revolves around young Martí and an attractive prostitute named Carolina who sells her charms to the political governor of Havana in return for military secrets, all in the name of Cuban patriotism. The author not only took liberties with dates but also with facts, even advancing Martí from a tender sixteen at the time of his arrest by the colonial regime to a more manly eighteen years of age. Carolina is shown as trying to save Martí from prison by bargaining her wares with the governor.[24] There is no evidence to prove this, although Wenceslao Gálvez writing in 1897 refers to "Carolina the patriot," gray-haired and then living in Tampa. Gálvez asserts that Martí "professed an immense and holy affection" for her.[25] The book was popular enough to call for a second edition, undated, and also anonymous. In 1915 it again appeared, this time with a new title, *José Martí, reseña histórica (José Martí, Biographical Sketch)*, and an author, Franco Rander (a pseudonym).[26] A second edition of the book under Rander's name appeared in 1929,[27] and a third in 1931,[28] making five editions in all of this spurious work.

This is a near record so far as reprints of biographical treatments of Martí are concerned, although authorities on Martí in Cuba would probably not deign to give the work the name of a biography.

A year after the first appearance of this novel in 1901, a sounder voice spoke for José Martí. It was that of Máximo Gómez responding to an invitation to take part in a ceremony honoring his old Cuban friend. In the letter, he wrote that he appreciated being called upon to attend since he was the first, after all, "to suffer the deep pain of seeing Martí disappear in that gloomy hour for the nation." He added:

José Martí was very little known by his compatriots the Cubans, in the true, splendid apogee of his glory. It is a blessed fact: I have not known another like him in the more than thirty years which I have found myself at the side of the Cubans in their struggle for the independence of their nation.[29]

In the same year that Máximo Gómez wrote this letter, 1902, Cuba became a republic after United States occupation forces under General Leonard Wood withdrew. The following year a treaty was signed putting into force the Platt Amendment to the Cuban Constitution. Tomás Estrada Palma became the new Republic's first President.

With the gaining of independence from Spain in 1898, the Cuban Revolutionary party had ceased to function as a militant political organization. Numerous groups occupied the void until 1903. In that year two new political parties based on a reorganization of those already in existence made their appearance: the Conservative Republican party, and the National Liberal party.[30] They remained the two major parties until the downfall of Machado in 1933.

The new Republic began auspiciously under Estrada Palma, but was soon in difficulties. In 1906 election irregularities and internal insurrection caused the resignation of Estrada Palma. The President's action resulted in the second United States occupation of the island. The North American Provisional government, first under the direction of Secretary of War William H. Taft, and then Charles E. Magoon, lasted until 1909.[31]

In preparation for the withdrawal of United States forces, elections were held in 1908. The Liberal candidate for President, José

Miguel Gómez, was elected. The date expected to be chosen for the restoration of the Republic was May 20, 1909, the anniversary of Cuba's becoming a republic. General Enrique Loynaz del Castillo, a veteran of the War of Independence and one of the leaders of the insurrection of 1906,[32] which had brought on the occupation, suggested, however, that the anniversary of the birth of Martí, January 28, 1909, should be chosen. The request was forwarded to President Theodore Roosevelt, who acceded.[33] By virtue of Martí's name, therefore, the Republic was back in Cuban hands four months earlier than planned. One can only speculate whether Martí would have been thus honored if his birthday had fallen after May 20.

In 1909 homage was paid to Martí in the Cuban House of Representatives by Miguel F. Viondi, in whose law office Martí had worked as a clerk in 1878. Viondi particularly praised Martí's oratory:

Although the stern grammarian or classical academician analyzing Martí's speeches may discover defects, it is undeniable that when Martí spoke from the rostrum, the same before linguists as before the public, the enthusiasm which he awoke had no equal. Everyone who heard him in the Lyceum of Guanabacoa attests to this.[34]

The difficulties of rehabilitating Martí for the welfare of the nation found expression in a pamphlet by H. C. Brito. Writing one year after the reestablishment of the Cuban Republic, he complained about the corruption, and lack of faith and love of country existing in Cuba. He said:

And those who wish to raise him up and re-establish moral equilibrium, for otherwise it will not appear, are apostrophized and censured because they create divisions and awaken ill-feeling to the harm of the nation.[35]

Recognition of the usefulness of a cult to Martí, however, was made in a speech paying homage to him in 1910. Mario García Kohly said before the City Council of Havana:

The cult to the great men who form a nation is the purest dedication to the grandeurs and virtues of it, because no one like these men incarnate and symbolize in their aspirations and griefs, the concept and life of that nation.[36]

In 1911 Roque E. Garrigó wrote a laudatory biography of Martí

showing that a direct line of victors ran from Christ through Cavour of Italy to Martí.[37]

In 1913 Néstor Carbonell, who had known and worked with Martí, said in a speech on his friend's life and work:

Poor poet, dweller in immense solitude! The people of whom you sang and to whom you offered your whole life scarcely know you because they need the time for dancing or vote-hunting in their districts.[38]

This speech was delivered at the beginning of the administration of Mario G. Menocal, the Conservative President of Cuba from 1913 to 1921.

Apparently there was no change in public attitude in the intervening five years, at least according to Napoleón Gálvez, writing on the anniversary of Martí's death May 19, 1918:

If [Martí] . . . could leave his tomb and return to life to see what is happening in this beautiful land . . . surely he would die again of sadness, grief, and shame. . . . This surely cannot be Martí's Republic. A republic without democracy. A republic without guarantees. A republic of licentiousness and waste. A republic where suffrage is a joke and liberty the melancholy memory of a lost cause; this it not, it cannot be, the radiant ideal of the Martyr of Dos Ríos.[39]

Judicious admiration for Martí was not lacking abroad, however. Gabriela Mistral, the Chilean poet who won the Nobel prize for Literature in 1945, wrote to Federico Henríquez y Carvajal in 1921:

I venerate Martí, I have a tender and penetrating admiration for him, and when I mention his name, it is more than just four syllables that I speak. His was the beautiful soul supreme and the true initiator of modernism—of a renovation of spirit and form—in our American literature.

She then went on to say that Martí, among the moderns, was one of the greatest influences in her writings, particularly in his "live words" and in the "freshness of a pure heart." She expressed her astonishment that Martí had not yet been granted the high place that he deserved in Latin American literary circles.[40] In the same year, however, Arturo R. de Carricarte asserted it was not true that Cuba was ungratefully neglecting Martí.[41]

In 1923, during the administration of the Liberal President Al-

fredo Zayas (1921-25), a masterful article written by Pedro José Cohucelo appeared in a Havana newspaper. It scourged those Cubans masquerading as men of letters who were taking the sacred memory of the Apostle and Martyr José Martí as the pedestal to raise up their own mediocre figures in the name of homage to him. Cohucelo wrote:

At all hours, at all moments, they speak to us of the surpassing merit of Martí, of the oblivion in which we have his memory, of the necessity of building a sacrosanct memory to his name.

He then asked the purpose of all the verbiage expended in marking out the route of Martí from his landing in Cuba to his death in Dos Ríos,[42] the declaration of his birthplace as a national monument, and the erection of a new monument that would be the "eighth wonder of the world." To Cohucelo, Martí was a man of ideas. "While they were raising monuments and consecrating everything that belonged to Martí in life," he declared, "they were insulting his memory with unrestrained ferocity." Cohucelo squarely laid down his charges:

Martí preached truth and honor, and we are friends of frivolity and imposture. He eulogized the excellence of disinterest in governmental functions, and we orient all action by the government for the benefit of the lowest appetites. He wanted a Republic "with all and for the benefit of all," and we have converted it into a wretched satrapy where some few oligarchs devour the very foundations of our history. He abominated peoples who begged or accepted favors from intermeddling foreigners, and we have converted ourselves into a colony enslaved by Uncle Sam. . . . He called for honest politics, and we have obeyed him by elevating a band of thieves [to office] who do not even have a concept of their own villainy. He dreamed and sought something very great, and we have belittled everything.

Cohucelo concluded that with every day that passed Cuba was widening the distance between itself and the true spirit of Martí. He scorned the raising of marble and bronze statues in favor of imitating his good works and ideals.[43]

Charles E. Chapman, the North American historian, writing of José Miguel Gómez, President of Cuba (1909-13), confirms the relative lack of regard in which Martí was held during the 1920's: "Not even the name of Martí, Máximo Gómez, or Maceo can to this

day [1927] rouse the Cuban masses to such enthusiasm as can that of José Miguel."[44]

While Martí was being neglected by the Cuban people, according to this charge, he was attracting attention in Spain. One of the first serious biographies to appear on Martí was that of M. Isidro Méndez, whose work was published in Madrid in 1925.[45]

In 1928 Fernando de los Ríos, an eminent Spanish writer, paid tribute to Martí:

My pretensions are humble: I come to give my offering to the memory of the most moving, profound, and compassionate personality that the Spanish soul has produced up to now in the Americas.

In addition, Fernando de los Ríos included Martí among those Great Men who were the key to "deciphering the historical enigma of peoples." He added: "In them [Great Men] we can measure the height of the spiritual level attained by the most exquisite forces of a people." De los Ríos found that the directing forces or values of Martí's life were to be found in his dedication to honor, love, grief, justice, liberty, and heroism. Borrowing a parable from the province of Oriente to express his opinion about the place of Martí in the hearts of his countrymen, de los Ríos wrote picturesquely, if somewhat inaccurately from the point of view of chemistry:

When one throws a chunk of salt into the water it can no longer be separated from it. Where is the salt? It is there, blended, like the rivers in the ocean, without name and form. This is what happens to great spirits; they are dissolved in the soul of all to flourish in the most hidden and intimate places of the spirit.

Thus it was, he felt, with Martí, who was present in all Cubans, idealistically, whether they realized it or not.[46]

Fernando de los Ríos expressed his appreciation during the administration of the Liberal President Gerardo Machado (1926-33). The speech sounded the knell of what is usually referred to as a long period of indifference toward Martí, although it can not be given credit for having awakened the Cubans to an acknowledgment of the Apostle for the first time. It is evident that this was a period of only relative indifference.

In 1929 four books appeared on Martí. Joaquín Llaverías, late

Director of the National Archives of Cuba, published an edition of Martí's articles and newspapers with facsimiles and commentary.[47] Another work on Martí as a newspaperman appeared under the authorship of Gonzalo de Quesada y Miranda. Since Quesada wrote this work with the major portion of Martí's personal papers in his possession, and since he was a journalist himself, he was able to turn out a competent study.[48] The Cuban diplomat and author, Alfonso Hernández Catá, produced a long work on Martí that was printed in Madrid.[49] In Havana Raimundo Lazo, a Cuban literary historian, did a study of Martí's writings.[50]

In 1929 the *Revista Martí,* a children's magazine under the direction of Gabriel García Galán, came into print to spread the word of Martí. It is still published.

In 1930 José T. Oñate, following Lubián's work in 1922, carefully plotted out with maps and photographs the route of Martí from Las Playitas to Dos Ríos.[51]

The beginning of the renaissance of interest in Martí may be conveniently dated from the time of Jorge Mañach's biography, *Martí, el apóstol,* published in 1933. Written in elegant Spanish, the book is probably the best known of all the biographies of Martí. It was translated into English in 1950. At the time the translation appeared Hubert Herring, a North American historian, wrote:

This excellent translation of the ablest biography of the Cuban liberator is a welcome addition to the Latin American shelf.... There have been a dozen lives [a conservative estimate] of Martí in Spanish; of these Jorge Mañach's comes nearest to that objectivity for which we beg. Good as it is Mañach's work confirms the peril of writing about heroes.... Gabriela Mistral in her glowing foreword on Martí unwittingly [through unrestrained poetic enthusiasm for Mañach and Martí] gives away the secret of why even the best biographies produced in Latin America fail to satisfy.[52]

At the time of publication of the biography in 1933, however, it was not yet clear to some that a revival of interest in Martí was occurring. Although Carricarte had asserted in 1921 that it was not true that the Cubans were neglecting Martí, by 1934 he was gloomily citing library statistics to demonstrate public apathy toward the Apostle for the period 1925-34. Carricarte noted in the nine years that he was

head of the Municipal Library of Havana, out of a total of 200,000 requests for books, only 300 had been for works on or about Martí. Comparing these figures with those for Caibarién, he found that the public library in Las Villas province in 1927 showed that out of 3,418 readers, only 36 had requested material on Martí. Likewise in the city of Santa Clara in the same province, out of 17,500 readers, only 4 asked for any work on Martí in 1927.[53]

Renaissance of Martí, 1933-55

Nevertheless, in retrospect, it may be seen that the renaissance had begun. After 1934 a great avalanche of biographies and studies was released in pursuit of Martí. Since it is impossible to mention all the books produced on the Apostle, references will be limited largely to volume rather than to individual works in this period. Works of most interest to the study are, of course, cited elsewhere in full. Many works on Martí are merely rewordings of other studies.

Although no major study has been published on Martí in the United States, two doctoral dissertations have been written on him, one by Esther E. Shuler at the University of Minnesota in 1946,[54] and the other by Alan M. Gordon at Harvard University in 1956.[55]

Published material on Martí by North Americans is notably lacking. Perhaps one of the reasons for this scarcity is the problem of translation. Manuel Pedro González has written of Martí, "Unfortunately, his prose is one of the most difficult to render into English that could be found in the Spanish world."[56] A selection of Martí's writings was translated into English by Juan de Onís and published in 1954.[57] The biographies of Lizaso[58] and Mañach help, but a third Cuban biography should be added to this list, that of Quesada y Miranda's *Martí, hombre* (*Martí, the Man*), since Quesada is the recognized authority on Martí.

In considering the need for a diffusion of knowledge of Martí in the United States, the statement of Andrés Iduarte, the Mexican writer, is worthy of note:

No other Hispanic American has known the United States so well nor has admired and divulged so much the grandeur of its institutions and its men of letters and its government. . . . With regard to his life, so fun-

damentally American because of his status as a well-rounded Hispanic American and a New Yorker in action, there is in Martí a continental spirit which we do not find in any other man of his time.[59]

Juan Ramón Jiménez, Spanish poet in exile in Puerto Rico and winner of the Nobel Prize for Literature for 1956, once gave his estimate of Martí. Jiménez reads:

Darío owed him [Martí] a great deal, Unamuno [a famous Spanish philosopher] quite a bit, and Spain and Spanish America, in large part, are indebted to him for making known the poets of the United States. Martí, in his travels of exile . . . incorporated the very best of the United States into Hispanic America and Spain better than any other writer in the Spanish language.[60]

In deference to the stature of Rubén Darío, Gabriela Mistral, Rufino Blanco Fombona, Amado Nervo, Justo Sierra, Fernando de los Ríos, and Juan Ramón Jiménez in the world of Spanish and Latin American letters, further commentary seems unnecessary to establish Martí's importance in the eyes of foreign writers. The Cubans are justified in their expressions of regret that the North Americans have neglected Martí.

Works of Martí in Print, 1895-1955

A fairly certain way of gauging interest in Martí is to measure the extent and time of the collection and publication of his writings. One of the major bibliographers of Martí, Fermín Peraza Sarausa, has produced a chronology of the work of the Apostle. Discounting errors and omissions, it is useful as a representative sample in documenting the volume of interest evidenced in Martí's own works.[61] Aside from various editions of collected works which were published in 1900-19, 1918-20, and 1925?-29, the chronology shows a marked lack of interest on the part of editors in bringing forth unpublished writings and reprints of Martí until the early 1930's. Two of the three sets of works mentioned were published at the expense of their compilers. Thus a brief review of the date of emergence of Martí's writings will show a casual, if not indifferent, demand for his works for several decades after his death.

According to Peraza's chronology, the first of Martí's works published after 1895 was an English translation in 1898 of selections from Martí's poetry by a North American, Cecil Charles.[62] One year later Martí's letter of farewell to his mother upon his last departure for Cuba was printed in Havana.[63]

The first major attempt to collect Martí's works was in 1900 in the first of sixteen volumes to be edited under the impulse of Gonzalo de Quesada y Aróstegui, the literary heir of Martí. Fourteen volumes in all were eventually brought out by Quesada himself. After his death in 1915, Quesada's wife edited and had published the fifteenth volume in 1919, and his son Gonzalo saw to the editing and publishing of the sixteenth volume in 1933.[64] At the time of publication of the sixth volume in 1909 Martí's disciple Quesada, complaining of indifference toward the Apostle, wrote:

In spite of the difficulties which I have had in collecting the materials to make the literary work of José Martí known in Cuba—certainly not as disheartening as the apathy with which our people receives them—I am not dismayed, since with its publication at the same time that I keep alive his venerable memory, I serve my country.[65]

From 1900 to 1910, in addition to Quesada's volumes, reprints of Martí's poems, articles, and letters appeared at the rate of about one item a year.[66] In 1910 an edition of selected works appeared in Paris with Américo Lugo, the Dominican litterateur, as editor.[67]

From 1911 to 1920 scattered articles and poems appeared in Havana newspapers and magazines. Collections of Martí's works were published in Paris and Madrid, and several editions appeared in Cuba.[68] In 1918 Rafael G. Argilagos brought out his first volume of selected thoughts of Martí. He eventually edited other works under the general title of *Granos de oro* (*Grains of Gold*). Quesada y Miranda considers that Argilagos' efforts helped very much to make Martí popular.[69] In 1919 Max Henríquez Ureña, the Dominican literary historian, edited a volume of Martí's works in Paris.[70] In the same year Rubén Darío edited a volume of Martí's poetry, also in Paris.[71] In Havana Néstor Carbonell published an eight-volume set of Martí's works, which appeared from 1918 to 1920.[72] In 1919 his brother, Miguel Angel Carbonell, brought out an anthology of Martí's works.[73]

From 1921 to 1930 the output on Martí did not increase notably. In Paris Ventura García Calderón edited a collection of Martí's writings.[74] Paris also saw translations of a few of Martí's poems in 1929 under the editorship of Armando Godoy.[75] Less than a handful of articles and letters of Martí appeared yearly in Cuba during this period, although Néstor Carbonell followed his eight-volume edition with two collections of Martí's writings, one in 1923,[76] and the other in 1926.[77]

In 1926 Martí's article "Vindicación de Cuba" appeared in an edition of twenty thousand copies paid for by the President of Cuba, General Gerardo Machado.[78] The selection of this particular article for widespread distribution was clearly a demonstration of anti-American sentiment on the part of the government and a recognition of the usefulness of Martí as a national symbol.

In Paris in 1926 Armando Godoy and Ventura García Calderón brought out their "complete works" of Martí in a two-volume edition.[79] Not to be outdone, in Madrid from 1925 to 1929, Alberto Ghiraldo edited another "complete works" of Martí in eight volumes.[80]

The year 1930 saw several dozen reprints of articles and poems, a collection of letters edited by Félix Lizaso,[81] and a selection of Martí's thoughts organized by M. Isidro Méndez.[82] In 1930 the Venezuelan government ordered the publication of a volume of Martí's writings on Venezuelan matters.[83]

Renaissance of Martí, 1933-55

During the years 1931 and 1932 less than half a dozen articles appeared under the increasingly harsh regime of General Machado. In 1933, however, Gonzalo de Quesada y Miranda brought out the final volume of his late father's edition of Martí's works.[84] In addition, in 1933 Quesada began publication of three volumes of other papers of Martí in his father's collection, finishing this task in 1935.[85]

The *opus magnum* in the field of publication of the works of Martí has already been cited many times and is, of course, the *Obras completas de Martí* edited by Gonzalo de Quesada y Miranda in seventy-four volumes and published by Emeterio S. Santovenia from

1936 to 1949.[86] This work has the greatest right to being called "complete," although several volumes are still to be added. With the publication of this set of Martí's writings the Cubans recovered their hero from the hands of foreign intellectuals, compilers, and commentators. As far as availability of Martí's work is concerned, this is the apex of a period of four decades of sporadic publication of articles, poems, letters, and "complete works." Thus the last request of José Martí to his favorite disciple was amply carried out by the son. The difference in attitude of the publishers as late as 1933 and the period of publication of the *Obras completas de Martí* (1936-49) may be noted in the following comment by Gonzalo de Quesada y Miranda:

Today [1947] publishing houses fight for an opportunity to make known the works of Martí, and at that time [1933] nobody wanted to aid me in the task of finishing the work begun by my father![87]

In 1946 another edition of Martí's works was published, this one in four volumes, by M. Isidro Méndez.[88] It became sixth in the line of "complete works." Single editions or compilations, such as those by Carlos Martínez-Fortún and Lilia Castro de Morales, have appeared since this date, without the pretense, however, of being complete.

Works about Martí in Print, 1895-1955

A rough examination of Peraza Sarausa's *Bibliografía martiana* was helpful in determining the volume of interest in Cuba and abroad in Martí as shown by the date of appearance of articles and books about him. It is not to be expected that this work contains references to every item that has appeared on Martí, but in its scope of 10,201 entries it furnished the best source available for a general appraisal. Books of over 100 pages were tabulated as "A" and books and studies of less than that number as "B."

The bibliography verified the assertion that the major volume of production on Martí has appeared within the last twenty-five or thirty years of the Republic, culminating in a great number of books, articles, and poems written shortly prior to and during the 1953 Centenary. That Martí was not wholly forgotten in Cuba before 1934 is

attested to by the appearance of 16 books (A); 40 (B); and 405 articles, most of which are recorded as being printed in Havana. This compares with production outside of Cuba in the same period: 6 (A); 16 (B); and 199 articles.

The total for Cuba from 1934 to 1955 was: 66 (A); 137 (B); and 5,840 articles. Most of this production took place in Havana, although a sharp increase of interest in Martí was noted outside the capital as the Centenary approached. The total production outside of Cuba for the same period was 26 (A); 34 (B); and 1,066 articles.

Total production on Martí at home and abroad in the period 1895-1955 was: 114 (A); 227 (B); and 7,510 articles. These figures do not include 1,740 items of reproductions of Martí's writings, such as entries on the appearance of newspaper articles as he wrote them, anthologies, and collected works. Some 500 book reviews, as well as duplicate entries, were also not counted. Taking these figures into consideration, the total production on and about Martí thus approximately reaches the figure of the 10,201 entries listed in Peraza's bibliography.

ANALYSIS: 1895-1955

Quantitatively speaking, the record of Martí's works reproduced and the material written about him from 1895 to 1955 is impressive, particularly during the latter half of the period. A qualitative analysis of the material written about him from 1895 to 1955, with a few exceptions, does not reveal a similarly impressive degree of scholarship. For the most part inordinate praise has been the rule at home and abroad.

Still Life: Martí in Marble, Stamps, and Metal

It is not possible to take the measure of a national hero without also considering his representation in statuary, stamps, and metal. The planning and building of Martí's monuments have been the focus of much acrimonious debate, which is revealing of the difference of opinion as to how his apotheosis could best be accomplished.

In 1925 a substantial and deluxe edition of iconography was brought out by the Cuban government as homage to Martí upon

the dedication of his birthplace at 102 Paula Street, Havana.[89] The book, the work of Arturo R. de Carricarte, consists of the reproductions of 137 photographs in life and death, statuary, and medals and coins struck off in Martí's honor. As such it constitutes a fairly complete record of the Apostle in pictures and effigy up to 1925. Most of the photographs show Martí as a serious, bushy-haired, slight individual with baggy trousers. Representations in bronze and marble have tended to be faithful to this picture of him.

MARTÍ IN STATUARY

As early as 1890 Gonzalo Zaldo, a young Puerto Rican admirer of Martí, molded a statue of his hero about eighteen inches high, basing it on a photograph of Martí as a prisoner at the age of sixteen. The first bust after Martí's death was modeled in 1895 by a North American sculptor, Fred B. Clarke. The most famous statue of Martí, however, was erected ten years after his death in Central Park, Havana, in spite of the lack of interest shown in 1899. The statue is the work of Villata Saavedra and an Italian sculptor, Giuseppe Neri. The editorial comment in the book on Martí's iconography is that the sculpture was begun by popular subscription in 1900, and, in a tone of amazement, that the collection was carried on "without intervention by the authorities of the nation . . . in the period of complete North American occupation."[90] On the occasion of the erection of the statue Félix Matos Bernier advised the Cuban public:

Do not look for the moral profile of Martí in these days. His brother [also] lives [only] in legend: his brother is Jesus Christ. . . . The souls of Christ and Martí beat together in the shining design of eternal progress.[91]

It was a design, however, that was temporarily obscured from view.

In 1906 a statue sculptured by the Italian Carlo Nicoli was erected in the Central Park of Cienfuegos, Las Villas province.[92]

In 1907 the remains of Martí were moved to a modest tomb, the work of José Bofill, erected in the Civil Cemetery in Santiago de Cuba. It eventually became a shrine, where, as it was noted in 1925, every day the teachers and students of the Spencer School in Santiago made a pilgrimage to lay flowers.[93]

In 1909 a statue was erected in the Central Park of Matanzas,

the capital of the province of the same name. The sculptor was Salvatore Buemi. The national symbol of Cuba, a half-nude and warlike woman with flowing hair and billowing skirts, strides ahead of Martí at the base of the statue. With flashing eyes and a shout on her lips she triumphantly holds aloft in outstretched arms a set of broken chains. The contrast with the figure of Martí, calmly standing with his hand slightly raised in a mild gesture, is striking.[94]

No more statues are reproduced as appearing from 1909 to 1925, but numerous busts were set up in his memory. One appeared in Palma Soriano, Oriente province, in 1912, and one was sculptured by Lucia Bacardí de Grau in 1916 and presented to the National University in 1923.[95]

In 1918 Ugo Luisi did a bust of Martí which was acquired by the National Museum in 1919. It later served as a model for gold coins minted by the Republic. The artist also did another bust of Martí in the same year, one which is considered to be quite unlike his subject.[96]

In 1922 Martí's appearance in statuary received an important stimulus with the proposal in the Congress by Pastor del Río that every municipality in Cuba dedicate a statue in the Apostle's memory.[97] Consequently a law of April 20, 1922, required every municipality to dedicate a statue, bust, or appropriate tablet to him. The law also specified that a street was to be named after Martí in each municipality. January 28, Martí's birthday, was declared a national holiday.[98] This last action, however, was rescinded by the Cuban Constitution of 1940.

More statues and busts were sculptured, one for instance by Alberto Sabas Magurcía, a Cuban, in 1924,[99] and another by Jilma Madera, in 1952.[100] Recent busts worthy of note are those of Teodoro Ramos Blanco, Rita Longa, and Juan José Sicre. The work of Sicre, a meditative Martí, is the best known and most often reproduced of the sculpture of the Apostle. It is the official bust placed in all the public schools.

The Martí Mausoleum.—The first massive undertaking in Martí's honor was a new tomb to which he was removed in Santiago de Cuba in 1951. It is the work of sculptor Mario Santí and architect Jaime Benavente, and was provided for with a grant of $100,000 by

the Congress in 1945.[101] The tomb is in the shape of a hexagon, and is located in the Civil Cemetery of Santiago. Six gigantic statues resembling the Caryatids of Greek mythology represent the six provinces of Cuba. The structure is open at the base and supported by thick columns. The ponderosity of the work is in open contrast to the simplicity desired by Martí for his tomb. He had written that all he wished was a bouquet of flowers and a flag on his grave.[102]

The Monument to Martí in Havana.—The most impressive and ambitious monument to Martí, after the tomb in Santiago de Cuba, is the monument in the Plaza Cívica in Havana. A law-decree (promulgated by the President while the Congress is not in session) in 1935 called for the erection of a suitable monument to Martí.[103] Two years later the "Comisión Central Pro-Monumento a Martí" was created to undertake the building of the monument. After a site had been chosen, the Commission announced an international contest for the best plan. Any architect or sculptor was permitted to enter, provided that he was residing in one of the countries of the Western Hemisphere. A first prize of $10,000, a gold medal, and a certificate were offered for the best design.[104] After all the plans had been submitted, the jury found that none of the proposals were suitable for what it considered an adequate representation of Martí. For one reason or another most of the foreign entries were disqualified. As a result in 1938 the first prize was declared forfeited, and the second of $5,000, a gold medal, and a certificate were awarded to architects Jean Labatut, Raúl Otero, and Enrique Luis Varela.[105]

Not satisfied with the results of the first contest, the Commission announced a second one. This time the project of Aquiles Maza y Santos and Juan José Sicre won in 1942. Cubans continued to win the top honors. Luis Bay Sevilla, editor of the magazine *Arquitectura,* criticized the jury for its composition, inasmuch as of the twenty-three persons, nine were high-ranking military officers, three were engineers, seven were lawyers, and the rest were veterans, newspapermen, bankers, and industrialists. Not a single architect or sculptor had a vote in the deliberations of the jury.[106]

The plan of the two artists contained the model of a statue of Martí that was to be the center of focus for the monument, itself done in the style of a Greek temple. Martí was represented in such a way

that Sicre's statue invited sharp criticism. Quesada y Miranda declared that the figure of Martí, half-naked and sitting up in the midst of flowing robes, represented a Greek and not a Cuban Martí. Quesada wrote:

What is, nevertheless, the greatest error of the project of Sicre and Maza? In my judgment, as for the sculpture, it is that of presenting a meditative, philosophical, and static Martí; and as for the architecture, its predominantly horizontal lines. Martí was above all a great rebel, always agitated, completely a man of action, an ascending figure. And that impression only may be given with a statue of Martí in life, with architectural lines in which height and the vertical predominate.[107]

Construction of the monument was delayed during Fulgencio Batista's first term as President (1941-45), and during that of his successor, Ramón Grau San Martín (1945-49), but opposition to the Sicre-Maza project did not abate.[108] In 1949 J. de la Cruz referred to their Greek temple as unaesthetic and resembling a "cage to catch song-birds."[109] In the same year the secretary of the Commission, Roberto Netto, made the startling revelation that all the papers referring to the project of Sicre and Maza had disappeared from the files of the former secretary of public works, Gustavo Moreno Lastres. Netto declared, however, that he was not accusing the Grau administration (which had just left office) of destroying the papers.[110] An anonymous letter was printed in a Havana newspaper asserting, however, that the papers had not really disappeared, but were hidden in an attempt to thwart the project of Sicre and Maza.[111] The location of the papers has never been publicly disclosed.

In 1949 a law-decree in the newly-inaugurated administration of Carlos Prío Socarrás reactivated the Commission to undertake the building of the monument in view of the approaching Centennial of Martí in 1953.[112] In spite of the mystery surrounding the missing papers, the Sicre-Maza project seemed at the point of being realized when a *coup d'état* by Senator Batista March 10, 1952, brought the downfall of the Prío government. In August of the same year the Commission was reorganized.[113] The new secretary of public works in the Batista cabinet was Enrique Luis Varela, one of the authors of the first project to win approval by the Commission. After reorganization

the Commission reversed the previous decision in favor of Sicre and Maza and awarded the final contract to architects Varela, Otero, and Labatut. Sicre and Maza were outraged and exclaimed, "We have been the victims of plunder, and we will exhaust every legal means to attain justice for our cause."[114] Although they did not achieve success by legal means to force acceptance of their plan for the monument, Sicre's fifty-five-foot-tall statue of Martí is located at the main entrance to the monument.

The monument is in the form of an obelisk reaching an altitude of 465 feet. The major portion of the structure is completed. An elevator transports sightseers to an observation tower at the top. In the base of the monument there is space for a museum and library. The entire structure is faced with 600 tons of marble, most of which has been taken from quarries on the estate "El Abra" in the Isle of Pines, where Martí spent time as a prisoner.[115]

The monument is jokingly called the "Raspadura de Santa Clara" (the "Candy Tower of Santa Clara"), since its shape resembles a molded pan-sugar candy made in the city of Santa Clara, Las Villas province.

The monument has been financed in part from a general government levy of one day's salary on all working people in the Republic to defray the costs of the Centenary. Additional levies have also been made.[116] The budget for the National Commission to Organize the Acts and Editions of the Centenary and Monument of Martí was at the high figure of $1,989,209 for the fiscal year 1955-56.[117] The total cost of the monument will be more than $3,000,000.[118] A brief visit by the author to Cuba in June, 1960, revealed that the monument was largely completed, but not yet open to the public. The monument faces the new Martí Library, completed during the regime of Batista, but put into use by Castro.

A Statue in the United States.—Although Martí has been neglected by North American writers, efforts have been made to erect statues and busts to his memory. In 1956, for example, the Park Commission of the City of New York designated a location on the Avenue of the Americas for a statue of Martí to be placed between those of José de San Martín and Simón Bolívar. The sculptor and donor is Anna H. Huntington, widow of the well-known philanthro-

pist and Hispanic scholar, Archer M. Huntington.[119] In 1957 the Cuban government sent a check for $100,000 to the city of New York to help finance the statue.

Three years later the statue was still missing from its intended pedestal in Central Park. The park commissioner, Robert Moses, insisted it was not ready, but this statement was refuted by the sculptor who asserted that the statue had been ready for two years. The possibility of a riot between Castro supporters and opponents may have caused the delay.[120]

MARTÍ ON STAMPS

Often the "arrival" of a public figure to national prominence can be plotted by his first appearance on postage stamps. General Antonio Maceo appeared on a Cuban stamp in 1907, ten years before Martí was so honored. In 1917-18, however, Martí appeared on a one-cent green stamp. It was reissued with slight changes from 1925 to 1928 and again from 1930 to 1935. Although the engraving of Martí has been changed in the meantime, a one-cent green stamp is still being issued. Maceo, as well as other Cuban patriots, was honored with different issues, but Martí did not appear on a new issue until 1945, at the time of the celebration of the fiftieth anniversary of his death. The Ministry of Communications ordered the issuance of two stamps on that occasion.[121] In 1952, after a suggestion by the Ninth National Congress of History, the Ministry authorized a series of twenty-one stamps in preparation for the Centennial year.[122] The issues became a kind of pictorial biography of Martí by showing his birthplace, Martí as a prisoner, as a poet, and as a writer, and his monument, among other high points in his career.[123]

In 1959 Senator George Smathers of Florida recommended to the Post Office Department that it honor José Martí with a commemorative stamp in its "Champions of Liberty" series. Although the department promised "early consideration," no stamp has appeared as yet.[124]

MARTÍ IN METAL

In 1913 a medal was struck off by presidential decree to be presented to members of the society of Emigrados Revolucionarios (Rev-

olutionary Emigrants) in recognition of their services to the nation in the liberation movement. The head of Martí occupied one side of the medal and the shield of the Republic the other. In the same year José Santos Verdú engraved a medal to submit in competition for gold coins to be issued by the government. Although another model was used, Santos' work was reproduced and the copies served as souvenirs for the seventieth anniversary of Martí's birth in 1923.[125]

In 1915 a collection of gold coins in the value of one, two, four, five, ten, and twenty dollars was minted in Cuba. The image used of Martí was based on the work of Ugo Luisi.[126]

The *Revista Martiniana* (the *Martian Magazine*), organ of the Sociedad Martiniana (1921-27), under the direction of Arturo R. de Carricarte, ordered a brass medal struck off in 1921 as a "Martí Award" to the best students graduated from the six provincial high schools. A similar medal was awarded to the outstanding graduate of the Havana High School with the title of "Annual Award." The first person to receive this medal was Pablo F. Lavín in 1922.[127] Lavín subsequently justified the award by becoming a devoted follower of Martí, writing[128] and giving series of lectures about him.[129]

In 1921 another medal was ordered by the city of Havana as a "José Martí Award" to be contested for in debate by the ten best graduates of the Havana High School. A sample is shown in the Iconografía as having been issued in 1924.[130]

For the Centennial Martí appeared on a silver dollar (1,000,000 issued); a fifty-cent piece (2,000,000 issued); a twenty-five cent coin (19,000,000 issued); and a penny (50,000,000 issued). The law stated that Martí's appearance on coins was one of the imperishable ways of commemorating the Centenary.[131] José Martí has appeared on the one-peso note since 1934.[132]

Conclusions

What conclusions can be drawn from the record of homage paid to Martí in literary works, busts, monuments, stamps, and metal?

First, after his death Martí was highly praised by his followers in terms that expressed religious veneration. Many of these admirers,

however, were persons, some of them Cubans in exile, who were writing and speaking outside of Cuba.

Second, the period that Martí is alleged to have been forgotten in Cuba corresponds to the years during which the Platt Amendment to the Cuban Constitution was in force. Although there seems to be no particular connection, Martí did serve as a symbol of nationalism, as when Machado ordered the reprinting of thousands of copies of Martí's anti-United States article, "Vindicación de Cuba."

Third, interest in Martí during the period 1895-1933 was marked outside of Cuba by the literary fame of such individuals as Gabriela Mistral, Rubén Darío, Miguel de Unamuno, Fernando de los Ríos, Rufino Blanco Fombona, and Amado Nervo. In Cuba Martí was generally neglected by the best writers, although the popularity of a spurious biography of the Apostle is attested to by its five reprintings.

Fourth, from 1895 to 1933 Cuban publishers showed a general reluctance to bring out reprints of Martí's works, while abroad numerous editions appeared. After this period the Cubans began a campaign to publicize Martí, culminating in the seventy-four-volume edition of Martí's works edited by Quesada y Miranda.

Fifth, during the Martí renaissance many biographies and studies appeared, mostly unobjective and lacking in originality.

Sixth, although Martí was neglected by the better writers in Cuba during the period 1895-1933, the record of homage paid to him in busts, monuments, stamps, and metal indicates that he was by no means forgotten. The conflicts that later raged around the choice of an appropriate design for the monument in the Plaza Cívica, disappearance of official papers, and other acts of dissemblance created an atmosphere that discredited the general purpose of paying honor to Martí. The history of the representation of Martí in busts and monuments shows the conflict existing between those who felt that this was an appropriate way to honor him, and those who urged that Martí was better honored by following his ideas for an honest government. Martí has frequently been used as a symbol of morality in public life. Complaints were made from the very first days of the Republic that everybody talked about him, but no one practiced his example. As will be seen in later chapters, this is a strong current in the promotion of Martí as a national hero.

Chapter 5

SYMBOLISM IN SOCIAL GROUPS

7HE RECORD of promotion of José Martí as a national hero through literary production and representation in marble, stamps, and coins has been recorded in Chapter Four. Prior to Martí's renaissance the names that stand out are those of Gonzalo de Quesada y Aróstegui, Néstor Carbonell, Arturo R. de Carricarte, Rafael Argilagos, and Emilio Roig de Leuchsenring. These Cubans continued to write during the renaissance and were joined by Félix Lizaso, Jorge Mañach, Emeterio S. Santovenia, M. Isidro Méndez, Carlos Martínez-Fortún y Foyo, and Gonzalo de Quesada y Miranda. Add the statement by Quesada y Miranda that scarcely a Cuban intellectual exists who has not written or projected writing about Martí at some time or other, and you have a picture of intensive individual interest and effort in discussing the Apostle. Writing as individuals these persons have contributed to what will later be discussed as the cult of Martí. In their zeal to spread the gospel some of these individuals have founded and worked through public and private organizations. Martiana has been fostered through the media of politics, education, the press, fraternal organizations, youth groups, professional societies, patriotic clubs, and organizations devoted exclusively to Martí.

Societies Dedicated to Martí

One of the first private organizations devoted entirely to Martí, the "Sociedad Martiniana," was established by Arturo R. de Carricarte in 1921. It was founded for the purpose of "exalting the memory

110

of the Apostle, and consecrating his efforts by enriching and spreading as much as belongs to the bibliography of his life."[1] The organization, never one of great vitality, lasted until 1927.

THE ASSOCIATION OF FORMER STUDENTS OF THE MARTÍ SEMINAR, AND THE FRAGUA MARTIANA

The leading patriotic organization in Cuba devoted exclusively to the furthering of Martí's teachings is composed of a group of former students of Gonzalo de Quesada y Miranda, head of the Martí Seminar, begun in 1941 in the Extension Division of the University of Havana. Students are invited to join a group called "La Asociación de Antiguos Alumnos del Seminario Martiano" ("The Association of Former Students of the Martí Seminar"). This group was established June 3, 1944, with "the supreme objective to maintain and intensify the cult of José Martí and the most elevated patriotism by means of the best knowledge of his life and work." In addition it was to perform for Cuban society Martian acts of a nonpolitical nature that would render a faithful interpretation of the doctrines of the Apostle.[2] Active membership in the Association is restricted to those who have joined the Martí Seminar as students, since it is assumed that only those who have a basic knowledge of the Apostle are competent to carry out his work.

The Alumni Association has performed its constitutional mandate to spread the word of Martí by establishing a *Boletín Oficial*, the first number of which appeared August 15, 1945. In 1947 the *Boletín* was changed in name to *Patria* in honor of Martí's newspaper published in New York. In addition the Association inaugurated a radio program in 1945 to give biographical sketches of the life of Martí and to read some of his writings. This program was on the air intermittently until 1952.

The Association was hardly under way before it began looking for suitable quarters. A likely spot in Havana was found in the area of the stone quarry ("Las Canteras de San Lázaro") where Martí had worked as a political prisoner. A remnant of the quarry still existed in the block bounded by Hospital and Príncipe streets. In 1944 this area had been secured by the administration of President Fulgencio Batista with a grant of $20,000 for the construction of a "Rincón

Martiano" ("Martian Corner") as a small park.[3] The Association chose a location at the other end of the block adjoining the park. With the support of the Rotary Club of Havana under the presidency of José Borrell Tudurí, other Rotary clubs, and funds furnished by the Administration of President Carlos Prío Socarrás, ground was broken by the Department of Public Works January 28, 1950, for the "Fragua Martiana" ("Martian Forge"). Plans for the Fragua included a museum, library, and cultural center for the promulgation of the doctrine of Martí. In 1952 a decree by President Prío declared the Rincón Martiano and the Fragua Martiana as national monuments. Their custody was turned over to the Association.[4] The Fragua was inaugurated January 28, 1952.

In the same year the Association acquired a small piece of property outside of Havana with the aid of the Cuban government to establish a rural recreation center for Martian groups. It was officially inaugurated in 1953 with the name of "Los Pinos Nuevos" ("The New Pines") in recognition of the famous speech of Martí's at Tampa, Florida, in 1891.[5]

Through one of its earliest activities the Association has achieved much publicity in its sponsoring gifts of bassinets each January 28. The idea originated with Carmelina Reyes de Pérez Cubillas, who proposed to a Rotary club in Cienfuegos in 1932 that a bassinet be given to any baby born in humble circumstances on Martí's birthday.[6] The idea was later promoted by the Rotary clubs of Havana. Under the impulse of Nena Acevedo the Association also undertook the task of donating bassinets, delivering its first baby crib to a child born January 28, 1945. The following year two bassinets were presented. In 1948 clothing was added, as was the donation of monthly gifts of clothing to the maternity ward of the University of Havana hospital. When a child is benefited with a bassinet, a dossier is opened for it by the Bassinet and Clothing Committee at the Fragua. The record contains information, pictures, and a "social security card" entitling the child to medical or social assistance from the Association.[7] Several Cuban physicians donate their services to this end. The main difference from other bassinet-donating organizations, therefore, is that under the sponsorship of the Association the child continues to receive benefits until at least twelve years of age.

The custom of giving bassinets on January 28 has spread to other groups in the city of Havana and the provinces. The week preceding Martí's birthday in 1956 a large automobile distributing firm in Havana furnished a show window for a display of twenty bassinets provided by the Rotary clubs of Havana.[8] This is a yearly occurrence. Other Rotary groups throughout the Republic contributed their share of bassinets. One of Havana's leading department stores devoted show window space to bassinets. A large-scale advertisement in the newspapers offered not only merchandise for the newly-born under the heading of "Week of the Martian Bassinet," but also offered maternity gowns for purchase by the expectant mother.[9] The mayor of Marianao, a large suburb of Havana, donated two bassinets to the cause in the same year.[10] Charitable organizations, such as the Feminine Club of Cuba, added their contribution during Martí week by distributing shopping bags of food to needy families in Havana.[11]

The custom of the Martian bassinet is widely practiced. Since the committee at the Fragua does not coordinate donations of other organizations, it is difficult to arrive at any total figure, but Quesada y Miranda estimates that perhaps several hundred bassinets were given away throughout the island in 1956. In fact, in Havana there is often a scramble by bassinet-dealing groups to be the first to reach the new infant since the supply of bassinets sometimes outreaches demand.[12]

In what way does the donation of bassinets further the ideals of Martí? The sponsor of the idea in the Association, Nena Acevedo, wrote that to shelter the bodies and souls of children was a supreme maxim of the Apostle. She asserted:

He knew that there was no warmth sufficient for the soul of man who felt cold at birth. He knew that cold, all of his life he carried it in his soul, for that reason God permitted him to die with his face to the Sun, so that he might receive the warmth which men had denied him.

She explained that Martí loved children, that he knew that they were the root of the tree of life, and that it was necessary to nourish them with affection and comprehension so that the fruit might issue strong and secure.[13]

In accordance with the motto of the Association, "Martianism is Action in Behalf of Collective Society," a plan to establish Martian

children's groups in the schools of the Republic was undertaken in 1945. The idea of children's groups for the purpose of spreading the doctrine of Martí had been put into practice in the early 1930's under the initiative of Juan Pérez Abreu de la Torre, a Mexican resident in Cuba. Centers were established in Remedios, Caibarién, and Sagua la Grande in Las Villas province,[14] but these "Grupos Infantiles," as they were called, were not widely promoted nor did they last.

The Martian groups established under the initiative of the Association in the schools of the Republic are to meet at least one Friday a month to evoke the memory of the Apostle and the other founding fathers. They are to "render a beneficial and humanitarian work for collective society, principally among the poor and humble with whom the Apostle wanted to throw his lot."[15] The official anthem of the groups is that of the Association.

In addition Martian youth groups are organized for secondary schools.[16] The constitutions of the groups are officially authorized by the Ministry of Education, which controls all public schools throughout Cuba.[17]

The activity of the Martian youth groups seems to lie mainly in donating bassinets, helping sick and needy students, giving books to prisoners, and being present at acts honoring Martí and the patriots of the war of liberation. The Association sponsors nearly four hundred groups in the schools of the Republic.[18]

The activities and philosophy of a typical Martian youth group have been described by Hilda Castro Vidal, its leader in a public school in Havana. She wrote that in the monthly meetings each member answered the roll by citing a thought by Martí. Then one of the group gave a brief talk on some aspect of the life of Martí. Once the doctrinal part had been concluded, practical activities were considered. Cases of financial distress were examined and the most urgent one then selected. A modest contribution was solicited from each member in the following fashion: each student introduced his fist holding a contribution into the money bag and then removed it, this time opened up, thus avoiding embarrassment to the member who was unable to contribute anything.

Quoting then from a saying by Martí, "Blessed be the hand which is lowered to the poor," Hilda Castro said that the group that

month had given clothes to a baby born in poverty. Quoting again from Martí, "There is nothing more beautiful than loving old people," she stated that their group had been knitting woolen scarves to present to elderly and indigent Cubans. She added that she could assure the parents of the children in her group that the group's program of activities would be realized because of the great faith of the girls in the importance of following the teachings of Martí.[19]

Among other campaigns of a civic nature engaged in by the Association was an attempt to have the capital city officially designated as "La Habana, Capital Martí." This idea originated with Alfonso de la Torre. Although publications of the Association bear this stamp, the suggestion has never been acted upon by the City Council of Havana.[20]

When the project for a new tomb for Martí was under way in Santiago de Cuba, the Association opposed it on the grounds that the modest one in which he was then buried was more in keeping with his wishes for simplicity. Once the monument was completed, however, the Association offered to call off its polemics against construction in view of the "love demonstrated in the realization of this work and the fervor of the townspeople of Santiago in its impressive inauguration, for this alone extenuates or pardons any errors in interpretation in Martian feeling or artistic conception." *Patria* added in its editorial that the Association felt, however, that the most worthy tomb for Martí would not be achieved by marble and bronze, but in "giving as a final rest for his sacred bones a fatherland as he conceived it and for which he struggled and died, for which each Cuban must work to translate his noble example and his wise doctrines into reality in accordance with our motto: 'Martianism is Action.' "[21]

The Association has assumed a kind of watchdog responsibility in alerting public opinion to acts which trespass upon true Martian grounds. In 1947 a column of the "Believe It or Not" type was established in *Patria* to call attention to "the constant errors which are published about the life and work of Martí, especially by persons and institutions that should be better informed." In the first article of this nature the Association lamented the fact that it had to point out the serious error made by another patriotic society dedicated to Martí, "La Orden de la Rosa Blanca" ("The Order of the White Rose").

In publishing its statutes the Order had made a mistake in quoting from the poem of Martí which had given its name to the Order by saying, "cardo ni ortiga cultivo" instead of "cardo ni oruga cultivo."[22] "Ortiga" in Spanish is a kind of nettle, and "oruga," although most commonly known as a caterpillar, is a term which is also applied to a certain weed in Spain.[23] The column of "Believe It or Not" concluded:

Only a lack of knowledge of these verses and of their true essence would have made such an error possible. It is incomprehensible that the Order should commit such an error, especially since it announces that it is endeavoring to spread the work of Martí throughout the whole world.[24]

Lest this be considered as an isolated incident, it is interesting to observe that the controversy over "ortiga vs. oruga" has been waged in other quarters. No less a person than the Communist leader Juan Marinello pronounced in favor of "ortiga." One writer refutes this position, asserting unequivocably that the word that Martí meant, wrote, and printed was "oruga."[25]

Another red flag arousing the antagonism of the Association was a proposal in 1951 by a group of Cubans to re-establish bullfights in Cuba. This sport had been abolished by the first North American administration in the Island. *Patria* vigorously condemned the proposal as completely anti-Martian inasmuch as Martí had referred to bullfighting as "a futile bloody spectacle . . . and against Cuban sentiment for being intimately linked with our colonial past." *Patria* was particularly indignant toward the bullfighting group for accusing its opponents of an "inferiority complex" in not wishing to revoke a disposition of the first North American occupation. Joining forces with the Bando de Piedad (a Cuban humane society) and the Sociedad de Estudios Históricos e Internacionales, the Association won the ear, not of the bull, but of enough public opinion to discourage the proposal.[26]

Almost everybody has his day in Cuba. There is a "Doctors' Day," a "Dentists' Day," and many others. In 1951 the Minister of the Interior, Tebelio Rodríguez del Haya, established a "Prisoners' Day" to honor all malefactors under lock and key. Had the Minister been content with merely decreeing the day there would probably have

been a minimum amount of protest, but he made the mistake of designating April 4 as a commemoration of the day on which Martí was taken prisoner. The Association, writers, and the two academies of history of Cuba immediately launched protests against this "profanation of the august memory" of Martí. The Association pointed out that Martí was a "POLITICAL PRISONER" and not a common criminal. Although the Association lamented the misfortune that brought persons to jail, and in the true Martian spirit could only hope for a civilized prison administration, on no account, it declared, should the name of Martí be associated with common prisoners. A change in Ministers brought a revocation of the designation of "Prisoners' Day."[27]

Another thorn in the side of the Association is a marble bust of Martí that reposes next to a discarded marble bathtub and other odd pieces of sculpture in front of a monument workshop in a busy street in Havana.[28] The bust represents an antiquated and insipid Martí. The Association carried on a running attack on it over a period of several years from 1945 to 1947. An editorial in the Association's bulletin stated:

The profuseness of busts of Martí that overwhelms us without the sanction of masters in the art of sculpture has caused amateurs in chiseling blocks of marble to present us with pseudo-Martian heads, worthy only of being pulverized as an auto-da-fé. . . . This is the head of a man who in no respect resembles our Martí; it is unfortunate and ill-proportioned in its desire to be called a "bust of Martí."

The editorial then urged all institutions of history and fine arts to be alert to insist upon the truth in every phase of representation of Martí, especially when he was being ridiculed.[29] Oblivious to the controversy, this bust still presided over the marble works in 1957.

Another target for the Association's campaign against un-Martian acts is the yearly parade of school children sponsored by the Ministry of Education. In 1948 Quesada y Miranda wrote:

Once more our children have been martyrized in the famous school parades January 28 in honor of Martí. . . . It is an absurd and hollow type of homage, which has been fought by physicians and conscientious educators. We consider these parades as anti-instructive, anti-hygienic, anti-democratic, and anti-Martian.

The writer then said that there was a rising wave of protest against these parades in which teachers and children suffered from the sun and became fatigued after waiting and marching for long hours, while "high authorities comfortably installed in the grandstand chatted and laughed."[30] The celebration of the parade of school children nevertheless has continued. An article in a Havana newspaper in 1956 described the parade of 10,000 school children before the statue of Martí, the President of the Republic, Fulgencio Batista, and other high officials of the government as a "very emotional tribute to Martí."[31] Other cities on the island also continued to honor Martí with similar parades.[32] The Association feels, however, that it has won a victory in that the parades are now shorter, more solemn, and unpolitical in nature.[33]

The Association is dependent upon dues contributed by a small number of former students and a subsidy of less than $100 a month paid by the government through the Instituto Nacional de Cultura to maintain the Fragua as a national monument. A tiny group of four benefactors, only one of whom is a Cuban, also aids the Association. Through its former students, most of whom are teachers in the schools of the Republic, and the Martian children's groups, the Association, under the direction of Gonzalo de Quesada y Miranda, wields an influence on behalf of Martí that is out of proportion to its small yearly income.

THE ORDER OF THE WHITE ROSE

Another patriotic group that has as its central objective the spreading of the Martí doctrine is "La Orden de la Rosa Blanca" ("The Order of the White Rose"). The Order was begun in 1946 by Carlos Martínez-Fortún y Foyo to "create Martiana and honest citizens." An article in the Order's monthly publication *La Rosa Blanca* (no longer published) elaborated on its purpose.

The Order of the White Rose proposes to realize the Apostle's ideal by preaching love for mankind, concord, and good will among brothers, trying to wipe out from Cuban land the evil seed of hatred and fratricidal division that may carry us to serious and irreparable wrongs.[34]

The Order set up five branch groups in other parts of the Republic and embarked upon a program of honoring Martí through the yearly

donation of bassinets, and the establishment of about a dozen children's groups in schools in the Republic. In 1950 the Order began a weekly half-hour radio program devoted to readings from Martí's poems, articles, and stories. It lasted until 1956. In many respects the activities of the Order resemble those of the Association, although on a much reduced scale. The Order's answer to the Association's terming Havana as "Capital Martí" was to call Cuba "Archipiélago Martí."[35]

The Order of the White Rose had a three-phase program. The first was to popularize the Martí doctrine; the second, to encourage interpretations of that doctrine; and the third, to promote "Martian action."[36] Martínez-Fortún is a scholar who gives an organic interpretation to the organization, likening these three functions to the brain, the heart, and the arm. He noted that the Order of the White Rose resembled the far-reaching roots of the rose plant in the Order's announced desire to make the group a universal body. He declared that one of the activities of the organization that corresponded to the third, or action phase, of the Order was the enshrinement in 1953 in a large glass housing of the spot in the Lyceum at Guanabacoa where Martí delivered a famous speech in 1879.

Martínez-Fortún asserted that in order to receive Martí one's "receptive antenna" had to be acute, otherwise the Apostle would remain on the surface. The activities of the Order, he declared, had practically been suspended in the past few years because of an unfavorable political atmosphere.

Martí as a Symbol in Fraternal Organizations

MASONS

The *Havana Post* reported July 1, 1956, that members of the Mystic Order of the Veiled Prophet of the Enchanted Realm from all over the United States paid tribute to José Martí at a brief ceremony at Martí's statue in Central Park. The Americans were in Havana on a holiday from their national convention in New Orleans.[37] In paying homage to Martí they indicated the general high respect that Masons accord Martí in Cuba. Martí, in fact, is the chosen hero of the Cuban branch of Masonry, which consists of over thirty thousand

members. The Apostle's statue, a massive piece of sculpture in white marble by Mario Santí, dominates the entrance to the Masons' new eleven-story building on Carlos III Avenue in Havana.

Documentary evidence of the esteem of the Masons for Martí is to be found in numerous articles on him in their magazine *Mundo Masónico*. For example, the January-March, 1953, issue is dedicated to Martí. On the cover is a composite picture showing the familiar Jamaica photograph of Martí, and superimposed upon it are a Mason's apron and sash, with all the symbols of office around the Apostle. Underneath is the inscription:

To honor and exalt him is the unavoidable duty
of every citizen of America, and very especially
of those of us who belong to the universal
Masonry that he honored and made famous.[38]

Sometimes doubt is cast that Martí was a Mason, since there is no written evidence that he ever belonged to a regular lodge. The Roman Catholic writer Juan Luis Martín, for instance, has made this allegation.[39] The answers given by Masons vary, but an article by Ricardo F. Rubio gives the essentials of the Masonic argument. This writer asserts that the lack of evidence is explained by the fact that in 1871 it was very dangerous in Spain to belong to Masonry, and therefore there is no record that Martí was registered in a regular lodge. Rubio refutes the charge that Martí was not a Mason, that he only used the meetings of Masons to carry on a conspiracy against Spain. Rubio said that in the first place no one could attend a meeting of Masons unless he was a certified member, and second that it was "completely forbidden to speak about politics or religion at a meeting." Therefore anybody who thinks that Martí did this, Rubio insists, is very badly mistaken.

Rubio declares that Martí joined the "Harmony Lodge" in Spain in the first part of 1871, where he became a Master and Orator of the Lodge. Rubio then shows how Martí spoke so harshly against Spanish rule in Cuba that the presiding officer had to pound the gavel to cause the Apostle to be more discreet. Although this is an interesting, if imaginative, picture, it invalidates Rubio's argument that Martí did not use Masonry as a source for political oratory.

Rubio further asserts that Martí reached Grade Eighteen (Sover-

eign Prince of the Red Cross), and that he eventually turned over his regalia to Fermín Valdés Domínguez, who later presented it to a local lodge in Havana.[40] The regalia is now enshrined in the museum of the Grand Lodge.

The presence of Martí's philosophy is to be seen clearly in all of the points listed in a Masons' creed published in *Mundo Masónico*. It reads:

1. To be a Mason is to love Light, Virtue, Wisdom, Justice, and Humanity.
2. To be a Mason is to love family harmony, concord among peoples, and peace for the human race.
3. To be a Mason is to forget the offenses that are committed against us, to be good to our adversaries and enemies, not to hate anybody, to practice virtue constantly, and to return good for evil.
4. To be a Mason is to preach tolerance, exercise charity, without considerations of race, belief, or opinions, to struggle against hypocrisy and fanaticisms.
5. To be a Mason is to be a friend of the poor and of the unfortunate, of those who suffer and of those who weep, of those who are hungry and thirst for justice, of those who propose as the only norm of conduct the well-being of all, their growth, and progress.
6. To be a Mason is to spread everywhere the divine lights of our Institution, to educate for the improvement of the Intelligence; to think about the most beautiful ideals of Law, of Morality, of Love, and to practice them.[41]

This creed appeared at the time of the Martí Centenary.

One of the ways in which the Masons pay tribute to Martí is through the construction and inauguration of Martian Corners. These are in the nature of little shrines set up in public parks, and are patterned after the one in the park beside the Fragua. They usually consist of a bust of Martí on a pedestal displaying an aphorism of the Apostle. Two such Corners were inaugurated on Martí's birthday in 1956 in Matanzas,[42] and Cumanayagua, Santa Clara province.[43]

An interview with Enrique Viciana Pérez, national president (1950-51) of the "Asociación de Jóvenes Esperanzas de la Fraternidad" ("Association of Youthful Hopes for Fraternity"), an organization corresponding to the De Molay branch of Masonry in the United States, revealed that Viciana had his own Martian Corner in his home. The Corner consisted of a bust of Martí, a picture of

Martí in Jamaica, and the Cuban flag. In his office he also had a picture of Martí and a bookcase with his works. In addition he had bought over a dozen books on Martí and numerous pamphlets. Several other Masons, he declared, have their own Corners, which they brighten with Martiana. In general, however, Viciana admitted, "The Cuban prefers to display a picture showing some invention of man rather than the portrait of the man who gave them their independence."

The reason for the numerous busts of Martí set up in Martian Corners, in Viciana's opinion, is that the Latin American responds most readily to impressions, in this respect differing from the Anglo-Saxon. For this reason the Cuban needs a representation of Martí constantly in front of him to remind him of the presence of the National Hero. Viciana declared that Martí was presented to Masonry through lectures, public acts of a patriotic nature, through articles in *Mundo Masónico,* and the Martian Corners. In general, however, Viciana said that it was difficult to carry out the ideas of Martí because of the difference in cultural levels among the Masons.[44]

One member of Masonry who is not ready to accept Martí as a full-fledged Mason is Jesús Fernández Lamas, a former Deputy Grand Master in Cuba. Fernández declared that Martí could not have been a good Mason simply because he did not have time. In the absence of documentation this Cuban was unwilling to say that Martí was a member of any lodge. Fernández believes that the Martian Corners are not a suitable way to approach Martí, since there is too much adoration of the Apostle, and not enough emulation. He believes, however, that within the next twenty to thirty years in Cuba there will be a completely developed school of Martian philosophy based on humanitarianism and love. Fernández declared that the role of Cuban Masonry in preparing the way for this school would be through constant efforts on behalf of the rights of man and the freedom of the people.[45] Fernández asserted that one of the major factors making Martí attractive to Masons was the Apostle's anticlericalism.[46]

One of the projects of the Masons in expression of their admiration for Martí was the establishment of the National Masonic University "José Martí" in 1951. Its purpose was to provide higher educa-

tional facilities that would have no religious or political background, thus serving an objective not achieved on the one hand by the Roman Catholic University of Villanueva, and on the other by the University of Havana. The founding president of the Mason's university was José T. Oñate, an engineer who in 1930 published his work following the route of Martí from Playitas to Dos Ríos. In 1954 the Masons for economic and political reasons severed connections with the university, which then dropped reference to its founders from its title. The university has maintained its original orientation, however, in avoiding political manifestations by its students and any religious connections. The university grew rapidly, expanding into homes converted into classrooms located throughout the city of Havana. A branch has been established in Cienfuegos, Las Villas province. In 1957 a total of 2,000 students registered in both cities. Since tuition is low, the university administration feels that it is fulfilling a distinct Martian social function in bringing education to persons who might not otherwise be able to have it. Anniversaries of Martí's birth are duly celebrated.[47]

Martí and the Rotary and Lions Clubs

Other organizations in Cuba identify themselves with and pay homage to José Martí. Among them are the Rotarians and Lions. The Rotarians take pride in the origin in one of their units in Cienfuegos of the custom of donating a bassinet in honor of Martí's birthday. In addition, the Rotary Club of Havana played an important part in promoting the building of the Fragua Martiana, already mentioned in this chapter.

Luis Angulo Pintado, once secretary of the Rotary International in Havana, made some points of identification of the Rotarians with José Martí. Angulo said that unquestionably he had to admit that Martí had inspired many Rotary doctrines. Quoting from Martí on the satisfaction that comes in old age from having lived a meaningful and productive life, he said that one of the purposes in founding Rotary clubs was to stimulate those who worked to find meaning in their lives through gaining friends, helping those in suffering, watching over the sacred nation of Cuba, and maintaining an ethical relationship in all actions of life. Then quoting from a work by Martí full

of admiration for Christ, Angulo said that it exactly characterized the ideals that the Rotarians stood for, and what good Rotarians practiced—friendship and love for mankind.[48]

The Lions clubs in Cuba also feel their share of admiration for Martí. The Apostle has been honored in ceremonies in club meetings held throughout the island. Carlos Iñiguez declared, "If Martí had lived in these times he would have been a Lion."[49]

Martí as a Symbol in Other Groups

Naturally many other organizations in Cuba honor José Martí in one way or another. For instance, the National College of Lawyers of Cuba established a $500 prize for the best essay on Martí by one of its members in 1953, plus a $250 prize for a law student in any of the universities of Havana writing on the same subject.[50]

Martí is honored in the world of sports. In 1948 a work on this subject was published in Mexico.[51] In Havana in 1956 the Cerro Hunting Club published a full-page advertisement in the *Diario de la Marina* announcing a new contest for the "Grand Prize José Martí Cup."[52] The club neglected to include Martí's reflection on this subject, "Hunting is wrong, unless it be to hunt foxes and wolves."[53] For the followers of the "sport of kings" in 1957 a local racing group announced the "Handicap José Martí."[54]

Martí and the Roman Catholic Church in Cuba

The anti-Roman Catholic writings of Martí are sometimes a cause for embarrassment to the Church in Cuba, but a source of profound satisfaction to Masons, Communists, and anyone else who happens to be anticlerical. An incident that illustrates the conflict between the Church and those opposed to it occurred in 1940. Early in the year a meeting of Catholics in the Hotel Nacional in Havana roundly condemned Communist activities in Havana. The Communists replied by citing Martí's anti-Roman Catholic article on Father Edward McGlynn in the United States.[55] Communist sniping accelerated during the year, finally causing the Church to reply through an anonymous article in one of its local journals. The author

was later revealed as Father Ignacio Biaín, a Spanish Franciscan monk stationed in Havana. He titled his article, "Martí, unjust and passionate." In it Father Biaín said that in reading the Communist attack on the Church the quotations used did not really sound at all as if it were Martí speaking, but more like some fanatic. He stated that anti-Church insinuations and internal contradictions with respect to religion were to be found in Martí's writings, but such a direct and thundering broadside against the official Church surprised him.

The Franciscan maintained that the Communists by their action had not "de-Catholicized" Martí, since the Patriot's religious definitions had never really been very clear. He admitted that Martí at times was frankly heterodoxical, but this was because he was a product of the times, a victim of laic liberalism. This was regrettable, he said, because Martí had a streak of saintliness in him that could have made him a great churchman. In Father Biaín's opinion Martí's anticlericalism did not add any new feature to criticism of the Church, since others before him had "shouted the same things." All that Martí contributed was ardor, "the vehemence of one who was convinced, and the nobility of one who was mistaken."

Referring to the McGlynn episode, the Franciscan said that he could sympathize with Martí's concern over a possible miscarriage of justice, but that "Martí's truth" was not necessarily historical truth. After all, he said, Martí listened only to Father McGlynn, not the archbishop. Besides, Father Biaín added, whatever reasons Father McGlynn had for acting as he did, his performance was to be censured by a Church that "has as substantive norms discipline and obedience." He concluded:

We have nothing against Martí the patriot; we admire his spiritual context and his heroism; we accept his dedication and high calling; but as far as Catholic matters are concerned, he is neither "Maestro" nor "Apostle"![56]

Father Biaín thought that he was replying to the Communists, but his article brought down on his head the wrath of Martians and anticlericals in general. The Communist issue paled beside the onslaught of the outraged opposition. Emilio Roig de Leuchsenring, biographer of Martí, led the offense. Pointing to numerous anti-Roman Catholic writings of Martí, the historian denied the validity

of Father Biaín's assertion that Martí's treatment of this subject was "in dispersed and forgotten pages." Roig insisted as a second point that it was false that Martí was accustomed to avoid Church subjects, as Father Biaín had written. In the third place, the historian declared, it simply was not true that Martí's anticlericalism was no more than a reflection of the atmosphere of the nineteenth century. Martí's direct experiences in Mexico, Guatemala, and Venezuela were proof of that. Roig also objected to the insulting tone of the article, which had referred to Martí's writings as "spittings, audacious, and ignorant—a repugnant diatribe without any historical basis!" Finally the historian protested against what he called the Franciscan's attempt to establish Roman Catholicism as the civic duty of every Cuban.[57]

Father Biaín was defended in the *Diario de la Marina* by Emilio Ballagas, who wrote that he was a fervent admirer of the friar. Although admitting that Father Biaín's reference to Martí's anticlerical writings as "red ochre and turpentine" was unfortunate, he asserted that the friar's praise of Martí's supreme idealism should have removed some of the bitterness being shown by the critics.[58]

The members of the Cuban Society of Historical and International Studies were in no mood to let any insult to Martí go unpunished. Meeting in solemn session this group of learned historians and writers proceeded to "excommunicate" Father Biaín for his heresy. Only one member voted against the proposal. Rafael Esténger, a biographer of Martí, discussing the excommunication of the Franciscan said that although the society of historians had taken Father Biaín's article seriously, it should forget the outburst because the friar "could not blemish or shake the glory of our Apostle, just as the blasphemies of knaves did not diminish the loftiness of Christ." Nor did Esténger consider that Father Biaín's article was "inadmissible to Cuban dignity." In his opinion the controversy was just not that important.[59]

Father Biaín, some sixteen years after the incident, declared that he had not changed his opinion of Martí. He maintained that as long as persons used Martí to criticize the Church he would reply in kind. The article, according to Father Biaín, was written upon the request of Cardinal Manuel Arteaga y Betancourt of Cuba to answer Communists who were using Martí to attack the clergy. The Franciscan

believed that if Martí had lived another fifty years he would have become "completely Catholic." According to Father Biaín, Martí was
a guiding spiritual force, with morals much superior to those of the
present time in Cuba. Although he himself felt very closely identified
with Martí, in his opinion most of the Spanish clergy in Cuba did not
feel the influence of Martí.[60]

Another point of view toward Martí was expressed in an article by
Francisco R. Ferrán y Rivero in the *Diario de la Marina* in 1945.
In many respects it echoed the Biaín article, saying that the "demo-
liberalism" of the nineteenth century was dead, and that it would be
anti-Martian to insist on an individualistic conception of democracy
just to follow Martí. Ferrán asserted that it also would be anti-Martian to use Martí's writings against the Church. He declared:

Those who slyly use sentences from Martí to defame our religious creed,
take from the Apostle that which is accidental and subject to revision,
thus slandering the essence of Martí.[61]

In defense of the Church, then, Ferrán would like to feel that if Martí
were writing today he would revise many of the statements that he
made against the Church. The author, however, seemed oblivious to
the dangers of this kind of speculation.

Ferrán wrote that if Cuba as a nation were going to progress it
would have to follow Martí; that there was no better way of giving
Cubans a feeling of belonging to the world at large than for them to
identify themselves with Martí, who admitted no boundaries to the
spirit. He wrote:

Only when great saints and great citizens meet in the same person is
national morality produced for the masses of its people. . . . We can still
not count on having any saints. But Martí possesses much of that which
is Catholic.[62]

The author said that Cuba, if it were going to progress as a nation,
would have to follow Martí's political vision, which had nothing anti-
Spanish about it. In fact, Ferrán declared that Spanish attitudes lay
very deep in Martí's thinking, in the sense that Ramiro de Maeztu
would give to these characteristics. Maeztu was a Spanish writer
whose works have been very popular among the most conservative
elements in Spain. His writings have been used to promote the

"Hispanidad" movement in Latin America of closer identification with Spain. Sympathizers of Francisco Franco, the Spanish dictator, used Maeztu's writings in Latin America during the late 1930's and early 1940's to promote a feeling of solidarity among admirers of strong men. Although Martí exalted great men, it is a mistake to identify him with "Hispanidad" in Maeztu's use of the term.

Ferrán added that because some Catholics had not learned to feel the influence of Martí's idea of the Republic, the nation at times had shunned them, believing itself only theoretically loved. He wrote that the Catholics had "a delicate task of reconciling, of harmonizing the Cuban nation with our doctrine, which does not recognize any frontiers for love and well-being, and which is to be the work of Cuban Catholic writers doing a useful work in their lives." Ferrán ended by saying that by following Martí Catholicism would be able to save Cuba for God, for America, and for itself.[63]

During official ceremonies in 1952 commemorating the fiftieth anniversary of the Republic, Monsignor José Burzio in a speech before Martí's statue in Central Park in Havana declared:

I do not believe that we have chosen a more adequate or eloquent way of expressing our adhesion to the young Republic of Cuba in these patriotic celebrations than to render tribute to the memory of the man who synthesizes all the ideals of the Cuban soul: José Martí. The people that has chosen as a model and a guide a maestro of the stature of José Martí will not stray away from the road of honor and glory.[64]

The following year various Roman Catholic lay organizations such as the Casa Cultural de Católicas (a cultural organization for women), Cuban Catholic Action, the Knights of Columbus, and others all joined in paying their respects to Martí. The Communists kept up their hit-and-run attacks on the Church, and were answered in full. Juan Luis Martín wrote in a local Roman Catholic journal denouncing Communist "attempts to make Martí practically a disciple of Marx." Martín said about Communistic tactics:

These do not constitute more than propaganda maneuvers, an insult to Martí, monstrous boldness of mental insufficiency, of ideological infantilism, if not an expression of bad faith.[65]

Each year on Martí's anniversary the Cathedral of Havana opens

its doors to honor the man who once wrote that Christianity had "died under the hands of Roman Catholicism." Sponsored by the Movement of Catholic Professionals and Intellectuals, the ceremony is attended by most of the high dignitaries of the Roman Catholic Church in Cuba, and representatives of the most important Church lay groups. For several years José Manuel Pérez Cabrera, a distinguished Cuban historian, has given the appreciation of Martí.[66] In essence his point of view, which he says is apparently shared by the Church since they have not corrected him, is that Martí, although not a church-going Roman Catholic, was deeply religious in his manner. Pérez Cabrera said that Martí was married in the Church and had his son baptized in the Church. He insisted that Martí's attacks on the clergy were secondary to the patriot's deeply religious faith, which was essentially Catholic.[67]

Martí is freely used on posters as a symbol to attract support for the Cuban equivalent of Father Edward J. Flanagan's Boys' Town, Nebraska. Largely the work of Father Ismael Testé, the Cuban center is called "Ciudad de los Niños" ("Boys' Town"), and is located outside of Havana. Its purpose is to take care of Cuban orphans. The use of Martí as a symbol is a legitimate expression for a worthy cause.

Elsewhere, however, occasional chippings away at the stature of Martí do take place among Roman Catholic writers. For instance, an Augustinian cleric, in writing praises of that order's University of Villanueva in Havana, wrote of the promising future of "this fair Isle of Maceo."[68] Although Maceo is given a share of the credit in the liberation of Cuba, the friar avoided the more obvious reference to Martí, since Cuba is very seldom referred to simply as the "land of Maceo."

Another method used by writers friendly to the Roman Catholic Church to undermine Martí's attack is to cast doubt on the authenticity of the Apostle's "Hombre del campo." Although the Cuban Academy of History has certified to the authenticity of the document, a recent attempt was made by José María Chacón y Calvo, president of the Ateneo, one of Cuba's most important literary societies, to question the document's origin.[69] Chacón's attitude leaves no doubt that although homages may be paid in the Cathedral of Havana, sectors of Roman Catholic opinion are still irked by Martí's anticlericalism.

The Cuban Church's role in reducing somewhat the saintliness of the Apostle will be discussed in the next chapter.

Martí in the Cuban Hebrew Community

The Hebrew community showed its respect for José Martí by honoring him during his Centenary. A score of articles and brief works were published, such as the one by Abraham M. Matterín on Martí and racial discrimination.[70] Other interpretations of Martí appeared in the "Voices of the Nation" column of *El Mundo*. A roving reporter asked the question: "What meaning does José Martí have for the Hebrews?" Felix Reyler, president of the Agrupación Cultural Hebreo-Cubana, answered that many Jews had contributed materially and spiritually to the Cuban independence movement. He cited the North American lawyer Horacio S. Rubens, a close friend of Martí, as an example. Matterín, also questioned, replied that Martí, imbued from childhood with readings from the Bible, reflected the Old Testament patriarchs in their zeal for justice and social progress.[71] As his contribution to the Centenary, Abraham Z. Vainstein translated a selection of Martí's works into Yiddish,[72] and a "José Martí Forest" was promoted in Israel in 1953 under the impulse of Matterín and Boris Shames, the head of a Zionist society in Cuba.[73]

Matterín stated that the funds to establish the forest came from the proceeds of a special contest held in 1953 by the Hebrew community in Cuba. The Martí Forest has been planted between the José de San Martín and Simón Bolívar forests near Jerusalem.[74]

A Hebrew organization that has used Martí as a symbol of international admiration and unity is the B'nai B'rith Maimonides in Havana. Its director, Marco Pitchon, declared that this group's homage to Martí in 1953 had resulted in a lengthy collection of foreign tributes to Martí by heads of state, university presidents, and leaders of political and social groups, mostly statements made outside of Cuba. The collection is being published in book form.[75]

In general it may be seen that Hebrew writers prefer to emphasize Martí's writings against racial discrimination, his thoughts on universal brotherhood, and citation of Jewish friends of the Apostle.

Postscript to Martí and Social Institutions in Cuba

Martí once wrote, "The love of union for mutual help belongs to strong peoples."[76] For a nation composed of persons noted for their individuality, Cuba has shown that it also has a people devoted to participation in societies. The usefulness of Martí as a symbol among these groups varies from what is considered a minimum requirement in paying homage, such as the laying of a wreath on the Apostle's statue once a year, to the full-fledged activities of an organization like the Association of Former Students of the Martí Seminar, whose activities are mainly directed toward "Martianism in Action." Other social and patriotic groups might have been considered in this chapter, but space did not permit their inclusion.

Chapter 6

THE APOTHEOSIS OF JOSÉ MARTÍ

*T*HE REVERENCE displayed by José Martí's early followers, the large volume of literary production and reprinting of his
works, his representation in monuments, busts, coins, and stamps, the
special societies dedicated to him, and fraternal organizations have
all contributed to the apotheosis of the Apostle. He has been promoted
beyond the rank of a "mere" national hero. He has achieved a stature
greater than that of Antonio Maceo, Manuel de Céspedes, and
Ignacio Agramonte, and the other heroes of Cuban independence.
One of the manifestations of hero worship that makes Martí unique
among Cuban heroes, and among many other heroes besides, is the
expression of esteem for him in word descriptions. The degree of religious symbolism in the cult of Martí is to be found in the "Martian
Suppers."

Attempts that have been made to represent Martí on film indicate the extent to which he, as a legendary figure, is the center of
controversy. The promotion of Martí has led to statements that he is
not only the ideal Cuban, but also the "universal man." A few individuals have dared to protest against the exaltation of Martí, particularly a few in the Roman Catholic Church, but as it will be seen,
even the Church embraces the man who often bitterly condemned it.

Language of the Martian Apotheosis

The words used to describe Martí are words that are seldom used
to describe other figures in Cuban history. On the contrary, they are

132

terms usually reserved for saints. Some that are typically and frequently associated with the name of Martí are: Apostle, Martyr, and Maestro. The first to call Martí "Apostle" was Gonzalo de Quesada y Aróstegui in a speech in New York in 1889,[1] later writing of Martí, "like Christ, he was the victim of mockery, he suffered injuries and ingratitude from the very ones whom he proposed to save."[2] One of the major biographies, as already noted, is *Martí, Apostle of Freedom,* by Jorge Mañach. Another "saintly" work is *José Martí, el santo de América,* by Luis Rodríguez Embil.[3]

Martí has been called "Captain of Archangels,"[4] "My Saint Joseph,"[5] "Redeemer,"[6] "The second son of God,"[7] "The Evangel of Tenderness,"[8] "The American Christ,"[9] "Jesus-Martí,"[10] and "Martí, the Savior."[11] His life and works have been referred to as "A Liturgy of the Martian Nativity,"[12] "The Martian Vigil,"[13] "The Martian Pilgrimage,"[14] "The Consecration at Dos Ríos,"[15] "Martian Litany,"[16] "Resurrection,"[17] "My Martian Breviary,"[18] and "I Read in the Bible of Martí."[19] Other terms of the Christian religion are to be found in use when writers refer to Martí: "agony," "oblation," "passion and death," and *"via crucis."* One author wrote of Martí's excursion from Playitas to Dos Ríos as his "Calvary."[20] The subject of Martí's death as a martyr has attracted over three hundred articles alone. One writer refers to Martí as the "divine antenna."[21] Luisa, the daughter of Manuel Mercado, Martí's friend, declared in retrospect that if a soul as beautiful as that of Martí existed there must be a God.[22] Néstor Carbonell was so carried away that he wrote, "As an orator José Martí was so unique that one would have thought that he was a supernatural being, since his words were worthy of a God."[23]

Various words have been derived from Martí's name, and are in frequent use among admirers of the Apostle. The most common one is the adjective, "martiano," referring to a person, act, or work that may be characterized as reflecting the ideals of Martí. The eighteenth edition of the Spanish dictionary of the Academy of the Spanish Language in Madrid has added the adjective "martiniano" as applying to Martí.[24] This has disappointed those followers of the Apostle who wanted the shorter adjectival form to be given the honor of appearing officially.[25] From a Guatemalan, Orozco Posadas, comes the noun "Martista," applied to a person who acts politically in benefit of

the community.[26] This word has not become popular in Cuba, however. Other words are "Martiolatría" (the worship of Martí), the adjective "martiense," and the noun "Martianismo."[27]

An example of the way in which a familiar phrase of Martí's has become a synonym is the substitution of a "Rosa Blanca" for a compliment.[28]

Besides the geographical terms "La Habana, Capital Martí," and "Archipiélago Martí," already mentioned, the word "Martilandia," has been used to refer to "El Abra," the estate on the Isle of Pines where Martí spent a period of semiconfinement.[29]

Representative Samples of Apotheosis

From the very extensive number of references to Martí in connection with religious symbolism and direct references to his divinity the following samples have been chosen as representative.

Wrote Rafael Mohedano:

On Christ's nativity the star that shone in the infinite night of Bethlehem announced to the world the coming of one who, with the bitterness and tribulations of Humanity, was to create the marvelous rosary of human redemptions. On Martí's nativity the powerful brain was born that later was to conceive the Manifiesto de Montecristi, and with the bitterness and grief of his enslaved nation, was to create the gospel of Cuban redemption.[30]

Declared Alberto de J. Calvo:

Perhaps with the single exception of that well-loved prince . . . Buddha, the greatest one to give us the example of his life was, in truth, extremely humble Martí, whose humility, like that of Christ's, came to him from the depth of his soul.[31]

Juan E. Bory, who knew Martí in Montecristi, said:

You were a saint of civilian holiness! You did not look for that genteel sacrifice that is visible and material, you went in search of that Christian sacrifice that is spiritual, profound, and ineffable. Really yours was a sacrifice of saintly legend. . . . [W]hen your heart was pierced with thorns, you did not hate those who wounded you because the white dove and the sacred host of your holiness was in your soul. . . . To understand your work, oh Great Maestro, is to love it and to love you![32]

A frequent vehicle for the apotheosis of Martí is in the over eight hundred poems written to and about him. An example of the exaltation of Martí in this medium is the stanza composed by Francisco Sixto Piedra, cited in a ceremony before Martí's remains in 1951:

> *Sublime Christ of the fatherland,*
> *Whose Jews were the Spanish soldiers,*
> *You also had your cross, your false apostle,*
> *And your terrible Golgotha: Dos Ríos!*[33]

Pánfilo D. Camacho, a Cuban biographer, wrote:

I am in favor of the thesis that we should speak and write about Martí every day. I believe that every Cuban is obliged to know him and to imitate him, and at least to follow his maxims of love toward others. . . . His indifference toward earthly possessions places him very near the sublime son of Galilee.

Señor Camacho then said that a new religion should be established not only for Cuba but for the whole world—the Martian religion.[34]

The end of comparisons of the life of José Martí with that of Christ is not in sight. In 1956 Alberto Entralgo Cancio published his work relating the experience of José Martí to the trial of Jesus.[35]

The Martian Suppers

A yearly ceremony celebrated in many towns and cities of Cuba that has taken on overtones of a religious rite is what is called "La Cena Martiana" ("The Martian Supper"). The event is also referred to as the "Martian Nativity," and "Christmas Eve." It is held once a year on the night before Martí's birthday. The custom originated in Manzanillo, Oriente province, in 1926, under the impetus and direction of Juan Francisco Sariol, the editor of the magazine *Orto*.[36] The original intent of the Supper was to have a banquet followed by speeches in honor of the Apostle. The custom was taken over by numerous groups of Masons and Lions, who thus faithfully paid sober homage to Martí.

The religious nature of the Martian Supper is to be found in an address at one of them by Rafael G. Argilagos, an early Martian anthologist. He said:

The Nativity of José Martí is an extraordinary event of honest jubilation and of constructive effort. It evokes, through its immortal symbolism, the sublime Biblical act of Jesus and his Apostles, although complete identification here is altered by the number of table companions and by the evident absence of the traitor Judas. . . . Here, also, the bread is his flesh; here, also, the wine is his blood; here, also, his creative thought is his life. Let us eat his flesh to make ourselves stronger; let us drink his blood to make ourselves worthier; and let us receive the sacrament of his creative thought to make ourselves better.[37]

At times, however, the ceremonies took on characteristics of conviviality that had dedicated Martians protesting with indignation. Abuse of the Suppers in 1946 brought concentrated fire from those who were outraged not by the religious tone of the event, but by the lack of it. One observer of a Martian Supper attended by the President of the Republic wrote:

[Among] a numerous group of cultured men (one supposes that they were cultured since they were officials of a department of public security) after dining gluttonously, and believe me, eating voraciously is the opposite of what the poor Cuban public does, some gentlemen spoke of the life of Martí, of his work, there were jokes and applause, but the worst of all this was . . . the presentation of Garrido y Piñero [a comedy team].

This critic said that the vaudeville act had the same effect as opening the Supper with the national anthem, and then closing it with a conga. All the while that this was happening the writer maintained that in another part of the city in a dilapidated school building children were collecting their pennies, which they later gave to a tubercular woman who lived in poverty near the school. He noted that after realizing this gesture the children cried out, "Our duty is fulfilled!" As a concluding reproach to the Martian Supper group, the author added a postscript that the woman suffering from tuberculosis had died.[38]

Another Cuban writer wrote that the Suppers were commendable in principle, but that it was lamentable when the observation of Martí's anniversary ended in scandalous bacchanalia.[39]

Finally the Sociedad de Estudios Históricos e Internacionales registered a severe protest in 1946 by declaring:

This grievous perversion is not to be wondered at . . . since we see how

the Christian Christmas Eve itself, instituted in the memory of the birth of Christ, and in imitation of which they initiated the "Martian Suppers," has been converted with the passage of time into the occasion for such unlimited profane pleasures that they create a scandal, provoking disapproval by those who are deeply religious.

The Society declared that to remedy the situation banqueting should be eliminated from the ceremony, and that participants should render homage to Martí with simple acts such as the reading of his works.[40]

The Society was joined in its protest by veterans' organizations, and representatives from the National Archives, the National Academy of Arts and Letters, the National Museum, the Masons, the National Library, the National School of Journalism, the Order of the White Rose, and other worthy organizations.[41] Suppers held by decorous groups in Artemisa, Piñar del Rio, and Manzanillo, however, were not criticized by the aforementioned organizations.

Under this barrage of criticism the Martian Supper revelers were subdued, although the ceremonies, with supper, are still held in many parts of the island.[42]

Martí in Motion Pictures

An example of the extremes to which Cuban nationalism is committed in its idealization of Martí is to be seen in two attempts, one major and the other minor, made to represent Martí on the screen. One of the tasks of the commission organized to celebrate the Centenary in 1953 was to choose a company to make a picture on the Apostle's life. In consideration of limited film production facilities in Cuba, the commission chose a Mexican company. The main actor was a Mexican, and the writer of the script was Mauricio Magdaleno, a Mexican author and biographer of Martí. The Cuban technical representatives were Francisco Ichaso, Félix Lizaso, José M. Pérez Cabrera, and Emeterio S. Santovenia. The producing company planned to film half the picture in Cuba and half in Mexico. The critics were all Cubans. Their complaint was that the picture should be filmed completely in Cuba, and that only Cuban actors should be used. They did not like the fact that "Martí" would be speaking with a Mexican accent, or that he would look like an "Aztec." The polemic

sustained over a period of months in 1953 about the film, called "La Rosa Blanca," was almost more dramatic than the picture itself.

One of the leading critics was Gonzalo de Quesada y Miranda, who felt that his advice should have been sought in the production of the picture. The leading defender of "La Rosa Blanca" was Francisco Ichaso, political writer and drama critic. Quesada charged that there was too much "mystery" involved in financial arrangements made for the picture, in addition to the criticisms noted above. Ichaso replied that there was a "conspiracy" to prevent the filming of the picture, and he accused the opposition of "gratuitous assertions, sophisms, falsification of the facts, and malicious insinuations."[43]

To add to the general furor the Cuban Association of Artists and the Union of Artists and Cinematographical Technicians of Cuba refused to have anything to do with the picture unless it was completely filmed in Cuba, had a Cuban as an adult Martí, and distributed part of the earnings from the film to charitable institutions that carried the name of "José Martí." One supporter of the film in noting that forty-four of the main actors in the picture were Cubans and that 60 per cent of the action was being filmed in Cuba said that their demand was a "chauvinistic explosion."[44] Ichaso also referred to the union action as "rabid chauvinism." He asked, "Since when is it the function of unions to dictate who is to appear in a picture and how they are to act?"[45]

With respect to the other criticisms of the film, Ichaso said that he hoped that the accusation that Martí would be an "Aztec" was nothing more than the kind of joke that appealed so much to the Cubans. In answer to those who thought that Martí would speak with a Mexican accent he cited a report by a woman who had known Martí that the Apostle spoke slowly, articulating with care, and that he pronounced his final "s's" in the Mexican style. Ichaso found that the criticism that the José Martí of the film was taller than the real Martí was of little consequence, since a good spiritual representation was much more important.[46] At any rate the film was produced by the commission as planned.

Aside from minor technical mistakes, the picture actually was not a bad representation of the life of Martí. The producers perhaps gave

undue emphasis to the romantic side of Martí's life, but this phase has also been emphasized by those most critical of the film.[47] The photography was excellent. "La Rosa Blanca" is generally shown once a year on Martí's birthday anniversary through the medium of television and one of the low-admission theaters of Havana. In 1956 the film was very poorly attended at this particular theater and subject to ribald comments and laughter from the gallery.

In the controversy over "La Rosa Blanca" the protagonists were Cubans versus Cubans, with a strong mixture of chauvinism added for good measure. In 1956 Warner Brothers produced a film titled "Santiago," a story about the Spanish-American War (the term used in Cuba is the Hispanic-Cuban-American War). Hollywood chose to represent Martí as living in 1898 (actually three years after his death) in an elaborate residence in Haiti, where he was interviewed by American adventurers taking part in the fight to free Cuba. The producer's presentation of Martí in luxurious surroundings was somewhat farfetched. The reaction of the Cuban reviewers was immediate and angry. Herminio Portell-Vilá referred to the plot as one of "the most typically idiotic models of the American film capital," adding, "Isn't there anything sacred or respectable for Hollywood?"[48] *Patria* declared that the film was an extravaganza that made one think that its authors "must have produced it under the happy effects of 'Bacardee,' as the Yankees say."[49] One Cuban critic of the film wrote in *Bohemia* that whoever injured Martí could not be a friend of Cuba. He said that all of Cuba should rise up against the outrageous insult of "Santiago." Although he had not seen the film, he felt that the report by Portell-Vilá left no room for doubt. "We are," he added darkly, "face to face with a case of open aggression."[50]

Quesada y Miranda criticized the film for its historical inaccuracies, but asked what could one expect from Hollywood if Cuban direction of "La Rosa Blanca" had made such a botch of Martí's life.[51] Judging from the virulence of some of the comments on the film, however, one would gain the impression that a small group of Cubans think that there must be a special department in Hollywood dedicated to the sole task of confecting insults against Cuba. The film was freely shown in Havana during the first months of 1957 without provoking public demonstrations against it. Perhaps one of the rea-

sons for this was that attendance at movies had dropped off somewhat during this period because of a wave of opposition to the government through the explosion of bombs in public places, including a few theaters. Probably the more basic reason for the lack of hysteria over the film is that the public at large has a less serious approach than movie critics.

When this reviewer saw the film the Cuban audience roared with laughter accompanied with good-natured sarcasm as soon as the actor representing Martí appeared on the screen. The sober-minded personality of Martí was in marked contrast to the fun-loving spectators.

In real life Martí was a thin individual, bushy-haired, slightly cross-eyed, and had a mustache. He usually wore a threadbare, black frock coat, and trousers that bagged around his ankles. Perhaps Martí's unprepossessing presentation adds to the difficulty of making a film about him.

Martí—Example of Cuban Virtues

The reaction by some Cubans against any tampering with the representation of Martí via the screen may be explained in part by the fact that he is often considered as the archetype of the Cuban. Soon after Martí's death the poet Diego Vicente Tejera declared in 1897 in Key West that Martí united all the Cuban virtues. He found that physically Martí was that typical Cuban whose flesh had been parched by the sun to give it a tropical tone. Although Martí was thin, "his slenderness had the flexibility of a Toledo steel blade." Tejera wrote that in morality Martí possessed Cuban goodness in all its grandeur. He said of the Apostle:

In intellect he had the full Cuban capacity; he was intelligent, but in such a brilliant degree that in the nations where he travelled or with those with whom he communicated, he left the impression of being a genius.[52]

Gastón Baquero, chief editorial writer of the *Diario de la Marina*, asked how Martí had accomplished so much in such a brief span of life. His answer was that Martí was a typical Cuban in that he was a son of the tropics, sensual, impressionable, and retentive. Baquero

wrote about Martí (ignoring what persons who knew Martí had said about his speech):

Rapid in his replies, vivacious in his conversation, an unceasing fountain of speech once he began to speak, he was completely Cuban, the ultimate, the very most.[53]

Martí Among Great Men

One of the ways of elevating the stature of Martí has been extensive writing by Cubans to associate their hero with other great leaders and patriots. One of the persons with whom Martí is most frequently compared is Simón Bolívar, the great South American liberator. The person who has done the most to promote this field of hero worship is Emeterio S. Santovenia y Echaide, formerly president of the Cuban Academy of History. In addition to the work on Bolívar, he has written comparing Martí with Abraham Lincoln, Giuseppe Mazzini, and Domingo Sarmiento, a book for each. Santovenia's latest revelation is a study comparing Martí with Benjamin Franklin.[54] Of all the North American presidents, Lincoln is perhaps the most widely admired by the Cubans. His name is often mentioned in connection with that of Martí.

Besides Sarmiento other Latin American patriots who are sometimes compared with Martí are Benito Juárez (president of Mexico, 1858-63, 1867-72),[55] Miguel Hidalgo (Mexican priest and liberator in the early nineteenth century),[56] José de San Martín (Argentine patriot and liberator),[57] and Eugenio Hostos (the nineteenth century educator in the Dominican Republic).[58]

Martí has also been compared with George Washington,[59] Mahatma Gandhi,[60] Sun Yat-sen,[61] Franklin D. Roosevelt,[62] and the Hungarian patriot Sandor Petoefi.[63] The list could be extended. For instance, that follower of the lives of great men, Emil Ludwig, found that Martí did not resemble Bolívar so much as he did Jan Masaryk, the Czechoslovakian statesman.[64] It does, indeed, take the many-sided personality of Martí to be identified with so many individuals. Perhaps the most that can be distilled from these comparisons is that all the figures are of national importance, and were great leaders and humanitarians.

Martí—the Universal Man

Another frequent theme woven around Martí is the one that his qualities make him not only the perfect Cuban prototype but also the ideal man. Armando Cruz Cobos wrote:

José Martí grows more and more in American and universal time-space. So much so that it may be affirmed about him that his continuity in the hereafter projects him beyond us Cubans as more than the mere political tool of our independence. . . . Martí personifies the extra-national hero of the human race.[65]

Martí is the "complete hero" to M. Isidro Méndez, the distinguished biographer and anthologist of the Apostle. He said that although Martí has been very much abused and deformed in the eyes of the public, he still unites all the virtues of the ideal man. Méndez's advice to the person seeking information is that he should always compare his findings with what Martí had to say on the subject in order to know the final word.[66]

The universality of Martí has been treated by numerous writers. Félix Lizaso wrote that Martí was a precursor of UNESCO,[67] and Raúl José Fajardo discussed at length the "universal conscience" of Martí.[68]

The Pervasiveness of Martí

Cubans are constantly reminded of the Apostle's presence. It is perfectly possible to imagine that a Cuban devotee of Martí might begin the day by consulting his watch with the figure of Martí on it, listen to any number of songs composed from the Apostle's poems,[69] and fry his breakfast egg in "Martí" Olive Oil, after, of course, having lit the stove with matches from a box with maxims of the Maestro on the back. He might even burn his toast from a loaf of bread labeled "The New Pines." On the way to work he might stop for gasoline at the "Martí Service Station." If he could find an empty place in downtown Havana, he might park near the "Martí Theater." Passing by a newsstand on the way to his office, he might decide to buy a comic book on the life of Martí for consumption by his children. Upon arrival at his office this Cuban would undoubtedly confront a Martian

expression on his daily calendar. As he faced the prospect of another eight hours of his average $120-a-month job, he might just possibly receive deep satisfaction by reminding himself that Martí once said, "Poverty is a good companion and one lives in peace with it."[70]

The Reaction to the Cult

The cult of Martí is often referred to by Cuban writers as the proper devotion to be paid to a great hero. It is seldom mentioned with the meaning that that term is sometimes used in English, that is, as worship as an emotional fad. There have been some voices, however, raised in protest against the excesses of hero-worship to which Martí has been subjected.

One such writer, who was important in advancing the Martí cult, Arturo R. de Carricarte, later wrote brusquely to correct some notions that had been developing around the figure of the Apostle. The subject of one article of this nature was that there was really nothing Cuban about Martí, in spite of all the talk about his "Cubanity." Carricarte pointed out that Martí's parents were Spanish, with no real permanent roots in Cuba. He showed that Martí's education was predominantly Spanish, and that his culture was also fundamentally Spanish. Carricarte then asserted that although Martí in his devotion to Cuba could not be excelled by anyone, nevertheless any Cuban characteristics that he might be credited with were nil.[71]

Carricarte also censured writers on Martí. He began by saying that naturally criticism should be directed at those politicians who publicly proclaimed that they were Martians, but never carried out his ideas. Carricarte added, however, that commenting on this had become so commonplace, in fact had been repeated to such a saturation point that he would not dwell on the point. Referring to the Martiophiles, who instead of being modest, affable, generous, humble, and honest—with a few exceptions—he said, "look upon each other not as colleagues, but as malevolent rivals, as irreconcilable enemies. . . . There are very few of us who really follow Martí. To defamation and belittling of character they add the negation of every good quality and a refusal to work toward the common good." Carricarte said that twenty years previously he had founded the

Sociedad Martiniana for a fraternal effort on behalf of Martí, but that he had begun to see the formation of a society of Martiophobes, if not precisely of Martí-haters, at least of persecutors of those who were trying to spread the word of Martí.[72]

In the same year another voice was heard in protest against the excessive adulation heard everywhere of Martí. Wrote Mariblanca Sabas Alomá:

In truth, because of wanting to make Martí sublime, by this very act we are dangerously bordering on ridicule, or, what is worse, on vulgarity. I feel in the deepest reaches of my conscience an uncontrollable desire some day to go out on these streets of God begging at the top of my voice to leave him [Martí] alone, not to mention him any more, that he be honored in the effective and constructive reality of DEEDS, not in hypocritical WORDS.

Miss Sabas Alomá then said that if it were in her power she would prohibit the mention of Martí's name for at least five years. In a torrent of well-chosen words she described the omnipresence of Martí in all phases of Cuban life. She was particularly depressed by the overwhelming association of Martí's name with all the minute commonplaces of everyday life.[73]

One Cuban critic of the cult of Martí, Evelio Alvarez del Real, wrote that he knew of entire families which over a period of many years had had no better source of income than the exaltation of the Apostle. About Martí himself he asked:

Who dares to criticize his poetry, to say that his oratory became tiresome at times, and that his tempestuous style is sometimes just too much for us? It would be a sacrilege.

Alvarez added that there were two kinds of biographers of Martí, those who added something new, and those who only knew how to splurge their adoration in flowery prose. He said that if he ever chose to write sometime on Martí he would like to do a psychological study to find out how men become saints by preaching war. Alvarez said:

His entire life was a gospel alive with Christian charity and love for his fellow man—that is well understood. But between that and his fall in full combat as a soldier there is a contradiction that confuses me.[74]

An apologist for the cult of Martí was G. Alvarez Gallego, writing

in 1946 upon the appearance of another edition of Martí's works. After criticizing all the lavish praise heaped upon it, he commented, however:

I would dare to say that abuse of Martí, such as in fact taking him sometimes as a national industry and commercial slogan, even using him for political armor plate, should not annoy us. Peoples need heroic myths. If the Martí of flesh and blood did not lend himself for that purpose—which he does—it would be necessary to invent or transform somebody . . . who had less gigantic stature.

He added that nations need great men who come to be a kind of byword that better identifies national characteristics. Alvarez said that Cuba had found in Martí the ideal that it needed, but he was not critical of this phenomenon.[75] Elsewhere the same writer referred to the sublimation of Martí as an expression of "the Terminal-God of the national laic religion."[76]

THE ROMAN CATHOLIC CHURCH

The only organized body in Cuba expressing its opposition to the exaltation of José Martí as a saint is, as is to be expected, the Roman Catholic Church. The opinion of Juan Luis Martín is representative in this respect. This writer states:

We lament the fact that Martí was not Catholic, and we regret it because we know perfectly well that Martí would have been the very same Martí even if he had been a good Catholic. To count him among the nation's heroes, to honor him as the greatest of those heroes, is the duty of all Cubans of all religious creeds. . . . We Catholics also place flowers before his statue, but we do not do it as an act of religious veneration or adoration, we take flowers there as a symbol of our political and civic loyalty to his memory.

Martín added that comparing Martí with Jesus Christ was a sacrilege and made Martí seem ridiculous.[77]

Another Roman Catholic critic of the cult of Martí, Alí Presalde, said that Martí's doctrine and action did not by any means represent the complete ideological content and emotional vitality of Cuba, nor did his polished thoughts encompass all the facets of the spiritual grandeur of the nation. Presalde wrote of Martí:

Many of his eulogies have gone beyond the limits that history and human

truth permit, offering us an inhuman and mythical Martí. This elevation of Martí to divinity is a misconstruction of the facts and makes it impossible for his life to serve as an example. Surely we would gain more if we presented Martí in a real existence as a man of flesh and blood, with his faults and limitations as he had them.

This writer then said that the best way to honor Martí was not to exalt him as a saint, but to follow one of his directives, "It is necessary to make virtue fashionable."[78]

The Inviolability of Martí

In a round-table discussion of the Martí "doctrine" held in Havana in 1956 the sacredness of the personage of Martí was well demonstrated. With one or two exceptions the participants were all elementary level teachers in the public schools of the Republic. The point at issue was the question whether the "Martí religion" should be taught in the schools. Almost all were in agreement, with minor variations on methodology, that his doctrine should be taught. One participant commented, however, that it would be unwise to teach Martí doctrine in the schools, specifically with regard to Martí's religion, since there seemed to be many contradictory phases to the way Martí felt on this subject. Which Martí would be taught, Martí-Buddhist, Martí-pantheist, Martí-anti-Roman Catholic, Martí-free-thinker? In addition the widely held belief that Martí had fathered an illegitimate child made him an incongruous figure to present to school children to follow as a moral example. This observer said that when the pupils grew up they would find out these references to the life of Martí and would become disillusioned about him. Instead, he emphasized, why not concentrate on Martí's truly prodigious efforts on behalf of Cuban liberation, but not hold him up necessarily as a moral guide in all phases of human conduct. At that point the roof caved in. Whether the argument is valid is not germane. The reaction of the teachers was swift and retributive, showing how emotionally charged are Cuban interpretations of Martí.

One critic politely but lethally said that the North American making these observations, she regretted very much to have to say it, apparently after almost a year in Cuba knew nothing about José

Martí, and the fact that he was an Anglo-Saxon was probably responsible for this. Another took his comments as a vicious insult by a Yankee imperialist, thereupon launching into a bitter attack on racial segregation in the United States.

The incident serves as an example of the "hands-off" policy of criticism of Martí, the personalistic nature that discussion of Martí often seems to take, and a kind of corrosive anti-Americanism that is easily aroused when criticism of Martí is implied.

Conclusions

To those who unqualifiedly support him Martí has become the supreme patriot, the Martyr of Dos Ríos, the golden-tongued orator, the friend of the poor, a colleague of the best of the great men, a guide for every situation, the image of Christ, the founder of a new religion, the typical Cuban, and the universal man. Consequently there is little agreement when it comes to representing such an idealized figure in plastic form, as in monuments or on the screen. Most of the criticism of the abuse of Martí is not directed toward his exaltation as a saint, but toward any earthly manifestations in that hero-worship. A few, but very few, Cubans have reacted bravely against the apotheosis of Martí in the deluge of Martiana, but their voices have been drowned in the flood. Supporters of the Roman Catholic Church are the least enthusiastic Cubans in the apotheosis of Martí, but they are inclined to row gently, perhaps remembering the furor over the "excommunication" of Father Ignacio Biaín.

Chapter 7

SYMBOLISM IN POLITICS

*J*osé Martí serves as a convenient, even necessary, symbol of identification for many politicians who wish to gain high office. Once there, party leaders find it indispensable to justify their acts by associating them with Martí's name. On the other hand the opposition attacks that identification as being misplaced, and would transfer the Apostle's mantle to its own shoulders. From the sidelines those who revere Martí cry, "A plague on both your houses! Everybody talks about Martí, but no one does anything to fulfill his ideals."

The purpose of this chapter is to examine viewpoints of leading politicians, political events, and party platforms to determine to what extent Martí's ideals have been reiterated and followed in the recent history of Cuba. Since Martí was very much preoccupied with the corruption existing in the Spanish colonial government, and since it is often said that corruption continues to be the major shortcoming of modern Cuban government, particular attention will be given to these charges. In addition a large share of the chapter will be devoted to an examination of the degree of success achieved in political reform, an important feature of Martí's philosophy of government.

Political Background in Cuba, 1933-1940

When President Gerardo Machado fell from power in 1933, the traditional Liberal and Conservative parties of Cuba fell with him. Popular antagonism to their support of the dictator forced them to

148

disband, although some Liberals later reorganized with the same name. Up to the time of Machado the Liberal and Conservative parties had alternated with reasonable frequency in furnishing chiefs of state, but support of Machado by both parties had helped to undermine the two-party system. For the next twenty-five years the Cuban political scene was to be marked by a series of shifting coalitions of parties dominated by three men, Fulgencio Batista y Zaldívar, Ramón Grau San Martín, and Carlos Prío Socarrás.

The downfall of Machado was effected by the intervention of Sumner Welles, the special envoy of President Franklin D. Roosevelt. Later Welles sought a replacement in the person of General Alberto Herrera, but the army officer was not acceptable to the leaders of the revolt. A compromise candidate, Carlos Manuel de Céspedes y Quesada, was chosen and took office August 13, 1933. The new President dissolved Congress, abrogated constitutional reforms made in 1928, and declared the Constitution of 1901 to be in effect. However, as one historian writes:

The lack of cohesion in the government, of discipline in the armed forces, and of a plan worked out in advance and immediately applied, aided in a bubbling over of passions, of a spirit of vengeance, and of the most absolute anarchy.[1]

Within three weeks sergeants, corporals, and soldiers of the army, led by Sergeant Fulgencio Batista in the Agrupación Revolucionaria de Cuba (Cuban Revolutionary Group), joined with civilians and overthrew President Céspedes. In his stead they named Ramón Grau San Martín, a professor at the University of Havana and leader of a group that organized later as the Partido Revolucionario Cubano (Cuban Revolutionary Party), named after Martí's long defunct party. To distinguish themselves its members said that they were "Auténticos" ("Authentic Revolutionaries"), since they intended to cause deep social changes in Cuba. The orientation of the party's program at that time has been described by Dr. Manuel Costales Latatú, a professor of surgery at the University of Havana, and a member of Grau's 1933 cabinet. Costales said:

We worked night and day without rest, organizing administrative institutions, studying the most pressing national problems for the good of the country, dictating decrees of social justice and of economic benefit

for all the needy classes of the nation, especially workers and farmers, realizing from our position of power what the people called an *authentic revolution* that remained moulded in 132 law-decrees studied with patriotism and honesty.[2]

Costales maintained that in less than four months the antiquated legislation of Cuba was changed to have a human and progressive content. One of the most important was the Law of Nationalization of Work, which required employers to hire Cubans in place of importing labor forces. The Law also called for an eight-hour day, a minimum wage law, retirement benefits, universal suffrage, and scaling down of usury, among others.[3] Grau, however, in spite of his progressive program, lacked popular support, and in addition was not acceptable to Welles. Although the United States was soon to give up its right to intervene in Cuban affairs, it was unwilling to see a new government that did not respond to its interests.

Early in 1934 Batista, as head of the Army, forced Grau's resignation, naming as his successor Carlos Hevia, who also turned out to be unacceptable to the public at large and to the United States representative. Finally a candidate suitable to the powers concerned, Colonel Carlos Mendieta Montefur, became President on January 18, 1934. International recognition followed, but the new government met many difficulties, including a general strike in March, 1935. It was at this point that the personality of Batista, now a colonel, began to "project its influence with greater force in public destinies."[4]

Mendieta's original followers began to leave him as opposition to the regime grew. Late in 1935 the President resigned, and his Secretary of State, José A. Barnet, replaced him. In the January elections of the following year a coalition formed by the Liberal, Nationalist, and Acción Republicana Constitucionalista (Republican Constitutional Action) parties succeeded in putting their candidate Miguel Mariano Gómez (son of former President José Miguel Gómez), into office as President. Federico Laredo Bru was elected Vice-President. The major opposition was the Conjunto Nacional Democrático (National Democratic Alliance). Among the parties refusing to take part in the elections was Grau's Cuban Revolutionary party (A).

Miguel Mariano Gómez made the mistake of thinking that he was actually Chief of State. As a Cuban historian says, "He tried to

work against the realities of the Cuban scene, acting as if he did not understand at all the meaning and influence of Batista."[5]

Under Batista's initiative a law was passed by the Congress assigning a tax of 9 cents on each 100-pound bag of sugar to support civic-military schools throughout the country. A pet project of Batista, these institutions were designed to provide for the education of children of workers, public employees, and members of the armed forces. Since benefits under this system were directed largely toward children whose fathers had been soldiers or veterans of the armed services, President Gómez felt that the law was inconsistent with a civilian administration; consequently he vetoed it. Although this veto was a presidential prerogative, members of Congress felt that Gómez was trying to "coerce, with his announced veto, congressional free will."[6] Congress lost no time in deposing him on the day before Christmas, 1936, and substituting Federico Laredo Bru as President.

Laredo was an astute and moderate politician who recognized that Batista as head of the army was the real power in Cuba. The new President conducted himself accordingly.

In 1939 a Constituent Assembly was called to prepare a new constitution. The opposition triumphed in the elections. Ramón Grau San Martín, who had been in exile, assumed the presidency of the Assembly. Much of the Cuban Revolutionary party's (A) forward-looking legislation of 1933, which had never been carried out, was incorporated into the Constitution of 1940. Later Carlos Márquez Sterling occupied Grau's place in the Assembly.

In July the Constitution of 1940 was promulgated by the Congress, and general elections followed shortly. Batista was the candidate of the CND, composed of seven parties. His opponent was Grau, who, in addition to his own party, received support from the ABC party,[7] and from ARC. Batista won. The new President's administration (1941-45) initiated the semiparliamentary type of government established by the Constitution of 1940.[8]

Martí Viewed by Batista

Martí was the subject of an address by Batista, then Army Chief of Staff, to a North American radio audience in 1938. The Colonel

said that Martí constituted a complete guide from the cradle to the grave in matters of citizenship and conscience. As such he was an example not only for the worker, but also for the statesman, not only for the Cuban, but for all members of those nations belonging to the American community. He quoted from Martí, and then added the following:

Those of us who have a great historic responsibility such as that which has corresponded to us during these recent years of republican life, have had our lives fixed on his exemplary conduct. We wish to leave a record of our devotion to Martí not only on the written page and in speeches, but in concrete and evident accomplishments.[9]

During Batista's administration the greatest controversy over Martí came from opposition to the projected multimillion dollar monument in his honor in Havana, and the relationship of the obelisk to national elections and the general state of affairs of the nation under Batista. Commenting late in 1943 that voting credits for millions of dollars to build the monument came on the eve of general elections in 1944, Sergio Carbó, the editor of the Havana newspaper *Prensa Libre,* complained:

What would the fearless and spotless gentleman, index of honor and patriotism, say if he up there in outer space should be informed of the state of our sanitation, of the abandonment of our public services, how typhoid is spread because of a lack of water and sewer systems in his beloved land, how schoolhouses are tumbling down, and in the meantime the authorities continually exact money from the citizenry, ridiculing it with a prodigious monument to his memory?[10]

Before erecting such a temple to Martí, Carbó said, it would be better to honor the patriot with honest elections. Then directly addressing Batista, the editor asked him if he did not fear the inevitable public suspicion that he was using a display of public works for the monument to associate the governmental candidate for the presidency, Carlos Saladrigas, with the name of Martí. Carbó asserted that this would be an ignominious act in Martí's memory, and that it would be better to leave the monument unbuilt. The monument was not built at that time, and Batista held honest elections. Ramón Grau San Martín, the head of the Cuban Revolutionary party (A), won.

Martí Interpreted by Grau

In 1939 Grau gave an important speech, "José Martí and the Cuban Revolutionary party." In it he maintained that only one who, like Martí, had lived in exile could really appreciate the bitterness and injury of calumny from those at home. Grau said that he would answer his critics by using some of Martí's own writings, saying, "If my life accuses me, I will not be able to say anything that will answer for it." But then he added, "My life will defend me. . . . I know that I have been useful."[11]

Referring to the *Bases del Partido Revolucionario Cubano*, Grau found that Martí had foreseen and hoped to avoid election frauds, ignorance of real democracy, and constant injury to the free and cordial exercise of man's fullest capacities. Grau maintained that fraud had been perpetrated throughout the history of the unfortunate Republic and would continue until it was recognized that election of the Cuban Revolutionary party (A) was the only solution to the nation's ills. Grau called for an end to economic imperialism, especially in the form of foreign loans from powerful neighbors. He said that it was unthinkable that in Cuba, the richest land in the world, a hardworking and honest people should live in misery.[12]

Directing himself to those in power, Grau insisted that they should not "waste nor use for security or personal luxury the money that should be dedicated to the greatest development of all the nation's resources. Let them regulate relations between capital and labor, and assign to the Cuban, at the very least, an equitable share similar to that which the same foreigners who argue about their rights enjoy in their own country."

Grau responded to criticism for his having assumed the name of Martí's Cuban Revolutionary party by maintaining that his own followers had a right to use the name because they were in patriotic intent the "true interpreters" of the Martyr of Dos Ríos. He said that it was necessary to talk about Martí, but it was also necessary to follow what he preached. He added that there were many who invoked his name, but very few who actually followed him. Grau warned:

The able and scrupulous politician invokes his name to win followers in the campaign that is to bring him to power, and once there, to exploit the

unfortunate. False leaders invoke him as a recognized password to triumph, in order to hide their true intentions of personal gain. Dictators and petty traitors invoke him [to gain office], they always do, so that afterwards, in their greed for riches and power, they bargain with foreign oppressors.[13]

Grau asserted that if the Martian ideal had really been followed by those who had been in power, the natural riches of Cuba would not have been turned over to foreigners for exploitation, and in many cases not even developed but left to lie idle.

The orientation of Grau's interpretation of Martí in 1939 may be seen to rest mainly on anti-imperialism, Cuba for the Cubans, and censure of those who used Martí to gain office.

On the occasion of the anniversary of Martí's birth in January, 1944, toward the end of Batista's first term, Grau dropped all references to foreign imperialism in his speech on Martí. Instead he concentrated on a harsh indictment of the Batista regime by expressing some of the Martian ideals that "saturated his own spirit." How prophetic, he said, were Martí's warnings against an authoritarian and bureaucratic system of government. Worse yet, however, was the graft and corruption evident in Batista's administration. He then quoted at length Martí's exhortations to honesty and morality in government. He accused Batista of using false voting certificates, buying voters, and using public funds to further the candidacy of Batista's choice for President. He found it especially shocking that Batista was stifling democracy in Cuba by using the enormous prosperity resulting from the war of the world's democracies against dictatorships. It was a very great error, he said, for politicians without ideals to insist on thinking that the people also did not have them. For the Cuban Revolutionary party (A), he concluded, no cause would be sufficient to keep the party from carrying out its task of dedication to the Apostle's principles.[14]

Grau's target did not allow him a monopoly of the use of Martí's name in debate. A Batista supporter replied that if Grau were really such an advocate of Martí he would have had something to say in favor of unity, which Martí often called for and which was very much needed in Cuba at the time. He asserted that Grau instead enlisted Martí in his party merely to use him as an instrument of disunion

and discord. He charged that if Grau were serious about unity of factions in Cuba he would have accepted the cabinet post that Batista had offered him at the time of the state of emergency when Cuba entered World War II.[15]

Soon after Grau took office in 1945 he announced that the Republic of Martí was at last gaining its economic liberty. He was prepared, he said, to follow the teachings of Martí, who, it seemed, had wished to test the will of the people and the government by placing difficulties (shortages of finished goods) in its path. He then used a variation of his 1939 speech by again quoting Martí, "If my life is worth anything, let it speak for me." The President said that he felt just the same way and was prepared to give his life to resolve the problems facing the country.[16]

Grau mentioned difficulties, but not so emphatically as Alberto Salas Amaro, a Cuban newspaper editor, who commented on the political situation in Cuba in the same year as a "profanation of Martí." This critic saw Cuba as subjected to all kinds of political crime, chronic neglect of the farmer, unlimited discrimination against the Negro, a foundering economy, deception, opportunism, scurrilous demagoguery, and unselfish patriotism in decadence. If Martí could only see this state of affairs, declared Salas, his holy wrath would strike it down. "And still," he complained, " we continue treating the liberators as if they were Gods, until our Olympus has surpassed the one of Greek mythology."[17]

A year later another critic, a newspaperman, echoed these harsh words of reproval for the Cuba of Grau. He said:

Martí dreamed of a prosperous and happy Cuba. . . . And this Cuba is not the Cuba that its lover would dream of. . . . Let the soul of the great lover dream on up there in glory, while down here, very much awake, we Cubans, insincere, cowards, and egoists, continue exploiting the ideal of a prosperous, fortunate, and happy Cuba. . . .[18]

Félix Lizaso, writing in 1947 on the neglect into which the memorial to Martí in Dos Ríos had fallen, said, "We are, without doubt, the people that has least known how to appreciate the sacrifices of its great men."[19]

Numerous other Cubans criticized Grau for failing to follow the example of Martí, but none sounded quite so exasperated and bitter

as one writing an open letter in 1949 to Major General Enrique Loynaz del Castillo, veteran of the Revolution and elder statesman. This Cuban wrote to the General to protest against the Grau administration, which had ended earlier in the year. First of all he named Grau as the illegitimate usurper of the thought of Martí, and secondly denounced him in his constant profanation of the Apostle in his wishing to associate his "wretched and corrupt government with the pure ideals of Martí." Grau, he said, was living in Spain at the time of the War of Independence, and was seventeen years old, just the same age as Martí when the Apostle went to prison, but with what a difference! Grau, he declared, was then indifferent to the agonies of Cuba, but now claimed a closeness to Cuba that he really never felt. In his opinion Grau should not be allowed to continue insulting the "sacrosanct memory of Martí."[20]

Partially to find a reply to these charges the author asked the former President in 1957 just how his administration had tried to make Cuba the land of Martí. Specifically, a part of his 1939 speech on Martí was read:

And it is profoundly lamentable that [Martí] having offered everything for the land in which he was born, has not been able to see fulfilled, up to the present, a free and decent route for his beloved country.[21]

Grau was then asked whether anything had happened within the past eighteen years to change this estimate of his. The former professor replied that his administration had tried to fulfill the Martí ideal in many respects, but there were several points of progress that he especially wanted to mention. Since man was now living in the age of the automaton, he declared, it was one of his administration's main tasks to find ways of integrating the worker into a society where he would not be replaced by the machine. He said that it was essential to find and bring out the best qualities of the individual to correspond to the work that he was to do. One concrete accomplishment of his administration, Grau believes, was an attempt to make nations with a high standard of living, such as the United States, pay for the products of less wealthy nations at a rate that would allow a similar standard of living to be approached in labor areas furnishing raw materials for foreign trade. Another was the Grau doctrine of the

"integral salary," that is, one that would take into consideration the need to supply the working man with a balanced and adequate diet, sufficient clothing, housing, and education for himself and his family.

Grau insisted that from 1945 to 1949 he followed the Martí ideal by attempting to make the armed forces responsible to civilian control. This was done, he said, by training soldiers not only for military duties, but also preparing them for civilian occupations. He said that Cuba as a maritime nation, with thousands of miles of coastline and excellent harbors, was still inadequately adapted to take advantage of its natural riches. He established marine investigation centers of small groups of soldiery along the coast. Their duties included gathering of statistics not only on the fishing industry, but also census-taking of Cuba's animal population. When on leave the soldiers were not permitted to go around armed, as had been the practice in less civilian-minded administrations. There had been genuine good feeling, Grau insisted, between soldiery and citizenry because it was apparent that the military was there not only to defend the nation, but to contribute to its civilian progress. He said that now there was a barrier existing between the two. Although he was prepared to give more examples of how his administration had carried out the ideals of Martí, those he mentioned were particularly important. The former President concluded the interview by reciting a poem by Martí indicating the poet's deep religious beliefs.[22]

Grau has naturally received praise for certain features of his term in office. One Cuban historian considers him to have been "one of the governors who was most respectful of freedom of thought."[23]

In 1954 Grau made another try for the presidency, with a University of Havana professor of law, Antonio Lancís y Sánchez, as his running mate. Considering the presence of Batista's troops at the polls as an unwarranted intimidation, however, Grau at the last minute withdrew his party from participation in the elections.

Professor Lancís asserted that Martí had always had a profound influence on him; that he best remembered him for his purity and his deep feeling of sacrifice. He believes that Martí has had his deepest effect upon youth through the medium of schools, but when young people grow older they forget about him. When asked whether there was anyone in Cuba's past or present who approached the ideals of

Martí, he replied that Manuel Sanguily, a contemporary of Martí, would fill that specification with respect to the Apostle's prophetic vision. As for the present, he cited Grau as an example in his sense of nationalism and his constant warnings to be careful of the United States. Lancís believes that the influence of Spain has made a very deep impression on Cuba, and that for the most part it has been bad, particularly in its heritage of individualism that constantly tends toward anarchy. Dr. Lancís had a large portrait of Martí in his law office, and said that he had a large bust of Martí in his home, the only person so honored. Among the many articles and books written by Professor Lancís, one is on Martí and elections.[24]

The legislative program of the small group of Cuban Revolutionary party (A) legislators who managed to gain election to the Cuban Congress in 1954 consisted mainly in recommendations for improvements for workers and teachers. Their platform called for a 20 per cent across-the-board increase in salaries for all working people in Cuba; unemployment insurance; restoration of privileges enjoyed by public school teachers before March, 1952; a minimum salary of $200 a month for all government employees; a minimum salary of $150 a month for teachers in private schools; and repeal of laws dealing with the armed forces.[25] As a program of action these points respond to the ideals of Martí in promoting the dignity of man. Since the party has enjoyed no real power in Congress from 1952 to the present, however, their platform is no more than an aspiration.

Martí Seen by Prío

The second representative of the Cuban Revolutionary party (A) to hold power in Cuba was Carlos Prío Socarrás, the heir apparent to Grau in 1948. Prío had been associated with Grau since the overthrow of Machado. Prío was also Grau's Prime Minister, a post with little power under Cuba's semiparliamentary system, but a convenient steppingstone to the presidency. In the 1948 elections Prío won over Dr. Ricardo Núñez Portuondo, the Liberal-Democratic candidate and nearest rival.[26]

Soon after gaining the presidency Prío broke with Grau. At the time of the anniversary of Martí's birth in 1949 (a time that seems

to have become fashionable for a wringing of political hands and washing of dirty linen in public), Grau said:

I made Carlos Prío President of Cuba because I thought that he was capable of following the program of *autenticismo*, but it was a mistake. That's the way it goes![27]

The same day that this article appeared another on Martí could be read in Havana. Written by Francisco Ichaso, a political commentator and writer on Martí as a dramatist, it said that only one word could describe the state of politics then existing in Cuba— scandalous. He wrote that there was very little in Cuba after half a century to reflect the heroism of the Fathers of Independence. He found that as far as the external features of democracy were concerned, Cuba had progressed somewhat, but as far as the realities were concerned, "We are going from bad to worse." He wrote:

The cloud of scandal under which the regime of *cubanidad*[28] began continues fixed, immovable in the apparently new sky of *cordialidad*.[29] The venality of that government that had made so many protests in favor of decency in public affairs projects its foul shadow on the present one, and has condemned it to a kind of shameful inhibition, of deadly paralysis.[30]

Ichaso commented that Cuban politicians in power had always had a light-fingered touch with public funds, but the past was nothing to compare with the present. He noted that in the good old days politicians ingeniously invented "lost battalions" (that is, nonexistent government workers) in order to collect their salaries. He said, "The imagination of the native has always been very wide awake to this kind of political 'evolution.' " But now, he charged, there was just wholesale robbery from the Treasury. Ichaso was not optimistic about the future. He found that there was nothing more difficult in Cuba than to purify administrative activities. He said that it was very rare to find a judge or court of justice that would condemn an official charged with having stolen public funds. He commented, "It is a widely-held idea that crimes against property are not considered as such when that property belongs to the State." Such an attitude and the record of corruption in government, he declared, were making Cuba suffer from a very bad reputation abroad.

The avalanche of charges of corruption in Grau's government,

Ichaso explained, had finally caused the former President to insist that there had been "liberality" in the dispensation of public funds only at the *end* of his administration. He said that Grau maintained that the only object of the free spending was to elect Prío to prevent the government from falling into the hands of the followers of Machado in the Liberal-Democratic coalition. Charged Ichaso, "This recognition is tinged with that strange frankness that . . . [is] one of the characteristics of *cubanidad*."

At this time the Prío administration was accused by Jorge Mañach, one of Martí's chief biographers and also a leading politician in Cuba. Mañach asked what Martí would think if he should lift his head and see the Cuba of 1949 with its political cavalcade of adventurers and thieves "loaded with cynicism and millions of stolen dollars." He would see, according to Mañach, a despoiled Treasury, Congress sold, schoolrooms bought by the highest bidder, farmers still illiterate, high schools converted into cradles of rebellion, and an exodus of desperate and jobless youth to the United States. What would Martí do, he asked, with those who after reaching power by promising reform exceeded their predecessors in corruption? Mañach answered himself that the evil of Cuba was not, however, that its whole people was corrupt, but that the government had fallen into evil hands.[31]

In an imaginary conversation with Martí (resorting to tête-à-têtes with the Apostle is a popular pastime among writers on Martí), Mañach asked the patriot how it was possible to return decency to public life if the electorate put those men into office who insisted on robbing it of their very decorum. Mañach complained that the good people were not taking part in political parties, that they had become egoists unwilling to take on the added responsibility and inconvenience that participation implied. Martí's answer to all this, in Mañach's own words, was that the biographer should not despair, that once good men eventually did attain power they would act in such a way that by a display of honesty and good faith the people would respond.

That same year the *Diario de la Marina,* which was then the oldest Spanish newspaper in print in the world, and was conservative, pro-Roman Catholic, and pro-Spanish, printed a front-page picture

of Martí to honor the patriot on his birthday. What was unusual about a most famous picture, however, was that in this issue Martí displayed a perfectly developed black eye, perhaps a freak of printer's ink, but more eloquent than words.[32]

Another critic of the Cuban scene wrote the following year on Martí's birthday, "Chaotic in the economy, in social matters, and in politics, the nation shows no signs of improvement on the horizon." He said that every day Cuba was putting more distance between itself and the ideals of the founding fathers. He then insisted that Martí had never really been understood by the great mass of the Cuban people.[33]

When Carlos Prío Socarrás was Prime Minister of Cuba in 1946 he had spoken on Martí's birthday. Newspaper headlines acclaimed the participation of 200,000 Cubans in paying homage to the Apostle.[34] Prío began his speech with the modest hope that he would be forgiven any inadequacies since as Prime Minister he had had "neither the time nor the disposition to coordinate his thoughts about Martí." He composed himself, however, to the extent that he was able to compare Martí and Bolívar. He found that Bolívar was humanized when he descended from the heights to which hero worship had elevated him, to die in desperate and humble circumstances; on the contrary, Martí was deified when he died as a martyr. Prío said:

But this deification, the logical reply of the soul of his people before the injustice of his death, dissipates the true personality of the Apostle in the eyes of the great mass of the people. . . . The trend, nevertheless, has turned. We have seen in time that a José Martí situated far beyond us, in a kind of national niche whose only saint is he, was getting too far away from his people, for whom he alone lived and suffered.[35]

Prío then asserted that he had felt Martí's presence. In a direct invocation of the Apostle he proceeded to tell Martí that he had seen him watching over his dreams and "cherishing what little good there was in him." Addressing his protector he said:

I understood in time why I could not imitate you because it is not possible to compare oneself with you. But I aspired to win the approving silence of your august shade. And when calumny has tried to soil an act that I have tried to keep clean, I have remembered you, the sum total of all the purity that humanity can shelter, whom they wished to injure with [slander] without your permitting a single objection to come from your lips.

The touching, humble tone of Prío's speech as Prime Minister in 1946 is in marked contrast to another he gave as President in 1951. In this speech Prío adopted a rancorous and belligerent tone toward the outstanding apostate from the Cuban Revolutionary party (A), Eduardo R. Chibás, head of the Cuban People's party (Orthodox). Martí was merely the vial that Prío used to display the poison he held for Chibás. Nothing could better illustrate Martí's comment, "There is no greater fury than that between political rivals in the same party."[36] Prío began in all innocence by saying that he was not going to take Martí and convert him into a political instrument, as Chibás had done by proclaiming himself nothing less than Martí's heir. Prío said that he preferred to bow humbly before the great liberator and take his conduct and his work as an example. He then proceeded to the point:

Nothing is more opposed to the Martian spirit than Chibás and his party. In Cuban life Chibás represents hatred, low passions, calumny, and lies.[37]

Quoting in full from Martí's poem, "La Rosa Blanca," Prío lamented the fact that this display of unselfish friendship would be lost on Chibás. He said that one should always distrust anybody that claimed to be more honest than anyone else. He ridiculed Chibás and his party by asserting that they had taken honesty as their favorite motto, and that they had no other program than that of "being honest." Quoting from Martí he said, "Virtue is quiet in men as in peoples. A boasting party is a weak party." Prío stated that Chibás and his party were certainly the traitors about whom Martí had warned.

Then the President lapsed into the third person, maintaining a weird form of reference to himself for the rest of the speech, as if he had left for another engagement. He said that the trouble with Chibás was that he envied the patriotism, disinterest, and generosity of Dr. Carlos Prío. He declared:

Dr. Carlos Prío Socarrás has never bragged about his identification with the thought of Martí. I know, nevertheless, that he reads Martí constantly and that he makes an effort to follow his teachings. From his position as President of the Republic he has known how to be cordial with

everybody, respectful of his adversaries, and magnanimous with his enemies.

Prío then called for a kind of popularity contest in which he postulated his respectful conduct as Chief of State against the hateful conduct of Chibás, leaving it up to the people to judge the winner.

Prío then defended a recently floated government loan of large proportions as a very Martian act. To prove it he read off praise of his action by his ministers and aides. He continued:

President Prío did not complain about the vile abuse and the calumny daily let loose against his person or against the government by those who believe that the duty of the opposition is to try to cover one's adversary with mud. On the contrary he accepted it as one of the sacrifices—undoubtedly the most sorrowful—that democracy requires of the governor in his attempt to keep public liberties intact.

Prío asserted that he had floated the loan, first, because it was good and nobody attacked it right away, and secondly, because it was in part to pay veterans. He added with a display of startling candor, "Veterans have families, and they as well as their families vote. It was dangerous to vote against that loan, and then later on to repudiate it, for reason of election mathematics." He went on:

I have been very careful, Cubans, that politics should not be allowed to enter into the permanent work of the Republic. For the institutions that are going to last forever I have selected the best [individuals] . . . since I had the legitimate right to choose the men who think as I do and, as I, maintain a political doctrine or criterion.

By this time just what Prío's doctrine consisted of was a little unclear. Ending up in a long burst of self-righteousness, Prío left Martí ideologically far behind, not mentioning him again in the speech.

It would be difficult to find a political speech that more clearly demonstrates the split personality of some politicians, the duality of the spoken word and the record. It is a perfect example of the public expression of virtue, comparable to the cleansing of Richard M. Nixon in the 1952 presidential campaign in the United States.

Unfortunately for Prío there was one man in Cuba who forgave the President nothing—Senator Fulgencio Batista. With the aid of followers in the army Batista turned Prío out of power March 10,

1952.[38] Prío fled to Mexico. Shortly afterwards the exile is reported to have bemoaned the fact that he was almost without financial resources. When questioned about "La Chata" and several other country estates and possessions that he had in Cuba he admitted that these had not been confiscated. Then in a characteristic burst of frankness he is reported to have added, "I think being poor is a sin."[39] (In this statement he was not echoing the Martian ideal.) This account may be apocryphal, but even if it is, previous comments by the former President and the Alice-in-Wonderland aura of Cuban politics entitle the observer to put a large share of credence in it.

Prío remained in exile in Mexico and the United States until 1955. Part of the time he was involved in litigation with the United States government over charges of arms smuggling. When the former President returned to Cuba he dramatized his arrival by hieing himself and his followers off to Santiago de Cuba to pay homage at the tomb of Martí. Addressing Martí, the former President spoke as follows:

The nation is sad. But just as your fall shrouded Cuban hearts in mourning, and it was thought that without your word and will liberty would be impossible, at last your followers realized it [liberty], just so we, it does not matter what sadness restrains us, also will make our country free again, as you would wish.[40]

Within a matter of months Prío was publicly accused by the Cuban government of entering a conspiracy to overthrow the regime, and once again he was forced to leave the country for exile.

Martí—Symbol of Unity and Discord

Batista cancelled out any general good will that he had among the Cuban people when he left his post as senator of the Republic to take over the government by force March 10, 1952. He immediately dissolved Congress, suspended constitutional guarantees, and ruled by decree. It was an unfortunate choice of time considering the approaching celebrations for the Martí Centenary the following year, since the contrast between the President's act and the ideals of Martí came into the full glare of world-wide publicity.

The Martí Centenary in 1953

The President made a brave and modest attempt to open the celebrations. First of all he said that to find examples of the exemplary conduct of Martí it would be necessary to elevate oneself to the teaching of Jesus and to heed the political lessons of men like Abraham Lincoln and the Mexican patriot Miguel Hidalgo. He continued:

Martí wanted the best for Cuba—we all must confess it—it still has not been achieved in the land where he was born to serve. I appeal to all of my compatriots in this solemn hour to unite in the cult of that great guide for leaders, . . . who had in the devotion of his people and in every citizen a perpetual altar, the smile of an angel on every child, and a caress of glory on every flower in his land. Martí, our Apostle, said that in order to give tribute no one's voice was too weak. Mine is weak and so is that of everyone else to honor him.[41]

Just how weak many articulate citizens considered that voice was soon made evident. The Cuban Revolutionary party (A) honored Martí by criticizing the Batista regime, asserting that it lacked the moral authority to commemorate the Apostle.[42] Censure of the President even took poetic form in a "Lament for José Martí in his Centenary." Wrote this poet:

Wandering among the shades, Maestro, dove, eagle,
My voice is searching for thee to give us our direction.
I say among the shades because I feel in my Nation
The lengthening shadows of fatal tentacles.

.   .   .   .

Come to strengthen our hearts, come to dispel the shadows,
Come to cut out the cancer, come to sweeten our lips.
We must find our direction, we must purify our violent passions,
We must shed light upon thee. Oh Cuba, we must look higher![43]

Another Cuban wrote that one day was just like another in Cuba, where "La Rosa Blanca" could not blossom. He said that adulation of Martí was the work of demagogues; that the caste system and racial discrimination in Cuba prevented any real appreciation of the Apostle.[44]

Cubans extensively criticized the still unfinished monument to Martí in the Plaza Cívica of Havana. One writer said that the wealth

accumulated by Prío, Grau, and Batista while in office was in violent contrast to the forced contribution of one day's salary from workers and businessmen. Lack of compliance laid one open to arrest and imprisonment—a most commendable atmosphere, he added sarcastically, in which to be honoring Martí![45]

An editorial in the *Diario de la Marina* noted that Martí had looked for a system of land use that would provide a home for every good man. Martí's ideas in this respect had given rise to much talk by demagogues, but the editorial found that very few steps had been taken for a sound and contructive plan for agrarian and housing reform. The newspaper then quoted Martí on the dangers of a one-crop economy and economic dependence resulting from the sale of its products to only one nation. The editorial urged Cuba to follow Martí's economic ideas.[46]

Raimundo Lazo, a professor of literature at the University of Havana and writer on Martí, had some points of criticism for the persons chosen to speak in commemoration of Martí in the official ceremonies. José Vasconcelos, the Mexican writer, had been brought to Cuba to take part in the celebration. Lazo criticized Vasconcelos for supporting in the name of Martí Bastista's dictatorship by saying that the effects of a dictatorship could be good. Lazo was particularly bitter against Vasconcelos' visit to only one center of education and then proclaiming that in Cuba, thanks to the regime of Batista, there were no abandoned children. The fact was, said Lazo, that from one end of the Republic to the other, children existed in the most wretched state.

Lazo also censured Fernando Ortiz, the venerable Cuban sociologist, who was chosen to deliver the commemorative speech in the Senate of the Republic. Ortiz justified the Batista regime by quoting Martí who once said, "When a people sees itself floundering . . . blessed be the daring man who seizes hold of the rudder with a strong hand." Lazo asked how one could blame foreigners for favorably associating Martí and Batista when prominent Cubans themselves did it. The best homage to Martí, he said, would be to restore that which was most lacking in Cuba—Liberty.[47]

The basic question in the Centenary, according to Jorge Mañach, was whether the Cubans had been faithful to the ideals of Martí.

Trying to avoid either undue pessimism or optimism, he posed the question whether the Republic had been a success. He found that it had progressed in a formal and material way, but not in spiritual values. Progress was to be seen in the abrogation of the Platt Amendment, the recognition of workers' rights, and a lessening of race prejudice, he believed, but the Republic had been set back twenty years with the seizure of power by Batista in 1952, with the suspension of the Constitution, the strangulation of public liberties, and the resulting ominous tension. Under these circumstances the Centenary took on a tone of marked irony in Mañach's eyes. Martí would have been completely opposed, as the record of his life showed, he asserted, to the militarism present in Cuba. Wrote Mañach:

All the values and ethical norms that Martí preached are in crisis. One is dignity, because every day the number of Cubans who are ruled by instincts and not by conscience grows larger. . . . The idea of duty has been converted into mere allusion, rhetorical and almost ridiculous. Law is renounced in favor of personal advantage. Before the spectacle of those enriched by power, the great masses, although they cannot participate directly in the official atmosphere, feel nevertheless strong enough to find out the culprits, although at the same time they lack moral examples to fulfill their duties. We all make demands, but nobody demands anything of himself. The dramatization of that demand, which at times is accompanied by violence, is in direct proportion to the frivolity with which that demand is robbed of all realization.[48]

On this basis, Mañach insisted, it was impossible for a people to defend itself from illegitimate ambitions that were constantly in ferment. He concluded that the only solution to the crisis, which was essentially a moral one, was to encourage the establishment of a legion of followers of Martí. If they found themselves unable to act, they should at least faithfully preserve a Martian attitude.

Accusations and counteraccusations as to who was competent to observe the Martí Centenary attained such volume and acerbity that the Bloque Nacional de la Prensa (a national association of editors and publishers) and the Consejo Nacional de Veteranos (a veterans organization) called for a cease fire in the combat among the Martians during the "Great Week of Martí." Francisco Ichaso wrote that he did not dare to predict how the public would react to this request, but he could describe the scene of the conflict:

The national bedlam is of such a caliber that here nobody listens to anyone else, least of all when what is being said has the slightest tone of good advice. It is a time for inflamed tongues, of alarms and excursions, of vindictive burnings at the stake, and anyone who does not speak the rough, steely language of the agitator runs the risk of bloody mockery.[49]

Ichaso said that the least that could be asked was that hostilities be suspended for the purpose of common veneration of Martí. He pointed out that the press and veterans were not calling for a cancellation of the fighting, just an armistice for seven days. He said that in Batista's speech opening the Centenary there was not the slightest criticism of anybody, and he hoped that the rest would follow the President's example.

Others also took a calm and positive view, such as the editorial in a Havana daily applauding the action of the government in allowing so many organizations to take part in the Martí celebrations.[50] On the whole, however, the Centenary was marred by a discordant chorus of invective.

POLITICAL BACKGROUND IN CUBA, 1954-1957

In 1954 Batista stepped down temporarily from the presidency, entrusting it to Andrés Domingo y Morales del Castillo while he himself ran for the presidential term 1955-59. Batista's group was the Partido Acción Progresista (Progressive Action party), supported by the Liberals, the Democratic party, and the Partido Unión Radical (Radical Union party). These four groups became known collectively as the Coalición Progresista Nacional (National Progressive Coalition), although Batista's party was the only one with any real strength.

Batista's opposition came mainly from the two wings of the Cuban Revolutionary party (A), headed by Ramón Grau San Martín and Carlos Prío. From exile Prío refused to allow his wing to take part in the elections on the grounds that free elections had not been assured. Prío's action resulted in a split with Grau, although, as has been seen, the former professor himself withdrew at the last minute as a candidate for the presidency. In the face of negligible opposition Batista was elected for a four-year term.

Prior to the Bastista coup in 1952 an association called the

Sociedad de Amigos de la República (Society of Friends of the Republic) was established in Havana by a group of prominent citizens, among them leading writers on Martí. The purpose of the Society was to study public problems, check compliance of the government with the Constitution, encourage participation of good citizens in political parties, and promote morality in government. In its manifesto the Society commented upon the paradox existing between the Cubans who fought in the War of Independence and those in the subsequent history of the Republic. The manifesto reads:

> The Cubans who united to struggle and even to die epically for an ideal have not always known how to join together to consolidate and develop the dreamed of Republic in which liberty, justice, and decorous well-being also should have their base.[51]

Confronted with a situation calling for just such a display of coordination of all for the good of the Republic, the Society in 1955, minus some "friends" who had joined the government, issued a call to all opposition political parties and the Batista forces. The Society urged a series of talks to "arrive as soon as possible at a democratic reordering of the institutions of the Republic."[52] The magic words on the political airwaves for weeks were "national solution." Euphemistically this meant general elections the sooner the better to oust Batista. As a civic organization the Society seemed to meet some standards of Martian conduct. It managed to elicit a certain amount of cooperation from the opposition political parties while the head of the Society, old patriot Cosmé de la Torriente, held talks with the President. In view of the firm situation of Batista in power, however, and the splits among the opposition parties, no "solution" was forthcoming.

As usual taking a detached view, Carlos Márquez Sterling, constitutional expert and biographer of Martí, wrote that there would never be a solution unless political action was granted to all parties and unless they stopped feuding bitterly among themselves. Neither would there be any solution if the "caste of untouchables" refused to take part in politics for fear of being contaminated.[53] Upon the death of Cosmé de la Torriente in 1956 the Society seemed to lose its motivating force completely, although it may be said to have been on its way toward preceding its leader to the grave by several months.

Martí—Symbol of Insurrection

In view of the failure of a peaceful "solution" to the problem of Batista's government, a more radical solution was attempted with the landing of a small force of Cuban exiles in Oriente Province late in 1956. Led by Fidel Castro, a young belligerent offspring of the Cuban People's party (O), the group took as its name "Movimiento 26 de Julio" in reference to an abortive attempt made by some of its members on that date in 1953 in Santiago de Cuba to overthrow the government at the Moncada barracks. After the landing, Batista's troops were in pursuit of the rebels in the mountain region around Santiago de Cuba. For the next two years the country was in a state of tension. Crude, homemade bombs exploded daily in Havana, constitutional guarantees were suspended, and the press censored while the rebels continued to conduct guerrilla warfare from the Sierra Maestra Mountains in Oriente province. In a photograph taken during an interview between the Cuban journalist Benjamín de la Vega and Fidel Castro in Mexico sometime before the expedition set out, one could note a statue of Martí in the background of the rebel leader's headquarters.[54]

With reference to Castro's invasion of Cuba, the old politician Orestes Ferrara, in self-imposed exile in Europe since his association with Machado, declared that Martí had been very bad for Cuba. He said:

I say this because by believing that they are apostles, an infinite number of young men have done themselves a great amount of harm. What does all this being a "hero or martyr" amount to anyway?[55]

Martí—Symbol of Concord

In the midst of revolution and counterevolution in 1957 Senator Andrés Rivero Agüero, leader of the government-dominated parties in the Senate, arose to pay homage to Martí on the anniversary of his birth. Rivero's main theme was brotherly love. He began his speech by quoting the first stanza of Martí's "La Rosa Blanca," in which the poet refers to the gratitude he felt for a faithful friend. Cuba, according to the Senator, had not yet reached that political maturity to

which it was entitled because the Cubans put so much passion into their political struggles that they frustrated all attempts to consolidate their efforts for the good of the country. He said that political passion belittled and poisoned the collective conscience of the Cubans, causing more damage than all the hurricanes that periodically devastated parts of the island. He asked:

How is it possible if, as Martí said, it is necessary to manage the affairs of government with zeal, caution, and prudence, that passion is what gives the most characteristic coloring to the political questions of Cuba?[56]

The peacemaker then said that it was necessary to appeal to the living thought of Martí in every hour of existence of the nation, especially in the present state of troubles "saturated with low passions that carry us along the road of hate to the most barbarous manifestations." Finishing on a theme of forgiveness, he quoted the last stanza of Martí's "La Rosa Blanca":

> And for the cruel one who tears out
> The heart that gives me life,
> I cultivate neither thistle nor weed,
> I cultivate a white rose.

This note of brotherly love was somewhat marred by the suspension of constitutional guarantees in the nation, censorship of the press, and recent assassinations of the head of the military intelligence branch of the army and also of the head of the National Police. To many Cubans the thistles were more apparent than the white roses on the Cuban landscape.

President Batista did not lose the opportunity to call for Martian peace and concord, citing "La Rosa Blanca" in its entirety, when he spoke on the turbulent state of affairs in the nation March 10, 1957, the anniversary of his seizure of power.[57] An answer came from as far away as Guatemala City, Guatemala, where two Cuban exiles fired shots at the Cuban embassy and plastered its walls with posters reading, "Traitors and assassins of the fatherland of Martí celebrate the anniversary of the Tenth of March!"[58]

A much more serious outburst against the regime came three days later when a group of about one hundred rebels assaulted the presidential palace in downtown Havana. The assailants barely missed

killing the President. The attack was repelled, but forty persons were killed, most of them rebels.[59]

Some of the revolutionists fighting for Fidel Castro on the other end of the island were captured and brought to trial in April, 1957. Among them was a young Mexican, Alfonso Guillén Zelaya, who ended his defense by quoting Martí:

Every man of justice and honor fights for liberty wherever he may see it offended, because that is to fight for his integrity as a man; and the one who sees liberty offended and does not fight for it, or helps those who offend it, is not a whole man.[60]

The newspaper account of the trial stated that this reading caused fervent cries of "Long live Free Cuba!" and "Long live Mexico!" to ring out from spectators in the courtroom. The judge thereupon ordered a recess so that the accused might have light refreshments served by the "Committee of Civic Resistance."

In the midst of rebellion and discord the leader of the government parties in the Cuban House of Representatives, Rafael L. Díaz-Balart, echoed the theme of love, not insurrection, as being the most important in his opinion in the thought and action of Martí. Díaz-Balart said in an interview that for him Martí was the most perfect and real interpreter of the preachings of Christ, and that the Apostle could be compared with Lincoln and the Mexican President Benito Juárez. The Congressman pointed out that his middle name was Lincoln, and that one of his own sons bore this name. Comparing Lincoln and Martí, Díaz-Balart found that both had a sense of humanitarianism and Christianity.

The Congressman said that the passionate nature of the Cubans, along with their *personalismo,* both inherited from the Spaniards, had made it impossible to leave the epoch of the *caudillo* (man on horseback). Part of this was due to the Latin American admiration of force, also an inheritance from the Spaniards.

Responding to a question on the role of the platform in Cuban political parties, he said that all of them were beautiful, but who used them? He maintained that the opposition was always demanding honesty in government, but not one of their administrations ever turned out to be honest. Concluding with his favorite interpretation of Martí, Díaz-Balart said that Martí "preached love as a rationalization

of national integration." Since the passion of the Latin was so great, it was necessary to channel and emphasize love as the ideal emotion.[61] Uncouth opposition elements made an armed guard necessary at all times at the entrance to the lawmaker's home in Havana. However much they might have genuinely felt the force of the Martian precept of love, government leaders did not feel inclined to turn the other cheek.

Martí—Symbol of Anti-Americanism

An editorial in the liberal but not leftist Havana newspaper *El Mundo* in 1939 described the leader of the Popular Socialist party (Communist) in Cuba, Juan Marinello, as "an illustrious poet, writer, and distinguished figure in politics."[62] In that year the Communist-dominated party also enjoyed respectability by winning 87,802 votes in its bid to take part in Cuba's Constituent Assembly. Of the eleven parties taking part in the balloting, the Communists were in fifth place, with the Cuban Revolutionary party (A) on top with 207,637 votes. The Communist strength was impressive, and such was the prestige of Marinello that he was given an assignment as minister without portfolio in the cabinet in 1943 during Batista's first term (1941-45). Within ten years Batista had returned to power, the Popular Socialist party was outlawed, and Marinello was in hiding.

What makes this pertinent to the study is that Juan Marinello is one of Cuba's most outstanding scholars of José Martí. At the time of the Martí Centenary in 1953 Marinello wrote some words of advice to his fellow authorities on Martí. Marinello found that one of the main faults with the many scholars writing on the Apostle was that they spent so much time memorizing his sayings that these began to have an autonomous life of their own and to lose the reality of the situation in which Martí thought and spoke them. He said:

This is the reason why we have many Martians who tinkle like little bells in ecstasy before the surpassing beauty with which Martí writes upon the indispensable equality of all Cubans, but who, in their daily life discriminate against and offend our Negro population. This is the case of well-known devotees of Martí, punctilious experts in the most abstruse

detail of his body of ideas and of the utmost shading of his style, who although applauding vigorously the originality and elegant strength with which their hero rises against the imperialist penetration of the United States, continue to live in the shadow of that intervention and even persecute those who, inspired by Martí, denounce and fight it.[63]

He said that there were many "anti-Martiano Martianos" of this type, and that it was his fervent hope that none of them would be called upon to speak during the Centenary.

Marinello maintained that it was necessary to make sure that the Centenary would suppress the habitual falsifications of Martí sentiment. He was referring in this instance, he said, to the clergy who larded their sermons and comments with quotations from Martí. This, he asserted, was "as disloyal as to wish to attribute Marxist thought to our man." He continued:

To destroy such falsifications it would be enough to collect as much as Martí said—and he said a great deal—against teaching by religious interests . . . and [to show] how much he differed, and he differed very much, directly and indirectly, from the basic conceptions of Karl Marx.

Marinello lamented the fact that misstatements about Martí could be made with such impunity by persons who found whatever they wanted to say in him. Marinello pointed out how Martí was neglected for a long time in Cuba, first receiving his recognition in other countries of the Americas, then Spain, and last of all in Cuba. During the Centenary he showed how Martí was honored in Washington and Moscow, adding, "Of course, in Washington it was [only] to deny him his major significance as a liberator, and in Moscow to grant him his correct stature." He then praised the Russian writer Ilya Ehrenburg's writings on Martí.[64]

Marinello had some advice for Cuban writers on how best to fulfill the Martí ideal in the matter of writing. He said that they should follow Martí's cardinal teaching, which was to give unlimited rein to what was personal and spontaneous within themselves, resist submission to formulas, to live as a part of collective society, to submerge themselves in traditional sources as the only way to overcome them, and to make the office of writing a daily duty and inexhaustible service. In this way writers on Martí could pay their best homage to

him on the occasion of his Centenary. Marinello maintained that it was the duty of the intellectual to take part in the political struggle to gain freedom from economic slavery to the United States.[65] Although Marinello was objective in not trying to make a Marxist out of Martí, he ignored, nevertheless, the writings of the Apostle that were favorable to the United States.

AMERICAN SAILORS AND THE MARTÍ MONUMENT

Two sailors of the United States Navy on leave for a holiday in Havana in 1949 unwittingly furnished the Cuban Communits first-class ammunition in their sniping campaign against Yankee imperialism. The American sailors, to the discredit of their uniforms and to Martí, in a drunken spree urinated on the Apostle's statue in Central Park, and then climbed to the top. One of the sailors audaciously sat on Martí's shoulders. Unappreciative of this feat of agility, an indignant crowd of Cubans quickly gathered. Swift retribution would undoubtedly have been exacted if at that moment local authorities had not opportunely arrived and carried the rascals away. The fully justified wrath of the Cubans began to pour down on the heads of the chastened and bewildered sailors, who were sent to the brig. Extremists called for immediate execution of the hapless sailors.[66]

The Communists, whose newspapers oddly enough had photographers present just as the incident occurred, said, in effect, that this was the crowning insult to a long line of imperialist injuries. The Communist press, notably *Noticias de Hoy,* howled with indignation and wrath. Juan Marinello wrote, "The offense committed by these devils dressed as sailors is the same as that which is instigated daily against Cuba by the imperialists."[67]

Other manifestations of public opinion, however, came to the rescue of the sailors. One Cuban pointed out that just prior to the incident some Cubans themselves had profaned the memory of Martí without nearly so great a furor from the public. In one instance a member of the National Police had thrown stones at a bust of Martí in Havana, but his only punishment was to receive suspension for a few days. In addition, shortly thereafter a group of hoodlums had held an early-morning picnic on the steps leading up to the bust of Martí in Havana, scattering the greasy remains of meat, empty wine bottles,

and also urinating on the spot. Many other instances of this nature, according to the writer, had occurred in the Republic.[68]

Another Cuban, Jesús Fernández Lamas, took advantage of the incident of the sailors to philosophize. He suggested that the exaggerated love that Martí's followers held for their idol had caused them to run the risk of falling into the excesses of fanatics of other religions. Fernández pointed out that one of the prime virtues of Martí was a deep capacity for forgiveness, and in that respect he deeply identified himself with the patriot. He said:

As for me, as in every pure Martian, the body [of Martí] has entered the tomb, and my spirit has been blended with his. There is a dead man in Santa Efigenia [the cemetery where Martí is buried] that has been born in the spirit of many Cubans.[69]

Therefore the writer was deeply disturbed about the incident, and in the silence of meditation he asked Martí what he should do or think about what had happened. He found that Martí "smiled in a patriarchical way, and looking at me with his brown eyes full of sadness, like candles in agony, said to me: 'Do not hate, nor ever provoke useless quarrels; clasp to your breast all those whose hearts are neither clean nor strong.'" In a forgiving mood the thought occurred to this Cuban that perhaps the young American sailors had actually awakened the Cubans to an appreciation of Martí.

Although the incident was reprehensible to Gonzalo de Quesada y Miranda, he pointed out that the statue itself had been in an abandoned state for a long time.[70] The Academy of History of Cuba subsequently passed a resolution urging the President of the Republic to take the necessary action to make sure that all the monuments of the nation would be given better care. In addition, local distributors of an American automobile firm established a $500 scholarship at the summer school of the University of Havana for Americans who wanted to come to Cuba to study the life of Martí.[71] The American ambassador to Cuba, fervently hoping to lay the matter to rest, placed a wreath of flowers at the base of the statue.[72] Relations between the hospitable city of Havana and the United States Navy were fully restored when a delegation of sailors also placed a wreath of flowers on the statue. In the face of expressions of responsible opinion on

the incident, the Communist attack, as well as that of the other extremists, gradually was dissipated.

COMMUNISTS IN THE MARTÍ CENTENARY

The Communist front bided its time, waiting for the Martí Centenary to use the personality and writings of Martí to make an assault on the government of President Batista, the United States, the Roman Catholic Church, and the upper classes in Cuba. Editorialized *La Ultima Hora*:

During this year of 1953 José Martí will be undergoing incessant re-examination in our island. Although insincere voices will sound off to deny him, and the writers for profit merely cheapen him, the compelling teachings of Martí will float upon the dirty seas to show their clean light. And from this re-examination, however much some may wish to avoid it, the healthy forces of the people will secure the purification of their most progressive convictions. Because Martí is all in all a great revolutionary spirit watching over Cuba and our America, he is an inducement to patriotic rebellion whose influence no honest conscience can avoid reflecting upon.[73]

The editorial then charged that there were men in Cuba facing the Centennial year who had upon themselves the tremendous responsibility of having violated all of its republican institutions, of having disordered the nation, created a national climate of indignation and a lack of confidence, and who had set up the military over the civil, all the opposite of what Martí had wanted for the Republic. It asked whether these men would praise Martí and at the same time link Cuban destiny with a nearby powerful neighbor who despised it (Martí's phrase), and yet wanted "to drag Cubans to die in distant peninsulas [Korea] where imperialist hucksters without a conscience wanted by blood and fire to keep an Asiatic people from marking out its own political direction." It called for a return to constitutional government, and ended by quoting Martí in an exhortation to all Cubans, "Unification is the word for the day."

The imperialist theme was worked up into other articles by writers for the January, 1953, issue of *La Ultima Hora*, such as those by Sergio Aguirre, Carlos Rafael Rodríguez, Jorge Castellanos, and Jacinto Torras. These writers frequently mentioned Martí's "Vin-

dication of Cuba" article against the United States, as well as the overworked phrase of the Apostle, "I have lived in the monster's den and I know its ways." The incident of the American sailors was revived by *La Ultima Hora*, which printed a page of headlines of the event. In addition Martí's article on the Haymarket Massacre was reprinted under the new orientation, "The Assassination of the Italians." So that the Roman Catholic Church would not feel neglected, Martí's "Hombre del campo" was reproduced in its entirety.

To reprove the wealthy classes one writer noted that Martí was always without money, pointing out that the Apostle had written to his friend Manuel Mercado in Mexico seven different times between 1877 and 1889 asking for loans.[74] This is a touching example of the extremes to which Marxist scholarship will go, even though the argument is not very convincing.

No one can deny that these Communist writers, from Marinello to the lesser hewers, were all hacking out a familiar line—anti-Yankee imperialism, anti-Roman Catholicism, antiwealth, and propoverty—*ad nauseam* in their use of Martí. Interestingly enough none of them seemed to show that "spontaneity and resistance to formula" attributed to Martí that Marinello called for from writers on Martí during the Centenary. They appeared to form part of the very group that Marinello was hoping would not be asked to speak during the Centenary, parroting sayings of Martí that have, indeed, taken on an autonomous life of their own far from the situation in which Martí thought and spoke them.

Martí—Symbol of Political Reform

Martí's concept of the future Republic was that of a government run by devoted patriots supported by an enlightened electorate. Although he idealized that Republic, he had his feet on the ground when he wrote on the subject of reform: "A good government is constituted when, unhindered by the conviction of human infallibility, it includes only useful reforms in its base."[75]

Martí has frequently been cited by reformers as the model to follow for good government in Cuba. Two political parties, the Cuban People's party (Orthodox), and the Havana Municipal party, and a

so-called political "movement" have been chosen to illustrate the use of Martí's name and ideals as symbols for crusades for better government. As will be seen, the reformers have not fared very well. The record of their lack of accomplishment corroborates the charge that "Cuba is not the Republic of which Martí dreamed." Perhaps the answer to their failure lies in another statement by the Apostle, who warned: "All the good will of a governor will be useless if the will of the governed does not second it with vigor and intelligence."[76]

THE CUBAN PEOPLE'S PARTY (ORTHODOX)

The political party in Cuba that seemed embryonically best to represent the ideals of José Martí was the Cuban People's party (Orthodox). It is impossible to discuss the party without considering the man who in essence was the party, Senator Eduardo R. Chibás. Chibás was one of the student leaders in the fight against Machado in the 1930's, who fervently supported the political ideal of the university professor Ramón Grau San Martín. After Chibás broke with Grau in 1946, the Cuban People's party (Orthodox) was founded. Chibás explained the establishment of the party in this way:

The orthodox movement was born to save Cuba in an unusual moment in history. Grau was preparing for re-election. Sinecures, election deals, bribery, and violence prevailed in the political atmosphere; public affairs were ruled by irresponsibility, incompetence, and avarice; corruption predominated in the labor movement through labor leaders imposed by the government; greed, fraud, contraband, and illicit business characterized the official administration.[77]

Chibás said that the party arose in 1947 as a hope for the future of Cuba, not merely as a circumstance or the capricious work of a party chieftain. He said that Grau's party had entered into a period of decadence and political prostitution. With the motto of "Vergüenza contra Dinero" ("Honor versus Money"), the party "mobilized the country in fifteen days." The term "Orthodox" was added after the name of the party as the answer to the Cuban Revolutionary party's "Authentic," a kind of self-sealing approval. Although Chibás lost to Prío in the 1948 elections, the party managed to capture over 300,000 votes and asserted that it had gained the sympathy of the man in the street, the country, the factory, and the school.

The political methodology of the party consisted in a strident and aggressive attack on malefactors in the government, mainly through the broadcasts and publications of Chibás. He wrote:

The outcry and intransigence of the Cuban People's party (O) have formed part of its battle tactics, a sure way of breaking down the indifference and skepticism reigning in many of the healthy sections of the population. . . . This intransigence has had no other target than administrative corruption, political cabals, palace and street gangsterism, and all the other vices that corrode national public life.

When the party was organized it was necessary to present a program to the Superior Electoral Tribunal (a government body that certifies political parties). Although Martí is not often cited directly in the program, it is obvious that in many respects the leaders of the Cuban People's party (O) were consciously or unconsciously following many of the Apostle's exhortations.

The party platform characterized the situation in Cuba at that time as being one in which the nation had still not achieved its economic independence, saying, "Political liberty is possible only when it is accompanied by economic independence." This was, of course, one of Martí's main themes. In addition the platform noted that the natural resources of Cuba remained almost unexploited because of governmental neglect, and that technological advancement and education in agriculture had not taken place.

The platform declared that in national politics the vices and corruptions of Spanish colonialism still existed. It read:

Personalism and opportunism take the place of collective ideals, and personal interests conspire against the interests of the group as a whole. The lack of honesty weakens the government of the country, resulting in deception of the citizenry and the growing separation between government and the people.

The bureaucracy was found to be so overwhelmingly obstructive that it had resulted in administrative chaos. Compare these statements with Martí's writings on the Spanish bureaucracy in Cuba and the need to cleanse Cuba "like the Augean stables."

Among the points in its program for the economic betterment of the nation, the Cuban People's party (O) listed several that are ob-

viously reflections of Martí's teachings. It called for resolving the dramatic contradiction between Cuba's political independence and its economic dependence, and for the diversification and expansion of agricultural production through elimination of the one-crop economy based on sugar. Expanding the Martí thesis of the high honor to be accredited to the tiller of the soil, the party called for an end to *latifundismo* (large landed estates), urged the enforced use of idle lands, and the establishment of a plan to rescue the masses of *guajiros* (countryfolk) who were living in servitude. It insisted upon the need for contracts to protect the farmers, the organization of cooperatives, irrigation, rural electrification, protection of the farmer against exploitation by middlemen, a sound system of government credit, and economic assistance to compensate for risks in agriculture.

The platform reflected Martí's respect for the man who worked with his hands in its demands for bettering the living conditions of the majority of the inhabitants of Cuba, the need for a just wage, and plans to avoid unemployment. In the field of education the party declared that reliance on theory and imitation had retarded the educational process in Cuba (a favorite theme of Martí's). The party urged education for all of Cuba's children, plus the elimination of illiteracy at all ages. The platform read:

The Cuban People's party believes that illiteracy constitutes a defect in society and a blemish on the State. Illiteracy is the negation of democracy, which does not tolerate excluded groups.

To combat the high rate of illiteracy the party called for improved educational opportunities, especially in rural areas.

The party also insisted upon thoroughgoing reform in the Ministry of Education, inculcation of respect for moral values in the face of overwhelming adulation for materialism, obligatory school attendance, and a school lunch program. It envisioned cultural missions, public libraries, traveling museums for the general advancement of the populace, and increases in teachers' salaries.

Among numerous points in the party platform on social and political reform some are typically Martian, such as the need for a civil service system, an end to racial discrimination, adherence to the constitutional separation of church and state, freedom of the press

and free circulation of ideas, special care for children, prison reform, reforestation, and subordination of the armed forces to civil authority.

In foreign policy the Cuban People's party (O) declared unanimously at one of its national assemblies that the party would decidedly back the cause of democracy and free determination of peoples everywhere in the world, especially in the Americas. The party stated that it would "resolutely combat all tyrants, from Stalin to Trujillo, from Franco to Perón." Compare this with Martí's statement that the fight to free Cuba was the fight to maintain human liberty in all Hispanic America.

Characteristic of the polarization of the party leaders' attitude toward the very right and the very wrong was the stand agreed upon unanimously in 1951 by the National Executive Council of the party. In calling for the support of the democracies in world affairs it made this statement:

The dramatically established dilemma of this epoch has well-defined outlines: we must choose between democracy, a system of government that bases its vitality on the consent of the governed, and Communism, which maintains itself in power, suffocating all dissent without permitting any kind of public expression.

By posing the choice between such strict alternatives the party seemed to be ignoring the fact that a majority of the Latin American governments did not have at that time (and do not now have) governments that responded to either of those choices.

The party stoutly maintained that the renewal of the Monroe Doctrine under the Río de Janeiro Pact of Hemisphere Defense should be a matter for multilateral action as opposed to the "imperialist risk" from the United States. Although the party pledged its support to the United Nations on the basis of strict equality of nations, it reserved its cooperation and solidarity for only those Latin American nations that were "positively democratic."

Strange contradictions seem to arise from these stands. Apparently the United States was to be rigidly proscribed from any imperialist meddlings in the affairs of the Latin American nations, but Cuba under the control of the Cuban People's party (O) was to be left free to "combat all tyrants, from . . . Trujillo . . . to Perón." Either this

meant direct aggression, indirect intervention, or both, or else must be dismissed as well-meaning but ineffective expressions of sympathy toward suppressed democratic elements in Latin American dictatorships.

In pointedly omitting a pledge of cooperation with the Organization of American States, but calling for participation in the United Nations, the party found itself faced with the unusual situation of advocating dealing with each nation as an equal in a world organization but not in a regional one. Although it is Cuba's prerogative not to belong to any organization if it pleases, the administration of a foreign policy, even when not consistent, should make sense. In this distinction between the United Nations and the Organization of American States the party's inconsistency just did not seem clear.

One of the salient features of Chibás' program for the improvement of government in Cuba lay in an uncompromising campaign against all forms of government corruption, which Chibás maintained was a direct inheritance from the Spanish colony. In this respect he directly linked himself with Martí, saying,

Martí was radically irreconcilable toward anything that might imply trafficking with colonial vices. . . . We aspire to wipe out all pollution from national politics, the same with the new as well as with the old. . . . It is not our fault that there is so much corruption, just as it is not the fault of the broom that filth exists. When the old parties decay, the people have the right to manifest themselves through a new party.

One of the stands that the party marked out in a national assembly in 1950 was an unrelenting refusal to make concessions toward cooperating with any other party then existing in Cuba. In this Chibás asserted that his party was imitating the "intransigence of Martí" in adopting a heroic line of political independence before all other parties. The comparison is somewhat farfetched. The purpose of Martí's Cuban Revolutionary party was to overthrow the Spanish regime, and that of the Autonomists was only a certain amount of independence for Cuba. There was hardly any contact between the two or basis for agreement. Apparently Chibás, in seeing corruption all around him in other political parties, assumed that any kind of compromise meant contamination. Perhaps at the time it seemed to Chibás that the Cuban People's party (O) and the other political

parties of Cuba were even farther apart than the parties of Martí's day, but the determined stand against cooperation with other power forces seems to indicate that Chibás felt that his party had a monopoly on virtue precluding the appearance of honest elements in other parties.

It is imperative, however, that honest groups in every party should strive through collective effort toward compromise on differences for the greater good or else individually face disaster. Martí realized the need for compromise when he once said, "One must do at each moment that which is necessary."[78]

At any rate the crusade against vice became the shining hallmark of the Cuban People's party (O) with a quotation from Martí to point out the party's orientation. It read:

The rascals have made it fashionable to make fun of those who refuse to become knaves. It is urgent now, in these times of show-window politics, to stop being ashamed of being honest. Decency must be brought into style and shamelessness banished.[79]

Chibás selected for his attack former Presidents Batista and Grau; President Prío and his brother Antonio, Minister of the Treasury; José Manuel Alemán, Minister of Education under Grau; and Aureliano Sánchez Arango, Minister of Education under Prío. All were accused of having robbed millions of dollars from the Treasury. Chibás did not limit himself to vague charges of peculation, but made specific references to extensive properties owned by these politicians as a consequence of their holding office.[80]

The most notorious of the accusations was what has come to be known in Cuba as "Case 82." It was the charge presented to the Supreme Court in 1950 by Pelayo Cuervo Navarro, a senator and leader of the Cuban People's party (O), that embezzlement during the administration of President Grau amounted to the astounding figure of $174 million. The accusation stated that this sum was secured by raids on retirement pension funds, the Ministries of Education and Public Works, and the Treasury itself. Case 82 has been bandied around the courts, but up to mid-1957 no one had been brought to justice. A newspaper report in January, 1957, noted that the brief of 15,600 numbered pages had been turned over to the

Havana district attorney.[81] The assassination of Pelayo Cuervo by unknown hands in March, 1957, added another episode to the case.[82]

To dramatize his absolute inconformity with government corruption (he himself spent a large inheritance from his father in the fight for clean government), Chibás shot himself in October, 1951, at the end of one of his famous Sunday night radio programs. He died several weeks later.

His followers were crushed. Elections for President were to be held in 1952, and surveys of public opinion had placed Chibás far ahead of any other candidate. The mantle of succession fell on Roberto Agramonte, the son of a prominent patriot who had been a friend of Martí. In spite of the fact that Agramonte, a professor of sociology at the University of Havana, was not as spectacular a candidate as Chibás, the general feeling was that he would win the elections by riding the wave of enthusiasm engendered by the campaigning of Chibás. Batista's sudden seizure of power in March, 1952, changed the political hopes of the Cuban People's party (O). Since that time the party has been rent asunder by differences among its leaders.

Manuel Bisbé, a professor of Greek at the University of Havana and the unsuccessful candidate of the Cuban People's party (O) for mayor of Havana in 1950, maintained, however, that once democracy returned to Cuba the party would be reunited. He insisted in an interview that the disagreement was over tactics and not program, that the main body of the organization and its offshoots were dedicated above all to the principle of honesty in government. Bisbé affirmed that peculation was the basic problem of Cuban government; that it had its roots in Spanish tradition and the administration of Charles E. Magoon during the American occupation of Cuba. Bisbé traced the fight against corruption mainly to two forerunners of honest government, José Martí and Juan José Maza y Artola, a senator in the early years of the Republic and later leader of the Nationalist party.[83] Chibás, according to Bisbé, was their successor. Bisbé stated that Martí was alive in the Cuban conscience; that it was the duty of the Cuban People's party to make him felt.

Bisbé was asked whether the death of Chibás and the resulting splintering of the party was an indication that Latins follow men and not parties. He answered that this was true, that the people do not

respond to programs but to a leader. He added, however, that the *caudillo* type that drew the support of Latin Americans in the nineteenth century had since been somewhat refined. Reliance upon a leader rather than a program, in Bisbé's opinion, makes it that much more imperative that the leader serve as an impeccably honest example. Chibás, he felt, met that standard.

The professor of Greek explained the refusal of the Cuban People's party (O) to cooperate with other parties as an attempt to force a return to a two-party system in the hope that this would lead to party responsibility and promote democracy in Cuba. He felt that this would have been accomplished if fair elections had been held in 1952.[84]

In a joint interview with Roberto Agramonte and Bisbé, the former presidential candidate reaffirmed Bisbé's point that Cuba's ills stemmed mostly from one base, the colonial residue of corruption in government. "What we need," said Agramonte, "is a revolution to bring about the fulfillment of the law." Agramonte cited two anecdotes to show the contrast in Cuban politics then with the times of Martí. Alemán is alleged to have made his raids on public funds while Minister of Education by the simple means of stuffing suitcases full of money and carrying them off to Miami for safekeeping.[85] Agramonte contrasted that episode with the story told by a Cuban patriot of having met Martí carrying his suitcase in New York. When asked why he did not take a carriage, Martí is said to have replied that the money that he could save by walking could be used for the Cuban Revolution.

Bisbé added that one of the greatest evils in Cuba was the National Lottery operated by the government. The Lottery is publicly justified as income for charitable organizations, which do receive a share of the funds, but Bisbé declared that much of the money was used by the President to buy Congress. Bisbé asserted that the lottery should be eliminated from the Cuban social and political scene. (Martí was against a lottery on the grounds that a philosophy based upon getting something for nothing undermines national character.)[86]

Bisbé, declaring that the average Cuban really does believe in honesty, dignity, and democracy, hoped that a new generation would

assert a civic conscience. He pointed out that in the recent past, he and Salvador Massip, a Cuban geographer and dean of the Faculty of Letters and Sciences at the University of Havana, had been detained by the police for questioning on their political activities. Bisbé said, "They can take away our jobs, and they have, but they can not take away our dignity. We believe it is our duty in this respect to bring the university to politics, and not politics to the university."[87]

In view of the tendency of the Cuban populace to identify itself with leaders and not programs, and the differences among its leaders, the Cuban People's party (O) may serve only as a monument to the memory of Eduardo R. Chibás. What is certain, however, is that if Cuba is ever to enjoy good government, a party, if not with that name, at least dominated by the principles that Chibás and his followers expounded, and another leader must arise to capture the imagination and the backing of the honest elements of society.

FREE ORTHODOXY

When a Latin American politician of influence no longer finds himself in conformity with his party he is apt not to join another major group, but rather to establish himself either in a new party, or at least in a new "movement." An example of this in Cuba is Carlos Márquez Sterling, who left the Cuban People's party (O) to create what he called the Ortodoxia Libre (Free Orthodoxy). Under this somewhat paradoxical label Márquez Sterling preferred to adopt a reserved but articulate opposition to all other political parties. As president of the Constituent Assembly for the Constitution of 1940, as the grandson of the prominent journalist, Adolph Márquez Sterling, a friend of Martí, and as a writer of several biographies of Martí, Márquez Sterling, the leader of the Free Orthodoxy, is of particular interest to this study.

When Márquez Sterling was accused of being an isolationist in party affairs in 1950 and a dweller in an ivory tower, he answered his critics by quoting Martí, who contrasted fickle spirits and those who stuck to their principles. Márquez Sterling asserted that he was one of the latter. He found that in the political history of Cuba the one point that really stood out was the reliance upon a *caudillo* as an expression of the Cuban intellect, both by liberals and by conserva-

tives. For the majority, according to Márquez Sterling, it was much easier to rely on the efforts of someone else than on oneself.

Márquez Sterling wrote that the majority of the political parties of Cuba had no other aim except to gain power in order to distribute among themselves jobs on the government payroll and to benefit from corruption in the National Lottery. He saw that the best party would be the one that would be based on cleaning out rotten politics. He said: "In the midst of the disunion that grips the country and casts a shadow over the present, the Republic is a myth, and political parties a public calamity."[88]

Referring to Cuban politics as being attacked by "infantile paralysis," he said that the supreme lesson to be learned from them was that the disdain for the law and collective effort, individual greed, and embezzlement from the government had created a serious moral bankruptcy in the nation. He then warned against the appearance of a new Hannibal who might rise up to take over the nation. In the same year he declared that what was most needed was a "generous and creative political approach like that of José Martí's."[89] Two years later Márquez Sterling was proved right, only the Cuban Hannibal arrived with tanks and not elephants.

In 1956 Márquez Sterling declared that he did not see any immediate prospect for the Free Orthodoxy to become a full-fledged political party, but that if he ever should have any influence in the political economy of the nation he would institute a public works program similar to the Works Progress Administration of Franklin D. Roosevelt. Referring to the estimate of one million unemployed in Cuba he said, "There is no worse cause for social unrest than a man without work, and this should be taken care of immediately."[90]

Márquez Sterling said that in the Constitutional Assembly of 1940, over which he presided, Martí had an influence on the lawmakers, especially when they were drawing up the sections of the Constitution that had to do with labor and the family. In general, however, Márquez Sterling insists that Martí's influence is to be found in the spiritual values of liberty and democracy expressed in the document, rather than in phrasings taken directly from the Apostle.

Márquez Sterling characterized the political group that he led as a movement that had as its central orientation the proposition that a

political solution for the ills of the nation can only be reached by peaceful civic action rather than violence; that the central problem of Cuba was one of institutions and not persons. He explained that the withdrawal of his group from the Cuban People's party (O) occurred when Agramonte was imposed upon the party by the directorate. Márquez Sterling is of the opinion that Free Orthodoxy meant that all the officers were to be democratically chosen.[91]

THE MUNICIPAL PARTY OF HAVANA

A party produced as an offshoot of the Cuban People's party (O) is the Partido Municipal Habanero (Havana Municipal party), a political organization devoted to the betterment of the city government of Havana. The party owes its origin largely to a professor of history at the University of Havana, Herminio Portell-Vilá. As a member of the Cuban People's party (O) Portell-Vilá was elected to the City Council of Havana in 1950. Portell-Vilá wrote that he fought against the Batista-dominated city administration, which he found to be inept, arbitrary, and corrupt. Each councilman, in addition to his salary, was given more than $1,000 a month for office expenses for administering to the welfare of the councilman's constituents. Portell-Vilá asserted that he filled these positions with persons of flesh and blood, and did not take part in the "immoral practice of considering the payroll as a regular income of the councilman."[92]

Every Sunday Portell-Vilá broadcast a program devoted to informing the citizens of Havana about the activities of their city government. When Batista came to power in 1952 Portell-Vilá was required, along with other councilmen, to take an oath of loyalty to the new regime. He refused to do so, and accordingly was denied entrance to his seat in the Council by a guard armed with a submachine gun. At this time further disenchantment came with the "so-called civic societies" and his constituents in general who failed to protest against the violent manner in which he was dislodged from office. Portell-Vilá discovered that the Cuban People's party (O), in addition to the contribution it received from his regular salary, also expected a slice of his office expenses. Portell-Vilá considered that this money was to go to the office staff itself and not to the party. He wrote:

Disillusionment caused me to found the Havana Municipal party, constituted by more than a thousand citizens of Havana who understood that the right that we Cubans have to organize politically does not depend upon the government of the day and that it even constitutes a duty.[93]

In spite of a vigorous campaign by radio, press, and door-to-door visits, members of Portell-Vilá's party were able to secure only 551 registrations while more than 100,000 citizens of voting age in Havana remained unaffiliated with any party. He declared:

We began to work in search of public opinion, a public opinion that was discouraged, confused, hardly disposed to show any responsibility, and largely uninformed about its rights and its duties as voters, and reluctant to exercise or to fulfill either.[94]

A requirement of the electoral law of Havana stipulated that a registration center for each party be set up in each of the city's forty-three districts. Portell-Vilá wrote that day after day, from door to door, he went in search of places where he could establish local headquarters, and sometimes the door was slammed in his face, "as if I were proposing to establish a lottery, a house of prostitution, or a marijuana shop."[95] He found that the refusal was sometimes accompanied by the most specious and absurd reasoning, and that it was evident that the majority of the citizens visited had no idea what was meant by the establishment of a party registration locale.

When attempting to recruit persons to man the registration centers Portell-Vilá's experience was just as disheartening. Although he discovered a multitude of persons contrary to the regime in power, "their opposition did not reach the extreme of standing up against the dictatorship or of working for a proposition for good government." He wrote:

How many ridiculous excuses! How many flights of the imagination and how much hypocrisy to hide civic weakness and to flee all responsibility. It is just in this way that colonial despotism is going to last for such a long time among us.

Each citizen of voting age in Cuba (prior to Castro) was issued a voter's *cédula* (identification booklet), which is an official document to permit him to vote. In order to avoid standing in line at the

polls on election day many citizens perferred to turn over their cedulas to others in return for varying sums of money, and the recipient did the voting for them. Portell-Vilá wrote that when it became apparent that the so-called "good elements" of the population were not going to respond to registration in his party, a dealer in cedulas offered to sell him 10,000 party affiliations from his files! After he refused Portell-Vilá asserted that the man then asked him in astonishment if he really thought that he could get the people to undertake honest registration.[96]

Portell-Vilá reported numerous instances of the use of a voter's cedula for multiple registration. He showed that Eliodoro Acosta Guzmán, with voter's registration number 296883, "appears registered in the Democratic party with affiliation No. 1559; in the Radical Union party, four times, with numbers, 36, 39, 896, and 977; and in the Progressive Action party, twice more with numbers 1165 and 2478."[97] The professor of history then asked how it was possible for there to be a movement for making Cuban politics decent when the first step seemed to be the need to secure voters' cedulas and to twist population statistics to inflate the number of affiliations. Portell-Vilá believes that none of the presidents of Cuba have found the way to the national integrity that was desired so much by Martí, Céspedes, Maceo, and other early patriots. He declared:

Bad governors are the product of an incompetent, unthinking, egotistical, and indifferent electorate that feels a kind of patriotism of their own, one that does not require great sacrifices of well-being and comfort.[98]

Portell-Vilá thinks that good government is impossible for one person or a small group to achieve, that it is the work of a whole people who must want it. Unlike Bisbé, he came to the reluctant conclusion that Cuba has dictatorships and constitutional masquerades simply because that is the way that the majority of the Cuban people want it.[99]

The platform of the Havana Municipal party struck at some of the evils in the government of Havana. It called for the elimination of the notorious "botellas" ("bottles"), salaried officials whose duties are more apparent than real. Guarantees against the spoils system were demanded on the behalf of all honest and capable employees.

Compare Martí's indignation at an instance of the spoils system in the United States. He wrote:

There, in our native land, we are not going to do things in this way, we are not going to keep men corrupted by the lottery of public employment, putting them in an office from which they will be ejected at the end of four years! There we will see that the best people occupy positions of public service, assuring them that merit and not favor will keep them in office and that the disease of the bureaucrats will not corrupt the life-blood of the republic![100]

The platform of Portell-Vilá's party urged a credit union to free government servants from flagrant usury, a serious problem in Cuba. For instance, one money-lender in Havana was very successful in furnishing loans on automobiles, although his interest rate by the end of one year was 80 per cent of the principal.

Portell-Vilá's party platform urged improved accounting methods for public funds and publication of income and expenditures.

His demand for a modern building for the Municipal Library of Havana illuminates what is perhaps one of the most outstanding sorrows of a city that boasts some of the most modern and elegant buildings in Latin America. Guides to the National Capitol are quick to point out that the dome is the third highest in the world, but this height is meaningless when legislators are disinclined to match it by raising up the cultural level of the Cuban citizenry.

Although a magnificent building dedicated to José Martí has been constructed in the Plaza Cívica to replace the picturesque but creaking facilities of the National Library, the Municipal Library of Havana occupied a depressing locale, dimly lighted, and inadequately provided with books and staff, in spite of efforts by the director, Fermín Peraza Sarausa, to make improvements. Some years ago the City Council appropriated funds for a new building, but somehow the money was dissipated before construction began. Now the Cuban populace sarcastically refers to Trillo Park, where the building should have been, as "The Trillo Library."

As in all official public libraries in Cuba (and most of Latin America, as a matter of fact), the custom prevails of forbidding the withdrawal of books for home use.[101] Nothing could be further from the aspirations of José Martí, who once wrote glowingly of the thrill

it gave him to see the Public Library of New York City circulating books for use away from the building.[102]

Another important plank in the platform of the Havana Municipal party was the one calling for a campaign against illiteracy through the coordination of the efforts of schools, workshops, factories, businesses, parents, schoolteachers, and, in fact, the entire citizenry.

Did the Havana Municipal party manage to bring about any reforms or achieve any of its goals in the brief time (1950-52) that it was represented in the City Council of Havana? The party claims some success, such as the erection of a new school building. In addition the reformers take credit for an unrelenting campaign to secure a new municipal hospital and an improvement in the water supply, both projects now close to realization.

After withdrawing from elections in 1953, Portell-Vilá concluded on the future of the party:

The Havana Municipal party will continue as an orienting force for public opinion and will act vigorously against usurpers and usurers of every ilk; but concerning elections it will wait until the people wake up from their degeneration and decide to act. If this happens while its organizers and directors, who will never relax in their civic crusade, are still alive, so much the better; if not, others will come who will succeed in taking advantage of that popular backing to save Cuba.[103]

The founder of the party once declared that Martí was not used as a symbol by his organization because misuse of the patriot was so widespread among other political parties in Cuba that it would seem like a mockery to name him.[104] The fact is, however, that the Havana Municipal party in its platform and its campaign for better government represented the ideals of Martí, specifically in regard to the elimination of usury, the spoils system, illiteracy, and inadequate library facilities, and generally in its frequently reiterated ideals of an honest and sound citizenry backing an equally honest and sound government.

Conclusions

This in essence has been a bird's-eye view of political parties in Cuba and the opinions of some of their leaders in the employment

of Martí as a political symbol. Although there are minor variations and themes, the use of Martí as a political symbol can be considered in two major categories. For those who are out of power Martí's extensive writings on morality are used as a weapon against corruption by the party in charge of the government. For those in power Martí's extensive writings on brotherly love, forgiveness, and unity for the good of all are employed to rebuke the clamorous criticism of politicians and parties on the sidelines. Once in power those who were on the outside switch emphasis in their use of Martí's writings from morality to unity. Thus Martí is the perfect tool to vindicate the split morality-versus-corruption personality of many of the Cuban politicians who have gained high office.

The crisis of Cuban politics was, is, and will be a moral one. Cubans recognize this. They see that corruption is rooted deep in Spanish colonial history, but more time is spent explaining its origin as an almost congenital disease than in any real attempt to progress in its eradication. Men and parties that have attempted reforms in line with Martí's teachings have not achieved much success. Part of the difficulty lies in the Cuban attitude of looking upon corruption in government in a spirit of *relajo* (a tendency toward making light of any situation). Some day the Cubans will have to confront the fact, however, that what is now comfortably referred to as a Spanish trait has become an essentially Cuban trait.

The extent of corruption in government in Cuba as a lack of the implementation of Martí's ideals has not been examined in a spirit of a North American "holier-than-thou" attitude. Although numerous instances of anti-American sentiment have been associated with the name of Martí, no desire for returning the compliment is made here. Any criticism of Cuban politics expressed or implied has been much more acrimoniously elaborated upon by the Cubans themselves. This in itself is a very good sign. In addition there is hope for the future, if the lessons of history count for anything, in that other nations have passed through periods of notorious graft on a wide scale, such as during the administration of President Ulysses S. Grant in the United States, and have then gone on to see honest administrations. Some of the other Latin American nations, such as Uruguay, Costa Rica, and Mexico have lately experienced governments that

have been relatively free from corruption. The complete and permanent impact of Castro and the establishment of communism in Cuba, to be examined in Chapter Nine, remains to be seen. The elimination of corruption and graft in government has been accomplished to some extent by the Castro reformers, but at a horrendous cost to life, liberty, and property.

Chapter 8

THE PEOPLE SPEAK

*F*ROM THE VIEWPOINT of politics it is clear that in many respects Cuba has not achieved the romantically democratic splendor that José Martí dreamed of for his Republic. Other areas of Cuban society were also examined to see whether Martí's ideals had been carried out up to 1957. In view of the Apostle's often reiterated, but not consistent, declarations of his identification with the common man, this chapter has included statements by union leaders to find to what extent labor has identified itself with its alleged champion. As will be seen, labor paid homage to Martí, but only superficially.

In consideration of Martí's two favorite occupations, education and journalism, this chapter has also examined statements by newspaper men and teachers as an assessment of their attitudes toward the fulfillment of Martí's ideals. As will be seen, neither of these professions fully represent Martian aspirations.

Finally, informal conversations with Cubans at various levels of society in Havana have been reported. These are impressions of Martí by persons speaking for themselves rather than as representatives of special groups. The study will show that the consensus of these views is that Cuba has not achieved Martí's ideal Republic.

Martí as Viewed by Labor Leaders

Since the downfall of Gerardo Machado in 1933 the labor movement in Cuba, organized as the Confederación de Trabajadores de Cuba (the Cuban Confederation of Workers, usually referred to as the CTC) has enjoyed a period of extensive growth. By 1944 that

expansion was completely dominated by the Popular Socialist party Communists. During the period 1946 to 1947 a fierce struggle ensued between a group of labor leaders sponsored by President Ramón Grau San Martín in the Workers' Commission of the Cuban Revolutionary party (A), and the Communists, who finally lost. Eusebio Mujal Barniol took over as secretary general of the CTC. By 1956 membership in the Confederation reached more than one million, distributed among thirty-three groups of workers. Battles continue to take place among factions within the unions. The Communists in 1957 claimed some twenty thousand members.[1] By 1962 they were again in control.

In the period of Communist influence and domination roughly lasting from 1937 to 1947, the use of Martí as a symbol in patriotic demonstrations was avoided. Such symbolism, according to one labor leader, Jesús Artigas, was considered by the Communists to detract from the international character of solidarity among workers.[2] (If true, this indicates that the Communists overlooked the "international aspects" of Martí's personality and philosophy.)

Artigas asserted that after the end of Communist domination of labor in 1947 Martí became a symbol in workers' unions, that tribute was always offered to the Apostle in national reunions of the CTC, and that there was a Martian Corner in the National Palace of Workers. Labor unions in Cuba did not, however, according to the labor leader, make a show of flag-waving on behalf of Martí.[3]

A practical attitude toward Martí was expressed by Prisciliano Falcón Lañú, head of the sugar-workers, Cuba's largest union (four hundred thousand members in 1957). He says simply, "When we struggle for a better life, we are fulfilling Martí's objectives. When sugar brings a high price on the world market there is happiness in Cuba." Falcón asserted that the unions in his confederation celebrated January 28, Martí's birthday, although they had no program of specific action to carry out his ideas.[4]

When Fulgencio Batista returned to power in 1952 the CTC dropped its affiliation with the Cuban Revolutionary party (A), Falcón stated, "to accord with political realities." The result was the replacement of the Workers' Commission with the National Workers' Union, also headed by Mujal and blessed by the Batista administra-

tion. The CTC came to terms with Batista since its philosophy, Falcón asserted, was to accept anything that helped labor.

Bernardo García Feito is one of the few labor leaders to have written on Martí. The material for this effort originally came from his articles in the trade magazine of the telephone workers' union. The book was widely distributed among laborers in order to propagate the teachings of Martí, although not, in the opinion of its author, in a spirit of contributing to the widespread "Martimanía," highly criticized by Juan Luis Martín, the Roman Catholic writer, in the prologue to the work.[5]

Martí has not been used more by the unions, García said, because for years the movement has been split between the anarcho-syndicalists and the Communists in a struggle for control. In this atmosphere, García believes, it has not been possible to develop an ideology influenced by the lofty conceptions of Martí.[6]

Most of the labor unions have their own trade journals, which often carry a photograph of Martí on the front cover for the month of January. These magazines sometimes contain poems to the Apostle, articles about him, and pages devoted to selected Martian thoughts. In *El Bancario,* the organ of the Federation of Bank Workers, Gladys García Ramírez de Fundora, for example, wrote about Martí:

We can be proud of having been loved by the greatest man that humanity has produced. He united the clear wisdom of Socrates and that love that Jesus had for mankind. Let us honor his name, not leaving him for foreigners who respectfully pronounce his name when they have come to know his country and to write his biography, in love with the personality of our Apostle.[7]

In another labor magazine, *Reportaje Gráfico,* an editorial declared in its January, 1957, issue:

Martí is the perpetual ratification of love and goodness. For that reason the great and glorious personality of the Apostle must represent for all Cubans decorum, dignity, sacrifice, and honor. . . . Compatriots: If we are honest and grateful, let us not look upon the Apostle as just one more patriot . . . let us see him as an immense and sacred God; like a CUBAN GOD.[8]

It is a long way, however, from this exhortation to the laborer to consider Martí a "Cuban God," to what is done in reality, at least

as shown by the outward manifestations of homage paid to him in the Cuban labor movement. This is to be explained, perhaps, by the time consumed within the unions in contests for leadership and in the need of their members to direct their energies toward the daily struggle for better salaries and working conditions. The labor unions, however, probably do no more nor less in celebrating Martí than many other groups in Cuban society. One area in which the labor movement might have bettered its status in society, as well as the welfare of the nation as a whole, would have been to use its collective power to honor Martí through improving the public schools of Cuba.

Martí as an Ideal in Education

Martí's ideal of education as raising man above the level of his time, of making him an abstract of the best of all that had preceded him, was far from realization in the public school system of Cuba in 1957. The fault is not Martí's, however, according to one critic, lawyer Juan S. Alvarez Pujals, but is the result of Cuba's having done everything contrary to what the Apostle called for in education.[9] In order to assess the validity of this statement an examination was made of school activities associated with the name of Martí, statements made by students and teachers, charges of corruption in the educational system, and consideration of Martí as a symbol of revolt to the youth of Cuba.

Martí's ideas on education, according to one authority, Gonzalo de Quesada y Miranda, were already fairly well spread among Cuban teachers and school children, although officially little was done to implement them. Quesada believes that women school teachers especially appreciate Martí.[10]

Teaching of Martí in the elementary schools takes the form of presenting certain poems of the Apostle for memorization, invariably "La Rosa Blanca," reading selections from Martí's La Edad de Oro about other nations' heroes such as Simón Bolívar, and instruction in Martí's patriotic efforts in the War of Independence. Often schools have essay contests about Martí. Sometimes these contests have been sponsored by social and cultural organizations such as the women's Lyceum and Lawn Tennis Club in Havana. Each year prizes were

awarded by the club to students in the fifth, sixth, seventh, and eighth grades in all the Havana public schools for the best essay on Martí. The first prize in 1953 went to María del Carmen Valle, fifth grade, for her essay, "Why Do We Love Martí?" She wrote:

I love Martí because he knew how to die for Cuba, he knew how to face life, to love justice, and to love children and mankind. For me Martí is a second God, but a God of his country, of liberty, to whom one directs a hymn instead of a prayer.[11]

Referring to the monument to Martí in the Plaza Cívica, the young author said that it was well to honor Martí with a monument, but there should be a monument to him in Cuban hearts.

In addition to essay contests there are, of course, patriotic acts performed in the schools, public and private, to honor Martí on his birthday. These are usually held in front of the bust of the Apostle, which is required to be located on the grounds of every school in the Republic. Parades of school children are also held.

Each year in May a parade of children from the rural schools throughout the Republic was held in Havana. Called "The Annual Salute of the Martian Flower," the project was initiated by President Batista. Each year it had as its object giving selected rural youth, who were brought to Havana on special trains, an opportunity to see the capital city in a period of three days of activities, while at the same time commemorating the day Martí fell in battle, May 19.[12]

Many schools have groups of children who are organized for special Martian activities. Some schools, in addition to the bust of Martí, have a Martian Corner. This might have, for instance, a photograph of Martí, the Cuban flag, and a shelf with some books by and about the National Hero. At the dedication of one of these corners in 1946 a social science high school teacher in Havana had some words to say on the extent to which Martí's influence had reached Cuban students. He asked:

What do our pupils know about Martí? Yes, they know his life, his accomplishments, his integrity, and his heroism. A grandiose figure shines in their minds, gilded in part by childish fancy that converts him into a kind of divinity. But, can we be sure that that deified Martí moves them to act, that he orients them in what they do, that he presides over their lives in some way? I am inclined to think not.[13]

It was necessary, this teacher said, to convert the static Martí to a dynamic one, to take his figure from the altar to make it act as a man through his admirers. He concluded that every student who visited a Martian Corner should at least take an idea away to derive some plan from it, and from the plan, some action.

Student Responses to Martí

The idealized Martí referred to by the social science teacher was clearly evident in the stereotyped replies reported in the "Voices of the Nation" column of a Havana newspaper on the occasion of Martí's birthday celebration in 1956. The only comments given were those of school teachers and students. One of the teachers, in reply to the question, "What do you think about our Apostle as a patriot, thinker, writer, poet, and teacher?" said:

José Martí as a poet had characteristic qualities: originality, liberty, and sincerity. His *Versos libres* are famous and his *Versos sencillos* are gentle and tender. Sometimes he expresses emotions so profound that they are capable of making the coldest heart feel emotion. Consider his poem "La Niña de Guatemala," a sad episode in the life of the poet, and the composition "Rose's Little Shoes." Martí was also a great patriot and excellent prose writer.

The other teacher interviewed replied to the same question:

The Apostle Martí wrote and looked for clear words so that he might be understood better by his readers. Only a Maestro's spirit so well gifted, so flexible, so capable of sympathizing with that which is human could write in such an open language about matters which, being of universal interest, are so completely adaptable to the mind of a child.

One of the young students interviewed, about nine years old, answered with his thoughts on Martí:

No one told so surely as our Apostle in his thoughts and in his writings about the feeling of duty, of justice, and of integrity. The worthy patriot counseled us children to be useful, making us see that Nature is beautiful, that life is a duty, that death is not ugly, that no one should be sad so long as there are books in the libraries, light in the sky, and parents and teachers.

The other student, about the same age, replied to the question of the interviewer:

Today is the birthday of our great patriot José Martí, of that Martí the child who wrote as a man, of that Martí the child who accepted like a man the rigors of prison, and of that Martí the child who was deported to Spain for feeling like a man. He gave everything as a patriot, he gave as much as he could give and he gave as much as he was and as much as he could be. Neither the generous, the wise, nor the heroes reach that point; it is reserved for the saints.[14]

Several anecdotes, more spontaneous in nature than the aforesaid responses, may be cited as characteristic of student attitudes toward Martí. A young Cuban servant, colored and originally from Santiago de Cuba, revealed that he had become interested in Martí in school, even winning first prize once in an essay contest for a brief biography of the Cuban hero. Asked what his opinion of Martí was, he replied that he never bothered to think very much about him. He declared that General Antonio Maceo was usually neglected in favor of Martí, but that both of them should be honored equally. Since Martí was white and Maceo colored, he felt that this was the reason for the supremacy of the Apostle over the General. He added, however, that Maceo was honored much more in Santiago de Cuba than Martí. He asserted that racism existed in Cuba although many people did not want to admit it.[15]

A conversation was held with a Cuban student about fourteen years of age traveling by plane from Havana to Miami. As many Cubans do, he replied in excellent English. He said that he was the grandson of an officer in the Cuban revolutionary movement, and vividly recalled his grandfather's account of the death of Maceo in battle. Although he greatly admired Maceo, he declared, he thought that Martí was just as great. Since he liked to read everything that Martí wrote, at that moment he was carrying in his suitcase one of Martí's works, which he planned to read on the way.[16] The poise and intelligence with which this young Cuban discussed Martí was impressive.

The outward signs of the promotion of Martí in the grade schools of the Republic thus show through class lessons, student responses, Martian Corners, parades, and all the patriotic paraphernalia that one expects to find in the school system of a nation proud of its history. The extent to which the student will feel Martí, however, will not be

determined so much by what he learns in school of the facts of Martí's life, as by realizing later how well the Republic has carried out the Maestro's ideas by having given him a good education.

CRITICISM AND PRAISE OF THE SCHOOLS VIA MARTÍ

Just as in politics, criticism of the educational system of Cuba was highlighted as the Martí Centenary approached. A noted Cuban historian, Ramiro Guerra y Sánchez, reported in 1952 on "Martí and the Schools of the Republic." Referring to the Apostle's interest in education for all, he wrote that it grieved him to report on the general breakdown in the public schools; that the special victims of it were the hundreds of thousands of children in the rural areas. He said that the terrible deficit of instruction in the country was a humiliation and a tremendous social injustice for the Republic, and one of the gravest threats to the well-being, the progress, and the stability of the people, and for the free and democratic institutions of the nation.[17]

Another critic wrote in 1953 that the rural school was one of the most important institutions of the nation, but unfortunately a true rural school system did not exist. He said:

The teachers who are in the rural schools at the present time have not received the technical preparation that would allow them to impart a proper rural education. And that grave error brings with it as a consequence a rural education that is deficient in not carrying out the task for which it was created.[18]

In Santiago de Cuba an inspector of drawing instruction for the province spoke out bitterly on the occasion of the Centenary celebrations for Martí. Year after year, she said, the schools had tolerated disordered administrations that had no respect for education laws. She asserted that the public school was ruined materially and spiritually, that it was rotten to the foundation; that it was a school in which instruction was faced with every kind of obstacle, and children and youth abandoned to the mercy of an atmosphere of materialism and passions. She then said, "Let us admit it, is this not the true picture, traced in bold strokes, that portrays the drama of the Cuban school?" The public school in Cuba, she charged, was a national scandal. Then directing a series of questions to the public school teachers so that

they might examine their consciences before paying homage to Martí in his Centenary, she asked:

1. Do you attend to the duty of teaching as the most sacred of duties?
2. Do you utilize the facilities of the school to which you belong exclusively for glorifying yourself and for attaining the rights that benefit you personally?
3. Are you afraid of losing your job if you face the sacred duties of your Apostleship?
4. Are you trying to evade, because of the bother that it brings with it, undertaking the civic campaign that the Cuban school demands?
5. Are you indebted to some political party that unrightfully gave you what does not belong to you?

The school inspector then called for action, not words, in praise of Martí in order to improve the school system.[19]

Praise by Teachers.—Gilberto Diago, one of the instructors in Education Mission No. 4 in Palma Soriano, Oriente province, wrote in 1955 on "The Presence of José Martí in the Rural Schools" for *Orientación Campesina,* the Ministry of Education's magazine for rural school teachers.[20] Commenting upon a celebration January 28 in honor of Martí, Diago stated that the program of rural teaching, whose beacon was President Batista, was intimately linked with the "Martian Apostleship." Quoting from Martí's definition "To educate is to deposit in each man all the human accomplishments that have preceded him. . . ." Diago declared that this was being done with respect to rural education in its program (through the Education Missions) of teaching hygiene, veterinary science, reforestation, manual arts, and building techniques. He wrote:

It really makes one feel good when one is doing something worth while, as when the presence of Martí infuses us with the unconquerable spirit that our labor brings forth. May God wish that in future commemorations of this day we may have the complete satisfaction of saying: MAESTRO, YOUR WORK IS FULFILLED.[21]

Some vocational schools have been established throughout the island in implementation, consciously or unconsciously, of the Martian exhortation to spend more time on practical studies. One of these is the Technical Industrial School "General José B. Alemán" outside of Havana. This is a high school that gives the children of

needy families vocational training in addition to regular courses. An interview was held with one of the instructors there. The word "Martí" was merely introduced into the conversation, and for the next fifteen minutes the instructor delivered a sincere lecture on the subject. Expressing a deep admiration for Abraham Lincoln, he asserted that Martí resembled this great North American in his intelligence, humanity, and patriotism. For the instructor, Martí had something of God in him because of all he was able to do for Cuba.

Referring to the invasion and revolt in Santiago de Cuba in December, 1956, the instructor said that two of the young rebels killed in the revolt had been former students of his and he personally could testify to the fact that they were devoted students of the ideals of Martí. It was also his firm conviction that the majority of the young people in the revolt against the Batista administration were fighting because they were inspired by the words of Martí to work for a better government in Cuba. He said that often his students came to ask his opinion about politics, but he felt unable to counsel them directly because he had taken an oath as a government employee to abstain from political issues. Instead he would refer them to Martí's works, telling them that they would find the answers to their questions in the Apostle's writings. This instructor had great praise for the work that his school was accomplishing.[22]

Criticism by Teachers.—A teacher in a public school in Havana revealed some facts about the nature of her work with a primary class. She stated that for four years she had been assigned as an interne, or substitute for the proprietor of the classroom. When asked what was meant by "proprietor," she replied that each classroom had a salary assigned to it, which belonged to the "owner" until she retired. In other words, the room was a kind of feudal benefice that could not be alienated except through prolonged absence. In the instance of the teacher interviewed, however, the proprietor had spent most of her time in Europe, entitling her to collect only half of her "fee," while the other half was paid to the interne who actually did the work. Sometimes a proprietor collected the whole salary without ever teaching. The only hope for the interne was that some day the proprietor would retire, leaving the benefice to the substitute, as the regulations provided.

Often, however, the regulations were disregarded from above, as happened with the teacher interviewed. When her proprietor "retired," instead of receiving the classroom as her own, an outsider was brought in. She would have been without a position had not the pleas of her students and of the principal of the school secured a classroom for her that was being vacated at the same time. Many positions were filled through a complicated rating scale that would break the morale of an IBM machine, but many were also filled by favoritism.

The pay scale for a four-hour teaching day five times a week, according to the teacher interviewed, was $112 to $120 a month, with the maximum being $150 in very rare instances. Most of those at the top of the scale received $130. She said that among the many problems the teacher had to face was the one of lack of supplies and outdated textbooks.

The teacher said that Martí was extensively taught in her school, beginning in the first grade with the reading of the *Versos sencillos*. Throughout the rest of the grades Martí's teachings appeared in courses entitled "education," "morals," "civics," "history," and "literature." Asked whether the precepts of Martí had been implemented in the educational system of Cuba, she replied emphatically, "Absolutely not!"[23]

A lively debate was held among a group of public school teachers in 1956 over the status of the Republic that Martí had hoped for, and in particular, how well it had fared in the field of public education, in which they had all had direct experience. One of the teachers maintained that compulsory attendance at school was not carried out. If children did not want to come to school there was no way to bring pressure on the parents. This teacher asserted that Roman Catholic groups undermined the public school system, and her charge included Roman Catholic public school teachers themselves. She also declared that many private schools would not admit colored children.

Another teacher confirmed the charge that there was racial discrimination in the private schools, but added that this could also be extended to the public high schools that refused to hire colored instructors. She pointed out that there were no Negro professors in the universities, and that in her school white children refused to sit next to colored students.

Another teacher heatedly denied that there was racial discrimination of any kind in Cuba, and then for the benefit of a North American in the audience proceeded to fulminate against the barbarisms of racial discrimination in the United States. There was general agreement, however, that there was very little in the way of vocational education for the majority of the Cuban students, and that the public school system was in a state of abandonment. Everyone agreed that very few of Martí's points on education for Cuba had been carried out.[24]

Report on Cuba.—Documentary evidence of the teachers' complaints exists. In 1951 a monumental report was published on the findings and recommendations of an economic and technical mission to Cuba organized by the International Bank for Reconstruction and Development. The mission was composed of a distinguished group of seventeen experts from the United States. The chief of the mission was Francis Adams Truslow. During 1950, in collaboration with the Cuban government, the mission delved deeply into the economic problems of Cuba, finally making frank recommendations for revolutionary changes in many branches of national activities. The scholars devoted one chapter of their report to education in the Republic.

They found that for the period 1949-50 only half of the total school population was enrolled in any kind of school. Compared with the figure of 63 per cent enrolled in the period 1925-26, this showed an actual drop in school attendance. The mission discovered that less than one Cuban in ten in the high school age group was enrolled in any school, with no high schools existing for the rural population. For the period 1931-43 no gains in percentage of literacy for the population as a whole were made.[25] From 1943 to 1953, however, illiteracy dropped from 28.7 per cent to 23.6 per cent.[26]

Among other problems noted in the educational system were the short school days for both students and teachers—only four hours. The report showed that teaching positions were bought and sold from $500 to $2,000 apiece. There was much unevenness, according to the *Report,* in the distribution of schools and teachers. Many areas had "show-window" schools located along main roads, but they served only small numbers of students. In some schools, the *Report* stated, teachers had as many as 120 pupils in one class. In the junior high

schools of Havana, on the other hand, 901 teachers looked after 5,000 students, an average of 5.5 pupils per teacher.

Among other shortcomings of the system the *Report* scored the low salaries of teachers, shortages of school supplies, dilapidated buildings, too many "inspectors," unreliable statistics on education, apathy and absenteeism on the part of both pupils and teachers, and the generally deplorable state of rural education. The mission summarized the major problems in its findings as follows:

1. Overcentralization of administration.
2. Discontinuity of administration.
3. Nonprofessional administration.
4. A demoralizing heritage of political patronage and graft.

It recommended:

1. Establishment of a nonpolitical National Board of Education, under the chairmanship of the Minister of Education, to direct policy and administration.
2. Authorization for the National Board of Education to place management of the school system in the hands of a professional Director of Schools appointed by—and responsible to—the Board.
3. Partly decentralize control and encourage local initiative by reviving the system of *elected,* local Boards of Education, with limited local powers.[27]

Corruption—Martí's Anathema.—The unhappy condition of the public school system referred to by the teachers and substantiated by the *Report on Cuba* has been further marked by charges of wholesale depredations on Ministry of Education funds. No area of governmental service seems to have been more contaminated by the heritage of colonial corruption than this one.

The size of the budget is revealing. For the fiscal year 1956-57, out of a total budget of $330 million for the national government, the Ministry of Education received $74 million, or 22 per cent.

Accusations of graft in 1956 resulted in investigations undertaken by the Tribunal de Cuentas (the Government Accounting office) to search for funds missing in the Ministry. The Tribunal charged that the chief paymaster from March, 1952, to February, 1955, had disappeared, along with all the financial records for the period. The Tribunal stated that the embezzlement amounted to more than $3

million, and that "there was no doubt but that superiors of the former paymaster were also involved in the systematic sleight of hand of money and documents." The report declared that the substitution of a new paymaster did not bring an end to the embezzlement. Stamped as "Case 30," the matter was turned over to the courts for that curious process known as Cuban justice that never convicted wholesale marauders on public funds. What is even stranger is that the Batista administration was accusing itself of the misuse of public money. The news account of the case stated that the scandal in the Ministry of Education was the greatest, but was only one of a series that invalidated the pretensions of honesty of the administration in power.[28]

THE UNIVERSITY OF HAVANA

The main center of higher education in Cuba is the University of Havana, founded in 1728.[29] The University has been the center from which have come many biographies and studies on the Apostle. In addition to its numerous faculty members—Jorge Mañach, Raimundo Lazo, Herminio Portell-Vilá, Raúl Roa, Manuel Bisbé, Roberto Agramonte, Ramón Infiesta, Salvador Massip, Pablo F. Lavín, and Antonio Lancís—who have contributed to Martiana through their extensive writings, the University has promoted special courses on Martí. One is the Seminario Martiano, established in 1941 through the initiative of Gonzalo de Quesada y Miranda, who has been its director since that date. It is a two-year course. In addition the University created the "Cátedra Martiana" ("Martí Chair"), first occupied in 1950 by Raimundo Lazo.[30] The Cátedra is composed of a series of lectures given each year by a different expert on Martí.

The University has also honored Martí by naming the new social sciences building after him. At the time of the dedication of the edifice Dean Raúl Roa said:

This building does not bear the name of José Martí as a mere matter of circumstance. The Faculty decided to put it under the aegis and benediction of José Martí for his having always paid deeply felt tribute to the sovereignty of the conscience, to democratic solidarity, and to social justice, normative ideals of the Apostle of our Independence, and upright principles of teaching that are imparted to youth in our classrooms.[31]

Martí—Symbol of Revolt to Youth.—From the idealistic presentation of Martí in the classroom beginning in the primary grades, the National Hero has eventually been captured by university students as the perfect vehicle to express their rebellious instincts. José Martí once wrote in his novel *Amistad funesta*:

Students are the ramparts and the strongest army of freedom. . . . When liberty is in danger, a newspaper threatened, a ballot box in peril, the students unite . . . and arm in arm they go through the streets demanding justice, or they run printing presses in cellars for what they cannot say.[32]

University of Havana students of the 1930's took this description of themselves literally. Discovering Martí, they printed his words and distributed them anonymously throughout the city. Angry officials sought to discover the gifted conspiratorial author.[33] After the overthrow of Machado, students for some time played an active role in the government of Grau. During the turbulent state of affairs in 1933 Martí's statue in Central Park was the scene of several instances of jubilation at the fall of the tyrant.

Ruby Hart Phillips, for many years correspondent for the *New York Times* in Havana, wrote that she witnessed thousands of persons streaming across Central Park in a burst of enthusiasm over the resignation of Machado. She declared that some of them, weeping with joy, climbed the statue of Martí. Another demonstration brought tears to her eyes, for "the sheer pathos of it." She reported:

A small group of boys of probably 10 to 12 years, poorly dressed, some of them barefooted, came solemnly across Zulueta street carrying a Cuban flag carefully between them. They marched quietly up to Martí's statue in Central Park and the rest waited silently while one of their number climbed the tall statue, a no small feat in itself, and put the flag in Martí's outstretched hand. Then the small boy climbed down and they all walked quietly away. That was their contribution to the celebration, while adults killed and mutilated two men on the next corner.[34]

Extremes of violence, which had been frequent occurrences against professors and students at the University of Havana during Machado's regime, did not end with his overthrow, nor with the University's receiving autonomy in 1940. Student political disturbances, often provoked by the government, have continued.

CONFLICT AT THE MARTÍ CENTENARY: A fortnight before the grand

celebrations to be held during the Martí Centenary, the statue of Julio Antonio Mella, a martyred hero of the revolt against Machado, was drenched with a can of red paint. The Federación Estudiantil Universitaria (Federation of University Students) declared that the incident was a deliberate insult by the Batista government. The students quickly assembled around the statue, posted a guard of honor, and waited for trouble, which was not long in coming. An effigy of Batista was made, paraded through the streets, and burned. The police intervened, and in the rioting sixteen students were wounded, some seriously.[35] This is what university students of that period remember of the general hue and cry that marked the Martí celebrations.

CONFLICT AT MARTÍ'S BIRTHDAY IN 1956: Three years later the date for another homage to Martí approached. For some time the Federation of University Students had been engaged in skirmishes with the government, and was waiting for an opportunity to make a show of protest by assembling students. January 28 the leaders of the Federation organized the distribution of handbills to the student body to assemble in Central Park "In homage to the Apostle." The students gathered in front of the statue to Martí, and as they were about to lay wreaths at the base a riot broke out between them and the police. Fifty-five homage-paying students were arrested and sent to jail. Elsewhere, around the University of Havana, students celebrated the day by setting fire to several cars bearing official license plates, stoned police cars, and built a bonfire in front of the steps leading up to the University.[36]

Everyone wanted to pay homage to Martí. Ramón Grau San Martín, the students' fallen idol, was denied permission to lead a group of followers to the statue. A group of workers belonging to a union within the CTC was also not permitted to bring its flowers to the Apostle. Students from the provinces of Oriente and Pinar del Río were refused permission to hold a parade in Martí's honor. The Frente Cívico de Mujeres Martianas (Civic Front of Martian Women) was not allowed to assemble to hear an address by Raúl Roa, Dean of the Faculty of Social Sciences at the University of Havana.[37] It was a day to remember.

HIGHER EDUCATION IN CRISIS: During the Batista regime the Univer-

sity was often closed because of political difficulties with the government. The academic year 1956-57 saw the University open for only one month before classes were again suspended by the University Council for the same reason. Students were not even permitted to use the library facilities during this period. Thus a student entering the University of Havana might well find his course of studies being indefinitely extended. The attitude of the authorities of the University may be seen in an official statement made at the opening of the academic year 1954-55. It read:

It is not the nature of the University to be converted into trenches for fighting, however lofty and great the ideal that inspires it. . . . We want students to become men of science . . . and at the same time to nourish their thought with the highest redeeming principles. . . . Let the students develop their civic life and political relations outside and come to the University in search of what it can give them in its nature as an educational institution, forming themselves in investigation and study, free from passions.[38]

An interview with Dean Raúl Roa brought to light some personal statements regarding the impasse between the University and the government. Although the University is nominally autonomous according to the Constitution of 1940, it receives its main support from the state in the form of 2¼ per cent of the total budget of the government. In 1956, however, the National Police invaded the grounds of the University in search of arms, smashing doors in the office of the rector (president), and tumbling the regalia and symbols of his high office onto the floor. This was in clear violation of the autonomy of the University, and a lack of respect. It was necessary to close the University to avoid extended bloodshed between students and police. In view of such incidents, Roa declared, it was difficult for the University to be a spiritual force immune to combat. Although he said that Martí's expression "To be educated is the only way to be free . . ." was the unofficial motto of the university, he could not say in general that Martí's body of ideals was alive in Cuba, or that the Republic had fulfilled what he so earnestly desired.[39]

Subsequently Dean Roa followed Agramonte as Castro's Minister of Foreign Relations. He has become a vociferous and severe critic of the United States.

A SINCERE PATRIOT MUST SACRIFICE EVERYTHING: Militantly interpreting this Martian precept of patriotism, the Federation of University Students continued to take an open part in opposition to the Batista regime. In March, 1957, when the presidential palace was stormed, the president of the student organization, José A. Echevarría, was killed after he had assaulted a radio station to arouse popular support for the revolt.[40] His successor, Fructuoso Rodríguez, was ambushed and killed by the police the following month. Another University of Havana student shot in the same encounter with Rodríguez was José Westbrook, a Cuban-American. Westbrook, according to a statement made by his bereaved mother, had left instructions that if he should die in the struggle for freedom, he wanted a set of Martí's works to be buried with him, since "his passion was José Martí." His request was fulfilled.[41]

Westbrook's death recalls the cynical statement by Orestes Ferrara, who said that Martí had done irreparable harm to the youth of Cuba by making them believe that they were apostles. Westbrook and Ferrara thus epitomize the gulf existing between those who censure the Apostle (decidedly a minority), and those who are willing to die for a Martian ideal.

Martí's Economic Theory Reflected.—In part the combativeness of the University students is to be explained by the lack of economic opportunity, which is linked to Martí's injunction against a one-crop economy. The Cuban economy is largely dependent upon sugar production, which furnishes the major source of the national income. During much of the year the sugar mills are not in operation while waiting for the harvest season. This creates a large number of persons who are "underemployed." That is, they work only during the sugar harvest and processing, and many must live on credit for the rest of the year.

In addition thousands of young people arrive on the labor market each year without finding jobs. The desperate economic situation of Cuban youth has been described by Rubén Ortiz-Lamadrid, a Cuban journalist. He saw the Cuban economy as one in which young generations pathetically searching for work were unable to find anything because there were not enough commercial, agricultural, and industrial activities to absorb them. He said:

With this accelerated rhythm of growth in population, uncompensated for by proportional opportunities for employment, that produces constantly increasing unemployment, and the bad examples of illicit opportunism that each new public administration offers to the public, Cuba cannot in any way enjoy political harmony nor social peace because the unadorned economic fact is that the very bad distribution of wealth, the exploitation of the supposedly common national endowment of wealth and commerce, impedes it.[42]

Faced with this situation, the Cuban youth were, he believed, without hope for the future. Ortiz-Lamadrid added that whoever did not see the picture as he painted it did not because the high rank of their positions, public or private, had taken them a long way from the body of Cuban citizenry.

In 1956 a message to Cuban youth came from the venerable patriot Major General Enrique Loynaz del Castillo. In assessing the Cuban scene he said that the years that had passed since the inauguration of the Republic had not served as much of a lesson for the Cubans. He declared:

I look backward with bitterness and disillusion, without hope that anything will change in the future. Politics instead of an honorable career has become a springboard to becoming rich. . . . I consider it, nevertheless, an inexcusable duty to urge the new generations to return to the ideals of Martí and to become inspired in that living fountain of patriotism and integrity, so that they might struggle without rest in wiping out the stains that have shamed the Republic, so that the day might arrive when those who caused them will be punished without pity.[43]

Martí's Education Theories Unfulfilled.—Part of the plight of the modern youth of Cuba may be due to a fault of the University of Havana. The *Report on Cuba* charged that the training program of the universities of Havana and Santiago were inadequate for modern requirements. It stated: "They produce too many men of letters for whom employment is scarce and too few with the technical qualifications needed for agricultural and industrial development." The mission suggested that independent foreign educational experts be called in to examine the policies, curricula, facilities, and methods of the universities of Havana and Oriente to make recommendations for improvement.[44]

José Martí once asked:

How are governors to come from universities if in America there is no university where the rudiments of the art of government, which is the analysis of the peculiar elements of the peoples of America, are taught?

That question is still valid for the Cuban universities as institutions of society. The traditional courses on political theory are, of course, taught, as well as many courses on law and theoretical public administration. But it cannot be said that there is any organized course of study in the roots of political behavior, power politics, or political parties as a logical extension of the Martian precept. This will be possible, of course, only when democratic processes are restored in Cuba.

This was the panorama of education in the Cuban Republic up to 1959. Public education, if not abandoned, subject to deep-rooted corruption, the University of Havana in continual crisis, and Cuban youth without much hope for the future. Primed with Martí's teachings of equality, justice, and economic opportunity for all, the Cuban youth may be expected to suffer disillusionment with a nation that sponsors the teaching of such high ideals but produces little evidence of fulfilling them. Thus, in their minds, revolt against that government was justified in the name of Martí.

One of the simplest but most important statements to be remembered in the *Report on Cuba* is:

An examination of the educational system in Cuba convinced the Mission that unless and until drastic improvements are effected, the Cuban people cannot hope effectively to develop their country.[45]

Although many changes in education have been made since the colonial period to conform to Martí's precepts, such as the prohibition of religious instruction in the schools, with a corresponding departure from scholasticism, and the inauguration of technical schools in the cities and of vocational-type education missions in rural areas, on the whole the report confirms Alvarez Pujals' charge of unfulfilled Martian ideals. This is particularly true if one considers Martí's loathing for corruption. Although Martí did not precisely anticipate graft in the educational system, no mental gymnastics are necessary to ascertain how his moral philosophy could be extended to cover the public school.

Martí and the Press of Cuba

Once when José Martí had in mind the establishment of a newspaper he wrote in his notes:

Born in turbulent times . . . obeying instincts and impulses rather than wise judgments, we men of the present generation live in a pitiful and almost total lack of knowledge of the problem that we are supposed to solve. To study it, to establish it, and to clarify it is the purpose of this newspaper. We must become independent and prepared in such a way that we do not blindly serve base motivations or shameful interests. . . . Thus do we acquire the stature of free men.[46]

To what extent does the press as an institution in Cuba reflect the influence of the ideas of Martí? Since journalism was a major interest to Martí throughout his life, this field is worth examining briefly. Like every other institution in society the press is really no better nor worse than the individuals who form a part of it. In general it may be said that editors have freely given space for articles and poems on Martí.

Cuba, up to 1959, ranked after Argentina, Brazil, Chile, Mexico, and Peru in the number of daily newspapers published in relation to the size of its population. In Cuba about one person out of every fourteen bought a newspaper, compared with the neighboring island of Haiti, where only one person out of every 350 buys a daily.[47] Given the relatively high number of persons in Cuba who read the papers this may be considered an important medium for spreading the doctrine of Martí.

Several of the newspapers in Havana carried quotations from Martí on their front pages. *Pueblo,* for example, published by Octavio R. Costa, a frequent writer on Martí, reprinted Martí's comment: "People need to love something great. Nothing is destroyed without something arising in its place."[48] *El Mundo* heralded the Martian statement: "The written word is not to cover up the truth, but to say it." During a period of censorship of the press in January and February, 1957, *El Mundo* indicated inconformity with the government action by refusing to print Martí's words on its front page. As soon as the censorship was lifted Martí's saying was returned to its customary location.

As a newspaper catering to conservative, Spanish interests, the

Diario de la Marina has engaged in battle with the more liberal *El Mundo*. In 1952, on the eve of the anniversary of Martí's death, *El Mundo* referred to attacks made upon it by the editor of the *Diario de la Marina*. Asserting that their rival was quite correct in his statement that there were differences between the two papers, *El Mundo* published the other paper's statement on the death of Martí in 1895, which had said:

Martí has fallen forever, the civilian chief, the dreaming and delirious head of the separatist movement . . . in the ill-named cause of independence for Cuba . . . our most enthusiastic, patriotic applause, and our modest but excited congratulations to the nation.[49]

Referring to the boast of the *Diario de la Marina* that it had "served 120 years in the general and permanent interests of the nation," *El Mundo* sharply asked, "Which nation?" The editorial ended with the statement that *El Mundo*, on the other hand, founded with the Republic, had always served Cuba.

The following year at the time of the Martí Centenary the editor of the *Diario de la Marina,* José I. Rivero, seemed to make up for the un-Cuban attitude of his newspaper in the past by stating, "As a Cuban and as the editor of the *Diario de la Marina* . . . I have him [Martí] present in my every act."[50]

In Cuba there are three inseparable ingredients: the press, politics, and Martí. This was demonstrated early in 1957 with the announcement of the formation of a new political party by the editor of the Havana newspaper *Ataja*. In February blue headlines announced the formation of the party with 250,000 affiliations, a large figure even for Cuban election-inflated statistics. The emblem of the new group, the Partido Unión Cubana (Cuban Union party), displayed the heads of Martí and Maceo, and the familiar motto, "All together and for the well-being of all," taken from Martí's speech at Tampa in 1891.

The editor of *Ataja*, Alberto Salas Amaro, the founder of the party, wrote that its formation had taken a heroic effort in view of the censorship of the press, the suspension of constitutional guarantees, and lack of access to the radio then existing in the nation. But it was made possible, he declared, because a group of men had dedicated

themselves to the ideals of the generation that brought freedom to Cuba, and had persisted in a similar heroic methodology. Wrote Salas Amaro:

The secret is simple: will to conquer, faith and passion in the truth of a new idea, in the justice of a cause. Will and faith move mountains, they are the engines of progress, the only explanation of the iron tenacity that drags from Nature its most jealously guarded secrets.

Lining up the new party with an array of support from early patriots, especially Martí, Salas Amaro said that to those who asked what his party's program consisted of he would answer "with full lungs, with the oxygen and aroma of the *manigua* (the Cuban backwoods famous in the war of liberation), the cry that resounded in the veterans' encampments and that resounds today in the consciences of all good Cubans: Long Live Free Cuba!"[51]

When Martí was writing for newspapers in the United States and Latin America he seems to have had very little difficulty in getting his articles, many of a controversial nature, printed. The same cannot be said for many Cuban journalists. In the period 1956 to 1957 in Cuba, censorship of the press, along with the suspension of general constitutional guarantees, occurred on two different occasions for periods of forty-five days each.

Unfortunately many Cuban newspapers were dependent upon government aid to keep them out of debt. Since this help often went to a newspaper as a direct subsidy, it could be extended or withdrawn at will depending upon the political attitude of the paper toward the administration. This did not always encourage objective reporting.

The Dean of the Havana province branch of the National College of Newspapermen, Jorge Quintana, touched upon another hidden censorship of the press, the direct, personal subsidy, which they received in addition to their regular salary, paid to reporters assigned to government departments. Quintana asserted that the College was opposed to this practice and refused to support any newspaperman that was fired from such a position.

The press of Cuba, according to the Dean, has never really responded to Martí. He found that everyone talked about the Apostle, but no one practiced his teachings. Some of the obstacles in the way of Martí's ideal of an honorable press, the Dean believed, was the

high degree of commercialism which took away the best in reporting. Quintana was pessimistic about the past, but not about the future, since in the years to come, he believed, the press would have to take Martí's strong feelings for democracy and love of liberty into account. Newspapermen would have to emulate Martí's teaching, which is one of the mottoes of the College, "There is no monarch like an indignant journalist."[52]

Quesada y Miranda, a former full-time newspaperman, although critical of certain features of the Cuban press, insists that many individual reporters, oblivious to monetary rewards, have distinguished themselves in the past by attention to the principles of human justice, often risking injury and death to report the news faithfully.[53]

The most independent source of information in Cuba up to 1959 was the widely circulating (250,000 copies) weekly *Bohemia*. The editor and publisher, Miguel A. Quevedo, also published two other weeklies, *Carteles* and *Vanidades*. *Bohemia* promoted sensational news stories, but contained the political news that was not to be found elsewhere. Compared to many other Latin American newspapers, the Cuban press was quite outspoken. In fact, at times it seemed reckless since libel laws were seldom enforced.

The press perhaps may not be given a very high score in living up to the standards of Martí in the field of journalism. Any higher mark must wait until the press is free from governmental censorship.

Realization by Cuban publishers that they are not always free to report the news was perhaps best reflected in a simple cartoon drawn for *El Mundo* in 1956. It consisted of a drawing of a bust of the Apostle with their favorite quotation from him, "The written word is not to cover up the truth, but to say it." The drawing was headed, "Pastime for coloring."[54] Another cartoon in the *Diario de la Marina*, appearing at the time of Martí's birthday anniversary in 1957, under the title of "Logic," showed a boy seated on a rock asking, "And why, if Martí is so great, do we honor him only once a year?"[55]

A Collection of Comments on Martí

Thus far most attention in this study has been paid to those who

have been interested in Martí to the extent that they have written articles, books, and poems about him, and to those who have attained stature in the social, economic, and political life of the nation. Their influence in the establishment of José Martí as the National Hero has probably been a decisive one. During the author's studies in Cuba, however, he listened to many informal conversations in which Martí was the main subject. It might be helpful to have a few views reported of some Cubans as they have discussed the moral, social, and political themes pertaining to the figure of Martí.[56]

A Beggar

Along the streets of Havana wander many beggars, from ragged urchins to ragged elders, furnishing a sharp contrast to many well-dressed individuals, fine homes, and expensive cars. Representatives of the indigent class are accustomed to take up nightly headquarters in front of the better theaters to prey upon the cinema trade. One was a grey-haired old woman, whose request for alms was met by a question on the Apostle. Had she ever heard of Martí? "Ah, yes," she replied, "the little old man!" When asked what else she knew about him, she added, "They say he loved everybody." With that she gratefully took the alms proffered and scurried away, never again stopping the interviewer for money.[57]

A Boatman

Another representative of the lower classes of Havana offered his views on Martí midstream in the Havana harbor. As the owner of a small rowboat, this Cuban gained his living ferrying tourists to Morro Castle on the other side of the bay from Havana. Asked what he thought of Martí, his countenance brightened and he seemed to be transported to a realm beyond the reality of his menial task. In reverent tones he said that Martí was a very great man, that he was very intelligent, very pure, and very clean. When one of the passengers commented that Martí seemed a man not only for Cuba, but for all of Latin America, the boatman exclaimed, "For the whole world!"[58]

A Policeman

A policeman on duty at a public building in Havana furnished

the subject for another interview. When asked what he thought of Martí, he pointed to some of the librarians leaving and said that they could tell more about the Apostle than he could. Upon being urged to reveal his own feelings, he replied, "Well, sir, imagine, I don't have much to say about him. He was a great patriot and helped to win our independence, like Maceo." Asked whom he thought was the greater of the two, he replied, "Well, sir, both were great, the one was a fighter and the other a thinker." Which of the two did he prefer? "Martí," he answered, "because he was white and Maceo was black." Then he expressed his admiration for the United States, not because the person speaking to him was an American, but because, he said, "In the United States people respect each other, obey the laws, and can earn a decent living."[59]

A Waiter

A restaurant worker waiting for the bus on a Havana corner revealed his thoughts about Martí. He said that he had a very high opinion of Martí because he had started the Cuban freedom movement, adding that the Americans, of course, had later helped. Although he declared that he had no special feelings about Martí, he said with a wink, "He was quite a lover, though. Tell me if that isn't the honest truth!"[60]

A Store Clerk

Conversation between a store clerk in a Havana record shop and an elderly customer was overheard. Upon being thanked by the old gentleman for having done him a favor, the girl who had waited on him replied jokingly, "Don't mention it, 'Love is repaid with love.' " (A reference to Martí's play, *Amor con amor se paga*.)[61]

A Washroom Artist

The aphorisms of Martí continue to turn up in unexpected places. In a washroom that belied its name in a fourth-rate Havana restaurant, someone had scrawled in misspelled words, "Maceo died by treachery [referring to the popular belief that Maceo was killed by one of his own men], but Batista will die with his face to the sun." This last reference is to the often quoted line from a poem by Martí

that he himself would die in this manner. It is hard to tell from this cryptic message in the washroom whether the writer was pro-Batista or just sarcastic.[62]

THE UPPER MIDDLE CLASS

Several dozen swimming clubs are to be found along an aristocratic section of Havana's Caribbean shore. Persons who belonged to these clubs prior to Castro were upper middle class and upper class. The subject of Martí was introduced into the conversation of a mixed group of persons at one of these clubs. No Cuban is loath to talk about Martí. Soon talk was animated over Martí's status as a thinker. A participant made the flat statement that he thought that Martí was one of the greatest thinkers in the world. Another added that he thought that Martí was one of the greatest poets in the world. This point was not supported wholeheartedly by every member of the group, although there was general agreement that the Apostle was at least a great poet.

As such discussions often developed, one of the Cubans made the point that Martí's ideals had not been carried out in view of the fact that every single administration in Cuba had been headed by thieves who had robbed millions from the Cuban people. One of the group made the statement that no honest or decent person would go into politics—they all went into medicine, law, or commerce. Asked why the honest Cubans did not meet the challenge of this low state of affairs by demanding an honest government, they replied that Cubans never take anything seriously. Every theft from the government is treated as a joke. In addition they maintained that Cuba is, for the most part, a rich country, and the people have not had to undergo those trying experiences of war, hunger, and privation that mold character. The final explanation was that the corruption of their Spanish heritage left the Cubans unable to better themselves.[63]

The comment is often made among members of the upper classes that Martí is not liked because of the lack of stability in his family relations; that is, the abandonment of his wife and son, and his affair with Carmen Mantilla. A great-nephew of Carmen Zayas-Bazán indicated on one occasion that members of his family did not respect or like Martí because of his treatment of his wife and child.[64]

This attitude of disapprobation of Martí's family relations by the upper classes was affirmed by a young corporation lawyer belonging to that group,[65] and by the wife of a leading expert on Martí.[66] Since many families in the Cuban aristocracy are composed of descendants of Spanish nobility (some still preserve titles), and also since the influence of the Roman Catholic Church is strong among them, this attitude is understandable. Even with the record of a model family life, Martí in his role in the downfall of the Spanish colony could hardly be expected to inspire enthusiasm in this group. One is led to suspect that criticism of Martí's family life is a pious and oblique way of sniping at an otherwise inviolable national hero.

A BRICKLAYER

The work that Martí did for Cuba, according to a Havana bricklayer, has turned out to be a failure because no one has fulfilled the mission he set forth for the Republic—freedom and independence. He said that for him Martí was a hero, but that malicious Cubans asserted that if Martí had lived he would have been a degenerate just like the rest. He added, however, that there is a *dicho* (saying) that runs:

> *If Maceo and Martí should come back to life*
> *And contemplate their unhappy country*
> *Surely shame would kill them.*
> *Either the Cuban would be reborn,*
> *Or else they would die again.*

The bricklayer said that the monument to Martí in the Plaza Cívica had been a disgusting waste of money; that a full-sized gold statue of Martí could have been made with all the wasted contributions. He felt that the simple statue in the Central Park in Havana was more appropriate homage.

He pointed out that honesty was to be found not among those who had access to great amounts of money, but rather among the workers. The reason for this was simple—the worker who did not establish a good credit rating in a restaurant would die of hunger when he had no work. He added that there were many Cubans who ate only one meal a day, and others who worked with only a five-cent sweet roll, a cigarette, and a glass of water to sustain them.

Pointing to a drive being constructed along the sea that had required a detour around a fashionable tennis club, the bricklayer commented sarcastically that if it had been a schoolhouse the city would have torn it down to make way for the road. The worker said that for him Martí was like a God. He repeated the statement for emphasis.

Another Cuban joined the conversation on Martí, which lasted for another hour. Politics was the main theme; especially the disillusionment that the people suffered after Ramón Grau San Martín's term in office. The bricklayer, on the other hand, had words of praise for some United States Presidents, adding, "Give us the worst President that the United States has ever had, and we would gladly accept him as an improvement over anything we have had." The new participant in the conversation said that one of the greatest vices in Cuba was the lottery; that Martí had fought against it. He said, "How can one think about Martí when the government permits such corruption?" This Cuban felt that one of the happiest strokes of luck for the United States had been in the moral influence of the Puritans. At that point two rats came running along the sea wall and the speaker commented ironically, "Representatives of our sanitary facilities here in Cuba!"

A third Cuban, announcing that he was a *guajiro* (man from the country), joined the conversation. He had some definite ideas on the way in which Cuba had progressed since the time of Martí. This man declared that in many localities in the interior there had been little progress since 1900, that most of the advancements were to be found in Havana and the larger cities of Cuba.

One of the participants in the conversation then commented upon Martí and racial discrimination, without seeming to take into account Martí's opposition to it. Referring to race wars in Santiago de Cuba in 1912, this Cuban came to the un-Martian conclusion that one white man was worth one hundred Negroes. The discussion on Martí was still intense when the interviewer slipped away.[67]

A TAILOR

A colored tailor had some definite ideas about Martí. He declared that he had attempted all of his life to follow the teachings of

Martí, and that for him Martí was a God. As a fellow Mason he agreed with Martí that the Roman Catholic Church exploited the people. He found, however, that Martí suffered from a weakness not to be found in Antonio Maceo, that of trying to please everybody. He said that if Martí had been more like Maceo in this respect he would not have felt required to come to Cuba to fight on the battlefields; that he would have been more useful in New York.[68]

A Banker

An elderly, retired banker, a veteran of the War of Independence, showed that he was an enthusiastic follower of Martí. He said that Martí was a genius whose teachings should be expounded more and more in the schools. Martí, he felt, was a perfect example to be followed in the political life of the country, but not necessarily as a moral example. He said, "Martí was not a perfect man in his love affairs, but at least he never failed to be a gentleman in this respect."

The banker laughed when the matter of the monument in the Plaza Cívica was raised. He said that Martí should be a monument in the soul of every Cuban, and not in the sacrilege of millions spent in an operation that had not been moral or clean in any respect. He said that the majority of the Cubans wanted honest government, especially those in the interior who had very good intentions but whose necessity often carried them into the hands of immoral politicians. He insisted that it was necessary to instill respect for law in the Cuban mind; that in this regard the Cuban Revolution had not yet taken place. He pointed out that it would be healthful for Cuba to return to the War of Independence practice of hanging malefactors.

The retired banker asserted that the influence of the Spaniards had been very bad for Cuba, above all in their commercial practices. As an illustration of Spanish character in this respect he cited an experience he had had many years ago when he was a customs inspector. A Spanish merchant had declared that the boxes he was importing contained beans, whereas in reality investigation showed that they held hams, which paid more duty. The merchant thereupon tried to bribe the customs inspector. When told that this in the long run might result in far greater cost to the merchant than paying the

duty, the smuggler is reported to have replied, "No amount of money that I might have to pay can equal the thrill of cheating the government!"[69]

A University Student

A young university student of the upper classes felt just the opposite, however, about Spanish influence in Cuba, saying that it had been good, adding, "I'm all for Spain." His generation, he declared, was sick and tired of Martí; they had simply been forced to study and hear too much about him. He insisted that many of his friends felt the same way. His brother, however, did not agree, and expressed a deep admiration for Martí.[70]

A Music Teacher

Conversation with a middle-aged Cuban music schoolteacher, a great-niece of one of Martí's close associates, brought out the allegation that she was acquainted with the socially prominent Cuban woman, whose first name was also María, who was Martí's second illegitimate child by a woman in Cuba. As to this reflecting a defect in Martí's character, however, she laughed and said that in view of Martí's greatness one could forget anything. He was, after all, she added, "very gallant with the ladies." The music teacher's mother, who was listening to the conversation, said that she had been living in Tampa, Florida, when Martí came to visit, and everyone there idolized him. Her daughter added that the influence of Spain on Cuba had been unfortunate in that it had left a heritage of absolutism and patrimony. She found that the custom of inheriting posts that prevailed during Spanish colonial days was reflected among some government officials who seemed to think that the income from their posts was their personal property.[71]

An Illiterate Vendor

An illiterate lemon seller was the subject of another informal interview. He was reluctant at first to offer his views because he was unable to read or write, but he soon warmed to the subject. He declared that Martí's greatest mistake was to go into battle since he was betrayed as a result and killed. The vendor was of the opinion that there

were many traitors in Cuba and very few good persons. He was bitter about the money spent on Martí's monument in the Plaza Cívica. He declared that it was a vast scheme to exploit the people, and that the money should have been used instead for the benefit of the poor, for whom Martí had so much sympathy. The lemon seller had some kind words for the Spaniards. According to what he had heard from his elders (he emphasized the fact several times that he could not read or write), at least during colonial times Spanish grocers gave out samples of food. He concluded by saying that he had profound respect for Martí because one should feel kindly toward all persons who have a good heart.[72]

A Psychiatrist

Although a number of persons indicated indifference toward Martí, very few showed outright hostility toward him. An exception was one of Cuba's leading neurosurgeons. The reason he gave for his attitude was that he never could stand the "supposedly idealistic type." He declared that Martí had no particular originality in his writings, or any definite plan of government for Cuba. He asserted that Martí just took what other people were writing at the time, used it, and pretended that it was his own. Speaking as a psychiatrist he labeled Martí an abnormal psychopath who preached morality and practiced immorality. The Cuban physician indicated that he did not like Abraham Lincoln, either. The neurosurgeon's brother, a lawyer, joined the conversation, saying that he shared these views, although perhaps not in such an extreme way. What irritated the lawyer more than anything else was the religious symbolism surrounding the Martian Suppers held on the eve of Martí's birthday anniversary. He declared frankly and in vivid English, "If you have an independent mind, they stink!"[73]

Conclusions

Many other conversations were held with Cubans on the subject of Martí. Opinion often differed widely on certain aspects of his life, his writings, and his use by politicians. In general, however, it may be said that of the Cubans queried, everyone knew him in some way. Many felt that Martí was a very great patriot, some that he was a

genius, others that he was a superman, and many that he was a saint, or almost God.

Most of them had a rudimentary knowledge of Martí's life, and showed particular interest in his early imprisonment and eventual death as a martyr. It was a rare Cuban who was not able to cite "La Rosa Blanca" from memory, although Martí's other poems were less known to him. Cynical smiles lightened the countenances of most Cubans when asked to name the political party that best seemed to have carried out the teachings of Martí. The invariable answer was that none of them had done so. All felt that Cuba was not the Republic Martí had desired.

Almost everyone said that the monument in the Plaza Cívica was nothing more than a scheme to steal money; that a much more appropriate way to honor Martí would be to follow his teachings. The assertion was often made that Martí was continually cited, but nobody practiced what he preached. Opinion was quite evenly divided between those who felt that the Spaniards had had a good influence on Cuba and those who felt that they had left a legacy of waste and corruption.

Martí's anti-Roman Catholicism was most often explained on the basis that Martí was a Mason, although a number of Cubans asserted that there was no deep conflict between being a Mason and a Catholic. The subject of Martí's extramarital relations very frequently brought forth a smile when it was mentioned to a Cuban, who, more often than not, was inclined to be indulgent in this matter.

One fact seems clear. There is enough difference of opinion on Martí among Cubans to ensure a lively debate whenever he is mentioned. Considering the apathy of many North American John Does toward George Washington, or Thomas Jefferson, for example, the Cubans' dynamic and disputatious nature is somewhat to be envied.

In time it would be very useful to conduct scientific studies of public opinion in Cuba on various topics associated with the name of Martí. Obviously, however, public opinion in a dictatorship is not easy to find. Investigation along these lines in Cuba is now closed indefinitely. Evidence exists, however, that Martí continues to be used as a symbol by the regime of Fidel Castro, who assumed power on January 1, 1959.

Chapter 9

AFTERMATH OF THE REVOLUTION

*F*ROM FIDEL CASTRO'S LANDING in Oriente province in 1956 to the sudden departure of Batista from Cuba on January 1, 1959, Cuba underwent a bitter civil war that resulted in the loss of thousands of lives. The victorious rebels claimed that Batista had sanctioned the murder of at least 10,000 victims. It is not the purpose of this book to examine this period extensively nor is it possible to elaborate in detail on the profound turmoil created by the social, economic, and political changes that have occurred in Cuba since Castro seized power. In one respect this latter period is no different from preceding periods in Cuban history—José Martí continues to be used often as a political symbol. In fact, criticisms by Martí against North American politics and economic policies have lent themselves to frequent repetition. Some representative samples of statements by leading politicians quickly show how Martí is still being used to justify action of all kinds.

Martí and Fidel Castro

Castro had scarcely taken over the reins of government before the printing presses began to reproduce his famous speech "La historia me absolverá" ("History will vindicate me"). This was his address to the court in Santiago de Cuba after he had been arrested for his abortive attack on the Moncada barracks on July 26, 1953. Castro's liberation movement took its name from this date.

In this speech Castro complained to the court that his jailers had

refused to let him read any works of Martí, seemingly because the prison censor considered Martí too subversive. "Or was it," he added, "because I said that Martí was the intellectual author of the Twenty-sixth of July?" He also charged that he was prevented from reading other matter, but he found that this was really of no importance. "I bear in my heart the Maestro's doctrines and in my thoughts the noble ideas of all men who have defended the people's liberty."

Castro concluded his long address with another tribute to Martí, quoting him as follows,

A man who is content to obey unjust laws and who allows the country in which he was born to be oppressed, and men to mistreat him, is not an honorable man. . . . In the world there must be a certain amount of decency just as there must be a certain amount of light. When there are many men without decency, there are always others who have in themselves the decency of many men. Those are the ones who violently rebel against those who rob the people of their liberty, which means to rob men of their decency. In those men exist thousands of men, a whole people, human dignity. . . .

Castro then elaborated on the influence of Martí,

He taught us that the 10th of October and the 24th of February are noteworthy events for patriotic rejoicing because they mark the days in which the Cubans rebelled against the yoke of an infamous tyranny; he taught us to love and to defend the beautiful Cuban flag and every afternoon to sing an anthem whose verses tell us that to live in chains is to live in base ignominy and effrontery, and that to die for country is to live. We learned all that and we will not forget it even though today in our country men are being assassinated for practicing the ideas that they were taught from the cradle. . . . It seemed that the Apostle would die in the very year of his centenary, that his memory would be extinguished forever, so great was the insult! But he lives, he has not died, his people are in rebellion, his people are faithful to his memory; there are Cubans who have fallen defending his doctrines, there are young men who have come to die next to his tomb in magnificent vindication, to give their blood and lives so that he may continue living in the soul of the father-land. Cuba, what would have become of you if you had allowed the Apostle to die?[1]

A former close associate of Fidel Castro, Teresa Casuso, later commented on the trial and the influence of Martí: "Fidel showed that he had read a great deal of José Martí, who seemed, indeed, to be

the guiding spirit of his life. That Fidel was by his nature a man of war, and Martí a man of peace, was a fundamental contradiction which time has brought into sharp relief. . . ."[2]

Castro in the United States

One of the judges at the trial, Manuel Urrutia Lleó, declared himself in favor of Castro. This caused him to lose his job, but Castro in gratitude later made him the Provisional President of Cuba on January 9, 1959. Urrutia then proceeded to dissolve Congress, political parties, and the courts. The United States recognized the new regime within a week after the flight of Batista. On February 13 Castro's first premier, José Miró Cardona, resigned and was replaced by the bearded revolutionary himself. Roberto Agramonte, sociologist and writer on Martí, became Foreign Minister.

Responding to an invitation by the American Society of Newspaper Editors, Fidel Castro made a triumphant visit to the United States in April, 1959. He had informal visits in Washington with Secretary of State Christian Herter and Vice-President Richard M. Nixon, but he was not officially welcomed. Teresa Casuso, who was in charge of press relations for Castro, reported that Castro had refused to allow the Cuban ambassador to arrange for an official reception. Castro reasoned that such recognition was common for the "sold-out" presidents and dictators of Latin America and he preferred not to go in the capacity of an official guest. Casuso writes, "That this was his decision is certain. But it is no less certain that not the slightest initiative was taken on the Washington side. If Fidel had been invited, he would have accepted in spite of what he had said; but he could not go looking for an invitation."[3] Castro was widely acclaimed in a visit to New York, and then went on to Canada.

While in Washington the Premier appeared on a "Meet the Press" program. He denied that either he, his brother Raúl, or Raúl's wife, were Communists, and said that his heart lay with the democracies and that he did not agree with Communism. He also mentioned that elections would be postponed about four years because it would take that long to solve Cuba's problems. Castro commented, "Real democracy is not possible for hungry people. Real democracy

ought to be established over social justice and work for everybody."[4]

Old-line Communists Reappear

Although Castro spoke against Communism in Washington, developments in Cuba belied his words. A rebel criminal code drawn up during the conflict with Batista was being used to deal out summary justice to hundreds of opponents of the regime. In many instances justice was done, but in others the charge was made that Castro was using this means to rid himself of political opponents. Furthermore, drastic rent reductions, lowering of land values, and forced sale of vacant lands caused many members of the middle class, which had supported Castro, to feel that Communism was indeed the aim of the new government. Former prominent Communists were now openly active. The Communist newspaper *Hoy* resumed publication under the editorship of Carlos Rafael Rodríguez, a leader of the Communist party in the 1940's, and a minister in Batista's government from 1940 to 1944.

Juan Marinello, Blas Roca, and Lázaro Peña, all prominent Communists, reappeared on the scene and began to reorganize the Popular Socialist party. Communist influence in the labor unions increased, in spite of the efforts of some leaders of the Twenty-sixth of July movement to combat it. Major Ernesto "Ché" Guevara, Argentinian physician, supporter of the former leftist government of Jacobo Arbenz in Guatemala and Castro's close associate, also seemed to be pushing the country far to the left. The leftist inclinations of Raúl Castro were also to be seen.

On June 3, 1959, the Agrarian Reform Law was passed, providing for sweeping land reforms and expropriation of large estates. The handwriting on the wall was unusually clear. When President Urrutia expressed dissatisfaction with the growing influence of the Communists in government, Castro summarily dismissed him in a radio broadcast and replaced him on July 17 with Osvaldo Dorticós Torrado, a small-town lawyer. Castro himself resigned as Premier.[5]

Within ten days, however, Castro resumed the premiership. Meanwhile invasion scares and attempts were reported in Nicaragua, Panama, and the Dominican Republic, with Castro singled out as

the instigator. Castro responded to a warning by President Eisenhower in July that the United States was closely watching the situation, by commenting that Cuba would never accept any interference in her domestic affairs by any international organization or nation, including the United States.[6]

The Disenchanted

Disillusionment with Castro continued to grow within Cuba. Major Pedro Luis Díaz Lanz defected to the United States, and appeared as a witness before the U. S. Senate Internal Security Committee, charging Communist influence in Cuba. This did not endear either Díaz Lanz or the U. S. Senate to Castro. Meanwhile the ties between Cuba and the Soviet Union were growing, as well as with the People's Republic of China. In July the New China Democratic Alliance, a Communist group, announced that it was establishing a Chinese newspaper in Havana.

Castro seemed to find traitors everywhere. Major Huberto Matos, one of his closest associates in the struggle against Batista, was arrested for alleged antigovernment activities. One of the first anti-Castro organizations to be established was that sponsored by Rafael Díaz-Balart, former brother-in-law of Castro.

Díaz-Balart, who had fled into exile in January, 1959, called his group "La Rosa Blanca." A revolutionary pamphlet circulated by a pro-Castro group in New York City answered Díaz-Balart by reproducing Martí's poem of the same name, and charging,

Martí did not live to see his political and social work betrayed by bad Cubans. He could not foresee that the best of our youth, men and women, would be outraged and murdered with impunity by men of the lowest character, exalted in power by brute force. . . . And now those bad Cubans, who, after having dishonored and violated the national honor, instead of lowering their heads and asking for pardon from an offended fatherland, attempt also to dishonor the sacred memory of the Apostle.

The tract then declared that the true name of a traitorous group associated with the Batista regime should be "The Black Rose," which signified desolation and death. This then was an answer to Díaz-Balart's use of "La Rosa Blanca" for his group.[7]

At its tenth National Labor Congress in November, 1959, the Cuban Confederation of Workers withdrew from the anti-Communist Inter-American Regional Organization of Labor, calling it an "agency of American imperialism."[8] In the same month Guevara replaced Felipe Pazos as head of the National Bank of Cuba. Pazos had been a leading moderate in the Castro regime and highly respected in banking circles inside and outside of Cuba. This was just one more instance of moderates being replaced by aggressive leftists. Another important change that had occurred earlier, in June, was the resignation of Roberto Agramonte as foreign minister, and his replacement by Dr. Raúl Roa, former Dean of Social Sciences at the University of Havana, and an aid to this writer in his researches on Martí. Roa once told the author that Batista police had broken into his home and held him at bay with machine guns as they searched for proof of his collaboration with Castro. He laughed and commented that they accused him of being the bearded revolutionary's main contact in Havana. "Wasn't that ridiculous?" Roa asked me. It seemed so at the time, but not now.

In September Dr. Roa's campaign against the United States was brought into sharp relief, when he abstained in the General Assembly from voting on the question of admitting Communist China to the United Nations. In the past the United States had been able to command the lead in directing the voting of the Latin American bloc in such matters, but this was a distinct and shocking reversal.[9]

By the end of 1959 and early in 1960 Cuban attacks against the United States increased in intensity. The President was called "the little old golf player who misrules the United States," and Christian Herter, Secretary of State, was referred to as "a robust wolf of the imperialist den."[10]

Martí Commemorated

Meanwhile the anniversary of Martí's birth was once more commemorated January 28, 1960. An editorial in *Bohemia* commented on the significance of the celebrations,

Our people loves in Martí the human synthesis of its best sentiments, of its dearest desires, of its highest destiny. Martí is a living example of all

civic virtues. He incorporated the whole past history of the struggle for liberty, he brought this beautiful tradition to life with his inflammatory words and his heroic will, and he outlined a future of dignity, democracy, and justice, toward which our people are surely moving, in spite of the obstacles that error and evil have strewn in their path.

The article continued,

Not infrequently it was necessary to express one's love for Martí merely in observance of the important dates in his life and in those of our country's history, concealing one's true feelings, so as not to confuse the healthy devotion of the people with the farcical "official devotion" of bureaucrats whose conduct was unworthy of honoring the Apostle. That happened in the tragic seven years of the dictatorship. But ever since last year the cult to Martí has again become external without injury to its deep emotional content, because an atmosphere of liberty is breathed in the country. . . .

The editorial then commented favorably upon the many ceremonies being conducted in Martí's honor throughout the country, and above all, the best to be observed was the return of the Martí Suppers, which had been suppressed for so long.[11]

Henceforth a parade of new admirers began to appear before the statue of Martí in Central Park, Havana, to pay homage. One was Deputy Premier Anastas Mikoyan, who early in February laid a big floral wreath bearing the red hammer and sickle at the foot of Martí's statue.

"Martí said it."

The University of Havana was also the scene of homage to Martí on his anniversary. Roberto Agramonte, the ex-foreign minister, opened the series of ten lectures of the Seventh Martí Lectureship. The President of the Republic, Osvaldo Dorticós, spoke at the end of the Martí Week, which included the lectures. Dorticós told his audience that Martí's call for action for a bright future for Cuba had fallen into a void and that it was "necessary to repeat Martí, not only in a gesture of enthusiastic recollection, but also in bringing his thought to life, by refreshing the mentality of our people and reminding them again and again, today and every day, that what he asked for in Cuba is still left to be done in our land, and that the same

danger that he anticipated still exists on the American continent."
The President then repeated the well-worn phrases of Martí
about the dangers of economic domination by a single country (the
United States) becoming political domination. He continued,

Martí said this, and when we say it now, that we want to buy from and
sell to all nations, we are called Communists. Martí, not we, said that we
should join the whole world, and not just a part of it. . . . And José Martí
was no Communist when he said . . . 'If the family of republics of the
Americas has a special destiny, it should be that one will not strike away
from the rest.'[12]

In March the French freighter "La Coubre," loaded with munitions, exploded in the Havana harbor. It was reminiscent of the
famous explosion of the "Maine" in 1898. The "La Coubre" explosion was blamed on the United States by the government newspaper, *Revolución*. As a result relations became more strained than
ever, and the demand was increasingly heard in the United States
that sugar imports from Cuba should be drastically cut in order to
bring the rebels to order.

In June of 1960, President Dorticós made a whirlwind visit to
other Latin American countries. He held an extended press conference in Lima, Peru, outlining the accomplishments of the Revolution.
One enquiring reporter questioned him about freedom of the press
in Cuba, particularly the seizure and suppression of the *Diario de la
Marina*. Dorticós explained it away with the comment that Martí
was the first one to recognize the perfidy of the *Diario*, saying that
Cubans should combat everything the newspaper recommended. He
explained, "Lo dijo Martí." ("Martí said it.")[13] Thus a new phrase-
ology was introduced for an old rationale. Martí said it, and so it
must be sanctioned.

Meanwhile in Havana, Blas Roca, editor of the Communist newspaper *Hoy*, also defended the silencing of the *Diario de la Marina*
on the grounds that freedom of the press could not be allowed to
endanger the Revolution, and to permit the return of a semicolonial
regime to oppress nine-tenths of the population.[14]

In August of 1960, Fidel Castro ordered seizure of all United
States property in Cuba, estimated at around $750,000,000. In the
same month the Foreign Ministers of the Organization of American

States met in San José, Costa Rica, to consider demands by the United States that Cuba be condemned for allowing Communist infiltration into the Western Hemisphere. The Cuban Foreign Minister, Raúl Roa, answered the charges with a long, two-hour speech which was liberally laced with the expression, "No lo dijo Marx, lo dijo Martí." ("Marx didn't say it, Martí said it.") Herbert J. Mangham, a frequent writer on Mexico and Cuba, wrote from the conference that Roa preceded many quotations from Martí with this phrase and that he used Martí to justify all of the things for which Castro was criticized, especially his anti-Americanism. Mangham declared, "Dr. Roa, a brilliant polemicist, used the phrase with dramatic effect, and it was one of the reasons he got the biggest hand of the session."[15]

The OAS, Castro, and Trujillo

The United States was not successful, however, in persuading the foreign ministers to condemn Castro and Cuba by name, but the conference did pass a resolution opposing extracontinental domination by Communist power. Dictator Rafael Trujillo, however, was condemned by name, and the foreign ministers recommended severance of diplomatic ties with the Dominican Republic. Trujillo was still the greater menace in the eyes of the delegates.

This sentiment was confirmed later in 1960 by José Figueres, former president of Costa Rica, after a lecture to a group attending the Eleventh Annual Conference on the Caribbean at the University of Florida. In the question period the author asked the former president whom he considered the greater menace to the free institutions of the Americas, Trujillo or Castro, and Figueres responded, "Trujillo!"

Castro at the United Nations

The month following the San José meeting saw Fidel Castro delivering a diatribe against the United States in the General Assembly of the United Nations. The Premier lost an opportunity to elaborate on the sayings of Martí. However, Castro did end with a

quotation from "The Declaration of Havana," which is alleged to be based on the guiding spirit of Martí. The Premier repeated Article 6 of the proclamation of the National General Assembly,

The right of the farmers to the land; the right of the worker to the fruits of his labor; the right of children to education; the right of the sick to medical and hospital assistance; the right of the young to work; the right of students to free, experimental, and scientific instruction; the right of Negroes and Indians to the full dignity of man; the right of women to civic, social, and political equality; the right of old people to a secure old age; the right of intellectuals, artists, and scientists to struggle by means of their works for a better world; the right of nations to nationalization of imperialist monopolies, thus recovering the national wealth and resources; the right of countries to free commerce with all the peoples of the world; the right of nations to full sovereignty; the right of nations to convert their military fortresses to schools, and to arm their workers, their farmers, their students, their intellectuals, the Negro, the Indian, the woman, the young man, the old man, all the oppressed and exploited, so that they may defend, on their own, their rights and destinies.[16]

On October 14 the United States State Department answered Castro's many charges against the United States with some of its own. Castro's complaints had concerned U. S. relations with Cuba since 1898; American monopolies in Cuba; the U. S. naval base at Guantánamo Bay; support of Batista through military aid and friendly ambassadors; Cuba's balance of payments with the United States; terms of payment for expropriated lands in Cuba; Cuban sugar exports to the United States; anti-Castro Cubans in the United States; explosion of the munitions ship "La Coubre" in the Havana harbor; charges of aerial bombing of Cuba from United States territory; alleged propaganda and subversion on Swan Island (radio broadcasts to Cuba); "red smear" tactics of the American press against Castro's government; the use of Guantánamo Bay as a pretext for provoking an incident to justify "aggression" in Cuba; the destruction of Puerto Rico's nationality; confining of the Cuban delegation to Manhattan when it was attending the United Nations meetings in New York; difficulty of renting hotel rooms in New York; accusations against the Cuban delegation of involvement in the death of a young girl shot in an incident between anti-Castro Cubans and

Castro supporters; and finally, refusal of the United States to negotiate with Cuba.

The United States delegate to the United Nations answered these charges in detail, and then elaborated on the complaints of the United States against Cuba. These were as follows:

1. For openly announced political reasons Cuba's imports from the United States have been drastically reduced.

2. Property is not expropriated but confiscated without payment, to serve political rather than social ends.

3. Growing intervention in Cuban affairs by the Soviet Union and Communist China is welcomed by the government of Cuba.

4. The present Cuban government seeks to intervene in the internal affairs of other American states and to undermine the inter-American system.

5. The present Cuban government claims to speak for the Cuban people but denies them the right to choose their own spokesmen in free elections . . . only the Communist party is permitted to function . . . the Cuban jails are crowded with thousands of political prisoners.

6. The editors of the great Cuban papers are all in exile, while every expression of opposition to the policies of the government or to Communism is suppressed as counter-revolutionary.

7. It interferes with the free exercise of religion.

8. The right of a fair and impartial trial is denied those who differ with the government in power.

Although Castro's speech to the United Nations had not mentioned Martí by name, surprisingly the United States document did:

The great apostle of American liberty was Thomas Jefferson. The great Cuban apostle of liberty was José Martí, a man whose name and ideals are respected in the United States.

On the centenary of Martí's birth the Soviet Union tried to indicate some spiritual tie between Martí and Communism. No such tie exists, nor could exist. Martí's opinion of Marxism was expressed in his famous letter to Fermín Valdés Domínguez. The Marxian concept has two basic dangers, he said: "that of extraneous, confused, and incomplete interpretations, and that of the pride and dissimulated violence of ambitious men, who in order to raise themselves in the world begin by pretending—in order to have shoulders of other men on which to stand—to be impassioned defenders of the helpless."

Martí perceived correctly the dangers of Communist imperialism under a pretense of defending and succoring the oppressed. He perceived correctly that the strength of the Western Hemisphere depends on the

fraternal unity of its peoples. He perceived correctly that the true goal and glory of mankind is brotherhood, peace, dignity; and that unity is the key to strength and progress.[17]

And thus the United States State Department discovered and made use of the symbol of Martí as the Universal Man. It takes no stretch of the imagination to assume that Roa's frequent repetition of "Martí lo dijo" at the San José conference must have awakened the United States delegation to the usefulness of Martí as a symbol.

President John F. Kennedy also referred to Martí in a speech to Latin American diplomats in Washington on March 14, 1961. In his ten-point program for economic aid for Latin America he paid tribute to Simón Bolívar, José de San Martín, and Martí as social reformers in the spirit of Washington and Jefferson.

It is interesting to note, however, that at the time of the Martí Centenary two leading Cuban Communists had categorically denied that Martí was a Marxist. A statement by Juan Marinello in 1953 has already been referred to in Chapter Seven. Another leading Communist, Carlos Rafael Rodríguez, had written that Martí was remarkable not only for his part in gaining independence for Cuba, but also for seeing the dangers of exchanging one master, Spain, for another, the United States; but, he insisted,

One must not, let us make it clear once and for all, attribute to Martí ideological bases that are alien to him and that distort his real significance. It is plausible, but it is artificial to probe the great man to extract from him a pretended socialist streak; imagine what his stature would be if he had to cope with the problems that surround us today. This is true because in perspective we can see that no one was more the child of his times, more expressive of his class, more tied to the customs of his day, than José Martí. . . . The Republic of Martí, therefore, is democratic in its political aspect, and bourgeois in its social content.[18]

The United States Breaks with Cuba

Twenty days before the presidential elections in November, 1960, President Eisenhower sanctioned an economic embargo against Cuba. Cuba, supported by the Soviet Union, responded with a request that the General Assembly of the United Nations consider Cuba's charges that the United States was threatening aggression and that invasion

was imminent.[19] It was rejected. In the middle of December the President extended the ban on Cuban sugar imports, and the Department of Agriculture assigned no sugar quotas for 1961 to Cuba. The reason given was that Cuba was following a policy of deliberate hostility toward the United States and that it was steadily committing increasing amounts of its sugar crop to Communist countries.[20]

A break in relations between the United States and Cuba was imminent, and it came January 3, 1961, when the United States broke diplomatic ties with the Castro government. The action was taken after a demand by the Castro government that the United States Embassy in Havana reduce its staff from eighty-seven to eleven persons. Castro charged that 80 per cent of the employees were "spies of the Federal Bureau of Investigation."[21]

The CIA Invades Cuba

The *New York Times* in an editorial on the same day wrote, "It is incredible to us that the Cubans can believe we are about to invade their island."[22] Nevertheless, the Kennedy administration sanctioned an invasion of the island under the sponsorship of the Central Intelligence Agency and the National Revolutionary Council, the main Cuban refugee group in the United States. The Council was headed by José Miró Cardona, Castro's first premier, long since defected to the United States. The abortive invasion took place at Cochinos Bay on April 17, 1961, and the part officially played by the United States was disclosed a few days later.[23] If it was Soviet policy to dupe the Cubans into provoking the United States into attacking a Latin American country in order to undermine hemisphere solidarity, it was indeed a shrewd move. At any rate, the United States blundered badly. Over a thousand Cuban invaders were taken prisoners.

On May 1 the exultant Castro declared that Cuba was a socialist nation, and that elections would be barred. The next day he declared that Cuba would become a full-fledged member of the Communist bloc. Toward the end of the month the U. S. Central Intelligence Agency reported that the cost of the invasion to the United States had been $45,000,000. Meanwhile Castro offered to exchange 1,173 captives for 500 tractors. This immediately led to a widespread

campaign for funds for "Tractors for Freedom" throughout the United States. The relatives of the prisoners, however, were doomed to disappointment when the deal fell through later in the year because Castro raised the ransom terms.

The Advance of Marxism

Throughout 1961 the conversion of Cuba to Communism moved inexorably forward. Late in July Castro announced that Cuba would eventually have one party to build a socialist state. His opposition in Cuba seemed to be thoroughly crushed by the failure of the invasion attempt, and the Revolutionary Council in the United States was torn by dissension. The *New York Times* reported that only five of the two hundred groups in the United States seemed to be at all effective in working to oppose Castro.[24]

Early in December Fidel Castro avowed his faith in Marxism, saying that he would form a Socialist Revolution party with restricted membership to lead the nation to a "people's democracy." He also revealed that he had previously hidden his Marxist beliefs to avoid alienating the bourgeoisie before he was ready to fight them.[25] This finally put to rest extensive and immaterial speculation as to whether Castro was "actually a Communist or not."

Cuba Excluded from the OAS

Meanwhile the Kennedy administration, burned by criticism of the Cuban invasion attempt, had been working actively behind the scenes to obtain a specific condemnation of Fidel Castro's government and its association with the Soviet bloc. The test came at Punta del Este, Uruguay, when the foreign ministers of the Organization of American States met late in January, 1962, at the request of Colombia to consider the threat of Communism in the Western Hemisphere. At stake was President Kennedy's "Alliance for Progress," a massive, multibillion-dollar aid program for Latin America.

On January 31, 1962, the meeting of consultation of the foreign ministers voted twenty to one (Cuba against) that the principles of Communism were incompatible with the principles of the inter-

American political system. The action was hailed by President Kennedy as being the first time that the American republics had spoken with one voice against the perils of Marxism-Leninism to the Western Hemisphere system.[26]

The United States, although it succeeded in obtaining a resolution to exclude Cuba from participation in the inter-American system, found that abstentions by Argentina, Bolivia, Brazil, Chile, Ecuador, and Mexico made victory significantly less complete. A resolution was also passed calling for suspension of trade with Cuba in arms and implements of war, with instructions to the Council of the OAS to consider banning other items. Several days later President Kennedy announced a ban on all trade with Cuba, except for some foods and medicines.

Cuba promptly challenged the legality of being excluded from the OAS, inasmuch as there are no provisions for expulsion from the Organization.[27] The Soviet Union supported the complaint, asserting that it was incompatible with the principles of the United Nations Charter, which specifies in Article 53 that no enforcement action may be taken against a state by a regional organization without prior authorization by the Security Council of the United Nations.

On February 14, as the Council of the Organization of American States in Washington, D. C., was preparing to expel Cuba, the Cuban delegate, Ambassador Carlos M. Lechuga, peremptorily took a walk, Soviet-style. Expulsion thereupon became a mere formality. The following day the General Assembly's Political Committee at the United Nations overwhelmingly rejected by a vote of 50 to 11 Cuba's charge that the United States was planning aggression. Nineteen Latin American nations gave solid support to the United States. Cuba's isolation from the community of Western Hemisphere nations seemed virtually complete. The Security Council also denied Cuba's request for consideration of the charge. The solidarity that José Martí had called for in "Nuestra América" had failed to materialize in the image advocated by the Castro regime.

Marxist Directorate Formed

On March 9, the Havana government announced a 25-man

Communist-style directorate to form the leadership of the Integrated Revolutionary Organization, a committee to establish the single proletarian party that Castro had promised to form. At least ten Communists were in the group, including Blas Roca, Carlos Rafael Rodríguez, who had replaced Fidel Castro on February 14 as head of the all-powerful Agrarian Reform Institute, and Lázaro Peña, head of the Cuban Workers Federation.[28] Conspicuously absent was Juan Marinello, head of the University of Havana, but no longer president of the Popular Socialist party (Communist).

In three years, step by step, Fidel Castro and his fellow Marxists converted the freedom-loving people of Cuba into a tightly-knit socialist dictatorship. In typical fashion the end, social revolution, justified the means, deception, betrayal, terror, and destruction of human liberties. The use of Martí as a symbol is clearly evident; his abuse, tragic.

Chapter 10

SUMMARY AND CONCLUSIONS

THE LIFE OF JOSÉ MARTÍ was an odyssey, a wandering in exile, a life fraught with perennial anguish in its dedication to free Cuba from Spain. Poet, dramatist, political prisoner, pamphleteer, novelist, journalist, teacher, diplomat, filibusterer, and revolutionist— Martí was all of these and more. Yet he is probably best known for his writings and revolutionary activities. His fevered brain assimilated and converted into fluid Spanish prose some of the currents of social, political, and economic thought of the nineteenth century. He was a graphic reporter of great and little events in Europe, Latin America, and the United States during the 1880's and 1890's. He often wrote with such haste, however, that many of his observations remain in topical settings, where their usefulness is obscured. At worst in his writings he was obtuse, wordy, and flamboyant; at best he was sincere, sensitive, and acute in capturing the essence of the personality of a great man or reporting a human interest story. One can see originality of expression in much of his work, especially his poetry, but on the other hand much of his material, particularly on European affairs, came to him from other sources.

The Specter of Failure

Although Martí is given credit for having started the Revolution on its final journey to success, and therefore in the final analysis is identified with that success, no one element seemed to dominate in the personal history of Martí quite so much as failure. His relations

245

with his father were for the most part marked by misunderstanding. He failed as a young conspirator by allowing himself to be discovered. His teaching experience in Guatemala turned out unsuccessfully, as did his marriage to Carmen Zayas-Bazán. He ended in disaster as a conspirator for a second time in Cuba, when he was once again deported to Spain. The newspaper he started in Venezuela, as well as his reporting ventures for a newspaper there, ended unhappily. He began writing for numerous magazines and newspapers in New York, but he never seemed to last for more than a year or two on most of them. He had grandiose schemes for books, but he never carried them out. He was deficient as a novelist and dramatist, although he succeeded as a translator.

The Fernandina expedition, which was to invade Cuba, was a fiasco. When Martí finally did gather a group to go to Cuba, he and Gómez were unable to secure the original number of men, although the small party that set out did manage to reach the Cuban shore. Martí's relations with General Antonio Maceo were never smooth, and they were unable to reach an agreement on the establishment of the government that Cuba was going to have. Martí's final and decisive defeat was as a soldier. As a newly-created major general he knew less about fighting than the ordinary private. Apparently without having fired a shot he was cut down by the enemy. Yet it seems that he was not wholly unprepared for the death that came to him at Dos Ríos. Some assert that he committed suicide, which could indicate that he himself considered his life a failure, redeemable only by an act of self-sacrifice. To paraphrase an old French proverb, "Nothing succeeds like success," one might say that with respect to Martí's last act, which assured him his long-sought martyrdom, "Nothing succeeded like failure."

Despite Martí's record of inadequate performance in many endeavors, he still made decisive contributions to the Revolution. A hero by correspondence, he kept the spirit of the Revolution going by reminding its leaders of their duty, by encouraging the tobacco workers of Florida to give just a little more to the party, and by dedicating himself to the movement, writing, speaking, and traveling. As the friendly persuader he did not fail. He was the force behind the creation of the Cuban Revolutionary party. Therein lies one of

his greatest successes, a substantial contribution to the independence of Cuba.

Whether Martí's failures were the result of a lack of personal capacity at times, or of an inability to foresee or adapt himself to circumstances, or of merely innocent association with misfortune, it was precisely his everlasting faith in spite of adversity that led to his greatness. Although discouraged at times, he continually displayed a boundless optimism in believing that the revolutionary forces, poorly organized, poorly equipped, and poorly trained though they were, could overcome the Spaniards after so many abortive uprisings. With this record of defeats, carrying on the fight must have taken great courage. He never lost faith that the Revolution would be a success. This is the faith that moves nations. It brought independence to Cuba, although Martí did not live to see it fulfilled. Cubans may find it unpatriotic to speak of Martí's failures, but to point them out is only to emphasize his successes, and to explain his apotheosis. Most saints have undergone great tribulations in their lives.

Martí's Moral and Social Philosophy

Martí was not a philosopher, although this point has been the subject of contention among Cuban writers. Martí, rather, was a writer of homely moral phrases, many of them rephrasings from the Bible. An eclectic, he seldom gave the source for his philosophizings. It is difficult to coordinate his social and moral philosophy, but it is possible to detect certain "resonances," a favorite term with one biographer of Martí.

Martí constantly moralized about man—his mind, character, love, and friendship—the good life, and death. He felt that social conventions hampered the full development of the individual, and hoped that by exposing society's restrictions he could somehow ease them by means of his writings. He was torn in his concept of man between seeing him romantically as self-sufficient, intelligent, and self-sacrificing, and looking upon him as only a part of an ignorant mass, or as a sleeping beast. He wrote lovingly of all human virtues: truth, honesty, dignity, fraternity, compassion, piety, selflessness, justice, happiness, friendship, and love. His poem on friendship, "La

Rosa Blanca," has become a Cuban byword. One of the strongest threads running through Martí's personal philosophy was the concept of grief. He frequently wrote about it, preached it, rejoiced in it. Martí saw himself as the chosen son of stern Duty. He found satisfaction in the sacrifices that duty demanded, and he sought the martyrdom that excessive attention to this concept often brings. The emotion of love, whether it was for his own suffering or for his fellow man, never left Martí. It was probably a combination of these feelings that drove him on through disappointments and hardships to his final immolation at Dos Ríos.

Martí has been criticized for his apparent lack of a sense of humor, but it is probably just this shortcoming that permitted him to become a martyr. People who refuse to take themselves seriously are just not capable of bearing the cross. Nevertheless Martí was a vibrant individual who used every moment of his life in some kind of productive activity. It is therefore paradoxical that he wrote so often of death, and of the longing that he had for it. At times, however, he resisted the thought of dying, and perhaps for that very reason lived so actively.

Martí was often confused as to where he stood on religion. He was attracted by Oriental mysticism with its emphasis on transmigration of souls, pantheism, panentheism, Christianity, and agnosticism. Martí was perhaps at his best when expressing his sentiments about humanitarianism. He was certain of a life after death, finding evidence of it in the miracle of the brain, electricity, suffering, music, and the shortcomings of man. His greatest idol was Ralph Waldo Emerson, about whom he wrote his best piece of descriptive literature. Martí was hostile to the Roman Catholic Church, often making bitter statements about it, as in his reporting on the Church's censure of Father Edward McGlynn, and in his tract "Hombre del campo," which criticized the rural clergy in Latin America.

Martí's moral philosophy found expression in most of his writings on social institutions. He wrote not as a scientist but aphoristically about the home, husband and wife relationships, divorce, adultery, parental obligations to children, education, and race relationships. Although generally favorable to the institution of marriage, Martí often commented on the lack of understanding existing between hus-

bands and wives, undoubtedly influenced by his own unhappy experiences. He loved children, composing some of his most tender poems and stories for them.

In his concern for the younger generations he wanted to see them well educated, not with the traditional emphasis on theology and rhetoric, the main subjects of scholasticism, but more on practical subjects, such as mechanics, physics, and chemistry. He was particularly concerned about concentration on urban schooling to the detriment of scientific education in agriculture. He called for experiment stations and traveling teachers for the benefit of the rural population. Although Martí seems to have been influenced by Positivism in his ideas on education, no agreement among Cuban writers has been reached on this point.

Martí was conscious of problems of race in the Americas, writing of the difficulties of the assimilation of the Negroes in Cuba. He believed that the Negroes were intelligent and capable, and not to be scorned because of the color of their skin. Although he recognized the obstacles confronted in springing from slave status to freedom, he was confident that the problem could be solved by studying the history of the Negroes. He never specified, however, the way in which the transition was to be accomplished.

On the subject of Indians, Martí wrote articles, a novel, and a play, and translated a famous American novel on that subject, Helen Hunt Jackson's *Ramona*. He saw that the desperation of the Indians' status in the Americas could be traced to the devastation brought upon them by the Spanish conquerors, and that the Americas would never progress until the Indians had to stand upon their own feet.

Without too much difficulty it is possible to find almost any moral or social philosophy that one wants in Martí. It is partly for this reason that writers have found it so difficult to classify him as either a "philosopher" or a "thinker." In fact, this conflict of opinion over Martí's ideas is an indication of the vagueness and contradictory nature of many of them. The most that can be said, perhaps, is that Martí produced an extensive body of writings in matters of morals that has stimulated extensive comment and citation. That comment has included questioning the validity of Martí's serving as a moral example in view of certain aspects of his own private life.

Martí's Political Ideas

Martí frequently mentioned political philosophers in his writings, but as in his moral and social philosophy, he cannot be said to have held to any organized political system. His curiosity led him to many insights into the practical workings of politics, which he seemed to prefer to more formal study. He saw politics as a resolution of equations, an attempt to maintain a status of equilibrium among the power groups of society. He was first of all, however, a revolutionist bent on remolding the distribution of those powers in Cuba by the elimination of Spanish colonial forces from the island.

Three important sources for the expression of Martí's political philosophy exist in the documents of the Revolution: the *Resoluciones,* the *Bases del Partido Revolucionario Cubano,* and the *Manifiesto de Montecristi.* In them Martí called for a holy crusade to be marked by individual sacrifices to defeat the Spaniards, although it was to be a war without hatred and mistreatment of the vanquished. When the war was over no special group was to be allowed to rise to the top at the expense of the others. In particular the military was to remain subordinate to the civilian powers. The vestiges of Spanish corruption were to be rooted out, and with their disappearance the Cubans would be able to reassert their qualities of tolerance, culture, intelligence, humanity, and justice, which would help to prevent Cuba from falling into the errors committed by other Latin American nations after having won their independence. Cuba would then be dedicated to the principles of freedom, equality, and justice for all.

Martí's experience with colonial government, however, did not include firsthand knowledge of institutional operations. The three documents did not call for a constitution, nor did they show that Martí could see what institutions would be established after independence had been achieved. In this respect it is very clear that Martí was more the revolutionist than a student of institutions. He did, however, have some ideas about the "good governor," and, in general terms, about the nature of the new Republic. He insisted upon a careful study of the problems peculiar to the nation rather than reliance upon imitation of foreign governmental operations. He felt that too much was being copied in the Latin American nations.

In his political philosophizings he emphasized the concept of patriotism, which he declared was the most beautiful and vehement expression of man's love. He wanted the submission of the individual to the nation, in spite of his many declarations on the virtues of democracy and freedom, saying that the individual was to be wiped out and the nation served instead. He wrote ecstatically of liberty, influenced by the romanticism of the nineteenth century, but he felt uneasy at the thought of unrestrained freedom. Instead he concentrated on the duties of the citizen toward his government. He glorified public service, although he recognized that it called for numerous sacrifices that were not appreciated by the masses of the people. He was less emphatic about the rights of the citizen. He asserted that every citizen, and particularly the educated, had a clear responsibility to take part in politics. Martí exalted liberty as long as it seemed useful to encourage the Cubans to gain their freedom from Spain, but his writings elsewhere indicate that he would have considerably restricted that liberty once the Republic was in operation.

An admiration for great men stands out in Martí's political philosophy, particularly in the instances of Simón Bolívar, José de San Martín, George Washington, Abraham Lincoln, Benito Juárez, Ralph Waldo Emerson, Walt Whitman, Peter Cooper, Henry David Thoreau, Cecilio Acosta, and José de la Luz y Caballero. He thought that the common people, "the little packs of beasts," never pardoned the heroes that they were obliged to admire. Martí felt comfortable in the presence of great men, perhaps because he thought of himself in that category. His admiration did not go out unqualifiedly to the "man on horseback," however, but was rather directed toward those who had achieved great humanitarian accomplishments.

Martí saw Latin America as one great community of Spanish-speaking peoples with an identity of problems, particularly in their attempts to shed the detrimental aspects of the Spanish heritage.

Martí recognized the differences existing between the United States and Latin America. For that reason he urged the Latins not to rely too closely on their northern neighbor for economic relations, since domination of their economies by the United States would also bring political domination. He said that this was especially true in Cuba, which relied upon sugar for the major share of its national

income. He hoped that friendship would exist between North and South in the Western Hemisphere, but he believed that the Latin Americans could not be too careful.

Martí's economic ideas were a reflection of the classic economic liberalism of the nineteenth century. He held that wealth was produced more quickly in agriculture than in industry, which he thought was not so honest a source of work as that of tilling the soil. Martí glorified the manual laborer, in contrast to a formidable Latin American scorn for the man who works with his hands. He urged education as a means of solving agricultural problems, in particular diversification to avoid reliance on one crop, which often led to disaster in international economic relations.

Martí looked with sympathy upon the worker in society, demonstrating his concern for social justice through his articles on the Haymarket Massacre in Chicago in 1886, and his article on Peter Cooper, the North American philanthropist. Some writers have asserted that Martí was deeply inclined to socialism. Although he wrote a sympathetic obituary of Karl Marx, there is little evidence to support any particular socialistic philosophy on his part. What stands out is a general humanitarian approach undisturbed by reflections on socialistic doctrines. In fact, Martí's ideas on social phenomena and their solutions romantically envisioned a *deus ex machina* to "dissipate the clouds of combat, and channel the original forces of the new state."

Whatever Martí's moral, social, and political philosophy consisted of, it seems clear that one very important feature stands out— humanitarianism. Sometimes the thread becomes obscured, however, when, for example, Martí speaks contemptuously of the common people, and seeks personal identification with great men.

Martianism

Immediately after his death, Martí was praised by his followers in exile for his contributions to the freedom movement. For the next thirty years, with a few notable exceptions, he seemed to attract the attention and comments of prominent figures abroad like Rubén Darío, Miguel Unamuno, Fernando de los Ríos, and Gabriela Mis-

tral, while the best writers in Cuba neglected him. This did not mean, however, that Martí was unheralded at home by other segments of the population. His likeness received ample expression in busts, statues, monuments, and stamps. The abrogation of the Platt Amendment in 1934 came at a time that a renaissance of interest in Martí was beginning, undoubtedly stimulated by increased national pride in complete independence.

During the Martí renaissance the volume of literary production on Martí increased heavily up to the period of the Centenary in 1953, although for the most part it was repetitive and unobjective in quality. During this period his writings and a few basic studies became forage for hundreds of aspiring authors. Although many of the Latin American nations, like many parts of Cuba, wrote extensively on Martí as his Centenary approached, Havana has always been the center of literary production on him. He has been clearly, and unfortunately, neglected by North American scholars.

At the same time that Martí was being promoted as the National Hero, social organizations in Cuba began to adopt him as the symbol of their own particular organization, as in Masonry, the Rotary clubs, and the Hebrew community. Although there is no documentary evidence to prove that Martí was a member, Masonry secured him fast. Martí has been most useful to the Masons as a symbol of anti-Roman Catholicism and general good fellowship. Special organizations, such as the Association of Former Students of the Martí Seminar, and the Order of the White Rose were established by his followers to propagate the Martí doctrine through Martianism in action. In their promotion of the cult of Martí these organizations enjoy a spirit of disinterestedness not to be found in groups that emphasize only a few aspects of Martí's teachings that happen to coincide with the objectives of that particular organization.

Apotheosis

The beginning of the apotheosis of Martí may be conveniently dated from a speech by Gonzalo de Quesada y Aróstegui in 1889, when Martí's favorite disciple referred to his mentor as the "Apostle." At the time of his death in 1895 the word "apotheosis" had already

been applied to Martí's sacrifice at Dos Ríos. Evidence of Martí's elevation to "sainthood" is to be found in the neologisms associated with his name in the language describing him. Not the least of the religious symbolism surrounding Martí is to be found in the Martian Suppers, held on the eve of his birthday.

The difficulty of reaching agreement on the representation of Martí in as intimate a medium as the screen gives ample evidence of the degree to which he has taken idealistic or mythical proportions in the minds of many Cubans. The polemic over the film, "La Rosa Blanca," shows the extent to which belligerency forms the basis of many activities connected with the figure of Martí. This is particularly true when a completely foreign company tries to produce the film, as happened with "Santiago." Then a mere oversight on the part of the producers becomes a deliberate slight, with a resulting release of anti-Americanism. In the major representations, as in statues and monuments, no agreement can be reached on the best interpretation of Martí, with the result that an un-Martian atmosphere of spite, bitterness, slander, and trickery often mark the homage paid him.

Martí, in addition to being canonized by his followers, is represented as the ideal Cuban, with all the virtues, imagined and real, possessed by him. His enthusiasts have compared him not unfavorably with national heroes in the United States, Latin America, Italy, India, Hungary, and China. In fact, to some of his admirers he is the supreme example of the universal man, the precursor of UNESCO.

Such idolization eventually brought a reaction. The reactors may be divided into two groups. First are those who write that everybody talks about Martí but nobody does anything to show that they are real followers of his. In total number of words this group probably exceeds the production of those whom they criticize. The second group, much smaller, is composed of those who direct their criticism toward the excesses of hero worship that have brought many to the brink of absurdity.

One authority on Martí, for instance, denied that there was anything Cuban about Martí, that it was ridiculous to make this assertion, and that the cult-makers operated in an atmosphere of hate and jealousy, rather than practicing the Martian doctrine that they preached.

One critic wanted to curtail demonstrations in favor of Martí by pro-
hibiting the use of his name for at least five years. Another ventured to
state that anyone who dared to criticize Martí's poetry, or to say that
his oratory became tiresome at times would be guilty of sacrilege. One
critic wanted to know how a man could become a saint by preaching
war. No conflict seemed, however, to exist in Martí's mind. In the
historical background of the conquistadores these two concepts of the
cross and the sword had been married. Martí was a descendant of
this tradition.

The most significant group in Cuban society that is unwilling
to accept Martí as a saint is the Roman Catholic Church. Clerical
and lay leaders have objected to the extremes of Martí's statements
against the Church in terms that are usually not heard in connection
with the Apostle. Extremist opinion has tried to associate Martí with
ultraconservative Spanish thought. Other leaders have attempted to
minimize Martí's anti-Roman Catholicism, pointing out that Martí
never left the Church, was married in it, and had his son baptized
in it. Others have cast doubt on the originality of his tract, "Hombre
del campo." The Church embraces Martí with one arm, and generally tries to conceal some of his unorthodox blemishes with the other,
perhaps seeing in him a rival if he is completely rejected.

The giant conjured up by the builders of the figure of Martí has
become so great that they are no longer able to claim a controlling
share in him. When they brought about the extensive publication
of his works, the erection of monuments, the naming of streets, parks,
schools, libraries, and in general a widespread publicity campaign,
they made Martí a household word. They expected miracles to be
wrought in his name, but the result has been that to speak of Martí
is to speak in clichés. How did he die? "With his face to the sun, of
course." When Martí was in the United States where did he live? "In
the monster's den, and he knew its insides." Martí has become a
captive in his native land, the jinni of the magic lamp. Although
minus the magic, he is the agent of every Aladdin, patriot or huckster,
who wishes to call him up.

The publicists of Martí must accept a good share of the blame
for the abuse of Martí. They may assert that it is no fault of theirs
that Martí is mistreated, but the fact is that by making Martí seem to

be the answer to every social, moral, and political question others have come to the conclusion that it must be a good thing to quote him. The Martians sowed the fields with fertile seeds, but now they are indignant because the crows have moved in. The fields have become a polemicists' paradise. The agitation over Martí's representation in monuments, on film, and over who is the most competent to pay him homage was made only too clear at the time of the Centenary.

The Roman Catholic Church perhaps must accept some of the responsibility for the exaltation of Martí in that the elaborate ceremony, the profusion of saints, and extravagance of religious expression have come to be commonplace terms in the Spanish language in part through the influence of the Church. Thus it has been an easy transference of terms from the Catholic religion to the Martí religion. This would be a difficult hypothesis to prove, but if true, it would show that the Church has also contributed to the cult of Martí.

The publicists of Martí, unless they want to lose him completely to the chauvinists and persons whom they criticize for abuse of Martí, should themselves stop being jingoists, and seek instead scholarly detachment. Writers on Martí should not be censured by the government, but pressure must be brought to bear firmly on new literary works that add nothing original to the lore of Martiana. The task of critics and publishers is to show their mettle.

Real progress will be made when the embattled ivory towers of *personalismo* crumble and all the biographers and Martians can get together to cooperate amicably for the good of Martianism. For instance, an Institute of Martian Studies, rigidly proscribing political associations, might be created. Certain campaigns could be mapped out, such as narrowing the gap between excessive praise of Martí through unobjective biographies, and the unrelenting accusation that Cuba is not the Republic that Martí dreamed of. Another project might be to improve the public education system. The first serious test would be to see if the Martians were capable of cooperating.

Politics, Labor, Education, and the Press

Martí has had a very significant impact on the Cuban people as a symbol in their politics. Just about every concept that he wrote about

has been cited by one political party or another, and in some instances acted upon. His opposition to the lottery, corruption, bureaucracy, spoils system, usury, militarism, racial discrimination, and illiteracy have appeared as important themes of political platforms, speeches, and public acts of homage. His writings, for instance, have been used by major political parties, such as the Cuban Revolutionary party (A) and the Cuban Peoples' party (O) in their campaigns of nationalism and economic independence from the United States.

Martí's birthday, January 28, has frequently been the time for some writers to take an inventory of progress of the nation, generally with gloomy conclusions. A certain safety for the critic, however, seems to lie in associating his words with the name of Martí, thus softening the writer's personal responsibility, at the same time sharpening the criticism. This was particularly true of many statements made during the Centenary in 1953, coming as it did within the year after Batista's *coup d'état.*

The clearest use of Martí as a symbol is for the party out of power to employ the Martian precepts of morality in government as a stick to harass the party in power, while the latter responds by quoting "La Rosa Blanca" as an expression of brotherly love and unity. When the roles are reversed, so is the use of Martí as a symbol. The public confession of loyalty to Martí, humility, and personal purity seems to have become a frequent device to attract sympathy for the speaker, as demonstrated in speeches by Fulgencio Batista, Ramón Grau San Martín, and Carlos Prío Socarrás.

Martí has served as a masquerade for political parties to twist to their purposes, as when the Communists use him exclusively to criticize racial discrimination, American imperialism, the Roman Catholic Church, and the wealthy. The fact that Martí has been neglected by the United States, and in one instance abused by American sailors, has added fuel to the Communist program of anti-Americanism.

Corruption in government in Cuba, a revival of the spirit of the days of the Caribbean buccaneers, has reached a frightening degree. It has been accompanied by what is almost worse, an attitude of amusement and indifference on the part of many toward punishment of the offenders. The corruption that Martí recognized as a Spanish

heritage and warned against is conveniently used as an excuse to explain away Cuban peculation, which many political leaders declare is the major source of evil in Cuban government. In large measure Cubans are to blame for taking a negative attitude toward reform. Their approach, "Any party promising to clean up the government just wants to get in power so that it can steal," is followed by a kind of grim satisfaction when they are proved right. In this climate of opinion the new governors find it easier not to resist temptation, knowing that the people expect them to steal. New administrations in power have often been reluctant to prosecute embezzlers from the previous government for fear of setting a precedent for honesty. Any honest-intentioned administration would seem to be doomed from the start by the opposition, since whatever it does, somewhere in the writings of Martí something can be found to twist around to criticize it.

Unfortunately the lawbreaker is a hero to many. Dating from the days of the multifarious regulations of the early Spanish colonial regime, finding a way around the law became the smart thing to do. The familiar phrase, "I obey, but I do not comply," has left a favorable impression on the thinking of many Latin Americans. *El relajo,* mockery, the spirit so well described by Miguel de Cervantes in the figure of Sancho Panza in *Don Quixote,* carries the day in Cuba. Martí plays Don Quixote, the idealist tilting at windmills, to Cuba's cynical Juan Criollo, Sancho Panza in the Cuban drama. Nothing was further from Martí than the spirit of mockery. Ironically he becomes a victim of it. In many respects those who preach duty, sacrifice, honor, and honesty in his name tread the path of ridicule when they practice just the opposite. By failing to follow the message of Martí when it did sound clear, as against corruption in office, they reduce their hero to a pitiful heap of bones in the cemetery in Santiago. Assassination becomes the reward for those who would put Martí's words against corruption into action by initiating legal processes against offenders.

The failure of political parties led by the reformers is just one of the many instances to confirm the charge that Cuba has not attained Martí's ideal Republic. Ironically, the drastic "cures" introduced by the Castro regime have become worse than the disease.

Martí has been taken over as a symbol by labor groups, but in the

main these have been too occupied with achieving material gains of better wages and working conditions to pay the Apostle more than superficial homage. Labor in Cuba, in addition, has been undergoing internal struggles in its recent past which have militated against the development of a Martian ideology.

One of the most appalling lacks of Martian action in contrast to the extensive Martian propaganda that it puts forth has been found in bureaucratic and corrupt practices in the field of Cuban education. Apathy and absenteeism in the educational system of Cuba are more than accounted for by the sale of teaching positions, the "proprietors" of classrooms who collect their salaries but who never teach, "show window" schools, the high rate of illiteracy (almost 50 per cent among children of school age in rural areas), wholesale robbery of education funds, low salaries, short school days, high school education for just a few, an excessive number of "botellas," many of them inspectors, shortage of school supplies, and dilapidated buildings. There is a bitter irony to be found in that the area in public life in which Martí is regularly and fervently honored through parades, Martian school groups, and classroom teaching is the one that has not received the benefits of his lofty concepts. To repeat his fine definition of education:

To educate is to deposit in each man all the human work which has preceded him; it is to make each man the abstract of the living world up until the day of his death; it is to put him at the level of his time, so that he may float upon it . . . that is preparing man for life.

That definition in reality becomes:

To educate is to deposit in each man the record of corruption, cynicism, malice, opportunism, and bureaucracy that many top administrators and some of their political appointments in the field of education have represented.

Consequently the Martian teachings of governmental ethics that are learned in the schools by the Cuban youth become the spark that often symbolizes revolt against corruption and restraints on personal liberties.

Some progress has been made, as in the establishment by Batista of the Education Missions and technical schools, and Castro's cam-

paign against illiteracy. It may take some time to evaluate the results. A very good indication will be the next census, which should be taken around 1963, when it will be interesting to see whether figures of illiteracy for the nation as a whole, and especially of the rural population, will drop.

The press in Cuba has not measured up to Martí's definitions and standards. The press, of course, cannot avoid censorship by a stronger force. Quite rightly it finds ways, through the use of Martí as a symbol, to protest against restrictions imposed by the government. On the other hand, it does not seem to show the necessary Martian idealism when it gives itself over to excessive commercialism and direct governmental subsidies.

Some day a scientific survey of Cuban public opinion should be made to determine the extent of Martí's influence on the public at large, using as hypotheses the conclusions stated in this study. Meanwhile informal conversations with Cubans may be reported. Most of the Cubans queried about Martí responded by saying that he was a great patriot, some that he was a genius, others that he was a kind of superman, and many that he was a saint, or God. Most believed that Martí had become the supreme figure for exploitation by conscienceless politicians. Although most of those with whom conversations were held quickly declared that Martí was cited to satiation, it was unusual to find any resentment toward Martí because of it. They saw him as the unhappy victim; Cuba as an un-Martian nation.

The Future

Throughout the third part of this book the approach chosen has been to share the indignation of those who have used Martí as an example to point an accusing finger at malefactors in government. Without radically departing from that attitude, one must nevertheless point out that only to a limited extent can Martí be held up as an example to show that Cuba is not the Republic of which he dreamed. In his general propositions of duty, honesty, honor, and self-sacrifice, Martí called for the very best in disinterested service to the nation. But he did not have an answer to every problem, as enthusiastic admirers do think. To rely on Martí for everything is a fatal over-

simplification of complex social, economic, and political problems. For fifteen years a Latin from Manhattan, in many ways Martí lost contact with the Cuban scene. There is hardly any point, for instance, in harping on the fact that Cuba should change its one-crop economy just because Martí recognized the problem. The economic plight of the generations who enter the job market with little hope of employment will not be solved by searching for the proper quotation from Martí. That is to expect, albeit in true Martian fashion, the *deus ex machina*.

Martí in many respects is hardly the guide for a modern government hustling along in the second half of the twentieth century. His thoughts on the actual running of a government were extremely vague. Martí never logically developed his ideas of the national psychology and the institutions that are fundamental to a form of government based upon a democratic way of life. It is clear that good intentions are not enough to keep a nation in operation, and that a party cannot achieve success merely by appealing to the civic conscience of the electorate.

Unfortunately it does not seem to be clear in the minds of many Latin Americans whether democracy is possible, or desirable, for their nations. The author's personal experience has included conversations with many who have wanted democracy, but who have not really understood it. This can be explained in part by the hierarchical and authoritarian organization of their personal experiences through the family, society, the army, the Church, and their background of colonial history. The individualism and emotionalism of the Latin American must be taken into account as an obstacle to democracy. It is possible to love liberty too much—at heart many Latin Americans are anarchists, unwilling to make concessions for the greater good by giving up petty privileges. If it is granted that a sincere desire for democracy exists in the minds of many Latin Americans, each step forward must be hailed with more enthusiasm when the obstacles to that step are considered.

Those who have reached the depths of despair and cynicism about the future of Cuba should be reminded that in spite of many failures, Martí never lost faith in the Cuban people nor the hope that they would some day enjoy an honest, efficient, and humanitarian govern-

ment. By keeping this faith in the midst of discouragement Cubans may some day work to justify Martí's trust in Cuba, his Promised Land. Those who assert gloomily that Cuba is not the nation Martí dreamed of, and that nobody pays any attention to the Apostle's precepts of morality, should consider the thought that his ideas may have had their influence in an infinite number of anonymous ways. Although it was stated in the Introduction that it would be difficult to prove that people in Cuba who hold certain beliefs do so because Martí said them, it may be asserted that a very considerable number of these persons express those ideas in Martí's terms, thus making it *seem* as if there were some connection in their thinking with the idea and Martí. Surely Cubans are benefiting from his example, even if the evidence of it is obscure.

CHAPTER 1

1. Cuba, *El Archivo Nacional en la conmemoración del Centenario del natalicio de José Martí y Pérez, 1853-1953* (La Habana: Publicaciones del Archivo Nacional de Cuba, 1953), XXXVI, 3-4.

2. Joaquín Llaverías, "Mariano Martí y Navarro—algunos datos de su vida," *Boletín del Archivo Nacional,* XXVII (1928), 275-300.

3. Cuba, *El Archivo Nacional,* p. 492.   4. *Ibid.,* pp. 493-505.

5. Antonio Martínez Bello, *La adolescencia de Martí, notas para un ensayo de interpretación psicológica* (La Habana: Imp. P. Fernández y Cía., 1944), pp. 6-9.   6. "Ofrenda de hermano," *Revista Cubana,* XXIX (1951-52), 238.

7. *Ibid.,* p. 239.   8. Cuba, *El Archivo Nacional,* pp. 3-5.   9. *Ibid.,* pp. 5-10.

10. *Obras completas de Martí,* ed. Gonzalo de Quesada y Miranda (74 vols.; La Habana: Ed. Trópico, 1936-49), I, 21, ed. note, 26.   11. *Ibid.,* XXVI, 15.

12. Herminio Portell-Vilá, *Historia de Cuba en sus relaciones con los Estados Unidos y España* (4 vols.; La Habana: Ed. Jesús Montero, 1938-41), I, 424, 438, 457.

13. Ramiro Guerra y Sánchez, *Guerra de los Diez Años, 1868-1878* (La Habana: Cultural, S. A., 1950), p. 41.

14. Jorge Mañach, *Martí, el apóstol* (Bilbao: Espasa-Calpe, 1933) p. 38.

15. Cuba, *El Archivo Nacional,* pp. 15-16.

16. Gonzalo de Quesada y Miranda, *Martí, hombre* (La Habana: Seoane, Fernández y Cía., 1940), p. 38.   17. Cuba, *El Archivo Nacional,* p. 19.

18. Quesada y Miranda, *Martí, hombre,* pp. 36-39.

19. Cuba, *El Archivo Nacional,* p. 21.

20. Arturo R. de Carricarte, *Martí en Isla de Pinos* (La Habana: Imp. Ed. América, 1923), pp. 9-13.

21. Emilio Roig de Leuchsenring, *Martí en España* (La Habana: Cultural, S. A., 1938), Apéndice X, p. 265.

22. *Obras,* ed. Quesada y Miranda, LXV, 19.

23. Roig de Leuchsenring, pp. 111-135.

24. *Obras,* ed. Quesada y Miranda, I, 37.

25. Roig de Leuchsenring, pp. 97, 112-115.

26. *Obras,* ed. Quesada y Miranda, I, 91-96.

27. Valdés Domínguez, p. 248.   28. Roig de Leuchsenring, p. 276.

29. *Obras,* ed. Quesada y Miranda, XXVI, 27-123.

30. *Ibid.,* I, 99-113.   31. Roig de Leuchsenring, pp. 105, 109.

32. Félix Lizaso, *Martí, místico del deber* (3d ed.; Buenos Aires: Ed. Losada, 1952), pp. 91-99.

33. Mañach, pp. 97-99.   34. *Obras,* ed. Quesada y Miranda, XLVIII-L.

35. Camilo Carrancá y Trujillo, *Martí, traductor de Victor Hugo* (México: Talleres Gráficos de la Nación, 1933), p. 16. For the translation see *Obras,* ed. Quesada y Miranda, LXI, 141-179.

36. Quesada y Miranda, *Martí, hombre,* p. 85.

37. *Obras,* ed. Quesada y Miranda, XXVI, 169.   38. Lizaso, p. 112.

39. *Obras,* ed. Quesada y Miranda, LXVIII, 29.

40. Valdés Domínguez, p. 253.

41. David Vela, *Martí en Guatemala* (La Habana: Imp. Mundial, 1953), p. 215.

42. *Obras,* ed. Quesada y Miranda, LXVIII, 29.   43. *Ibid.,* p. 36.

44. Máximo Soto Hall, *La Niña de Guatemala, el idilio trágico de José Martí* (Guatemala: Tip. Nacional, 1942).

45. Gonzalo de Quesada y Miranda, *Mujeres de Martí* (La Habana: Ed. Indice, 1943), p. 52.

46. José de Jesús Núñez y Domínguez, *Martí en México* (México: Imp. de la Secretaría de Relaciones Exteriores, 1934), p. 188.　47. Vela, pp. 111-113.

48. Interview with Gonzalo de Quesada y Miranda, May 30, 1956.

49. *Obras,* ed. Quesada y Miranda, XLI, 64-65.

50. *Papeles de Martí,* ed. Gonzalo de Quesada y Miranda (3 vols.; La Habana: Academia de la Historia de Cuba, 1933-35), III, 118.

51. *Obras,* ed. Quesada y Miranda, LXVIII, 57.　52. *Ibid.,* p. 63.

53. *Ibid.,* pp. 70-74.　54. *Ibid.,* LXV, 39.

55. *Cartas inéditas de Martí,* ed. Joaquín Llaverías (La Habana: Imp. El Siglo XX, 1920), p. 27.

56. Cuba, *El Archivo Nacional,* pp. 129-139, 514-515.

57. Quesada y Miranda, *Martí, hombre,* p. 112.

58. *Obras,* ed. Quesada y Miranda, LXVIII, 79.

59. Cuba, *El Archivo Nacional,* pp. 288-290.

60. *Obras,* ed. Quesada y Miranda, LXII, 15-16.

61. Carlos Márquez Sterling, *Martí, maestro y apóstol* (La Habana: Seoane, Fernández y Cía., 1942), pp. 312-313.

62. Carlos Márquez Sterling, *Nueva y humana visión de Martí* (La Habana: Ed. Lex, 1953), pp. 261-262.

63. Roig de Leuchsenring, pp. 201-204, 237.

64. *Obras,* ed. Quesada y Miranda, LXV, 61.

65. Quesada y Miranda, *Martí, hombre,* pp. 126-129.

66. Portell-Vilá, p. 24.

67. *Obras,* ed. Quesada y Miranda, LXX, 21, ed. note, I, 186.

68. *Ibid.,* I, 199-200.

69. Gonzalo de Quesada y Miranda, *Martí, periodista* (La Habana: Rambla, Bouza y Cía., 1929), p. 195.

70. Quesada y Miranda, *Martí, hombre,* pp. 136-142.

71. Gonzalo de Quesada y Miranda, *Anecdotario martiano, nuevas facetas de Martí* (La Habana: Seoane, Fernández y Cía., 1948), p. 188.

72. Virgilio Ferrer Gutiérrez, "José Martí en César Romero," *Libertad* (La Habana), 25 de junio de 1944, pp. 6-7. Ferrer Gutiérrez reproduces in part in facsimile a letter dated May 30, 1944, from César Romero, Hollywood actor and son of María Mantilla Romero. Romero writes, "Undoubtedly Martí was the man of the Century, and the fact that I am his grandson fills me with great pride."

73. *Obras,* ed. Quesada y Miranda, LXII, 101.

74. Quesada y Miranda, *Martí, periodista,* pp. 87-91.

75. Mañach, pp. 184-185.　76. Quesada y Miranda, *Martí, hombre,* p. 164.

77. *Obras,* ed. Quesada y Miranda, LXX, 80-83.

78. Quoted in Quesada y Miranda, *Martí, periodista,* p. 113.

79. Manuel Pedro González, *Fuentes para el estudio de José Martí* (La Habana: Publicaciones del Ministerio de Educación, 1950), pp. 337-338.

80. *Ibid.,* p. 333.　81. *Obras,* ed. Quesada y Miranda, LXIII, 41.

82. *Ibid.,* I, 203-210.　83. *Ibid.,* I, 210-213.

84. Quesada y Miranda, *Martí, periodista,* p. 203.　85. Lizaso, p. 191.

86. *Obras,* ed. Quesada y Miranda, LXIII, 96.　87. *Ibid.,* XLII, 31.

88. Quesada y Miranda, *Martí, hombre,* p. 211.

89. Herminio Portell-Vilá, *Martí, diplomático* (La Habana: Cultural, S. A., 1934), pp. 10-11.

90. *Obras,* ed. Quesada y Miranda, I, 217-222.　91. *Ibid.,* XXV, 7, ed. note.

92. Andrés Iduarte, *Martí, escritor* (México: Cuadernos Americanos, 1945),

pp. 174-175.   93. Lizaso, p. 202.

94. *José Martí*, (*Fulgor de Martí*) (México: Ed. Botas, 1941), p. 186.

95. Mañach, p. 212.   96. Quesada y Miranda, *Martí, hombre*, pp. 187-188.

97. *Obras*, ed. Quesada y Miranda, XXV, 84.

98. *Ibid.*, LXVIII, 125, 131-32.   99. *Ibid.*, p. 150.   100. *Ibid.*, I, 237-246.

101. Gonzalo de Quesada y Miranda, *Significación martiana del 10 de Octubre* (La Habana: Academia de la Historia de Cuba, 1953), pp. 9, 24-25.

102. *Obras*, ed. Quesada y Miranda, LVII, LXX, 91, ed. note.

103. *Ibid.*, LXVIII, 167.

104. Quesada y Miranda, *Martí, periodista*, p. 195.

105. *Obras*, ed. Quesada y Miranda, LXVIII, 165-166.

106. *Ibid.*, II, 36-46.   107. *Ibid.*, LXVIII, 181.   108. *Ibid.*, p. 184.

109. *Ibid.*, LXX, 27, ed. note.   110. *Ibid.*, II, 63-72.

111. *Ibid.*, LXIX, 17.   112. *Ibid.*, pp. 28-29.

113. Quesada y Miranda, *Martí, hombre*, p. 202.

114. *Ibid.*, pp. 203-204.   115. *Obras*, ed. Quesada y Miranda, II, 80-87.

116. Cuba, *El Archivo Nacional*, p. 293.

117. *Papeles*, ed. Quesada y Miranda, III, 106.

118. Portell-Vilá, *Martí, diplomático*, Appendix 6, p. 27.

119. Manuel Pedro González, *José Martí, Epic Chronicler of the United States in the Eighties* (Chapel Hill: The University of North Carolina Press, 1953), pp. 58-60.   120. *Obras*, ed. Quesada y Miranda, XXII, 16-18.

121. González, *José Martí, Epic Chronicler*, p. 56.

122. Cuba, *El Archivo Nacional*, pp. 293-294.

123. Portell-Vilá, *Martí, diplomático*, p. 18.

124. *Obras*, ed. Quesada y Miranda, IX, 151-170.

125. *Ibid.*, pp. 171-179.   126. *Ibid.*, II, 107, 117, ed. notes.

127. *Ibid.*, LXIX, 47.   128. *Ibid.*, II, 237, III, 22.

129. Quesada y Miranda, *Martí, hombre*, p. 226.

130. Cuba, *El Archivo Nacional*, p. 182.

131. *Obras*, ed. Quesada y Miranda, III, 102-103; XIV, 84-87.

132. Emilio Rodríguez Demorizi, *Martí en Santo Domingo* (La Habana: Imp. Ucar García, 1953), p. 55.

133. *Obras*, ed. Quesada y Miranda, IV, 77.

134. Máximo Gómez, *Diario de campaña* (La Habana: Centro Superior Tecnológico, 1941), p. 273.

135. *Obras*, ed. Quesada y Miranda, IV, 194-195.   136. *Ibid.*, pp. 93-95.

137. Quesada y Miranda, *Martí, hombre*. p. 232.

138. *Obras*, ed. Quesada y Miranda, LXVI, 181-197.

139. *Ibid.*, IV, 216.

140. Gerardo Castellanos G., *Panorama histórico, ensayo de cronología cubana* (La Habana: Ucar García, 1934), p. 1031.

141. *Obras*, ed. Quesada y Miranda, V, 59, 178-179, 214.

142. Carlos Jinesta, *José Martí en Costa Rica* (San José: Librería Alsina, 1933), pp. 19-24.

143. "Actas del Cuerpo de Consejo de Nueva York," *Boletín del Archivo Nacional*, XXXV (1936), 81.

144. *Obras*, ed. Quesada y Miranda, V-VI.

145. Quesada y Miranda, *Martí, hombre*, p. 241.

146. *Papeles*, ed. Quesada y Miranda, I, 52.   147. Lizaso, p. 246.

148. Núñez y Domínguez, pp. 177-180.

149. *Epistolario de José Martí*, ed. Félix Lizaso (3 vols.; La Habana, Cultural, S. A., 1930-31), III, 118-119, ed. note.   150. *Ibid.*, p. 140.

151. Horatio S. Rubens, *Liberty, the Story of Cuba* (New York: Brewer, Warren and Putnam, Inc., 1932), pp. 72-75.

152. For a study of Martí and the Cuban cigar makers in Florida see Orlando Castañeda, *Martí, los tabaqueros y la Revolución de 1895* (La Habana: Ed. Lex, 1946). 153. Quesada y Miranda, *Martí, hombre*, p. 249.

154. *Obras*, ed. Quesada y Miranda, VIII, 97-98.

155. *Epistolario*, ed. Félix Lizaso, III, 162.

156. Rodríguez Demorizi, p. 125.

157. *Obras*, ed. Quesada y Miranda, VIII, 135-137.

158. Quesada y Miranda, *Martí, hombre*, p. 254.

159. *Obras*, ed. Quesada y Miranda, LXX, 43, ed. note.

160. *Ibid.*, VIII, 159.   161. *Ibid.*, p. 188.   162. *Ibid.*, I, 13.

163. Gómez, pp. 285-286.

164. Quesada y Miranda, *Martí, hombre*, pp. 254-255.

165. *Obras*, ed. Quesada y Miranda, LVI, 101-102.

166. *Ibid.*, LVI, 105; VIII, 204.

167. *Ibid.*, LVI, 109-111, 115-116, VIII, 221-222.

168. *Ibid.*, LVI, 123, VIII, 270-276.   169. *Ibid.*, LVI, 125-126.

170. Enrique H. Moreno Plá, "Tres conjunciones de astros," in *Memoria del Seminario Martiano de la Universidad de la Habana*, ed. Gonzalo de Quesada y Miranda (La Habana: Imp. Universitaria, 1953), p. 55.

171. Gómez, p. 333.

172. Gerardo Castellanos G., *Los últimos días de Martí* (La Habana: Ucar García y Cía., 1937), p. 288.

173. *Obras*, ed. Quesada y Miranda, VIII, 74, 270-271.

174. Gómez, p. 336.

175. Castellanos G., *Los últimos días de Martí*, pp. 293-307, 323-324.

176. Antonio Martínez Bello, "El 'Suicidio' de Martí—su 'Inadaptación,' " in *Archivo José Martí*, ed. Félix Lizaso (6 vols.; La Habana: El Ministerio de Educación, Dirección de Cultura, 1940-52), IV (junio-diciembre de 1948), 372-392.

177. Gonzalo de Quesada y Miranda, *Alrededor de la acción en Dos Ríos* (La Habana: Seoane, Fernández y Cía., 1942) pp. 7-8.

178. For a comprehensive history of Cuba from pre-Columbian to present times see Ramiro Guerra y Sánchez *et al.*, *Historia de la Nación cubana* (10 vols.; La Habana: Editorial Historia de la Nación Cubana, 1952).

179. Emeterio S. Santovenia, "Experiencias del Gobierno propio," in *Historia de la Nación cubana*, VIII, Libro 2°, cap. iii, 79.

180. Cosme de la Torriente, "Política exterior. Las relaciones entre la República de Cuba y los Estados Unidos de América," in *Historia de la Nación cubana*, VIII, Libro 4°, cap. iv, 231.

CHAPTER 2

1. A systematized short cut to the thoughts of José Martí is a selection of 2,460 of his observations in *Código martiano o de ética nacional*, ed. Carlos A. Martínez-Fortún y Foyo (La Habana: Seoane Fernández y Cía., 1943). This work has been used for some of the citations in this chapter. Also see *José Martí, esquema ideológico*, eds. Manuel Pedro González e Iván A. Schulman (México: Ed. Cultura, T. G., S. A., 1961).   2. *Obras*, ed. Quesada y Miranda, LXII, 105.

3. *Ibid.*, LXIV, 172, 193-194; LXIII, 75.   4. *Ibid.*, LXII, 127.

5. *Ibid.*, LXIV, 40-41.
6. *Diccionario del pensamiento de José Martí*, ed. Lilia Castro de Morales (La Habana: Ed. Selecta Librería, 1953).
7. *Obras*, ed. Quesada y Miranda, XXV, 183-185.
8. *Ibid.*, LXVIII, 27; XII, 50; XXX, 159, 148.
9. *Ibid.*, XX, 31; XXVI, 37; II, 90; XIX, 97; II, 220; IX, 155; LXIII, 75.
10. *Ibid.*, XXVIII, 146.   11. *Ibid.*, XVI, 145; XVIII, 41.
12. *Ibid.*, XII, 46.   13. *Ibid.*, XII, 136; XXIV, 119-120; XI, 135; X, 21.
14. *Ibid.*, XV, 60; XXVI, 73.   15. *Ibid.*, XVI, 107; XI, 93.
16. *Ibid.*, XLI, 97.   17. *Ibid.*, LXIX, 12; LXIV, 97, 67.
18. Cuba, *El Archivo Nacional*, p. 288.
19. *Obras*, ed. Quesada y Miranda, LXVIII, 105.
20. *Ibid.*, XXVI, 36; XVII, 217; LXII, 56, 128; LXIII, 175; LXIX, 25.
21. *Ibid.*, LXIV, 194, 96.
22. *Las ideas en Cuba* (2 vols.; La Habana: Ed. Trópico, 1938), II, 67.
23. *Posibilidades filosóficas en Martí* (La Habana: Molina y Cía., 1935), p. 20.   24. *Obras*, ed. Quesada y Miranda, LXII, 104.
25. *Ibid.*, LXIV, 187.   26. *Ibid.*, LXVIII, 67.
27. *Ibid.*, p. 76.   28. *Ibid.*, LXVIII, 115, 118; XXV, 28.
29. *Ibid.*, XXXI, 215.   30. *Posibilidades filosóficas*, p. 16.
31. *El pensamiento político y social de Martí* (La Habana: Edición Oficial del Senado, 1941), p. 27.
32. "Ideas religiosas, morales, y filosóficas de Martí," *La Nueva Democracia*, XXV (febrero de 1944), 26-28.
33. *Obras*, ed. Quesada y Miranda, LXII, 73, 128-129.
34. *Ibid.*, LXIII, 26.   35. *Ibid.*, LXVIII, 114-115.
36. *Ibid.*, III, 175; XIV, 85.   37. *Ibid.*, I, 222; VIII, 188.
38. *Ibid.*, LXIV, 28.   39. *Ibid.*, XVII, 211; XII, 20.
40. Ibid. LXIV, 151; LXII, 80, 134-135.
41. *Ibid.*, LXIV, 149.   42. *Ibid.*, p. 87.
43. "Las ideas políticas de José Martí," *Cuadernos Americanos*, XIV (marzo-abril de 1944), 157.
44. "Martí y el espiritualismo," in *Vida y pensamiento de Martí*, ed. Emilio Roig de Leuchsenring (2 vols.; La Habana: Municipio de la Habana, 1942), I, 312.   45. *Obras*, ed. Quesada y Miranda, LIV, 175-177.   46. *Ibid.*, I, 35.
47. *Martí y la filosofía* (La Habana: Cuadernos de Divulgación Cultural #11, Comisión Nacional Cubana de la UNESCO, 1954), pp. 10-11.
48. *Obras*, ed. Quesada y Miranda, XLI, 136.   49. *Ibid.*, I, 72-73.
50. Lizaso, *Posibilidades filosóficas*, p. 22.
51. *Obras*, ed. Quesada y Miranda, XV, 32; XX, 69; XXVI, 51.
52. *Ibid.*, XX, 69; XXVII, 43; XX, 68, 70; XIII, 137.
53. Jorrín, pp. 13-14.
54. "Karl Christian Krause," *Encyclopedia Britannica, 14th ed.*, XIII, 501.
55. *Martí y el krausismo* (La Habana: Companía Ed. de Libros y Folletos, 1944), p. 85.   56. *Posibilidades filosóficas*, p. 11.
57. *Obras*, ed. Quesada y Miranda, LXIV, 189-190.   58. Jorrín, p. 13.
59. *Obras*, ed. Quesada y Miranda, XV, 26.   60. Jorrín, p. 10.
61. *Obras*, ed. Quesada y Miranda, LXIV, 74.
62. *Posibilidades filosóficas*, p. 21.
63. *José Martí, obras completas*, ed. M. Isidro Méndez (4 vols.; 2d ed.; La Habana: Ed. Lex, 1948), I, Tomo II, 1964.
64. *Obras*, ed. Quesada y Miranda, LXIV, 75.
65. *Ibid.*, XLV, 92-93, 123-128; LXIV, 78.   66. *Ibid.*, LIV, 165.

67. *José Martí, obras,* ed. Méndez, II, Tomo I, 85.
68. *Obras,* ed. Quesada y Miranda, XXXIII, 194.   69. *Ibid.,* p. 204.
70. *Ibid.,* pp. 187-213; XXXIV, 111-132.
71. For an extended and sympathetic treatment of Martí and the McGlynn case see Emilio Roig de Leuchsenring, "Martí y las religiones," in *Vida y pensamiento de Martí,* I, 111-158. This author does not mention Emerson's influence on Martí nor the role of Hindu philosophy in his thought, but concentrates on Martí's anti-Roman Catholic writings.
72. *José Martí, obras,* ed. Méndez, II, Tomo I, 83.
73. *Obras,* ed. Quesada y Miranda, XXIX, 197-201.
74. *Ibid.,* LXIII, 19; XXIV, 50; XV, 37-38; LXIV, 194.
75. Catalá, p. 310.   76. *Vida y pensamiento de Martí,* I, 14.
77. *Obras,* ed. Quesada y Miranda, XI, 93; XXX, 159; XXV, 186.
78. *Ibid.,* XXV, 90; XXVIII, 167-168.
79. *Ibid.,* XXV, 142; LXIII, 24.   80. *Ibid.,* XXV, 142, 20.
81. *Ibid.,* XVI, 150; XII, 156.
82. *Ibid.,* XXVIII, 165; XXIX, 96; XXVIII, 168; XXIII, 52.
83. *Ibid.,* XXVI, 88, 66, 48.
84. *Ibid.,* LXIV, 186.   85. *Ibid.,* IX, 164; XII, 12; XIV, 65.
86. *Ibid.,* XXIX, 63.   87. *Ibid.,* XXV, 66.
88. *Ibid.,* LXII, 128.   89. *Ibid.,* XXII, 123.
90. *Ibid.,* pp. 120, 118; XXVIII, 222-223; LXIV, 169-170.
91. *Ibid.,* XX, 145.   92. *Ibid.,* XXII, 195; XIX, 123.
93. *Ibid.,* XXII, 133, 119; XIX, 177-178; XXII, 140.
94. Jorrín, p. 12.   95. Catalá, p. 300.
96. "La capacidad de magisterio en Martí," in *Vida y pensamiento de Martí,* II, 218-219.   97. Mañach, *El pensamiento político,* p. 11.
98. *Obras,* ed. Quesada y Miranda, XIII, 76; XII, 114-115.
99. For a poetic treatment in prose of Martí's admiration for the Negro, see Armando Guerra, *Martí y los negros* (La Habana: Imp. Arquimbau, 1947).
100. *Obras,* ed. Quesada y Miranda, II, 89-90; XVI, 121.
101. *Ibid.,* XIX, 21; V, 14-18.   102. *Ibid.,* XXV, 172-173.
103. "Martí y las razas," in *Vida y pensamiento de Martí,* II, 346.
104. *Obras,* ed. Quesada y Miranda, XXXI, 148-149.
105. *Ibid.,* XXV, 129, 181.
106. Quesada y Miranda, *Martí, hombre,* p. 98.
107. *Obras,* ed. Quesada y Miranda, XXIII, 113.
108. Author's class, Universidad de Villanueva, Marianao, La Habana, Cuba, October 8, 1956.
109. *Obras,* ed. Quesada y Miranda, VI, 43; IX, 239-240.
110. Jorrín, pp. 3-4.   111. Lizaso, *Posibilidades filosóficas,* p. 18.
112. Iduarte, *La Nueva Democracia,* XXV, 29.
113. Humberto Piñera, "Martí, pensador," in *Pensamiento y acción de José Martí,* Universidad de Oriente, ed. (Santiago de Cuba: Universidad de Oriente, 1953), pp. 168-169, 180-181.   114. Béguez César, p. 4.
115. For a collection of critical essays on Martí see *Antología crítica de José Martí,* ed. Manuel Pedro González (México: Ed. Cultura, T. G., S. A., 1960).

CHAPTER 3

1. *Obras,* ed. Quesada y Miranda, XLIV, 40-41.
2. *José Martí, obras,* ed. Méndez, I, Tomo II, 1907.
3. *Obras,* ed. Quesada y Miranda, XIX, 12.

4. José Martí, *obras,* ed. Méndez, I, Tomo I, 393-394.
5. *Obras,* ed. Quesada y Miranda, IV, 150.
6. Ramón Infiesta, "Martí, político," in *Pensamiento y acción de José Martí,* p. 51. Elsewhere the same author refers to Martí as an "encyclopedic genius." *El pensamiento político de Martí* (La Habana: Universidad de la Habana, 1953), p. 21.
7. *Obras,* ed. Quesada y Miranda, II, 107, 117; VIII, 161, ed. notes.
8. *Ibid.,* VIII, 161.   9. *Ibid.,* II, 121.
10. *Ibid.,* VIII, 172.   11. *Ibid.,* p. 162.   12. *Ibid.,* p. 173.
13. *Ibid.,* pp. 174, 163.   14. *Ibid.,* p. 169.   15. *Ibid.,* IV, 196.
16. *Ibid.,* VII, 171; VI, 203.   17. *Ibid.,* II, 150; VIII, 224.
18. *Ibid.,* XVIII, 110; XV, 174; IX, 128-129.
19. *Ibid.,* VIII, 168-169.   20. *Ibid.,* pp. 165-166.
21. *Política de Martí* (2d ed.; La Habana: Ed. Lex, 1944), pp. 77-78.
22. *El pensamiento político de Martí,* p. 108.
23. *Obras,* ed. Quesada y Miranda, VIII, 166-167; II, 120.
24. *Ibid.,* VIII, 163, 175.   25. *Política de Martí,* pp. 77-78.
26. *Obras,* ed. Quesada y Miranda, XLIII, 191; I, 106.
27. *Ibid.,* XX, 133.   28. *Ibid.,* XIV, 195.
29. *José Martí, obras,* ed. Méndez, II, Tomo I, 110.
30. *Obras,* ed. Quesada y Miranda, IX, 155.
31. *Ibid.,* LXIII, 80; XII, 75; LXIV, 32.
32. "Martí y la política," in *Archivo José Martí,* V (enero-junio de 1950), 33.
33. *Obras,* ed. Quesada y Miranda, IV, 200; VI, 64; III, 165; VI, 59; XXIV, 16; IV, 224; XV, 152.   34. *Ibid.,* XXX, 121; XXII, 128-129.
35. *Ibid.,* IX, 53; XV, 121.   36. *Ibid.,* XXIX, 231; XXX, 100.
37. *Ibid.,* IX, 119; X, 190.   38. *Ibid.,* IX, 12; XXX, 49; V, 11.
39. *Ibid.,* XIX, 216; I, 103.   40. *Ibid.,* XXII, 194.
41. *Ibid.,* XXX, 48-49.   42. *Ibid.,* p. 44.   43. *Ibid.,* II, 179-180.
44. *Ibid.,* XIX, 13.
45. For a presentation of Martí as a "lawgiver" see Emeterio S. Santovenia, *Martí, legislador* (Buenos Aires: Ed. Losada, S. A., 1943). For Martí's "juridical thought" see Leopoldo Horrego Estuch, *Martí, su pensamiento jurídico* (La Habana: Ed. Mecenas, 1954). Horrego writes that Martí, although not a juridical technician, was "devoted to justice," p. 156. José A. Pérez Gorrín writes: "Martí did not produce a work of methodical and complete law. His juridical ideas are like shining stars scattered here and there in the totality of his works." José A. Pérez Gorrín y Eloy G. Merino Brito, *Martí y el derecho* (La Habana: Jesús Montero, 1953), p. 18.   46. *Obras,* ed. Quesada y Miranda, XIX, 14.
47. *Ibid.,* XXIX, 231; XXX, 181.
48. "Martí y el mundo de lo colectivo," *Universidad de la Habana,* XII (diciembre de 1941), 27-28.
49. *Obras,* ed. Quesada y Miranda, XXIV, 14; XIX, 126; XXIX, 177.
50. *Ibid.,* III, 126; XIV, 161.   51. *Ibid.,* X, 95.   52. *Ibid.,* I, 99.
53. *Ibid.,* XXIX, 170; XIX, 189.
54. *Ibid.,* XXII, 136; XXX, 73-74; XIX, 136.
55. *Ibid.,* LXIII, 170; XXVIII, 138.   56. *Ibid.,* XXV, 180; LXIV, 179.
57. *Ibid.,* LXIV, 188.   58. *Ibid.,* LXIII, 39.   59. *Ibid.,* XXI, 17.
60. *Ibid.,* LXII, 95.   61. *Ibid.,* XXV, 86, 82; XIV, 133; XV, 84.
62. Andrés Iduarte, "Las ideas políticas de José Martí," *Cuadernos Americanos* (México), XIV (marzo-abril de 1944), 159.
63. Agramonte, *Universidad de la Habana,* XII (diciembre de 1941), 20, 36-37.

64. Martí's writings on "Nuestra América" are extensive. See *Obras*, ed. Quesada y Miranda, Vols. XIX-XXIII.   65. *Ibid.*, II, 155; XIV, 59.
66. *Ibid.*, XXI, 208; XIX, 16-17.   67. *Ibid.*, XXIII, 222.
68. *Ibid.*, LXIV, 173.   69. *Ibid.*, XIX, 12-13.   70. *Ibid.*, XX, 137.
71. *Ibid.*, XXII, 12-13.   72. *Ibid.*, XIX, 199; XXVIII, 195; LXIII, 54.
73. Infiesta, *El pensamiento político de Martí*, p. 88.
74. *Obras*, ed. Quesada y Miranda, XIX, 21.
75. *Ibid.*, XXII, 28-29.   76. *Ibid.*, XXIX, 71-75.
77. Agramonte, *Universidad de la Habana*, XII (diciembre de 1941), 37.
78. Felipe de Pazos y Roque, "Las ideas económicas de Martí," in *Vida y pensamiento de Martí*, p. 178.
79. *Obras*, ed. Quesada y Miranda, XIX, 173.   80. *Ibid.*, p. 135.
81. *Ibid.*, XV, 64; XXII, 115; XXX, 113; XXIII, 59.
82. José Antonio Portuondo, "Introducción al estudio de las ideas sociales de Martí," in *Vida y pensamiento de Martí*, II, 237.
83. *Obras*, ed. Quesada y Miranda, XXVIII, 73; XVII, 146; XIX, 70; XXII, 130; XXIII, 61.
84. *Ibid.*, XXXII, 171-172; XXXIII, 71.   85. *Ibid.*, XXXV, 53-54.
86. Antonio Martínez Bello, *Ideas sociales y económicas de José Martí* (La Habana: La Verónica, 1940), pp. 159-160.
87. *Obras*, ed. Quesada y Miranda, XV, 57-67.
88. Infiesta, *El pensamiento político de Martí*, p. 21.
89. Andrés Iduarte, "Ideas económicas de José Martí," *La Nueva Democracia*, XXVI (noviembre de 1945), 12.
90. Raúl Maestri, "Martí, político monetario," *Repertorio Americano*, 3 de diciembre de 1938, pp. 57-58.
91. *Obras*, ed. Quesada y Miranda, XXIX, 89.   92. *Ibid.*, LXII, 105.
93. *Ibid.*, XII, 48.   94. Martínez Bello, *Ideas sociales*, p. 57.
95. Portuondo, in *Vida y pensamiento de Martí*, p. 235.
96. Lizaso, *Posibilidades filosóficas*, p. 18.
97. Jorge Mañach, *El pensamiento político y social de Martí*, pp. 13-14.
98. Letter from Juan Marinello to Antonio Martínez Bello, La Habana, August 4, 1940, reproduced in *Ideas sociales*, p. 217.
99. *Obras*, ed. Quesada y Miranda, XXXII, 69.

CHAPTER 4

1. *La Discusión* (La Habana), 21 de mayo de 1895, Suplemento 4, p. 1.
2. Quoted in James H. Wilson, *The Life of Charles A. Dana* (New York: Harper and Brothers Publishers, 1907), pp. 408-409.
3. "José Martí," in *Martí*, ed. Quesada y Aróstegui, VII, 11-12.
4. "Duelo de América," *Letras y Ciencias* (Santo Domingo), 3 de agosto de 1895, in *Martí*, ed. Quesada y Aróstegui, IX, 48-49. A bust of Martí is now located there.
5. "La apoteosis de Martí," *Patria* (New York), 6 de noviembre de 1895, in *Revista Cubana*, XXIX (1951-52), 143.
6. "Homenajes a José Martí" in *Martí*, ed. Quesada y Aróstegui, VIII, 33-35.   7. "José Martí," in *Martí*, ed. Quesada y Aróstegui, VI, 11.
8. "José Martí," in *Martí*, ed. Quesada y Aróstegui, XV, 90-91.
9. "Homenajes a José Martí" in *Martí*, ed. Quesada y Aróstegui, VIII, 29-30.
10. "José Martí," in *Martí*, ed. Quesada y Aróstegui, II, 5.
11. Gonzalo de Quesada y Aróstegui and Henry D. Northrop, *The War in*

Cuba, Being a Full Account of Her Great Struggle for Freedom (Rev. ed.; Washington: Liberty Publishing Co., 1896), p. 514.

12. "Martí" *El Cubano Libre* (Provincia de Oriente, Cuba), 30 de junio de 1896, in *Revista Cubana,* XXIX (1951-52), 440-441.

13. "Martí y su obra política," in *Martí,* ed. Quesada y Aróstegui, IV, 45-46.

14. "José Martí (Fragmentos de un artículo)" in *Martí,* ed. Quesada y Aróstegui, VIII, 45.

15. *Los raros* (Madrid: [Imp. G. Hernández y G. Sáez, 1929]), pp. 235-236. This work is probably Vol. XVIII of *Obras completas,* ed. Alberto Ghiraldo y Andrés González-Blanco (Madrid: [Biblioteca Rubén Darío, 1924?]). Utter confusion exists as to the organization of most of the volumes of this "complete works." See ed. note by Henry G. Doyle, *A. Bibliography of Rubén Darío (1867-1916)* (Cambridge: Harvard University Press, 1935), p. 28.

16. "José Martí," in *Martí,* ed. Quesada y Aróstegui, IX, 53.

17. Wenceslao Gálvez y del Monte, *Tampa, impresiones de emigrado* (Tampa: Establecimiento Tip. Cuba, 1897), pp. 116-119.

18. *Cuba en la mano* (La Habana: Imp. Ucar, García y Cía., 1940), p. 706. This is a useful guide for basic information on all magazines and periodicals published in Cuba prior to 1940.

19. Emilio Roig de Leuchsenring, "En 1899 sólo 16 cubanos representativos comprendían y admiraban a Martí," *Carteles,* 29 de enero de 1939, p. 38.

20. *Martí, A Story of the Cuban War* (Chicago: David C. Cook Publishing Co., 1899).   21. *Cuba* (New York: A. A. Knopf, 1946), p. 196.

22. Fermín Peraza Sarausa, *Bibliografía martiana* (2d ed. rev.; La Habana: Ed. Anuario Bibliográfico Cubano, 1956), p. 207.

23. Anon. [Erasmo Pella], *Martí, novela histórica por un patriota* (La Habana: Imp. La Moderna Poesía, [1901]), p. 6.   24. *Ibid.,* p. 66.

25. Wenceslao Gálvez, *Tampa,* p. 149.

26. Franco Rander [Erasmo Pella], *José Martí, reseña histórica* (La Habana: Imp. de Juan A. de la Cámera, 1915). The real name of the author, a Dominican poet living in Havana, was Erasmo Pella.

27. Franco Rander [Erasmo Pella], *José Martí, reseña histórica* (2d ed.; La Habana: Litografía e Imp. Industrias Gráficas, 1929).

28. Franco Rander [Erasmo Pella], *José Martí, reseña histórica* (3d ed.; La Habana: Litografía e Imp. Industrias Gráficas, 1931).

29. Letter from Máximo Gómez to Francisco María González dated 18 de mayo de 1902 in *El Mundo* (La Habana), 19 de mayo de 1902, p. 1.

30. José M. Pérez Cabrera, "Presidencia de Estrada Palma," *Historia de la Nación cubana,* VIII, Libro 1°, cap. i, 15.

31. Enrique Gay-Calbó, "Insurrección de 1906 y eclipse de la República. Gobierno provisional norteamericano," *Historia de la Nación cubana,* VIII, Libro 1°, cap. ii, 24-36.   32. *Ibid.,* p. 23.

33. Emeterio S. Santovenia y Echaide, "Enero 28 de 1909," *Patria,* VI (enero de 1950), 25.

34. Miguel F. Viondi y Vera, Speech in the Cuban House of Representatives, 19 de mayo de 1909, Cuba Congreso, *Diario de Sesiones,* XI (21 de mayo de 1909), no. 20, p. 3.

35. *Suum cuique* (La Habana: Imp. de Rambla y Bouza, 1910), p. 16.

36. Cited in *Martí,* ed. Quesada y Aróstegui, IX, 60.

37. *América: José Martí* (La Habana: Imp. Papelería de Rambla y Bouza, 1911), pp. 3, 15.

38. *Martí: su vida y su obra. El poeta* (La Habana: Imp. Seoane y Alvarez, 1913), p. 22.

39. Napoleón Gálvez y Ayala, "Si Martí viviese," *El Triunfo* (La Habana), 19 de mayo de 1918, p. 2.

40. Letter from Gabriela Mistral to Federico Henríquez y Carvajal, Temuco, Chile, noviembre de 1920, in *Social,* VI (mayo de 1921), 64.

41. Carricarte, *Revista Martiniana,* I (octubre de 1921), 6.

42. Under the initiative of Carricarte, the route was marked out and followed in 1922 by Lt. Rafael Lubián y Arias. See Lubian's *Martí en los campos de Cuba Libre* (La Habana: Propagandas Angulo, 1953).

43. "Pinceladas: ¡ Imitémosle! Así es como se honra su memoria!" *El Triunfo* (La Habana), 3 de junio de 1923, p. 2.

44. *A History of the Cuban Republic, A Study in Hispanic American Politics* (New York: The Macmillan Co., 1927), p. 410.

45. *José Martí; estudio biográfico* (Madrid: Agénce mondiale de librairie, [1925]).

46. "Reflexiones en torno al sentido de la vida en Martí," in *Archivo José Martí,* IV (enero-diciembre de 1947), 21-30.

47. *Los periódicos de Martí* (La Habana: Imp. Pérez Sierra y Cía., 1929).

48. *Martí, periodista.*

49. *Mitología de Martí* (Madrid: Renacimiento, 1929).

50. *Martí y su obra literaria* (La Habana: La Propagandista, 1929).

51. *La senda del apóstol (crónicas y fotografías de la ruta seguida por Martí en 1895 de Playitas a Dos Ríos)* (Santiago de Cuba: Morales, Alvarez y Cía., 1930).

52. *New York Herald Tribune,* Book Review Section, June 4, 1950, p. 4.

53. *La cubanidad negativa del apóstol Martí* (La Habana: Manuel I. Mesa Rodríguez, 1934), pp. 14-23.

54. "Poesía y teorías poéticas de José Martí (con especial referencia a su crítica de autores norteamericanos)" (unpublished Ph.D. dissertation, Dept. of Spanish, University of Minnesota, 1946).

55. "Verb-Creation in the Works of José Martí: Method and Function" (unpublished Ph.D. dissertation, Dept. of Romance Languages and Literature, Harvard University, 1956).   56. González, *José Martí, Epic Chronicler,* p. 28.

57. *The America of José Martí,* trans. Juan de Onís (New York: Noonday, 1954).

58. Féliz Lizaso, *Martí, Martyr of Cuban Independence,* trans. Esther E. Shuler (Albuquerque: University of New Mexico Press, 1953).

59. Iduarte, *Martí, escritor,* p. 23.

60. Cited in Iduarte, *Martí, escritor,* p. 302.

61. *Cronología de la obra martiana* (La Habana: Ed. Anuario Bibliográfico Cubano, 1955), pp. 32-35. References cited by title only and code number. Full citations are in Peraza Sarausa's *Bibliografía martiana, 1853-1955* (2d ed. rev.; La Habana: Ed. Anuario Bibliográfico Cubano, 1956). A monumental work, this bibliography is to be used with care since it contains many inaccuracies.

62. *Translations from José Martí,* trans. Cecil Charles (New York: J. E. Richardson, 1898), and *Tuya, Other Verses and Translations from José Martí,* trans. Cecil Charles (New York: J. E. Richardson, 1898).

63. Peraza Sarausa, *Bibliografía martiana,* p. 64.

64. *Martí,* ed. Gonzalo de Quesada y Aróstegui (16 vols.; Vol. 1, Washington: Gonzalo de Quesada, 1900; Vols. II & III, La Habana: Gonzalo de Quesada, 1901-02; Vol. IV, La Habana: Imp. y Papelería Rambla y Bouza, 1905; Vol. V, Roma: Casa Ed. Nazionale, 1905; Vols. VI-IX, La Habana: Imp. y Papelería Rambla y Bouza, 1908-10; Vol. X, Berlín: Gonzalo de Quesada, 1911; Vols. XI-XIV, La Habana: Imp. y Papelería de Rambla, Bouza y Cía., 1913-15;

Vol. XV, ed. Angelina Miranda de Quesada; La Habana: Imp. y Papelería de Rambla, Bouza y Cía., 1919; Vol. XVI, ed. Gonzalo de Quesada y Miranda; La Habana, Imp. Molina y Cía., 1933).

65. *Ibid.*, VIII, 6.   66. Peraza Sarausa, *Cronología*, p. 32.

67. *Flor y lava*, ed. Américo Lugo (París: Sociedad de Ediciones Literarias y Artísticas, 1910).   68. Peraza Sarausa, *Cronología*, p. 32.

69. *Granos de oro*, ed. Rafael G. Argilagos (La Habana: Sociedad Ed. Cuba contemporánea, 1918). Interview with Gonzalo de Quesada y Miranda December 6, 1956.

70. *Páginas escogidas*, ed. Max Henríquez Ureña (París: Casa Ed. Garnier Hermanos, [1919]).

71. *Versos escogidos de Martí*, ed. Rubén Darío (París: Casa Ed. Franco-Ibero-americana [1919]).

72. *Obras completas de Martí*, ed. Néstor Carbonell (8 vols.; La Habana: Ed. Especial de la Prensa, 1918-20).

73. *Evocando al maestro*, ed. Miguel Angel Carbonell (La Habana: Imp. Seoane y Fernández, 1919).

74. *Madre América*, ed. Ventura García Calderón (Paris: Ed. Franco-Ibero-americana, [1922]).

75. *Poèmes choisis*, trans. Armando Godoy (París: Emil-Paul Frèses, 1929).

76. *Discursos*, ed. Néstor Carbonell (La Habana: Biblioteca de El Magazine de la raza, 1923).

77. *España*, ed. Néstor Carbonell ([La Habana]: Ed. de Guáimaro, 1926).

78. Peraza Sarausa, *Bibliografía martiana*, p. 164.

79. *Obras completas de Martí*, ed. Armando Godoy y Ventura García Calderón (2 vols.; París: Ed. Excelsior, [1926]).

80. *Obras completas*, ed. Alberto Ghiraldo (8 vols.; Madrid: [A. Ghiraldo, 1925]-29).   81. *Epistolario*, ed. Félix Lizaso.

82. *Ideario*, ed. M. Isidro Méndez (La Habana: Colección de libros cubanos, 1930).

83. *Martí en Venezuela*, ed. Venezuela, Ministerio de Relaciones Exteriores (Caracas: Tip. Americana, 1930).

84. *Flores del destierro*, ed. Gonzalo de Quesada y Miranda (La Habana: Imp. Molina y Cía., [1933]), Vol. XVI of *Martí*, ed. Quesada y Aróstegui.

85. *Papeles de Martí*, ed. Gonzalo de Quesada y Miranda (3 vols.; La Habana: Academie de la Historia de Cuba, 1933-35).

86. *Obras completas de Martí*, ed. Gonzalo de Quesada y Miranda (74 vols.; La Habana: Ed. Trópico, 1936-49).

87. *Obras*, ed. Quesada y Miranda, LXX, 13.

88. *José Martí, obras*, ed. Isidro.

89. Cuba, Secretaría de Instrucción Pública y Bellas Artes, *Iconografía del apóstol José Martí* (La Habana: Imp. El Siglo XX, 1925).

90. *Ibid.*, Nos. 85, 86, 87.

91. Félix Matos Bernier, "José Martí," *La Democracia*, abril de 1905, in *Martí*, ed. Quesada y Aróstegui, IX, 75.   92. Cuba, *Iconografía*, No. 89.

93. *Ibid.*, No. 91, ed. note.   94. *Ibid.*, No. 92.   95. *Ibid.*, No's. 94, 95.

96. *Ibid.*, No's. 96, 97.

97. Pastor del Río, "Un desfile: una calle; una estatua," *América*, XXXVIII (febrero de 1953), 72.

98. Cuba, *Gaceta Oficial de la República de Cuba*, Ley [Unnumbered] (Secretaría de Gobernación), XX (27 de abril de 1922), 8673.

99. Cuba, *Iconografía*, No. 101.   100. *Patria*, VIII (febrero de 1952), 6.

101. Cuba, *Gaceta Oficial*, Ley No. 12 (Hacienda), XLIII (29 de octubre

de 1945), 21538. 102. *Obras,* ed. Quesada y Miranda, XLI, 81.
103. Cuba, *Gaceta Oficial,* Ley-Decreto No. 448 (Educación), XXXIII (9 de diciembre de 1935), 3-5.
104. For the early legislation and plans see Cuba, Comisión Central Pro-Monumento, *En memoria de José Martí* (La Habana: P. Fernández y Cía., 1938).
105. Luis Bay Sevilla, "El concurso para el monumento a Martí," *Arquitectura,* XI (octubre de 1943), 380. 106. *Ibid.,* pp. 381-385.
107. Gonzalo de Quesada y Miranda, "El Monumento a Martí," *Arquitectura,* XI (octubre de 1943), 386-390.
108. Félix Lizaso, "¿Habrá monumento a Martí?" *Carteles,* 5 de febrero de 1950, p. 28. 109. *El Crisol* (La Habana), 20 de junio de 1949, p. 1.
110. *El Mundo* (La Habana), 28 de junio de 1949, p. 12.
111. Emilio Roig de Leuchsenring, "Dónde está el archivo del monumento a Martí?" *Pueblo* (La Habana), 15 de junio de 1949, p. 7.
112. Cuba, *Gaceta Oficial,* Decreto No. 1439 (Defensa Nacional), XLVII (14 de mayo de 1949), 9734-9735.
113. *Ibid.,* Decreto No. 3039 (Educación), L (23 de octubre de 1952), 20333.
114. Angel I. Augier, "El debate del monumento a Martí," *Bohemia,* 26 de abril de 1953, pp. 6-7.
115. Letter from Nicanor Díaz, Jefe de Despacho, Comisión Nacional Organizadora de los Actos y Ediciones del Centenario y del Monumento de Martí, La Habana, Cuba, 15 de noviembre de 1956.
116. Cuba, *Gaceta Oficial,* Ley-Decreto No. 421 (Hacienda), L (25 de septiembre de 1952), 18401-18403.
117. *Diario de la Marina* (La Habana), 28 de octubre de 1955, p. 1.
118. Letter from Nicanor Díaz.
119. *El Mundo* (La Habana), 10 de julio de 1956, p. A-1.
120. *New York Times,* April 13, 1960, p. 41.
121. Gonzalo de Quesada y Michelsen, "Filatélica martiana," *Patria,* VI (enero de 1949), 20-21.
122. Cuba, *Gaceto Oficial,* Decreto No. 3833 (Comunicaciones), L (10 de diciembre de 1952), 23955-23956.
123. José L. Guerra Aguiar, *Catálogo general de sellos de Cuba* (La Habana: By the author, 1956), pp. 139-145.
124. *Florida Times-Union,* April 15, 1959, p. 24.
125. Cuba, *Iconografía,* No's. 110, 111.
126. *Ibid.,* No. 112. 127. *Ibid.,* No. 117.
128. Pablo F. Lavín, *Reflexiones en torno a Martí* (La Habana: Ed. Lex, 1953).
129. Pablo F. Lavín, "La Cátedra Martiana de Marianao," *El Diario de la Marina,* 29 de enero de 1956, p. 4D. 130. Cuba, *Iconografía,* No. 119.
131. Cuba, *Gaceta Oficial,* Ley-Decreto No. 363 (Hacienda), L (28 de agosto de 1952), 16387-16388.
132. Henry C. Wallich, *Problemas monetarias de una economía de exportación (La experiencia cubana, 1914-1947),* trans. Ernesto Cuesta (La Habana: Banco Nacional de Cuba, 1953), pp. 129-130.

CHAPTER 5

1. Cuba, *Iconografía,* No. 118.
2. "Reglamento y Estatutos de la Asociación de Antiguos Alumnos del Sema-

nario Martiano," *Boletín Oficial de la Asociación de Antiguos Alumnos del Seminario Martiano,* I (15 de agosto de 1945), 3. Hereinafter referred to as *Boletín Oficial.*

3. Cuba, *Gaceta Oficial,* Decreto No. 270 (Hacienda), XLII (14 de febrero de 1944), 2273-2274. The idea for preserving the area as a national monument was launched in 1938 in an article by Quesada y Miranda. See his "Las canteras de San Lázaro donde trabajó Martí," *Carteles,* 30 de enero de 1938, pp. 22-23.

4. Cuba, *Gaceta Oficial,* Decreto No. 6066 (Educación), L (8 de febrero de 1952), 2555-2556.

5. Carmen Ceballos, "Los Pinos Nuevos," *Patria,* XI (enero de 1955), 8.

6. *Patria,* VI (enero de 1950), 13.

7. Julia Rodríguez del Rey, "Nuestra Comisión de Canastilla Martiana y Ropero," *Patria,* XI (enero de 1955), 13-15.

8. *El Mundo* (La Habana), 1 de febrero de 1956, p. A-4.

9. *Ibid.,* 27 de enero de 1956, p. A-11, 14.

10. *Ibid.,* 1 de febrero de 1956, p. A-5.

11. *Ibid.,* 28 de enero de 1956, p. A-6.

12. Interview with Quesada y Miranda, January 18, 1957.

13. Nena Acevedo, "Nuestra canastilla martiana," *Patria,* XI (enero de 1955), 12.

14. Emilio Roig de Leuchsenring, *Martí y los niños* (La Habana: Cultural, S. A., 1932), p. 11.

15. Andrea Carballosa Madero, "Nuestra Comisión de Educación," *Patria,* XI (enero de 1955), 16-17.   16. *Ibid.,* 17-18.

17. Resolución No. 023421, Dirección de la Enseñanza, Ministerio de Educación, 21 de noviembre de 1947, later modified by Resolución No. 026685, 25 de enero de 1948.

18. Interview with Quesada y Miranda, February 19, 1957.

19. *Patria,* V (enero de 1949), 29-32.   20. *Ibid.,* XI (enero de 1955), 6.

21. *Ibid.,* VII (julio de 1951), 3.   22. *Ibid.,* III (marzo de 1947), 6.

23. Antonio Ponce de León y Ayme, "La oruga que nombró Martí," *Patria,* VI (junio de 1950), 6.   24. *Patria,* III (marzo de 1947), 6.

25. Ponce de León, p. 6.   26. *Patria,* VII (diciembre de 1951), 3.

27. *Ibid.,* VII (marzo de 1951), 7.

28. At the corner of 23d and 12th streets, in the Vedado, Havana, Cuba.

29. *Boletín Oficial,* I (15 de septiembre de 1945), 11.

30. Gonzalo de Quesada y Miranda, "¡No más desfiles escolares!" *Patria,* IV (febrero de 1948), 11.

31. *Diario de la Marina* (La Habana), 29 de enero de 1956, p. 1-A.

32. *Ibid.,* p. 7-B.

33. Interview with Quesada y Miranda, January 18, 1957.

34. *La Rosa Blanca,* II (septiembre de 1948), 6-7.   35. *Ibid., et seq.*

36. Interview with Carlos Martínez-Fortún y Foyo, March 26, 1957.

37. *Havana Post,* July 1, 1956, p. 2.

38. *Mundo Masónico,* XXI (enero-marzo de 1953), cover.

39. Roger Fernández Callejas, "Juan Luis Martín y Martí Masón," *Mundo Masónico,* XXI (abril-mayo de 1953), 5-6.

40. "Martí Masón," *Mundo Masónico,* XXII (mayo-junio de 1954), 24.

41. "Ser Masón," *Mundo Masónico,* XXI (agosto-septiembre de 1953), 21.

42. *El Mundo* (La Habana), January 27, 1956, p. A-11.

43. *Ibid.,* January 18, 1956, p. A-11.

44. Interview with Enrique Viciana Pérez, February 6, 1956.

45. Interview with Jesús Fernández Lamas, March 12, 1957. See his *Presencia*

de José Martí en la Logia "Silencio" (Artemisa, Cuba: Hermanos Trujillo, 1953).

46. See Jesús Fernández Lamas, *Martí, el anticlerical* (Artemisa, Cuba: Hermanos Trujillo, 1951).

47. Interview with Gregorio Silva, Treasurer, Universidad Nacional "José Martí," January 28, 1957.

48. Speech in 1953 by Luis Angulo Pintado, "Martí fué un precursor del Rotarismo."

49. *Diario de la Marina* (La Habana), 28 de enero de 1953, p. 3.

50. *Ibid.,* 27 de enero de 1953, p. 2. Accompanying the newspaper announcement was a list of eleven detailed instructions that would have discouraged any applicant but a lawyer.

51. Celso Enríquez, *José Martí y los deportes* (México: Ed. y Distribuidores "Istmo," 1948).

52. *Diario de la Marina* (La Habana), 4 de mayo de 1956, p. 3-B.

53. *Obras,* ed. Quesada y Miranda, XXIX, 170.

54. *El Crisol* (La Habana), 28 de enero de 1957, Supl., p. 14.

55. Blas Roca, "Martí responde," *Noticias de Hoy* (La Habana), 27 de febrero de 1940, pp. 1, 6.

56. "Martí, injusto y apasionado," *Semanario Católico,* 3 de noviembre de 1940, p. 9.

57. Emilio Roig de Leuchsenring, "En defensa de Martí," *El Mundo* (La Habana), 29 de diciembre de 1940, p. 22.

58. Emilio Ballagas, "Martí y los cristianos," *Diario de la Marina* (La Habana) 28 de diciembre de 1940, p. A-4.

59. "Excomunión del Padre Biaín," *El Avance Criollo* (La Habana), 14 de diciembre de 1940, p. 2.

60. Interview with Father Ignacio Biaín, January 30, 1957.

61. "Crónica católica: martianicemos nuestro amor patrio," *Diario de la Marina* (La Habana), 30 de enero de 1945, p. 7.

62. *Ibid.* 63. *Ibid.* 64. *Diplomacia,* LXIII (junio de 1952), [1].

65. Juan Luis Martín, "Comentarios de actualidad. Un insulto a Martí," *Alerta Cubano* (La Habana), septiembre de 1953, pp. 1-2.

66. *Diario de la Marina* (La Habana), 29 de enero de 1957, p. 10-A.

67. Interview with José Manuel Pérez Cabrera, January 18, 1956. In 1958 Dr. Pérez Cabrera briefly held the post of Minister of Education.

68. Father Manuel Fernández, O. S. A., "An Outstanding Achievement: The University of St. Thomas of Villanueva," *Havana Post,* January 19, 1957, p. 10.

69. José María Chacón y Calvo, "Pasión cristiana de Martí," *Diario de la Marina* (La Habana), 2 de febrero de 1957, p. 4-A.

70. Abraham M. Matterín, *Martí y las discriminaciones raciales* (La Habana: Ed. de la Agrupación Cultural Hebreo-Cubana, 1953).

71. *El Mundo* (La Habana), 24 de enero de 1953, p. A-6.

72. *De cara al sol* (La Habana: Ed. de la Agrupación Cultural Hebreo-Cubana, 1954).

73. Félix Lizaso, "Martí y los hebreos," *El Mundo* (La Habana), 14 de julio de 1953, p. A-6.

74. Interview with Abraham M. Matterín, March 18, 1957.

75. Interview with Marco Pitchon, March 19, 1957.

76. *Obras,* ed. Quesada y Miranda, XIV, 112.

CHAPTER 6

1. *Mi primera ofrenda* (New York: Imp. de El Porvenir, 1892), p. 94.
2. *Martí,* ed. Quesada y Aróstegui, VIII, 6.
3. *José Martí, el santo de América* (La Habana: Imp. P. Fernández y Cía., 1941).
4. Waldo Medina, "Martí, capitán de arcángeles," *El Mundo* (La Habana), 30 de enero de 1951, p. 4.
5. Pedro Beroes, "Mi San José Martí," *La Rosa Blanca,* III (mayo de 1949), 4.
6. Agustín López de Armas, "Martí, redentor de los cubanos," *La Publicidad* (Santa Clara), 7 de febrero de 1938.
7. José Machado y Hernández, "José Martí, segundogénito de Dios," *Excelsior* (La Habana), 20 de mayo de 1953, p. 1.
8. Osvaldo Bazil, "El evangelio de la ternura," in his *Cabezas de América* (La Habana: Molína y Cía., 1933), pp. 15-23.
9. Pedro José Cohucelo, "El Cristo americano, José Martí," *La Tribuna Popular* (Montevideo), 8 de febrero de 1953, p. 5.
10. Augusto Martínez Pereira, "Jesús-Martí," *Información* (La Habana), 10 de febrero de 1953, p. 4.
11. María Feria de Varona, "Para Martí, el salvador," *El País Gráfico,* 7 de junio de 1953, p. 30.
12. Rafael G. Argilagos, "Liturgía de la Natividad Martiana," *Martí,* XVI (febrero de 1945), 18.
13. Alberto Baeza Flores, "Vigilia martiana," *Carteles,* 29 de enero de 1950, pp. 10-11.
14. Miguel E. Bestard, "Peregrinación martiana de la I. O. O. F.," *Selva Habanera,* 3 de enero de 1953, pp. 1, 6-7.
15. Arturo R. de Carricarte, "Apostillas martinianas. La consagración de Dos Ríos," *Diario de la Marina* (La Habana) 26 de abril de 1942, p. 4.
16. José Manuel Espín, "Letanía martiana; mi homenaje en el primer Centenario del natalicio de José Martí," *Revista Casino Español,* VIII (octubre de 1953), 13.
17. Rafael Esténger, "Resurrección," *Alerta* (La Habana), 28 de enero de 1950, p. 4.
18. Noé de la Flor Casanova, "Mi breviario martiano," *El Universal* (México), 3 de febrero de 1953.
19. Raúl Fernández Ceballos, "Yo leí en la Biblia de Martí," *El Mensajero,* L (junio de 1953), 20-21.
20. Rafael M. Senmanat, *El calvario de Martí (de Playitas a Dos Ríos)* (Regla, Cuba: Ed. América, 1925).
21. José Manuel Cortina, "Martí, divina antena," *El Tanameño* (Sagua de Tánamo), 29 de enero de 1949, p. 2.
22. Dolores Guiral, "Si existió un alma tan bella como la del señor Martí, Dios tiene que existir," *Carteles,* 1 de febrero de 1953, p. 126.
23. "José Martí, como orador, fué único, y se le hubiera creído un hombre sobrenatural, pues sus palabras eran dignas de un Dios," *La Noticia* (Managua, Nicaragua), 30 de enero de 1952.
24. Real Academia Española, *Diccionario de la lengua española* (18th ed.; Madrid: Ed. Espasa-Calpe, S. A., 1956), p. 852.
25. "¿Error o mala intención?" *Patria,* XII (diciembre de 1956), 5.
26. "Rincón criollo. Cosas de aquí y allá," *Patria,* VI (mayo de 1950), 39.
27. *Ibid.*

28. Juan Giró Rodés, "Confidencialmente," *El Mundo* (La Habana), 27 de septiembre de 1956, p. B-2.

29. Waldo Medina, "Martilandia en ruinas," *El Mundo* (La Habana), 3 de febrero de 1948, p. 10.

30. "El Manifiesto de Montecristi," *Boletín Oficial*, I (noviembre de 1945), 6.

31. "Martí," *Patria*, III (enero de 1947), 12.

32. "Invocación al Apóstol," *Patria*, VII (junio de 1951), 5.

33. Manuel Ferrer Cuevas, "Ante los restos de Martí," *Archivo José Martí*, V (julio-diciembre de 1951), 552.

34. "La religión martiana," *Boletín Oficial*, II (enero de 1946), 4.

35. *Martí ante el proceso de Jesús* (La Habana: La Verdad, 1956).

36. Rogelio González Ricardo, "Cómo y dónde surgió la Nochebuena Martiana," *Orto*, XXXI (enero-marzo de 1942), 32-33.

37. Argilagos, *Martí*, XVI (febrero de 1945), 18.

38. Jesús Fernández Lamas, "Cenas Martianas," *Boletín Oficial*, II (marzo de 1946), 8.

39. Rogelio A. Pujol, "Cenas Martianas mixtificadas," *Boletín Oficial*, II (marzo de 1946), 7.   40. *Boletín Oficial*, II (abril de 1946), 5-6.

41. *Patria*, III (febrero de 1947), 5-6.

42. *El Mundo* (La Habana), 26 de junio de 1956, p. A-11.

43. *Ibid.*, 26 de diciembre de 1953, p. A-8.

44. J. M. Valdés Rodríguez, "Dificultades para realizar la película 'La Rosa Blanca,'" *Cinema*, 1 de noviembre de 1953, p. 18.

45. "Inaudito boicot sindical a la película sobre la vida de Martí," *Cinema*, 1 de noviembre de 1953, p. 40.

46. "Realismo y poesía en la versión fílmica de la vida de José Martí," *Cinema*, 29 de noviembre de 1953, p. 16.

47. See Quesada y Miranda, *Mujeres de Martí*.

48. "Hollywood juega con Martí," *Bohemia*, 12 de agosto de 1956, p. 35.

49. *Patria*, XII (septiembre de 1956), 4.

50. Agustín Tamargo, "Quien injuria a Martí y a Maceo no puede ser amigo de Cuba," *Bohemia*, 26 de agosto de 1956, p. 49.

51. *Patria*, XII (septiembre de 1956), 4.

52. *Patria*, VI (enero de 1950), 9-10.

53. "Martí y lo cubano," *Diario de la Marina* (La Habana), 27 de enero de 1952, pp. 4, 6.

54. *Bolívar y Martí* (La Habana: Imp. El Siglo XX, 1934); *Lincoln en Martí* (La Habana: Ed. Trópico, [1948]); *Dos creadores: Mazzini y Martí* (La Habana: Ed. Trópico, 1936); *Genio y acción, Sarmiento y Martí* (La Habana: Ed. Trópico, 1938); "Universalidad de dos Americanos," *Journal of Inter-American Studies*, IV (January, 1962), 33-51.

55. Jesús Fernández Lamas, *Juárez en Martí* (Artemisa, Cuba: Imp. Hermanos Trujillo, 1953).

56. Benjamín Jarnes, *Escuela de libertad. Siete maestros: Bolívar, Hidalgo, Lincoln, Martí, San Martín, Sucre, Washington* (México: Ed. Continental, [1942]).

57. Félix Lizaso, "San Martín en Martí," *Mensuario de Arte, Literatura, Historia y Crítica*, I (noviembre de 1950), 14, 22-23.

58. Emilio Roig de Leuchsenring, "Hostos y Martí, dos ideologías antillanas concordantes," *Revista Bimestre Cubana*, XLIII (enero-febrero de 1939), 5-19.

59. *El País* (La Habana), 7 de febrero de 1953, pp. 1, 12.

60. Antonio Penichet Gómez, "Abraham Lincoln, Mahatma Gandhi y José Martí," *Lux* (enero de 1951), pp. 21, 24.

61. Juan Luís Martín, "Un paralelo: José Martí y Sun Yat-sen," *Pueblo* (La Habana), 27 de enero de 1941, p. 11.

62. Marta Vidaillet Paradela, "Paralelos entre Roosevelt y Martí," *La Semana* (Baracoa, Cuba), 6 de enero de 1949, pp. 10-11.

63. José Luis Galbe, "Petoefi, el Martí de Hungría," in his *Causas célebres y vidas extraordinarias* (La Habana: Cultural, S. A., 1953), pp. 311-328.

64. *Biografía de una isla,* trans. Gonzalo de Quesada y Miranda (México: Ed. Centauro, S. A., 1948), pp. 291-292.

65. "Martí prometecio," *Educación,* XIII (enero de 1953), 13.

66. Interview with M. Isidro Méndez, March 3, 1957.

67. *José Martí: precursor de la UNESCO* (La Habana: Publicaciones de la Comisión Nacional Cubana de UNESCO, 1953).

68. *La consciencia universal y Martí* (La Habana: Ed. Lex, 1952).

69. Rogelio Dihigo, *Martí "su verso hecho música"* (2 vols.; [Marianao, Cuba: Típ. Nemesio, 1950-53]).

70. *Obras,* ed. Quesada y Miranda, XLV, 165.

71. Carricarte, *La cubanidad,* pp. 14-23.

72. "Martiolatría y conducta," *Alfanje,* IV (febrero de 1941), 7.

73. "Atalaya: dejemos quieto a Martí," *El Avance Criollo* (La Habana), 23 de agosto de 1941, p. 3.

74. "¿Abuso de Martí?" *Siempre,* 30 de enero de 1946, pp. 1-2.

75. "¿Abuso de Martí?" *Siempre,* 5 de febrero de 1946, p. 1.

76. "Trasluz. ¿Abuso de Martí?" *El Avance Criollo* (La Habana), 19 de mayo de 1952, p. 3.

77. "José Martí y los católicos," *Semanario Católico,* 18 de enero de 1953, pp. 30-31.

78. "El Centenario de Martí," *Semanario Católico,* 18 de enero de 1953, p. 23.

CHAPTER 7

1. Juan J. Remos, "Experiencias del Gobierno propio," *Historia de la Nación cubana,* VIII, Libro 2°, cap. iv, 81.

2. *El Mundo* (La Habana), 10 de septiembre de 1955, p. A-7.

3. *Ibid.*

4. Remos, *Historia de la Nación cubana,* VIII, Libro 2°, cap. iv, 81.

5. *Ibid.,* p. 84.   6. *Ibid.,* p. 85.

7. So named in its underground existence under Machado.

8. See William S. Stokes, "The Cuban Parliamentary System in Action," *Journal of Politics,* XI (May, 1949), 335-364.

9. *El Crisol* (La Habana) 29 de enero de 1938, p. 1.

10. *Prensa Libre* (La Habana), 17 de octubre de 1943, p. 3.

11. *Martí y el Partido Revolucionario Cubano* (La Habana: Ediciones de la Comisión Nacional de Propaganda del Partido Revolucionario Cubana [Auténticos], 1939), p. 8.

12. *Ibid.,* pp. 8-9.   13. *Ibid.,* p. 13.

14. "Se oponen la maldad y el poder a la obra constructor del Apóstol," *Prensa Libre* (La Habana), 30 de enero de 1944, p. 1.

15. Ramón Rivero Aguiar, "De Martí a Grau," *El Avance Criollo* (La Habana), 29 de enero de 1944, p. 4.

16. *Información* (La Habana), 20 de mayo de 1945, pp. 1, 16.

17. "Profanación de Martí," *Prensa Libre* (La Habana), 28 de abril de 1945, p. 3.

18. F. Moreno de Ayala, "El sueño de Martí," *Boletín Oficial* II (mayo de 1946), 4.

19. "Ecos y reflejos: ¿Es así que honramos a Martí?" *El Mundo* (La Habana) 6 de mayo de 1946, p. 12.

20. Open letter from Andrés Lugo Martínez to Maj. Gen. Enrique Loynaz del Castillo, *Prensa Libra* (La Habana), 23 de junio de 1949.

21. Grau San Martín, *Martí y el Partido*, p. 4.

22. Interview with Ramón Grau San Martín, February 6, 1957.

23. Remos, *Historia de la Nación cubana*, VIII, Libro 2°, cap. iv, 92.

24. Interview with Professor Antonio Lancís y Sánchez, January 30, 1957. See Antonio Lancís y Sánchez, *Lo electoral en Martí: espectáculo y ansia* (La Habana: Ed. Lex, 1953).

25. *El Crisol* (La Habana), 19 de marzo de 1956, suppl. p. [2].

26. See William S. Stokes, "The 'Cuban Revolution' and the Presidential Elections of 1948," *Hispanic American Historical Review*, XXXI (February, 1951), 37-79.

27. Juan González Martínez, "Por qué hice Presidente a Carlos Prío," *Bohemia*, 30 de enero de 1949, p. 65.

28. "Strictly Cuban," as Grau called his administration.

29. "Cordiality," as Prío's administration was beginning to be called.

30. Francisco Ichaso, "Cabalgata política: la difícil situación del gobierno actual ante las malversaciones del anterior," *Bohemia*, 30 de enero de 1949, pp. 27, 80.

31. Jorge Mañach, "Si Martí levantara la cabeza," *Bohemia*, 30 de enero de 1949, pp. 44, 66.

32. *Diario de la Marina* (La Habana), 28 de enero de 1949, p. 1.

33. Agustín Guerra de la Piedra, "¿Tenemos la República que soñó Martí?" *Orto*, XXXVIII (febrero de 1950), 1.

34. *El País* (La Habana), 29 de enero de 1946, p. 1.

35. *Ibid.*

36. *Obras*, ed. Quesada y Miranda, XVI, 20.

37. *El Crisol* (La Habana), 29 de enero de 1951, p. 18.

38. See William S. Stokes, "National and Local Violence in Cuban Politics," *Southwestern Social Science Quarterly*, XXXIV (September, 1953), 57-63.

39. "Cuba: Winner Take All," *Time* (Latin American ed.), March 24, 1952, p. 28.

40. René Fiallo, "Con una estrella en la frente," *Bohemia*, 18 de septiembre de 1955, p. 71.

41. *El Mundo* (La Habana), 27 de enero de 1953, p. A-8.

42. *Diario de la Marina* (La Habana), 28 de enero de 1953, p. 2.

43. Angel Cuadra, "Lamento a José Martí en su Centenario," *El País Gráfico*, 15 de febrero de 1953, p. 17.

44. B. Jiménez Perdomo, "Un día tras otro. Dónde no se puede florecer la Rosa Blanca," *Información* (La Habana), 29 de enero de 1953, p. 2.

45. César García Pons, "Las honras que el Apóstol hubiera rechazado," *Bohemia*, 25 de enero de 1953, p. 68.

46. *Diario de la Marina* (La Habana), 28 de enero de 1953, p. 4.

47. "Centenario antimartiano," *Prensa Libre* (La Habana), 19 de febrero de 1953, p. 1.

48. "La República ante el legado de Martí," *Bohemia*, 14 de febrero de 1953, pp. 59, 80.

49. "Actualidad política: un alto al fuego en honor de Martí," *Diario de la Marina* (La Habana), 27 de enero de 1953, p. 2.

50. *Información* (La Habana), 29 de enero de 1953, p. 2.
51. Sociedad de Amigos de la República, *El momento político de Cuba, acuerdos, cartas, y discursos* (La Habana: Ed. Lex, 1955), pp. 8, 12-13.
52. *Ibid.*, p. 19.
53. *Diario Nacional* (La Habana), 17 de septiembre de 1955, pp. A-1, A-8.
54. *Alerta* (La Habana), 19 de noviembre de 1956, pp. 1, 24.
55. Bernardo Viera Trejo, "Cuba y seis personajes lejanos," *Bohemia,* 10 de marzo de 1957, p. 36.
56. *Diario de la Marina* (La Habana), 29 de enero de 1957, p. A-14.
57. *El Mundo* (La Habana), 12 de marzo de 1957, p. A-4.
58. *Ibid.*, pp. A-1, A-8.   59. *Ibid.*, 14 de marzo de 1957, pp. A-1, A-7.
60. Raúl Ibarra, "Gestaron el '26 de Julio' en el término de Artemisa," *Diario Nacional* (La Habana), 25 de abril de 1957, p. A-8.
61. Interview with Rafael L. Díaz-Balart, February 6, 1957.
62. *El Mundo* (La Habana), 4 de junio de 1939, p. 1.
63. *El caso literario de José Martí. Motivos de Centenario* (La Habana: Imp. Vega y Cía., 1954) pp. 24-27.
64. Ilya Ehrenburg *et al., Martí en Moscú: homenaje en su Centenario* (La Habana: Ed. Páginas, 1953). Martí even turned up in a memorial in Red China. See Comité del Pueblo Chino para la Defensa de la Paz Mundial, *Conmemoración de Chu Yuan, Nicolás Copernico, François Rabelais y José Martí* (Pekín: [Publisher?], 1953).
65. Marinello, *El caso literario,* pp. 49-50.
66. *Patria,* V (agosto de 1949), 8.
67. "La ofensa de los *energúmenos* vestidos de marinos es igual a la que a diario fomentan contra Cuba los imperialistas," *Noticias de Hoy* (La Habana), 15 de marzo de 1949, pp. 1, 6.
68. Francisco J. Argüelles, "Hecho escandaloso," *Patria,* V (agosto de 1949), 8.   69. "Perdón," *Patria,* V (abril de 1949), 5-6.
70. *Patria,* V (abril de 1949), 3-4.   71. *Ibid.,* p. 11.
72. Asociación Nacional de los Emigrados Revolucionarios Cubanos de la Independencia, "El sentimiento de los compañeros del Apóstol," *Patria,* V (abril de 1949), 17.   73. *La Ultima Hora,* 1 de enero de 1953, p. 5.
74. Miguel Loyola, "Martí y la pobreza," *La Ultima Hora,* 1 de enero de 1953, p. 53.   75. *Obras,* ed. Quesada y Miranda, XLVIII, 119.
76. *Ibid.,* XIX, 143.
77. Partido del Pueblo Cubano (Ortodoxo), *Doctrina del Partido Ortodoxo* (La Habana: P. Fernández y Cía., n. d.), p. 3.
78. *Obras,* ed. Quesada y Miranda, LXII, 15.   79. *Doctrina,* p. 23.
80. *Antología cívica de Eduardo R. Chibás,* ed. Hugo Mir (La Habana: Ed. Lex, n. d.), *passim.*
81. *Prensa Libre* (La Habana), 13 de enero de 1957, pp. 1, 14.
82. *El Mundo* (La Habana), 14 de marzo de 1957, p. A-1. In a television address May 2, 1957, Grau implied that the murder had been committed by the government.
83. "Maza y Artola como legislador," *Universidad de la Habana,* XXVI (1955), 222-262.
84. Interview with Manuel Bisbé, January 30, 1957. Bisbé's point of non-cooperation would seem to run counter to the theory that two-party systems are only possible when major opposition elements cooperate rather than hew to individual lines.
85. "Cuba: 'Dictator with the People,'" *Time* (Latin American ed.), April 21, 1952, p. 31.   86. *Obras,* ed. Quesada y Miranda, IV, 111.

87. Interview with Roberto Agramonte and Manuel Bisbé, January 31, 1957.
88. "La legitimidad de la oposición," *Bohemia,* 1 de enero de 1950, p. 52.
89. "Necesitamos una política generosa y creadora como la de José Martí," *Bohemia,* 29 de enero de 1950, p. 60.
90. *El Crisol* (La Habana), 16 de enero de 1956, pp. 1-2.
91. Interview with Carlos Márquez Sterling, February 20, 1957.
92. *Partido Municipal Habanero, Memoria sobre cuatro años de esfuerzo por el buen gobierno municipal de la Habana* (La Habana: Burgay y Cía., n.d.), pp. [2-3].   93. *Ibid.,* pp. [3-4].
94. Herminio Portell-Vilá, "Escuela de Ciudadanía: Formación de un partido político," *Bohemia,* 21 de marzo de 1954, p. 8.   95. *Ibid.,* p. 126.
96. Herminio Portell-Vilá, "Escuela de Ciudadanía: Proceso afiliatorio," *Bohemia,* 28 de marzo de 1954, p. 131.   97. *Ibid.,* p. 132.
98. Herminio Portell-Vilá, "Escuela de Ciudadanía: Lección aprendida," *Bohemia,* 11 de abril de 1954, p. 32.
99. Herminio Portell-Vilá, "Escuela de Ciudadanía: Duplicidades," *Bohemia,* 4 de abril de 1954, p. 111.
100. *Obras,* ed. Quesada y Miranda, XIV, 101-102.
101. The Instituto Cultural Cubano-Norteamericano, which Portell-Vilá founded in 1943, allowed books to be withdrawn for home circulation.
102. *Obras,* ed. Quesada y Miranda, XXVIII, 94.
103. Portell-Vilá, *Bohemia,* 11 de abril de 1954, p. 123.
104. Interview with Herminio Portell-Vilá, November 29, 1955.

CHAPTER 8

1. Interview with Jesús Artigas, Secretary General of the National Federation of Workers in Medicine, and Financial Secretary of the CTC, March 14, 1957.   2. *Ibid.*   3. *Ibid.*
4. Interview with Prisciliano Falcón Lañú, Secretary General of the National Federation of Sugar-Workers, March 15, 1957.
5. *Martí al alcance de los trabajadores* (La Habana: Ed. Unidad, 1949), p. 13.   6. Telephone interview with Bernardo García Feito, March 8, 1957.
7. "El natalicio de José Martí," *El Bancario,* [XII] (enero-febrero de 1957), 18-19.   8. *Reportaje Gráfico,* II (enero de 1957), 3, 38.
9. *Patria,* XII (agosto de 1956), 4.
10. Interview with Gonzalo de Quesada y Miranda, April 19, 1956. Among those given credit for having first begun the cult of Martí were the school teachers in the Republic. See Mercedes Alvarez de Rodón, "Eran maestras que iniciaron el culto de José Martí," *Prensa Libre* (La Habana), 14 de julio de 1950, p. 9.
11. "¿Por qué amamos a Martí?" *Revista Lyceum,* X (agosto de 1953), 100.
12. *Diario Nacional* (La Habana), 19 de abril de 1957, p. A-14.
13. Ricardo Colls, "¿Qué es un Rincón Martiano?" *Boletín Oficial,* II (junio de 1946), 10.   14. *El Mundo* (La Habana), 28 de enero de 1956, p. A-10.
15. Interview held March 9, 1956. Name withheld.
16. Interview with Anthony Smith y Franco, en route Havana to Miami, August 18, 1956.
17. "Martí y la escuela de la República," *Cuba Profesional,* [I] (marzo-mayo de 1952), 48.
18. Samuel Feijóo, "Acción de la escuela rural," *Bohemia,* 11 de enero de 1953, p. 30.
19. Amparo Soler Soler, "El Centenario de Martí y la escuela cubana," *Diario de Cuba* (Santiago de Cuba), 28 de enero de 1953, pp. 10-11.

20. The magazine *Orientación Campesina,* formerly called *Educación Rural,* has one un-Martian characteristic in its full-page advertisement for the National Lottery. It usually occupies the most prominent place for an advertisement—the back cover.

21. "Presencia de Martí en las escuelas rurales," *Orientación Campesina,* II (marzo-abril de 1955), 21-22.

22. Interview held in 1957, name withheld.

23. Interview held April 1, 1957. Name withheld.

24. Meetings of public school teachers attended in Havana in 1956. Names withheld.

25. International Bank for Reconstruction and Development, *Report on Cuba* (Baltimore: The Johns Hopkins Press, 1951), pp. 406, 411-415.

26. The Census for 1953 gives a total population for Cuba of 5,814,112. Of the 4.4 million ten years of age and above, 23.6 per cent are illiterate. Among the rural inhabitants of Cuba 41.7 per cent are illiterate. In the age group ten to fourteen the over-all figure of illiteracy for the nation is 31.8 per cent. In rural areas the situation is worse—49 per cent of this age group is listed as unable to read or write. See Cuba, Tribunal Superior Electoral, Oficina Nacional de los Censos Demográfico y Electoral, *Censos de población, viviendas, y electoral* (La Habana: P. Fernández y Cía., 1955), pp. xxviii, xxxix.

27. *Report on Cuba,* pp. 404-434, 439-440.

28. *Bohemia,* 26 de agosto de 1956, pp. 67-68.

29. Other public universities, of recent origin, are Oriente University, in Santiago de Cuba, and Central University, in Las Villas province.

30. Universidad de la Habana, *Cátedra Martiana* (La Habana: Departamento de Intercambio Cultural, 1950).

31. "Yunques sonad, enmudeced campanas," *Anuario de la Facultad de Ciencias Sociales y Derecho Público, 1955-1956* (La Habana: Universidad de la Habana, 1956), p. 50.   32. *Obras,* ed. Quesada y Miranda, XXV, 109.

33. Interview with Gonzalo de Quesada y Miranda, January 19, 1956.

34. Ruby Hart Phillips, *Cuban Sideshow* (La Habana: Cuban Press, 1935), pp. 52, 65-66.   35. *Bohemia,* 25 de enero de 1953, pp. 70-75.

36. *Diario de la Marina* (La Habana), 29 de enero de 1956, p. 7-B.

37. *El Mundo* (La Habana), 28 de enero de 1956, p. A-10.

38. "Alocuciones, declaraciones, acuerdos y pronunciamientos del Consejo Universitario," *Anuario de la Facultad,* p. 532.

39. Interview with Raúl Roa, January 31, 1957.

40. *El Mundo* (La Habana), 14 de marzo de 1957, p. A-1.

41. *Diario Nacional* (La Habana), 2 de mayo de 1957, p. A-4.

42. "El caso económico de la juventud," *El Mundo* (La Habana), 22 de diciembre de 1956, p. A-6.

43. Angel Quintero, "Hay que inspirar ideales a las nuevas generaciones cubanas," *Bohemia,* 5 de agosto de 1956, p. 105.

44. *Report on Cuba,* p. 18.   45. *Ibid.*

46. *Obras,* ed. Quesada y Miranda, LXII, 118.

47. UNESCO, *Basic Facts and Figures* (Paris: Imp. Letouzey et Ané, 1954), p. 61.   48. *Pueblo* (La Habana), 19 de septiembre de 1955, p. 1.

49. *El Mundo* (La Habana), 18 de mayo de 1952, p. A-1.

50. *Diario de la Marina* (La Habana), 28 de enero de 1953, p. 4.

51. "¡Viva Cuba Libre!" *Ataja* (La Habana), 10 de febrero de 1957, pp. 1, 4.   52. Interview with Jorge Quintana, March 19, 1957.

53. Interview with Gonzalo de Quesada y Miranda, January 18, 1957.

54. *El Mundo* (La Habana), 28 de septiembre de 1956, p. A-6.

55. *Diario de la Marina* (La Habana), 29 de enero de 1957, p. 4-A.
56. As cited in the Introduction, however, no attempt has been made to present this material as a scientific investigation along the lines of professional public opinion testing.
57. Interview held in Havana, March 3, 1956. Name withheld.
58. Interview held in Havana, April 1, 1956. Name withheld.
59. Interview held in Havana, March 9, 1956. Name withheld.
60. Interview held March 13, 1956. Name withheld.
61. Noted in Havana April 10, 1956.
62. Noted in Havana August 4, 1956.
63. Interview held July 8, 1956. Names withheld.
64. Interview held in March, 1956. Name withheld.
65. Interview held December 17, 1956. Name withheld.
66. Interview held December 5, 1956. Name withheld.
67. Interview held January 27, 1957. Names withheld.
68. Interview held January 27, 1957. Name withheld.
69. Interview held January 29, 1957. Name withheld.
70. Interview held February 10, 1957. Names withheld.
71. Interview held November 13, 1956. Name withheld.
72. Interview held January 19, 1957. Name withheld.
73. Interview held January 14, 1957. Name withheld.

CHAPTER 9

1. *La historia me absolverá* (La Habana: Imprenta Económica en General, n.d.), pp. 6, 47-48.
2. *Cuba and Castro* (translated from the Spanish by Elmer Grossberg, New York: Random House, 1961), p. 103.   3. *Ibid.*, p. 207.
4. *New York Times*, April 20, 1959, p. 1.
5. *Ibid.*, July 18, 1959, pp. 1, 8.   6. *Ibid.*, July 4, 1959, pp. 1, 5.
7. Movimiento 26 de Julio de Nueva York, *Martí, su Rosa Blanca y Cuba*, n.d., tract in possession of the author.
8. *New York Times*, November 23, 1959, pp. 1, 12.
9. *Ibid.*, November 29, 1959, V, p. 3.   10. *Ibid.*, January 27, 1960, p. 11.
11. *Bohemia*, 31 de enero de 1960, p. 63.
12. Universidad de la Habana, *Vida Universitaria*, XI (enero, febrero, marzo de 1960), 22-23.   13. *Revolución*, 7 de junio de 1960, p. 8.
14. "Sobre la libertad de Prensa," *Hoy*, 8 de junio de 1960, p. 2.
15. "Castro and His Catch Phrases," *Tallahassee Democrat*, September 30, 1960, p. 4.
16. Centro de Estudios Martianos, *Trayectoria y presencia de Martí, guía y temario para jornadas martianas* (La Habana: Unidad 19 de la Imprenta Nacional, 1961), pp. 42-46.   17. *New York Times*, October 15, 1960, p. 7.
18. "Martí, guía de su tiempo y anticipadora del nuestro," *La Ultima Hora*, (enero de 1953), p. 6.   19. *New York Times*, November 2, 1960, p. 1.
20. *Ibid.*, December 17, 1960, p. 6.   21. *Ibid.*, January 4, 1961, pp. 1, 3.
22. *Ibid.*, January 3, 1961, p. 28.   23. *Ibid.*, April 21, 1961, pp. 1, 7.
24. *Ibid.*, May 29, 1961, p. 6.   25. *Ibid.*, December 3, 1961, pp. 4, 1.
26. *Ibid.*, February 1, 1962, pp. 1, 2.   27. *Ibid.*, February 6, 1962, pp. 1, 3.
28. *Ibid.*, March 10, 1962, pp. 1, 6.

Bibliography

GENERAL REFERENCES

BARNES, Ana Maria. *Martí, a Story of the Cuban War.* Chicago: David C. Cook Publishing Co., 1899.

BRITO, H. C. *Suum cuique.* La Habana: Imp. de Rambla y Bouza, 1910.

CASTELLANOS G., Gerardo. *Panorama histórico, ensayo de cronología cubana.* La Habana: Ucar García, 1934.

CASTRO Ruz, Fidel. *La historia me absolverá.* La Habana: Imp. Económica en General, [n. d.]

CASUSO, Teresa. *Cuba and Castro.* Translated from the Spanish by Elmer Grossberg. New York: Random House, 1961.

CHAPMAN, Charles E. *A History of the Cuban Republic, a Study in Hispanic American Politics.* New York: The Macmillan Co., 1927.

CHIBÁS, Eduardo R. *Antología cívica de Eduardo R. Chibás.* Ed. Hugo Mir. La Habana, Ed. Lex, [n. d.].

Cuba en la mano. La Habana: Imp. Ucar, García y Cía., 1940.

DARÍO, Rubén. *Los raros.* Madrid: [Imp. G. Hernández y G. Sáez, 1929]. (Vol. XVIII of his *Obras completas,* ed. Alberto Ghiraldo y Andrés González-Blanco. Madrid: Biblioteca Rubén Darío, 1924?).

DOYLE, Henry G. *A Bibliography of Rubén Darío (1867-1916).* Cambridge: Harvard University Press, 1935.

Encyclopedia Britannica. 14th ed.

FERGUSON, Erna. *Cuba.* New York: A. A. Knopf, 1946.

GÁLVEZ y del Monte, Wenceslao. *Tampa, impresiones de emigrado.* Tampa: Establecimiento Tip. Cuba, 1897.

GÓMEZ, Máximo. *Diario de campaña.* La Habana: Centro Superior Tecnológico, 1941.

GONZÁLEZ, Manuel Pedro. *Fuentes para el estudio de José Martí.* La Habana: Publicaciones del Ministerio de Educación, 1950.

GUERRA Aguiar, José L. *Catálogo general de sellos de Cuba.* La Habana: By the author, 1956.

GUERRA y Sánchez, Ramiro. *Guerra de los Diez Años, 1868-1878.* La Habana: Cultural, S. A., 1950.

——————— *et al. Historia de la Nación cubana.* 10 vols. La Habana: Ed. Historia de la Nación Cubana, 1952.

International Bank for Reconstruction and Development. *Report on Cuba.* Baltimore: The Johns Hopkins Press, 1951.

LUDWIG, Emil. *Biografía de una isla.* [Trans. Gonzalo de Quesada y Miranda.] México: Ed. Centauro, S. A., 1948.

Partido del Pueblo Cubano (Ortodoxo). *Doctrina del Partido Ortodoxo.* La Habana: P. Fernández y Cía., [n. d.].

PERAZA Sarausa, Fermín. *Bibliografía martiana.* 2d ed. rev. Ed. Anuario Bibliográfico Cubano, 1956.

285

_____. *Cronología de la obra martiana.* La Habana: Ed. Anuario Bibliográfico Cubano, 1955.

PHILLIPS, Ruby Hart. *Cuban Sideshow.* La Habana: Cuban Press, 1935.

PORTELL-VILÁ, Herminio. *Historia de Cuba en sus relaciones con los Estados Unidos y España.* 4 vols. La Habana: Ed. Jesús Montero, 1938-41.

_____. *Partido Municipal Habanero, Memoria sobre cuatro años de esfuerzo por el buen gobierno municipal de la Habana.* La Habana: Burgay y Cía., [n. d.].

QUESADA y Aróstegui, Gonzalo de. *Mi primera ofrenda.* New York: Imp. de El Porvenir, 1892.

_____, and NORTHROP, Henry D. *The War in Cuba, Being a Full Account of Her Great Struggle for Freedom.* Rev. ed. Washington: Liberty Publishing Co., 1896.

Real Academia Española. *Diccionario de la lengua española.* 18th ed. Madrid: Ed. Espasa-Calpe, S. A., 1956.

RUBENS, Horatio S. *Liberty, the Story of Cuba.* New York: Brewer, Warren and Putnam, Inc., 1932.

Sociedad de Amigos de la República. *El momento político de Cuba, acuerdos, cartas y discursos.* La Habana: Ed. Lex, 1955.

Universidad de la Habana. *Cátedra Martiana.* La Habana: Departamento de Intercambio Cultural, 1950.

UNESCO. *Basic Facts and Figures.* Paris: Imp. Letouzey et Ané, 1954.

VITIER, Medardo. *Las ideas en Cuba.* 2 vols. La Habana: Ed. Trópico, 1938.

WALLICH, Henry C. *Problemas monetarias de una economía de exportación (La experiencia cubana, 1914-1947).* Trans. Ernesto Cuesta. La Habana: Banco Nacional de Cuba, 1953.

WILSON, James H. *The Life of Charles A. Dana.* New York: Harper and Brothers Publishers, 1907.

ANTHOLOGIES AND COLLECTED WORKS OF JOSÉ MARTÍ

MARTÍ y Pérez, José, J. *The America of José Martí.* Trans. Juan de Onís. New York: Noonday, 1954.

_____. *Cartas inéditas de Martí.* Ed. Joaquín Llaverías. La Habana: Imp. El Siglo XX, 1920.

_____. *Código martiano o de ética nacional.* Ed. Carlos Martínez-Fortún y Foyo. La Habana: Seoane Fernández y Cía., 1943.

_____. *Diccionario del pensamiento de José Martí.* Ed. Lilia Castro de Morales. La Habana: Ed. Selecta Librería, 1953.

_____. *Discursos.* Ed. Néstor Carbonell. La Habana: Biblioteca de El Magazine de la raza, 1923.

_____. *Epistolario de José Martí.* Ed. Félix Lizaso. 3 vols. La Habana: Cultural, S. A., 1930-31.

_____. *España.* Ed. Néstor Carbonell. La Habana: Ed. de Guáimaro, 1926.

_____. *Esquema ideológico.* Eds. Manuel Pedro González e Iván A. Schulman. México: Ed. Cultura, T. G., S. A., 1961.

_____. *Evocando al maestro.* Ed. Miguel Angel Carbonell. La Habana: Imp. Seoane y Fernández, 1919.

_____. *Flor y lava.* Ed. Américo Lugo. París: Sociedad de Ediciones Literarias y Artísticas, 1910.

_____. *Flores del destierro.* Ed. Gonzalo de Quesada y Miranda. La Habana: Imp. Molina y Cía., 1933. (Vol. XVI of *Martí,* ed. Quesada y Aróstegui.)

————. *Granos de oro.* Ed. Rafael G. Argilagos. La Habana: Sociedad Ed. Cuba Contemporánea, 1918.

————. *Ideario.* Ed. M. Isidro Méndez. La Habana: Colección de libros cubanos, 1930.

————. *José Martí, obras completas.* Ed. M. Isidro Méndez. 4 vols. 2d ed. La Habana: Ed. Lex, 1948.

————. *Madre América.* Ed. Ventura García Calderón. París: Ed. Franco-Ibero-americana, [1922].

————. *Martí.* Ed. Gonzalo de Quesada y Aróstegui. 16 vols. Vol. I, Washington: Gonzalo de Quesada, 1900; Vols. II and III, La Habana: Gonzalo de Quesada, 1901-02; Vol. IV, La Habana: Imp. y Papelería Rambla y Bouza, 1905; Vol. V, Roma: Casa Ed. Nazionale, 1905; Vols. VI-IX, La Habana: Imp. y Papelería Rambla y Bouza, 1908-10; Vol. X, Berlín: Gonzalo de Quesada, 1911; Vols. XI-XIV, La Habana: Imp. y Papelería de Rambla, Bouza y Cía., 1913-15; Vol. XV, ed. Angelina Miranda de Quesada; La Habana: Imp. y Papelería de Rambla, Bouza y Cía., 1919; Vol. XVI, ed. Gonzalo de Quesada y Miranda; La Habana, Imp. Molina y Cía., 1933.

————. *Martí en Venezuela.* Ed. Venezuela, Ministerio de Relaciones Exteriores. Caracas: Tip. Americana, 1930.

————. *Obras completas.* Ed. Alberto Ghiraldo. 8 vols. Madrid: [A. Ghiraldo, 1925]-29.

————. *Obras completas de Martí.* Ed. Néstor Carbonell. 8 vols. La Habana: Ed. Especial de la Prensa, 1918-20.

————. *Obras completas de Martí.* Ed. Armando Godoy y Ventura García Calderón. 2 vols. París: Ed. Excelsior, [1926].

————. *Obras completas de Martí.* Ed. Gonzalo de Quesada y Miranda. 74 vols. La Habana: Ed. Trópico, 1936-49.

————. *Páginas escogidas.* Ed. Max Henríquez Ureña. París: Casa Ed. Garnier Hermanos, [1919].

————. *Papeles de Martí.* Ed. Gonzalo de Quesada y Miranda. 3 vols. La Habana: Academia de la Historia de Cuba, 1933-35.

————. *Poèmes choisis.* Trans. Armando Godoy. París: Emil-Paul Frèses, 1929.

————. *Translations from José Martí.* Trans. Cecil Charles. New York: J. E. Richardson, 1898.

————. *Tuya, Other Verses and Translations from José Martí.* Trans. Cecil Charles. New York: J. E. Richardson, 1898.

————. *Versos escogidos de Martí.* Ed. Rubén Darío. París: Casa Ed. Franco-Ibero-americana, [1919].

BIOGRAPHIES OF JOSÉ MARTÍ

Anon. [Erasmo Pella]. *Martí, novela histórica por un patriota.* La Habana: Imp. La Moderna Poesía, [1901].

CARBONELL, Néstor. *Martí: su vida y su obra. El poeta.* La Habana: Imp. Seoane y Alvarez, 1913.

CASTELLANOS G., Gerardo. *Los últimos días de Martí.* La Habana: Ucar García y Cía., 1937.

GARRIGÓ, Roque E. *América: José Martí.* La Habana: Imp. Papelería de Rambla y Bouza, 1911.

HERNÁNDEZ Catá, Alfonso. *Mitología de Martí.* Madrid: Renacimiento, 1929.

LIZASO, Félix. *Martí, Martyr of Cuban Independence.* Trans. Esther E. Shuler. Albuquerque: University of New Mexico Press, 1953.

_____. *Martí, místico del deber.* 3d ed. Buenos Aires: Ed. Losada, 1952.

MAGDALENO, Mauricio. *José Martí, (Fulgor de Martí).* México: Ed. Botas, 1941.

MAÑACH, Jorge. *Martí: Apostle of Freedom.* Trans. Coley Taylor. New York: Devin-Adair, 1950.

_____. *Martí, el apóstol.* Bilbao: Espasa-Calpe, 1933.

MÁRQUEZ Sterling, Carlos. *Martí, maestro y apóstol.* La Habana: Seoane, Fernández y Cía., 1942.

_____. *Nueva y humana visión de Martí.* La Habana: Ed. Lex, 1953.

MÉNDEZ, M. Isidro. *José Martí: estudio biográfico.* Madrid: Agence mondiale de librairie, [1925].

QUESADA y Miranda, Gonzalo de, *Anecdotario martiano, nuevas facetas de Martí.* La Habana: Seoane, Fernández y Cía., 1948.

_____. *Martí, hombre.* La Habana: Seoane, Fernández y Cía., 1940.

RANDER, Franco [Erasmo Pella]. *José Martí, reseña histórica.* La Habana: Imp. de Juan A. de la Cámara, 1915.

_____. *José Martí, reseña histórica.* 2d ed. La Habana: Litografía e Imp. Industrias Gráficas, 1929.

_____. *José Martí, reseña histórica.* 3d ed. La Habana: Litografía e Imp. Industrias Gráficas, 1931.

RODRÍGUEZ Embil, Luis. *José Martí, el santo de América.* La Habana: Imp. P. Fernández y Cía., 1941.

MONOGRAPHS ON JOSÉ MARTÍ

BÉGUEZ César, José A. *Martí y el krausismo.* La Habana: Companía Ed. de Libros y Folletos, 1944.

CARRANCÁ y Trujillo, Camilo. *Martí, traductor de Victor Hugo.* México: Talleres Gráficos de la Nación, 1933.

CARRICARTE, Arturo R. de. *La cubanidad negativa del apóstol Martí.* La Habana: Manuel I. Mesa Rodríguez, 1934.

_____. *Martí en Isla de Pinos.* La Habana: Imp. Ed. América, 1923.

CASTAÑEDA, Orlando. *Martí, los tabaqueros y la Revolución de 1895.* La Habana: Ed. Lex, 1946.

Centro de Estudios Martianos. *Trayectoria y presencia de Martí, guía y temario para jornadas martianas.* La Habana: Unidad 19 de la Imp. Nacional, 1961.

Comité del Pueblo Chino para la Defensa de la Paz Mundial. *Conmemoración de Chu Yuan, Nicolás Copérnico, François Rabelais y José Martí.* Pekín: [Publisher?], 1953.

DIHIGO, Rogelio. *Martí "su verso hecho música."* 2 vols. [Marianao, Cuba: Tip. Nemesio, 1950-53].

EHRENBURG, Ilya *et al. Martí en Moscú: homenaje en su Centenario.* La Habana: Ed. Páginas, 1953.

ENRÍQUEZ, Celso. *José Martí y los deportes.* México: Ed. y Distribuidores "Istmo," 1948.

ENTRALGO Cancio, Alberto. *Martí ante el proceso de Jesús.* La Habana: La Verdad, 1956.

FAJARDO, Raúl José. *La consciencia universal y Martí.* La Habana: Ed. Lex, 1952.

FERNÁNDEZ Lamas, Jesús. *Juárez en Martí.* Artemisa, Cuba: Imp. Hermanos Trujillo, 1953.

_____. *Martí el anticlerical.* Artemisa, Cuba: Hermanos Trujillo, 1951.

————. *Presencia de José Martí en la Logia "Silencio."* Artemisa, Cuba: Hermanos Trujillo, 1953.

GARCÍA Feito, Bernardo. *Martí al alcance de los trabajadores.* La Habana: Ed. Unidad, 1949.

GONZÁLEZ, Manuel Pedro (ed.). *Antología crítica de José Martí.* México: Ed. Cultura, T.G., S.A., 1960.

GONZÁLEZ, Manuel Pedro. *José Martí, Epic Chronicler of the United States in the Eighties.* Chapel Hill: The University of North Carolina Press, 1953.

GRAU San Martín, Ramón. *Martí y el Partido Revolucionario Cubano.* La Habana: Ediciones de la Comisión Nacional de Propaganda del Partido Revolucionario Cubano (Auténticos), 1939.

GUERRA, Armando. *Martí y los negros.* La Habana: Imp. Arquimbau, 1947.

HORREGO Estuch, Leopoldo. *Martí, su pensamiento jurídico.* La Habana: Ed. Mecenas, 1954.

IDUARTE, Andrés. *Martí escritor.* México: Cuadernos Americanos, 1945.

INFIESTA, Ramón. *El pensamiento político de Martí.* La Habana: Universidad de la Habana, 1953.

JARNÉS, Benjamín. *Escuela de libertad. Siete maestros: Bolívar, Hidalgo, Lincoln, Martí, San Martín, Sucre, Washington.* México: Ed. Continental, [1942].

JINESTA, Carlos. *José Martí en Costa Rica.* San José: Librería Alsina, 1933.

JORRÍN, Miguel. *Martí y la filosofía.* La Habana: Cuadernos de Divulgación Cultural #11, Comisión Nacional Cubana de la UNESCO, 1954.

LANCÍS y Sánchez, Antonio. *Lo electoral en Martí: espectáculo y ansia.* La Habana: Ed. Lex, 1953.

LAVÍN, Pablo F. *Reflexiones en torno a Martí.* La Habana: Ed. Lex, 1953.

LAZO, Raimundo. *Martí y su obra literaria.* La Habana: La Propagandista, 1929.

LIZASO, Félix (ed.). *Archivo José Martí.* 6 vols. La Habana: El Ministerio de Educación, Dirección de Cultura, 1940-52.

LIZASO, Félix. *José Martí: precursor de la UNESCO.* La Habana: Publicaciones de la Comisión Nacional Cubana de UNESCO, 1953.

————. *Posibilidades filosóficas en Martí.* La Habana: Molina y Cía., 1935.

LLAVERÍAS, Joaquín. *Los periódicos de Martí.* La Habana: Imp. Pérez Sierra y Cía., 1929.

LUBIÁN y Arias, Rafael. *Martí en los campos de Cuba Libre.* La Habana: Propaganda Angulo, 1953.

MAÑACH, Jorge. *El pensamiento político y social de Martí.* La Habana: Edición Oficial del Senado, 1941.

MARINELLO, Juan. *El caso literario de Martí. Motivos de Centenario.* La Habana: Imp. Vega y Cía., 1954.

MARTÍNEZ Bello, Antonio. *La adolescencia de Martí, notas para un ensayo de interpretación psicológica.* La Habana: Imp. P. Fernández y Cía., 1944.

————. *Ideas sociales y económicas de José Martí.* La Habana: La Verónica, 1940.

MATTERÍN, Abraham M. *Martí y las discriminaciones raciales.* La Habana: Ed. de la Agrupación Cultural Hebreo-Cubana, 1953.

Movimiento 26 de Julio de Nueva York. *Martí, su Rosa Blanca y Cuba.* n.d. Tract in possession of author.

NÚÑEZ y Dóminguez, José de Jesús. *Martí en México.* México: Imp. de la Secretaría de Relaciones Exteriores, 1934.

OÑATE, José T. *La senda del apóstol (crónicas y fotografías de la ruta seguida por Martí en 1895 de Playitas a Dos Ríos.* Santiago de Cuba: Morales, Alvarez y Cía., 1930.

PÉREZ Gorrín, José A. y Merino Brito, Eloy G. *Martí y el derecho.* La Habana: Jesús Montero, 1953.

PORTELL-VILÁ, Herminio. *Martí, diplomático.* La Habana: Cultural, S. A., 1934.

QUESADA y Miranda, Gonzalo de. *Alrededor de la acción en Dos Ríos.* La Habana: Seoane, Fernández y Cía., 1942.

_____. *Martí, periodista.* La Habana: Rambla, Bouza y Cía., 1929.

_____. *Mujeres de Martí.* La Habana: Ed. Indice, 1943.

_____. *Significación martiana del 10 de Octubre.* La Habana: Academia de la Historia de Cuba, 1953.

RODRÍGUEZ Demorizi, Emilio. *Martí en Santo Domingo.* La Habana: Imp. Ucar García, 1953.

ROIG de Leuchsenring, Emilio. *Martí en España.* La Habana: Cultural, S. A., 1938.

_____. *Martí y los niños.* La Habana: Cultural, S. A., 1932.

_____ (ed.). *Vida y pensamiento de Martí.* 2 vols. La Habana: Municipio de la Habana, 1942.

SANTOVENIA y Echaide, Emeterio S. *Bolívar y Martí.* La Habana: Imp. El Siglo XX, 1934.

_____. *Dos creadores: Mazzini y Martí.* La Habana: Ed. Trópico, 1936.

_____. *Genio y acción, Sarmiento y Martí.* La Habana: Ed. Trópico, 1938.

_____. *Lincoln en Martí.* La Habana: Ed. Trópico, [1948].

_____. *Martí, legislador.* Buenos Aires: Ed. Losada, S. A., 1943.

_____. *Política de Martí.* 2d ed. La Habana: Ed. Lex, 1944.

SENMANAT, Rafael M. *El calvario de Martí (de Playitas a Dos Ríos).* Regla, Cuba: Ed. América, 1925.

SOTO Hall, Máximo. *La Niña de Guatemala, el idilio trágico de José Martí.* Guatemala: Tip. Nacional, 1942.

Universidad de Oriente (ed.). *Pensamiento y acción de José Martí.* Santiago de Cuba: Tip. San Román, 1953.

VAINSTEIN, Abraham Z. *De cara al sol.* La Habana: Ed. de la Agrupación Cultural Hebreo-Cubana, 1954.

VELA, David. *Martí en Guatemala.* La Habana: Imp. Mundial, 1953.

ARTICLES AND PERIODICALS

ACEVEDO, Nena. "Nuestra canastilla martiana," *Patria,* XI (enero de 1955), 12.

AGRAMONTE, Roberto. "Martí y el mundo de lo colectivo," *Universidad de la Habana,* XII (diciembre de 1941), 16-43.

Alerta (La Habana). 1956.

"Alocuciones, declaraciones, acuerdos y pronunciamientos del Consejo Universitario," *Anuario de la Facultad de Ciencias Sociales y Derecho Público, 1955-1956.* La Habana: Universidad de la Habana, 1956, pp. 531-556.

ALVAREZ del Real, Evelio. "¿Abuso de Martí?" *Siempre,* 30 de enero de 1946, pp. 1-2.

ALVAREZ de Rodón, Mercedes. "Eran maestras que iniciaron el culto de José Martí," *Prensa Libre* (La Habana), 14 de julio de 1950.

ALVAREZ Gallego, G., "¿Abuso de Martí?" *Siempre,* 5 de febrero de 1946, pp. 1-2.

_____. "Trasluz. ¿Abuso de Martí?" *El Avance Criollo* (La Habana), 19 de mayo de 1952.

ARGILAGOS, Rafael G. "Liturgía de la natividad martiana," *Martí,* XVI (febrero de 1945), 18.

ARGÜELLES, Francisco J. "Hecho escandaloso," *Patria,* V (agosto de 1949), 8.

Asociación Nacional de los Emigrados Revolucionarios Cubanos de la Independencia, "El sentimiento de los compañeros del apóstol," *Patria,* V (abril de 1949), 17.

Augier, Angel I. "El debate del monumento a Martí," *Bohemia,* 26 de abril de 1953, pp. 6-8, 112-115.

Baeza Flores, Alberto. "Vigilia martiana," *Carteles,* 29 de enero de 1950, pp. 10-11.

Baquero, Gastón. "Martí y lo Cubano," *Diario de la Marina* (La Habana), 27 de enero de 1952.

Ballagas, Emilio. "Martí y los cristianos," *Diario de la Marina* (La Habana), 28 de diciembre de 1940.

Bay Sevilla, Luis. "El concurso para el monumento a Martí," *Arquitectura,* XI (octubre de 1943), 380-385.

Bazil, Osvaldo. "El evangelio de la ternura," in his *Cabezas de América.* La Habana: Molina y Cía., 1933, pp. 15-23.

Beroes, Pedro. "Mi San José Martí," *La Rosa Blanca,* III (mayo de 1949), 4.

Bestard, Miguel E. "Peregrinación martiana de la I. O. O. F.," *Selva Habanera,* 3 de enero de 1953, pp. 1, 6-7.

Biaín, Ignacio. "Martí, injusto y apasionado," *Semanario Católico,* 3 de noviembre de 1940, p. 9.

Bisbé, Manuel. "Maza y Artola como legislador," *Universidad de la Habana,* XXVI (1955), 222-262.

Blanco Fombona, Rufino. "José Martí," in *Martí,* ed. Quesada y Aróstegui, IX, 53-56.

Bohemia. 1953. 1956. 1960.

Boletín Oficial de la Asociación de Antiguos Alumnos del Seminario Martiano. 1945-46. (Cited elsewhere as *Boletín Oficial.*)

Bory, Juan E. "Invocación al Apóstol," *Patria,* VII (junio de 1951), 5-7.

Calvo, Alberto de J. "Martí," *Patria,* III (enero de 1947), 12.

Camacho, Pánfilo D. "La religión martiana," *Boletín Oficial,* II (enero de 1946), 4.

Carballosa Madero, Andrea. "Nuestra Comisión de Educación," *Patria,* XI (enero de 1955), 16-18.

Carbonell, Nestor. "José Martí, como orador, fué único, y se le hubiera creído un hombre sobrenatural, pues sus palabras eran dignas de un Dios," *La Noticia* (Managua, Nicaragua), 30 de enero de 1952.

Carricarte, Arturo R. de. "Apostillas martinianas. La consagración de Dos Ríos," *Diario de la Marina* (La Habana), 26 de abril de 1942.

──────. "Martiolatría y conducta," *Alfanje,* IV (febrero de 1941), 7.

──────. *Revista Martiniana* (La Habana), I (octubre de 1921), 6.

Catalá, Raquel. "Martí y el espiritualismo," in Roig de Leuchsenring (ed.), *Vida y pensamiento de Martí,* I, 297-339.

Ceballos, Carmen. "Los Pinos Nuevos," *Patria,* XI (enero de 1955) 8-9.

Chacón y Calvo, José María. "Pasión cristiana de Martí," *Diario de la Marina* (La Habana), 2 de febrero de 1957.

Cohucelo, Pedro José. "El Cristo americano, José Martí," *La Tribuna Popular* (Montevideo), 8 de febrero de 1953.

──────. "Pinceladas: ¡Imitémosle! Así es como se honra su memoria!" *El Triunfo* (La Habana), 3 de junio de 1923.

Colls, Ricardo. "¿Qué es un Rincón Martiano?" *Boletín Oficial,* II (junio de 1946), 10.

Cortina, José Manuel. "Martí, divina antena," *El Tanameño* (Sagua de Tánamo), 29 de enero de 1949.

El Crisol (La Habana). 1938. 1949. 1951. 1956-57.

CRUZ, Manuel de la. "José Martí," in *Martí,* ed. Quesada y Aróstegui, II, 3-21.

CRUZ Cobos, Armando. "Martí prometecio," *Educación,* XIII (enero de 1953), 13, 23.

CUADRA, Angel, "Lamento a José Martí en su Centenario," *El País Gráfico,* 15 de febrero de 1953, p. 17.

"Cuba: 'Dictator with the People,'" *Time* (Latin American ed.), April 21, 1952, p. 31.

"Cuba: Winner Take All," *Time* (Latin American ed.), March 24, 1952, p. 28.

DIAGO, Gilberto. "Presencia de Martí en las escuelas rurales," *Orientación Campesina,* II (marzo-abril de 1955), 21-22.

Diario de la Marina (La Habana). 1949. 1953. 1955-57.

Diario Nacional (La Habana). 1955. 1957.

Diplomacia. 1952.

La Discusión (La Habana). 1895.

"Error o mala intención?" *Patria,* XII (diciembre de 1956), 5.

ESPÍN, José Manuel. "Letanía martiana," *Revista Casino Español,* VIII (octubre de 1953), 13.

ESTÉNGER, Rafael. "Excomunión del Padre Biaín," *El Avance Criollo* (La Habana), 14 de diciembre de 1940.

————. "Resurrección," *Alerta* (La Habana), 28 de enero de 1950.

ESTRADA Palma, Tomás. "José Martí," in *Martí,* ed. Quesada y Aróstegui, VII, 11-12.

FEIJóo, Samuel. "Acción de la escuela rural," *Bohemia,* 11 de enero de 1953, pp. 30-33.

FERIA de Varona, María. "Para Martí, el salvador," *El País Gráfico,* 7 de junio de 1953, p. 30.

FERNÁNDEZ, O. S. A., Father Manuel. "An Outstanding Achievement: The University of St. Thomas of Villanueva," *Havana Post,* January 19, 1957.

FERNÁNDEZ Callejas, Roger. "Juan Luis Martín y Martí Masón," *Mundo Masónico,* XXI (abril-mayo de 1953), 5-6.

FERNÁNDEZ Ceballos, Raúl. "Yo leí en la Biblia de Martí," *El Mensajero,* L (junio de 1953), 20-21.

FERNÁNDEZ Lamas, Jesús. "Cenas Martianas," *Boletín Oficial,* II (marzo de 1946), 8-9.

————. "Perdón," *Patria,* V (abril de 1949), 5-6.

FERRÁN y Rivero, Francisco R. "Crónica católica: martianicemos nuestro amor patrio," *Diario de la Marina* (La Habana), 30 de enero de 1945.

FERRER Cuevas, Manuel. "Ante los restos de Martí," in Lizaso (ed.), *Archivo José Martí,* V (julio-diciembre de 1951), 550-552.

FERRER Gutiérrez, Virgilio. "José Martí en César Romero," *Libertad* (La Habana), 25 de junio de 1944.

FIALLO, René. "Con una estrella en la frente," *Bohemia,* 18 de septiembre de 1955, pp. 70-71, 98.

FLOR Casanova, Noé de la. "Mi breviario martiano," *El Universal* (México), 3 de febrero de 1953.

Florida Times-Union. 1959.

GALBE, José Luis. "Petoefi, el Martí de Hungría," in his *Causas célebres y vidas extraordinarias.* La Habana: Cultural, S. A., 1953, pp. [311]-328.

GÁLVEZ y Ayala, Napoleón. "Si Martí viviese," *El Triunfo* (La Habana), 19 de mayo de 1918.

GARCÍA Pons, César. "Las honras que el Apóstol hubiera rechazado," *Bohemia,* 25 de enero de 1953, pp. 68-69.

García Ramirez de Fundora, Gladys. "El natalicio de José Martí," *El Bancario,* [XII] (enero-febrero de 1957), 18-19.

Gay-Calbó, Enrique. "Insurrección de 1906 y eclipse de la República. Gobierno provisional norteamericano," Guerra y Sánchez *et al, Historia de la Nación cubana,* VIII, Libro 1°, cap. ii, 17-37.

Giró Rodés, Juan. "Confidencialmente," *El Mundo* (La Habana), 27 de septiembre de 1956.

Gómez, Máximo, "José Martí (Fragmentos de un artículo)," in *Martí,* ed. Quesada y Aróstegui, VIII, 45-46.

_____. Letter to Francisco María González, 18 de mayo de 1902, in *El Mundo* (La Habana), 19 de mayo de 1902.

González Martínez, Juan. "Por qué hice Presidente a Carlos Prío," *Bohemia,* 30 de enero de 1949, pp. 58-59, 65-66.

González Ricardo, Rogelio. "Cómo y dónde surgió la Nochebuena Martiana," *Orto,* XXXI (enero-marzo de 1942), 32-33.

Grau San Martín, Ramón. "Se oponen la maldad y el poder a la obra constructor del Apóstol," *Prensa Libre* (La Habana), 30 de enero de 1944.

"Los graves sucesos del jueves, 15 de enero," *Bohemia,* 25 de enero de 1953, pp. 70-75.

Guerra de la Piedra, Agustín. "¿Tenemos la República que soñó Martí?" *Orto,* XXXVIII (febrero de 1950), 1-16.

Guerra y Sánchez, Ramiro. "Martí y la escuela de la República," *Cuba Profesional,* [I] (marzo-mayo de 1952), 45-48, 83.

Guiral, Dolores. "Si existió un alma tan bella como la del señor Martí, Dios tiene que existir," *Carteles,* 1 de febrero de 1953, p. 126.

The Havana Post. 1956-57.

Henríquez y Carvajal, Federico. "Duelo de America," *Letras y Ciencias* (Santo Domingo), 3 de agosto de 1895, in *Martí,* ed. Quesada y Aróstegui, IX, 47-49.

Herring, Hubert. Book Review Section, *New York Herald Tribune,* June 4, 1950.

Ibarra, Raúl. "Gestaron el '26 de Julio' en el término de Artemisa," *Diario Nacional* (La Habana), 25 de abril de 1957.

Ichaso, Francisco. "Actualidad política: un alto al fuego en honor de Martí," *Diario de la Marina* (La Habana), 27 de enero de 1953.

_____. "Cabalgata política: la difícil situación del gobierno actual ante las malversaciones del anterior," *Bohemia,* 30 de enero de 1949, pp. 27, 80.

_____. "Inaudito boicot sindical a la película sobre la vida de Martí," *Cinema,* 1 de noviembre de 1953, p. 40.

_____. "Realismo y poesía en la versión fílmica de la vida de José Martí," *Cinema,* 29 de noviembre de 1953, p. 16.

Iduarte, Andrés. "Ideas económicas de José Martí," *La Nueva Democracia,* XXVI (noviembre de 1945), 10-12, 29.

_____. "Las ideas políticas de José Martí," *Cuadernos Americanos,* XIV (marzo-abril de 1944), 155-177.

_____. "Ideas religiosas, morales, y filosóficas de Martí," *La Nueva Democracia,* XXV (febrero de 1944), 3-7, 26-32.

Infiesta, Ramón. "Martí, político," in Universidad de Oriente (ed.), *Pensamiento y acción de José Martí,* pp. 49-70.

Información (La Habana). 1945. 1953.

Jiménez Perdomo, B. "Un día tras otro. Dónde no se puede florecer la Rosa Blanca," *Información* (La Habana), 29 de enero de 1953.

Lavín, Pablo F. "La Cátedra Martiana de Marianao," *Diario de la Marina* (La Habana), 29 de enero de 1956.

Lazo, Raimundo. "Centenario antimartiano," *Prensa Libre* (La Habana), 19 de febrero de 1953.

_____. "Martí y la política," in Lizaso (ed.), *Archivo José Martí*, V (enero-junio de 1950), 29-43.

LEDUC, Alberto. "Homenajes a José Martí," in *Martí*, ed. Quesada y Aróstegui, VIII, 29-30.

LIZASO, Félix. "Ecos y reflejos: ¿Es así que honramos a Martí?" *El Mundo* (La Habana), 6 de mayo de 1946.

_____. "Martí y los hebreos," *El Mundo* (La Habana), 14 de julio de 1953.

_____. "¿Habrá monumento a Martí?" *Carteles*, 5 de febrero de 1950, pp. 26-29.

_____. "San Martín en Martí," *Mensuario de Arte, Literatura, Historia y Crítica*, I (noviembre de 1950), 14, 22-23.

LLAVERÍAS, Joaquín. "Mariano Martí y Navarro—algunos datos de su vida," *Boletín del Archivo Nacional*, XXVII (1928), 275-300.

LÓPEZ de Armas, Agustín. "Martí, redentor de los cubanos," *La Publicidad* (Santa Clara), 7 de febrero de 1938.

LOYOLA, Miguel. "Martí y la pobreza," *La Ultima Hora*, 1 de enero de 1953, p. 53.

LUGO Martínez, Andrés. Open letter to Maj. Gen. Enrique Loynaz del Castillo, *Prensa Libre* (La Habana), 23 de junio de 1949.

MACHADO y Hernández, José. José Martí, segundogénito de Dios," *Excelsior* (La Habana), 20 de mayo de 1953.

MAESTRI, Raúl. "Martí, político monetario," *Repertorio Americano*, 3 de diciembre de 1938, pp. 57-58.

MAÑACH, Jorge. "La República ante el legado de Martí," *Bohemia*, 14 de febrero de 1953, pp. 59, 80.

_____. "Si Martí levantara la cabeza," *Bohemia*, 30 de enero de 1949, pp. 44, 66.

MANGHAM, Herbert J. "Castro and His Catch Phrases," *Tallahassee Democrat*, September 30, 1960.

MARINELLO, Juan. Letter to Antonio Martínez Bello, La Habana, 4 de agosto de 1940, in Martínez Bello, *Ideas sociales y económicas de José Martí*, pp. 215-219.

_____. "La ofensa de los *energúmenos* vestidos de marinos es igual a la que a diario fomentan contra Cuba los imperialistas," *Noticias de Hoy* (La Habana), 15 de marzo de 1949.

MÁRQUEZ Sterling, Carlos. "La legitimidad de la oposición," *Bohemia*, 1 de enero de 1950, pp. 52-53.

_____. "Necesitamos una política generosa y creadora como la de José Martí," *Bohemia*, 29 de enero de 1950, pp. 60-61, 106-107, 113-114.

MARTÍN, Juan Luis. "Comentarios de actualidad. Un insulto a Martí," *Alerta Cubano* (La Habana), septiembre de 1953.

_____. "José Martí y los católicos," *Semanario Católico*, 18 de enero de 1953, pp. 30-31.

_____. "Un paralelo: José Martí y Sun Yat-sen," *Pueblo* (La Habana), 27 de enero de 1941.

MARTÍNEZ Bello, Antonio. "El 'Suicidio' de Martí—su 'Inadaptación,' " in Lizaso (ed.), *Archivo José Martí*, IV (junio-diciembre de 1948), 372-392.

MARTÍNEZ Pereira, Augusto. "Jesús-Martí," *Información* (La Habana), 10 de febrero de 1953.

MATOS Bernier, Félix. "José Martí," *La Democracia*, abril de 1905, in *Martí*, ed. Quesada y Aróstegui, IX, 71-75.

MEDINA, Waldo. "Martí, capitán de arcángeles," *El Mundo* (La Habana), 30 de enero de 1951.

_____. "Martilandia en ruinas," *El Mundo* (La Habana), 3 de febrero de 1948.

MISTRAL, Gabriela. Letter (Temuco, Chile) to Federico Henríquez y Carvajal, noviembre de 1920, in *Social*, VI (mayo de 1921), 64.

MOHEDANO, Rafael. "El Manifiesto de Montecristi," *Boletín Oficial*, I (noviembre de 1945), 6-7.

MORENO de Ayala, F. "El sueño de Martí," *Boletín Oficial*, II (mayo de 1946), 4.

MORENO Plá, Enrique H. "Tres conjunciones de astros," in Quesada y Miranda (ed.), *Memoria del Seminario Martiano de la Universidad de la Habana*. La Habana: Imp. Universitaria, 1953, pp. 51-61.

El Mundo (La Habana). 1939. 1949. 1952-53. 1955-57.

Mundo Masónico. 1953.

NERVO, Amado. "Homenajes a José Martí," in *Martí*, ed. Quesada y Aróstegui, VIII, 34-36.

New York Times. 1959. 1960. 1961.

ORTIZ, Fernando. "Martí y las razas," in Roig de Leuchsenring (ed.), *Vida y pensamiento de Martí*, II, 335-367.

ORTIZ-LAMADRID, Rubén. "El caso económico de la juventud," *El Mundo* (La Habana), 22 de diciembre de 1956.

El País (La Habana). 1946. 1953.

PAZOS y Roque, Felipe de. "Las ideas económicas de Martí," in Roig de Leuchsenring (ed.), *Vida y pensamiento de Martí*, II, 177-209.

Patria (La Habana). 1947. 1949-52. 1955-56.

PENICHET Gómez, Antonio. "Abraham Lincoln, Mahatma Ghandi y José Martí," *Lux*, (enero de 1951), 21, 24.

PÉREZ Cabrera, José M. "Presidencia de Estrada Palma," Guerra y Sánchez *et al.*, *Historia de la Nación cubana*, VIII, Libro 1°, cap. i, 3-16.

PIÑERA, Humberto. "Martí, pensador," in Universidad de Oriente (ed.), *Pensamiento y acción de José Martí*, pp. 167-188.

PONCE DE LEÓN y Ayme, Antonio. "La oruga que nombró Martí," *Patria*, VI (junio de 1950), 5-7.

PORTELL-VILÁ, "Escuela de Ciudadanía: Duplicidades," *Bohemia*, 4 de abril de 1954, pp. 22, 110-111.

_____. "Escuela de Ciudadanía: Formación de un partido político," *Bohemia*, 21 de marzo de 1954, pp. 8, 126-127.

_____. "Escuela de Ciudadanía: Lección aprendida," *Bohemia*, 11 de abril de 1954, pp. 32, 122-123.

_____. "Escuela de Ciudadanía: Proceso afiliatorio," *Bohemia*, 28 de marzo de 1954, pp. 6, 131-132.

_____. "Hollywood juega con Martí," *Bohemia*, 12 de agosto de 1956, pp. 35, 111.

PORTUONDO, José Antonio. "Introducción al estudio de las ideas sociales de Martí," in Roig de Leuchsenring (ed.), *Vida y pensamiento de Martí*, II, 227-263.

Prensa Libre (La Habana). 1943. 1957.

PRESALDE, Alí. "El Centenario de Martí," *Semanario Católico*, 18 de enero de 1953, p. 23.

Pueblo (La Habana). 1955.

PUJOL, Rogelio A. "Cenas Martianas mixtificadas," *Boletín Oficial*, II (marzo de 1946), 7-8.

QUESADA y Michelsen, Gonzalo de. "Filatélica martiana," *Patria*, VI (enero de 1949), 20-21.

QUESADA y Miranda, Gonzalo de. "Las canteras donde trabajó Martí," *Carteles*, 30 de enero de 1938, pp. 22-23.

_____. "El Monumento a Martí," *Arquitectura*, XI (octubre de 1943), 386-390.

_____. "¡No más desfiles escolares!" *Patria,* IV (febrero de 1948), 11-12.

QUINTERO, Angel. "Hay que inspirar ideales a las nuevas generaciones cubanas," *Bohemia,* 5 de agosto de 1956, p. 105.

"Reglamento y Estatutos de la Asociación de Antiguos Alumnos del Semanario Martiano," *Boletín Oficial,* I (agosto de 1945), 3.

REMOS, Juan J. "Experiencias del Gobierno propio," Guerra y Sánchez *et al., Historia de la Nación cubana,* VIII, Libro 2°, cap. iv, 81-87.

Reportaje Gráfico. 1957.

Revolución. 1960.

"Rincón criollo. Cosas de aquí y allá," *Patria,* VI (mayo de 1950), 39.

Río, Pastor del. "Un desfile; una calle; una estatua," *América,* XXXVIII (febrero de 1953), 72.

Ríos, Fernando de los. "Reflexiones en torno al sentido de la vida en Martí," in Lizaso (ed.), *Archivo José Martí,* IV (enero-diciembre de 1947), 21-30.

RIVERO Aguiar, Ramón. "De Martí a Grau," *El Avance Criollo* (La Habana), 29 de enero de 1944.

ROA, Raúl. "Yunques sonad, enmudeced campanas," *Anuario de la Facultad de Ciencias Sociales y Derecho Público, 1955-1956.* La Habana: Universidad de la Habana, 1956, pp. 33-54.

ROCA, Blas. "Martí responde," *Noticias de Hoy* (La Habana), 27 de febrero de 1940.

_____. "Sobre la libertad de Prensa," *Hoy,* 8 de junio de 1960.

RODRÍGUEZ, Carlos Rafael. "Martí, guía de su tiempo y anticipadora del nuestro," *La Ultima Hora,* enero de 1953, p. 6.

RODRÍGUEZ del Rey, Julia. "Nuestra Comisión de Canastilla Martiana y Ropero," *Patria,* XI (enero de 1955), 13-15.

ROIG de Leuchsenring, Emilio. "¿Dónde está el archivo del monumento a Martí?" *Pueblo* (La Habana), 15 de junio de 1949.

_____. "En defensa de Martí," *El Mundo* (La Habana), 29 de diciembre de 1940.

_____. "En 1899 solo 16 cubanos representativos comprendían y admiraban a Martí," *Carteles,* 29 de enero de 1939, pp. 38-39.

_____. "Hostos y Martí, dos ideologías antillanas concordantes," *Revista Bimestre Cubana,* XLIII (enero-febrero de 1939), 5-19.

_____. "Martí y las religiones," in Roig de Leuchsenring (ed.), *Vida y pensamiento de Martí,* I, 111-158.

La Rosa Blanca. 1948.

RUBIO, Ricardo F. "Martí Masón," *Mundo Masónico,* XXII (mayo-junio de 1954), 24.

SABAS Alomá, Mariblanca. "Atalaya: dejemos quieto a Martí," *El Avance Criollo* (La Habana), 23 de agosto de 1941.

SALAS Amaro, Alberto. "Profanación de Martí," *Prensa Libre* (La Habana), 28 de abril de 1945.

_____. "¡Viva Cuba Libre!" *Ataja* (La Habana), 10 de febrero de 1957.

SÁNCHEZ, Serafín. "Martí," *El Cubano Libre* (Provincia de Oriente, Cuba), 30 de junio de 1896, in *Revista Cubana,* XXIX (1951-52), 438-441.

SANTOVENIA y Echaide, Emeterio S. "Enero 28 de 1909," *Patria,* VI (enero de 1950), 25.

_____. "Experiencias del Gobierno propio," Guerra y Sánchez *et al, Historia de la Nación cubana,* VIII, Libro 2°, cap. iii, 41-96.

_____. "Universalidad de dos Americanos," *Journal of Inter-American Studies,* IV (January, 1962), 33-51.

"Ser Masón," *Mundo Masónico,* XXI (agosto-septiembre de 1953), 21.

Sierra, Justo. "José Martí," in *Martí*, ed. Quesada y Aróstegui, VI, [13].
Soler Soler, Amparo. "El Centenario de Martí y la escuela cubana," *Diario de Cuba* (Santiago de Cuba), 28 de enero de 1953.
Stokes, William S. "The Cuban Parliamentary System in Action," *Journal of Politics*, XI (May, 1949), 335-364.
————. "The 'Cuban Revolution' and the Presidential Elections of 1948," *Hispanic American Historical Review*, XXXI (February, 1951), 37-79.
————. "National and Local Violence in Cuban Politics," *Southwestern Social Science Quarterly*, XXXIV (September, 1953), 57-63.
Tamargo, Agustín. "Quien injuria a Martí y a Maceo no puede ser amigo de Cuba," *Bohemia*, 26 de agosto de 1956, pp. 49-50, 97-98.
Time (Latin American ed.). 1952.
Torriente, Cosme de la."Política exterior. Las relaciones entre la República de Cuba y los Estados Unidos de América," *Guerra y Sánchez et al., Historia de la Nación cubana*, VIII, Libro 4°, 191-264.
La Ultima Hora. 1953.
Universidad de la Habana. *Vida Universitaria*, XI (enero, febrero, marzo de 1960), 22-23.
Urbina, Luis G. "José Martí," in *Martí*, ed. Quesada y Aróstegui, XV, 85-93.
Valdés Domínguez, Fermín. "Ofrenda de hermano," *Revista Cubana*, XXIX (1951-52), 237-287.
Valdés Rodríguez, J. M. "Dificultades para realizar la película 'La Rosa Blanca,' " *Cinema*, 1 de noviembre de 1953, p. 18.
Valle, María del Carmen. "¿Por qué amamos a Martí?" *Revista Lyceum*, X (agosto de 1953), 99-101.
Varona, Enrique José. "Martí y su obra política," in *Martí*, ed. Quesada y Aróstegui, IV, 27-46.
Vidaillet Paradela, Marta. "Paralelos entre Roosevelt y Martí," *La Semana* (Baracoa, Cuba), 6 de enero de 1949, pp. 10-11.
Viera Trejo, Bernardo. "Cuba y seis personajes lejanos," *Bohemia*, 10 de marzo de 1957, pp. 36-38, 91-93.
Viondi y Vera, Miguel F. Speech in the Cuban House of Representatives, 19 de mayo de 1909, Cuba Congreso, Cámara de Representantes, *Diario de Sesiones*, XI, No. 20 (21 de mayo de 1909), 1-5.
Vitier, Medardo. "La capacidad de magisterio en Martí," in Roig de Leuchsenring (ed.), *Vida y pensamiento de Martí*, II, 211-225.
Zayas, Lincoln de. "La apoteosis de Martí," *Patria* (New York), 6 de noviembre de 1895, in *Revista Cubana*, XXIX (1951-52), 143-150.

GOVERNMENT PUBLICATIONS

"Actas del Cuerpo de Consejo de Nueva York," *Boletín del Archivo Nacional*, XXXV (1936), 64-96.
Cuba. *El Archivo Nacional en la conmemoración del Centenario del natalicio de José Martí y Pérez, 1853-1953.* La Habana: Publicaciones del Archivo Nacional de Cuba, 1953, XXXVI.
Cuba, Comisión Central Pro-Monumento. *En memoria de José Martí.* La Habana: P. Fernández y Cía., 1938.
Cuba. *Gaceta Oficial de la República de Cuba.* 1922. 1935. 1944-45. 1949. 1952.
Cuba, Secretaría de Instrucción Pública y Bellas Artes. *Iconografía del Apóstol José Martí.* La Habana: Imp. El Siglo XX, 1925.
Cuba. Tribunal Superior Electoral, Oficina Nacional de los Censos Demográfico

y Electoral. *Censos de población, viviendas y electoral.* La Habana: P. Fernández y Cía., 1955.

UNPUBLISHED MATERIAL

Angulo Pintado, Luis. "Martí fué un precursor del Rotarismo," Unpublished speech in 1953.

Cuba, Ministerio de Educación, Dirección de la Enseñanza, Resolución No. 023421, 21 de noviembre de 1947, and Resolución No. 026685, 25 de enero de 1948.

Díaz, Nicanor, Jefe de Despacho, Comisión Nacional Organizadora de los Actos y Ediciones del Centenario y del Monumento de Martí. Letter to author, La Habana, Cuba, November 15, 1956.

Gordon, Alan M. "Verb-Creation in the Works of José Martí: Method and Function." Unpublished Ph.D. dissertation, Dept. of Romance Languages and Literature, Harvard University, 1956.

Shuler, Esther E. "Poesía y teorías poéticas de José Martí (con especial referencia a su crítica de autores norteamericanos)." Unpublished Ph.D. dissertation, Dept. of Spanish, University of Minnesota, 1946.

OTHER SOURCES

_____. Interview with Roberto Agramonte and Manuel Bisbé, January 31, 1957.

_____. Interview with Jesús Artigas, March 14, 1957.

_____. Interview with Father Ignacio Biaín, January 30, 1957.

_____. Interview with Rafael L. Díaz-Balart, February 6, 1957.

_____. Interview with Prisciliano Falcón Lañú, Secretary General of the National Federation of Sugar-Workers, March 15, 1957.

_____. Interview with Jesús Fernández Lamas, March 12, 1957.

_____. Interview with Bernardo García Feito, March 8, 1957.

_____. Interview with Ramón Grau San Martín, February 6, 1957.

_____. Interview with Antonio Lancís y Sánchez, January 30, 1957.

_____. Interview with Carlos Márquez Sterling, February 20, 1957.

_____. Interview with Carlos Martínez-Fortún y Foyo, March 26, 1957.

_____. Interview with Abraham M. Matterín, March 18, 1957.

_____. Interview with M. Isidro Méndez, March 3, 1957.

_____. Interview with José Manuel Pérez Cabrera, January 18, 1956.

_____. Interview with Marco Pitchon, March 19, 1957.

_____. Interview with Herminio Portell-Vilá, November 29, 1955.

_____. Interviews with Gonzalo de Quesada y Miranda, 1955-57.

_____. Interview with Jorge Quintana, March 19, 1957.

_____. Interview with Raúl Roa, January 31, 1957.

_____. Interview with Gregorio Silva, Treasurer, Universidad Nacional "José Martí," January 28, 1957.

_____. Interview with Anthony Smith y Franco, en route Havana to Miami, August 18, 1956.

_____. Interview with Enrique Viciana Pérez, February 6, 1956.

_____. Interviews held 1956-57, names withheld.

_____. Meetings of public school teachers attended in Havana in 1956. Names withheld.